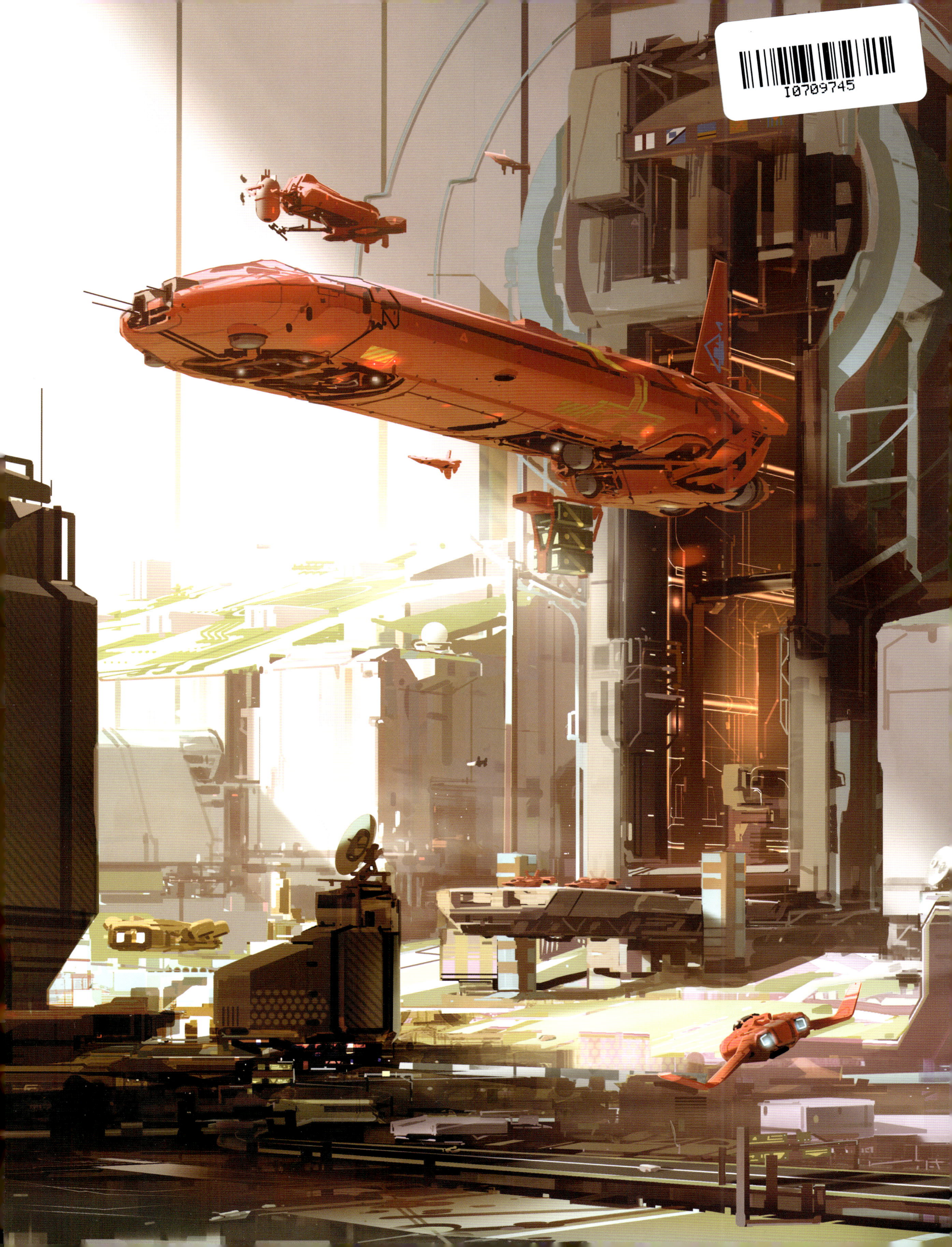
I0709745

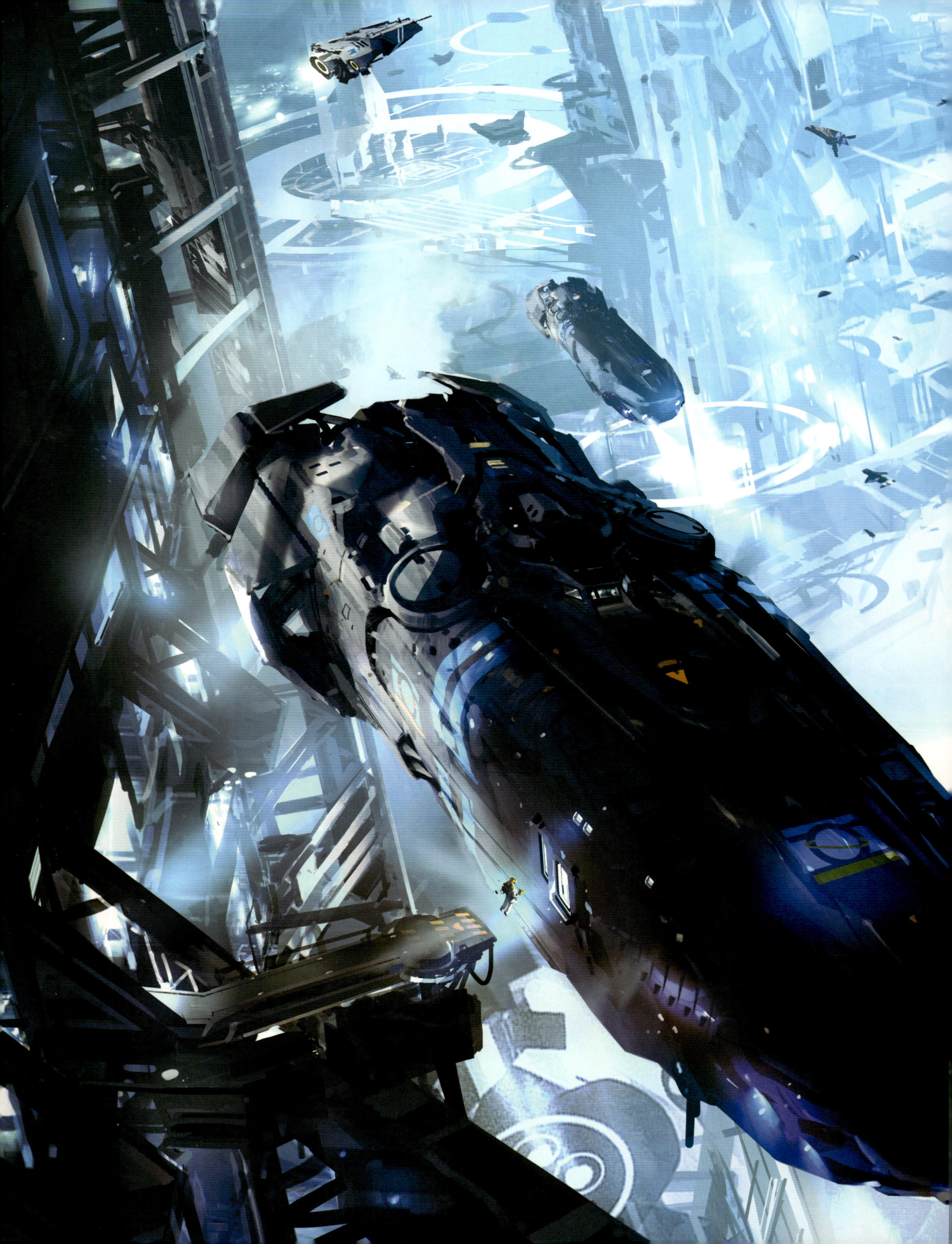

structura **3**

the art of sparth

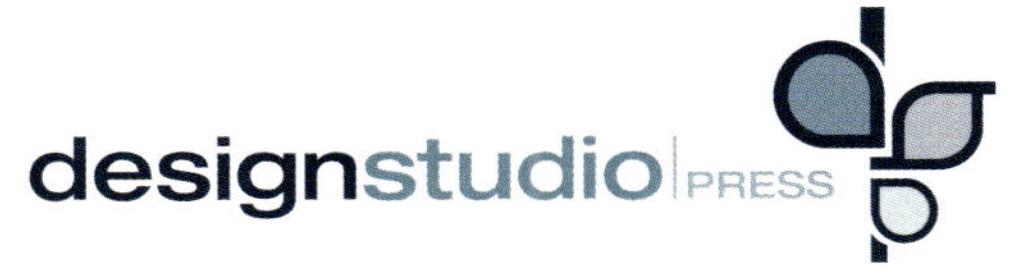
designstudio | PRESS

Structura3: The Art of Sparth
Copyright © 2015 Design Studio Press. All Rights Reserved.

All text and artwork in this book are copyright © 2015 Nicolas "Sparth" Bouvier unless otherwise noted.

Copyright © 2015 Microsoft Corporation. All Rights Reserved. Microsoft, 343 Industries, the 343 Industries logo, *Halo*, the *Halo* logo, Xbox, Xbox 360, and the Xbox logos, are trademarks of the Microsoft group of companies.

No part of this book may be reproduced or transmitted in any form or by any means, electronic or mechanical, including photocopying, xerography, and video recording, without the written permission from the publisher, Design Studio Press.

Graphic Design: Sparth (www.sparth.com) and Christopher J. De La Rosa
Art Direction: Scott Robertson
Copy Editor: Teena Apeles

Website: www.designstudiopress.com
Email: info@designstudiopress.com
10 9 8 7 6 5 4 3 2

Printed in Hong Kong
First edition, February 2015

Hardcover ISBN: 978-162465011-6
Paperback ISBN: 978-162465012-3
Library of Congress Control Number: 2014956844

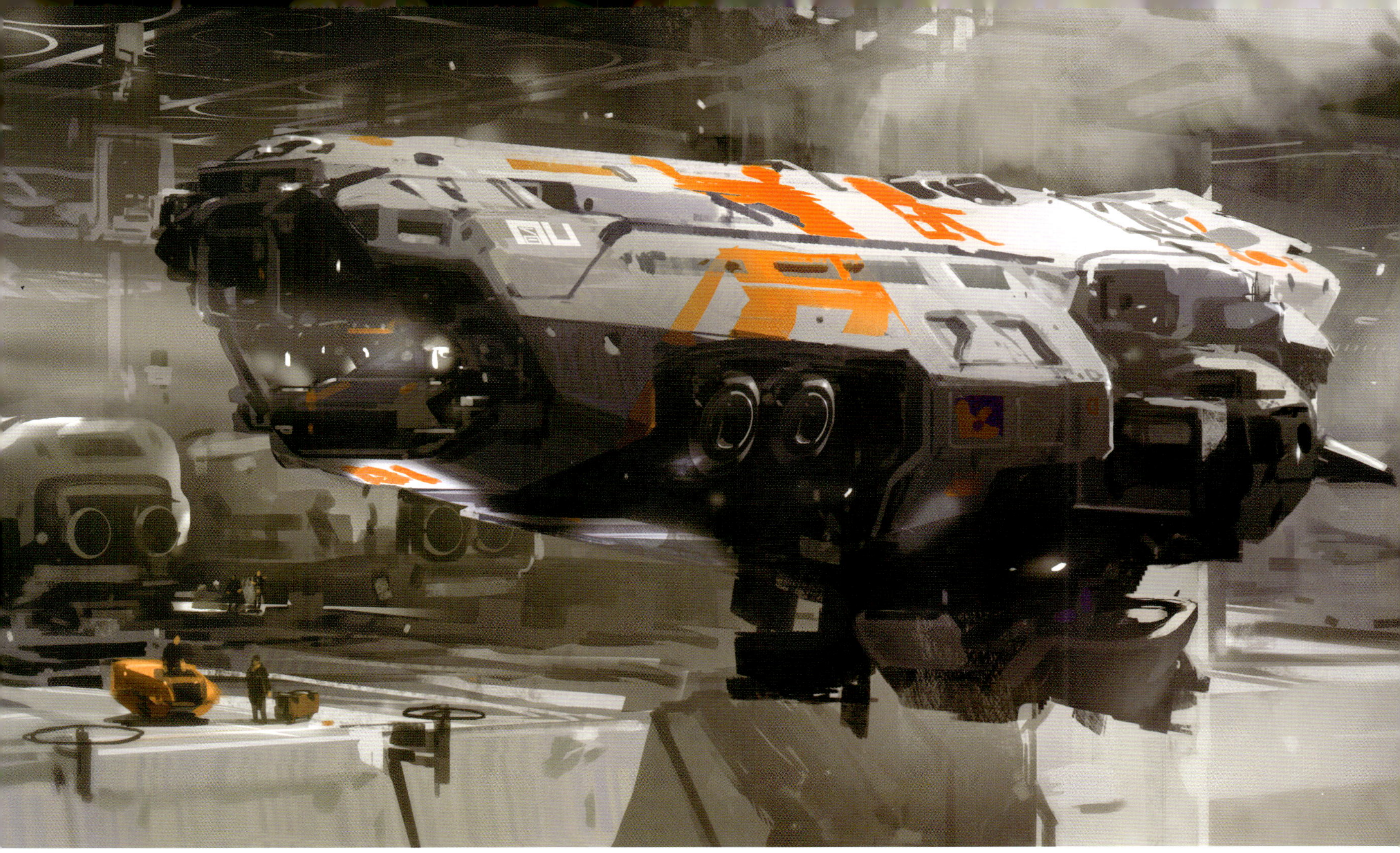

contents

foreword 6

introduction 7

chapter 1: visions 9

chapter 2: *halo 4* 46

chapter 3: 30-minute art 58

chapter 4: experimental and graphic . . 120

tutorials 138

foreword

Hulking space freighters hang weightless and thrumming above impossible geologic formations. Mechanical towers of unknown purpose stand vigil over frozen moons. A future megalopolis pulses with airships that shimmer in alien light. Sparth has a way of tapping into the vast, of conjuring moods and atmospheres that transport us through space and time. Whether it is a lone astronaut surveying a featureless plain, or a frenetic abstraction of shape and color, his scenes tend to stay open to interpretation, even demand our participation. It's one of the most compelling things about his work and it keeps me coming back again and again.

I remember falling in love with Sparth's work around 2002 on the Sijun Forums. Digital painting was relatively new at the time and just entering the mainstream as a tool. While most of us were just trying to get our heads around using a tablet and stylus, he was already pushing the boundaries of what could be done with the medium. Since then he has gone on to pioneer now ubiquitous digital painting techniques that we all rely on today; build a massive, vibrant body of work; and, in the process, deeply influence a generation of entertainment artists.

Sparth's work in this third volume of *Structura* is utterly luminous, rich in abstraction, and graphically built. The unusual economy of method, palettes, and simplicity of shapes at first suggests that he's moving into new stylistic territory. But I believe it is a return to his origins. Here is a renewed focus on the integrity of fundamentals, strong shape design, and drawing as an essential design tool.

This book represents the still-beating heart of one of concept art's great designers and an act of defiance in the face of the many obstacles encountered in the art-making life: artistically risk-averse art departments, difficulties balancing family and work life, struggles with health and other personal demons, and the challenge of navigating the currents of what is trending versus staying true to how and what one loves to paint. The potential barriers to artistic growth are many. But Sparth manages to press on at a mighty pace, fearless and inspired, with an adaptable talent, a curious nature, and an approach born of years of exploration that balances intuition with a dedication to craft.

If his work is not already a touchstone for you, it will be before you close this book.

Thom Tenery
Los Angeles, California
September 2014

Structura3 covers three years of personal and professional creative adventures, and expresses my constant urge to create and experiment inside and outside the boundaries of the concept art world by using innovative techniques and unique workflows.

One technique is using primitive shapes like cubes or triangles to make a successful composition, which I find fascinating. Simply put, I absolutely love throwing simple shapes on a canvas to create an interconnected world of visual rhythms and dynamics. There are shapes that work perfectly well together. Lines combined with squares or circles, for example, can produce great combinations. It's all about how forms interact into a single, unified flow. Of course, you need to extrapolate a tangible result out of the interplay, but the concept of primitive shapes prevails nonetheless. If they are put together successfully, they can potentially become the backbone of any thoughtful composition. True, these experiments are not always suitable for production and studio work, but they are vital additions to my explorations, feeding my design senses with new ideas every time I jump into a new painting session.

Limiting the amount of time spent on an image is another way to obtain groundbreaking results. The brain needs to process the image faster, leaving behind unnecessary strokes and rendering. You have to rely on a minimum amount of shapes and painting tricks to get straight to the point: a successful composition paired with great visual storytelling. There are several online art forums and groups applying these limitations, as well as random daily themes, and I've been having a lot of fun participating in these challenges. The third chapter of *Structura3* is entirely dedicated to my 30-minute paintings, which you could call "speed paintings," though I admit I don't really like the term. It's just a more straightforward approach where the initial impulse prevails.

Since 2009, apart from several book covers, my professional work has been entirely dedicated to 343 Industries, the Microsoft studio behind the *Halo* franchise. This means I have been de facto entirely committed to the future of the game, and have been doing so with continuous excitement and passion. The *Halo* world is huge and organic by nature, not only because of the tremendous amount of preexisting visual and narrative materials, but also thanks to the hundreds of artists, writers, animators, musicians, and game designers who contributed to the success of this unequaled franchise. The inclusion of a *Halo* chapter in this book will not come as a surprise.

And *Structura3* would not be complete without including a chapter about my art process. As it's fun changing the recipe, I decided to explain more about the key elements that are part of my daily workflow. The way I engage with an image, the way I compose. The obvious as well as the less obvious. It's all in there, as a complete list of design thoughts and reminder notes, ready to be implemented into any digital workflow.

Obviously my passion for science fiction is as alive as ever. The future of space can be abstract and figurative at the same time, and I love that aspect of it, playing with it from one image to the next. Space travel allows the reign of imagination. You can throw anything into the mix, from strange propulsions to improbable architecture. The universe becomes fully mine. But there's also this awareness that our time on Earth is way too short to see it all—and to create it all. I suppose that like *Blade Runner*'s Roy Batty, I simply need more life.

Enjoy the trip.

Sparth
Seattle, Washington
September 2014

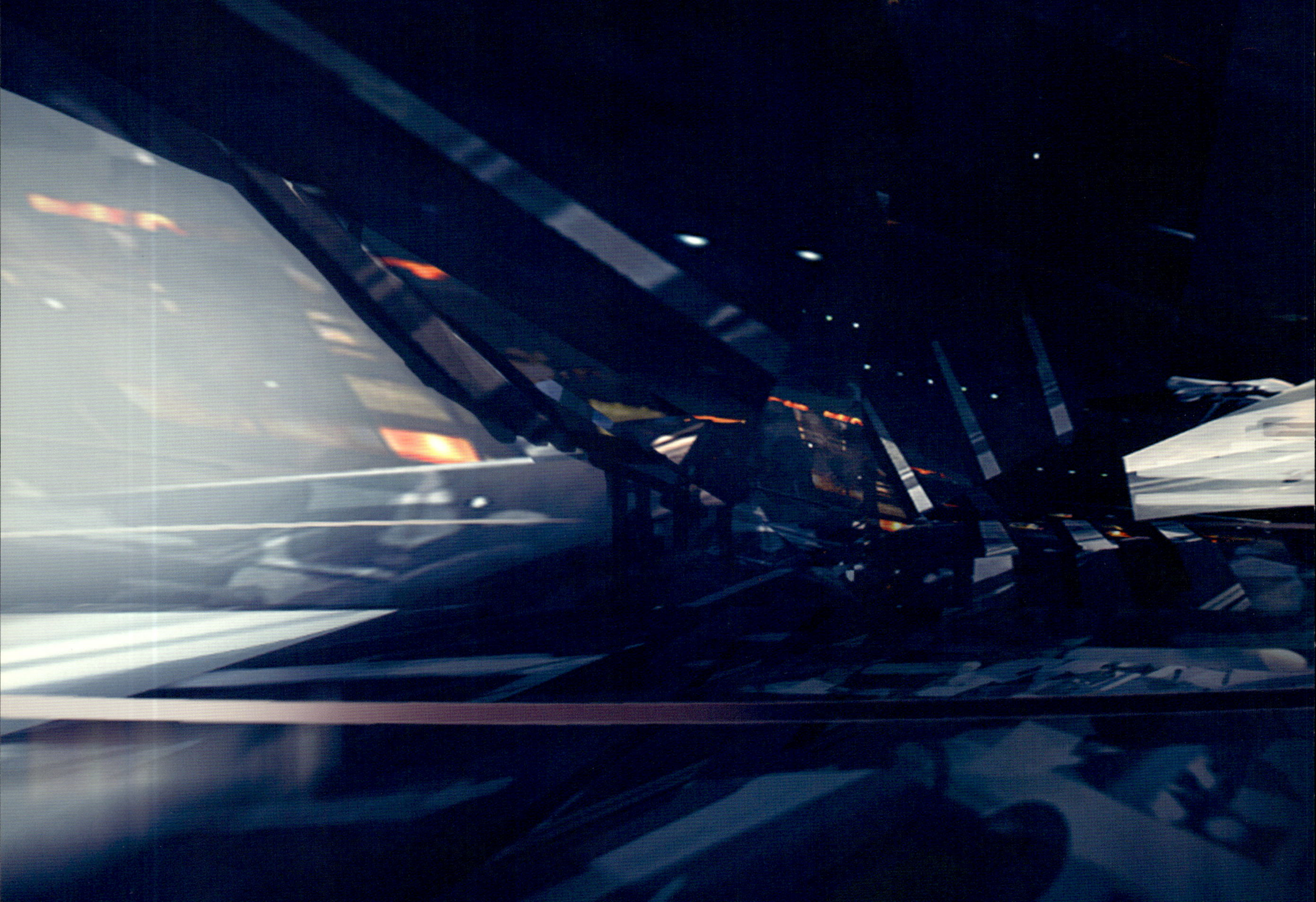

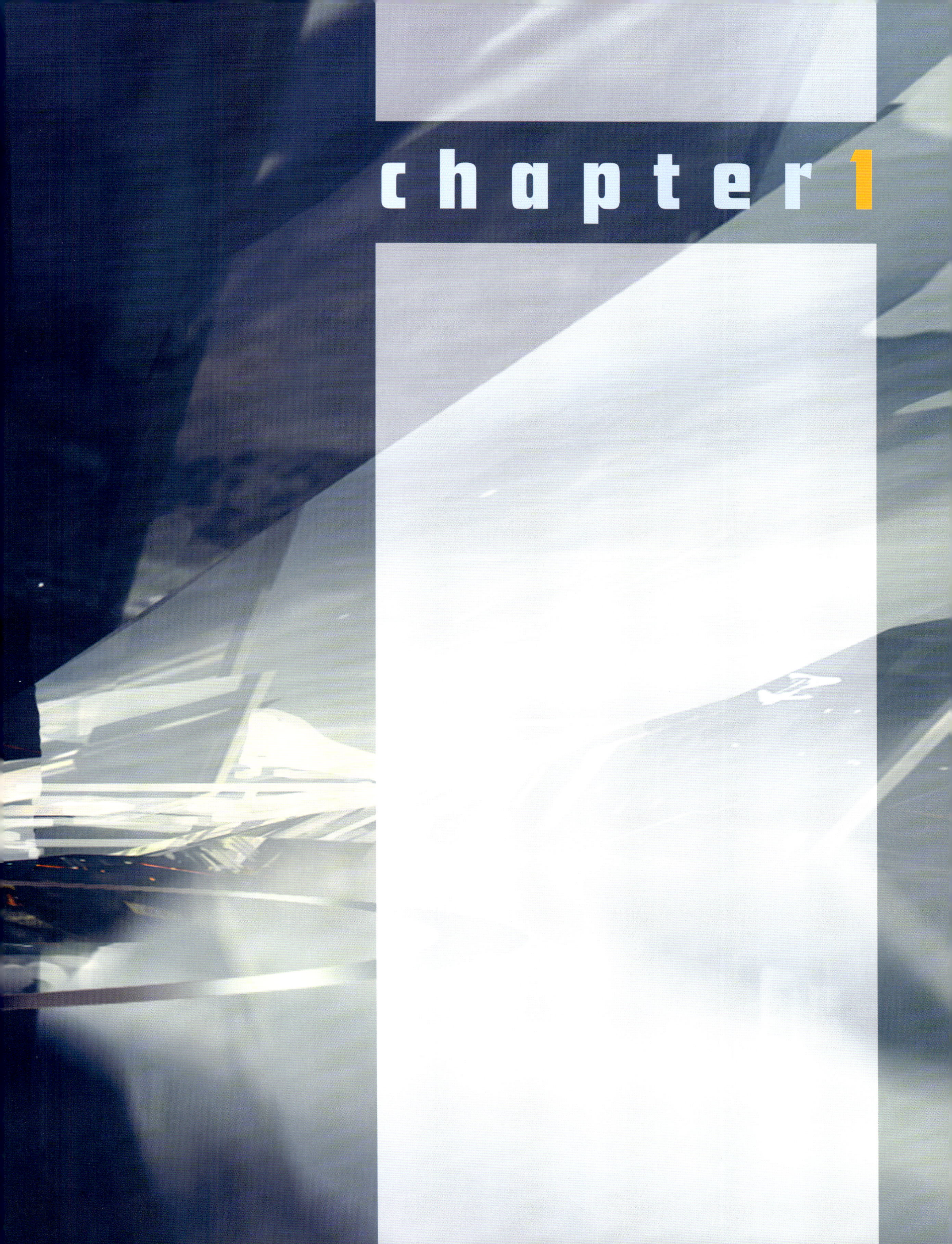
chapter1

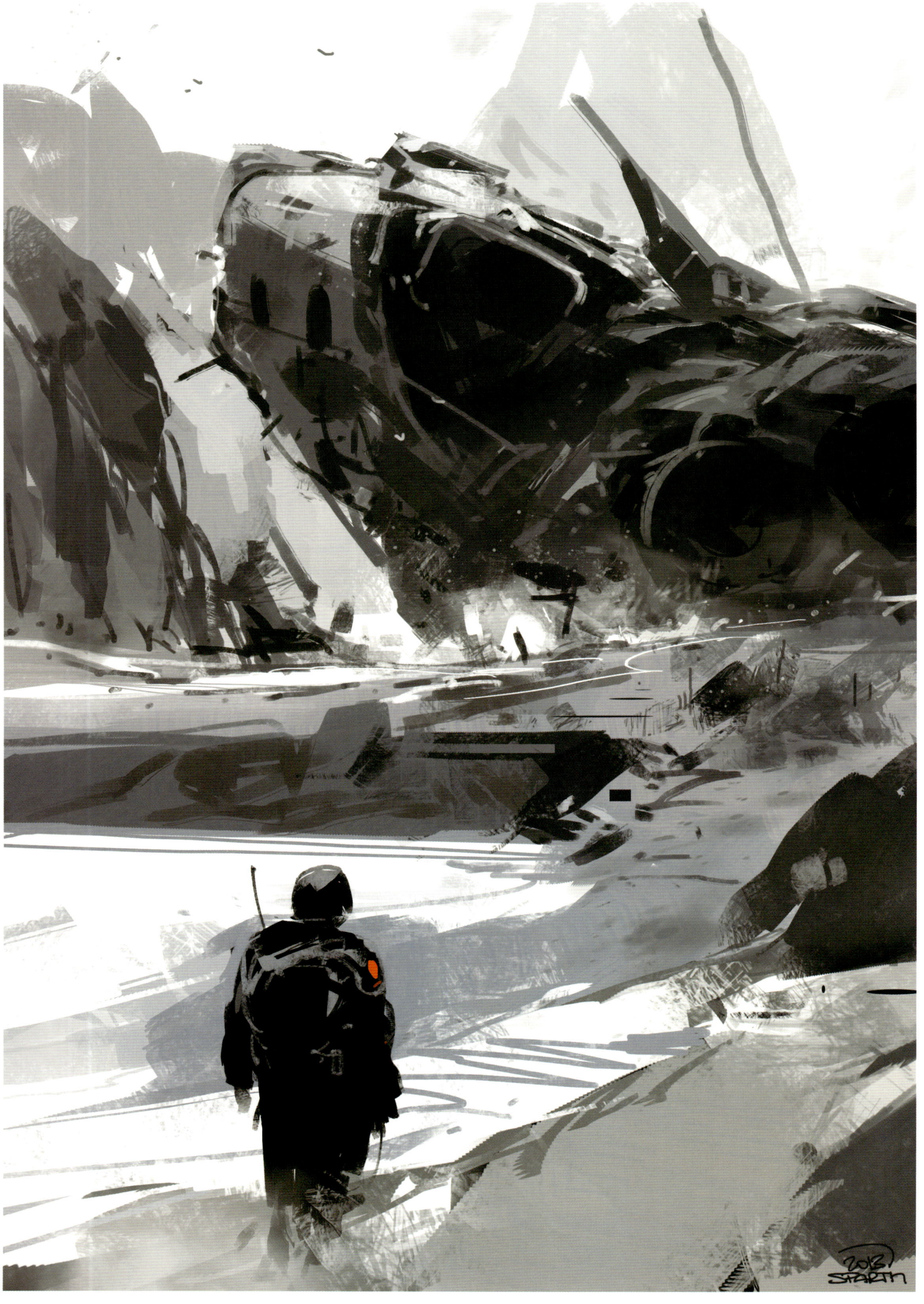

Ruin sketch, 2013

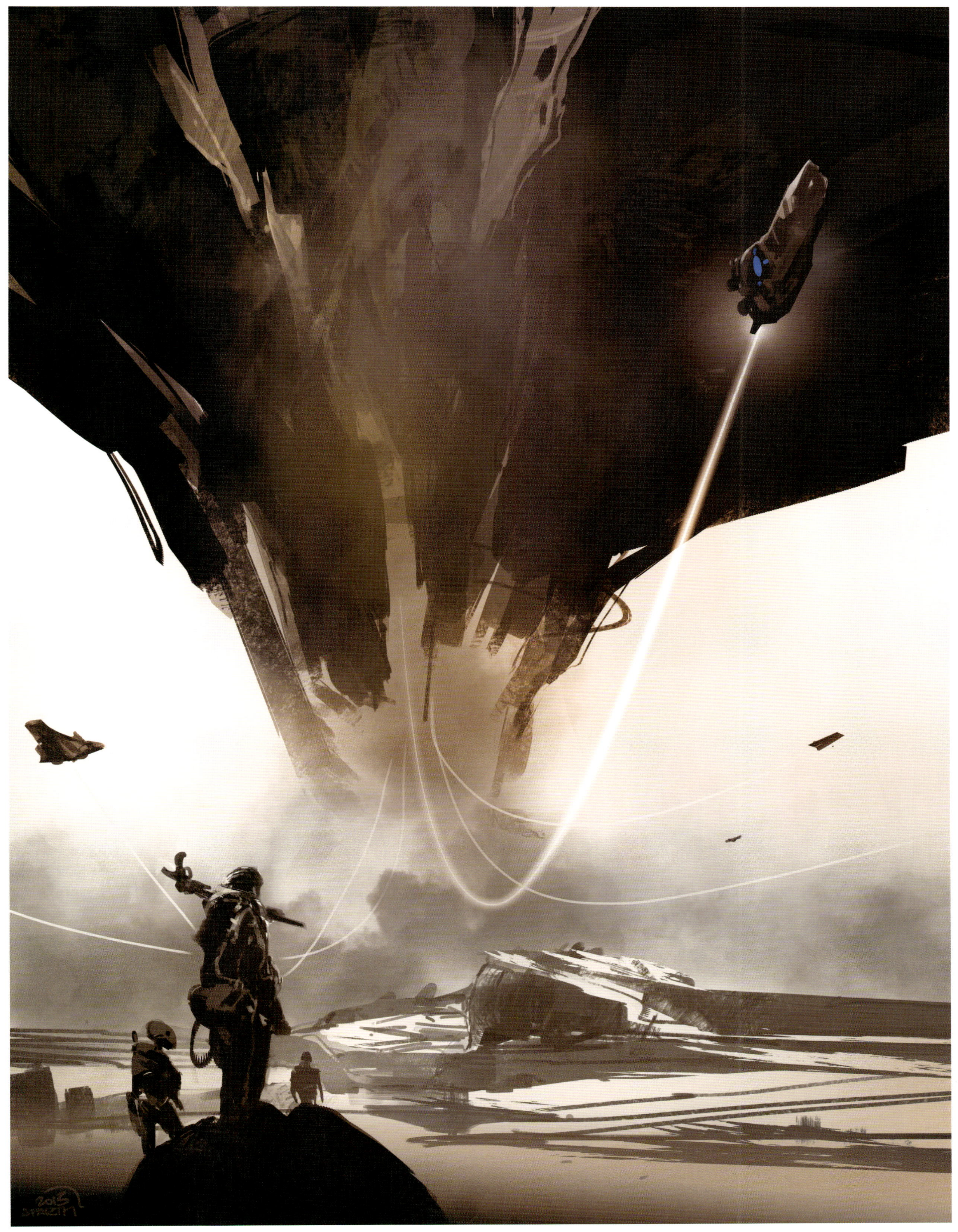

Opening, 2013

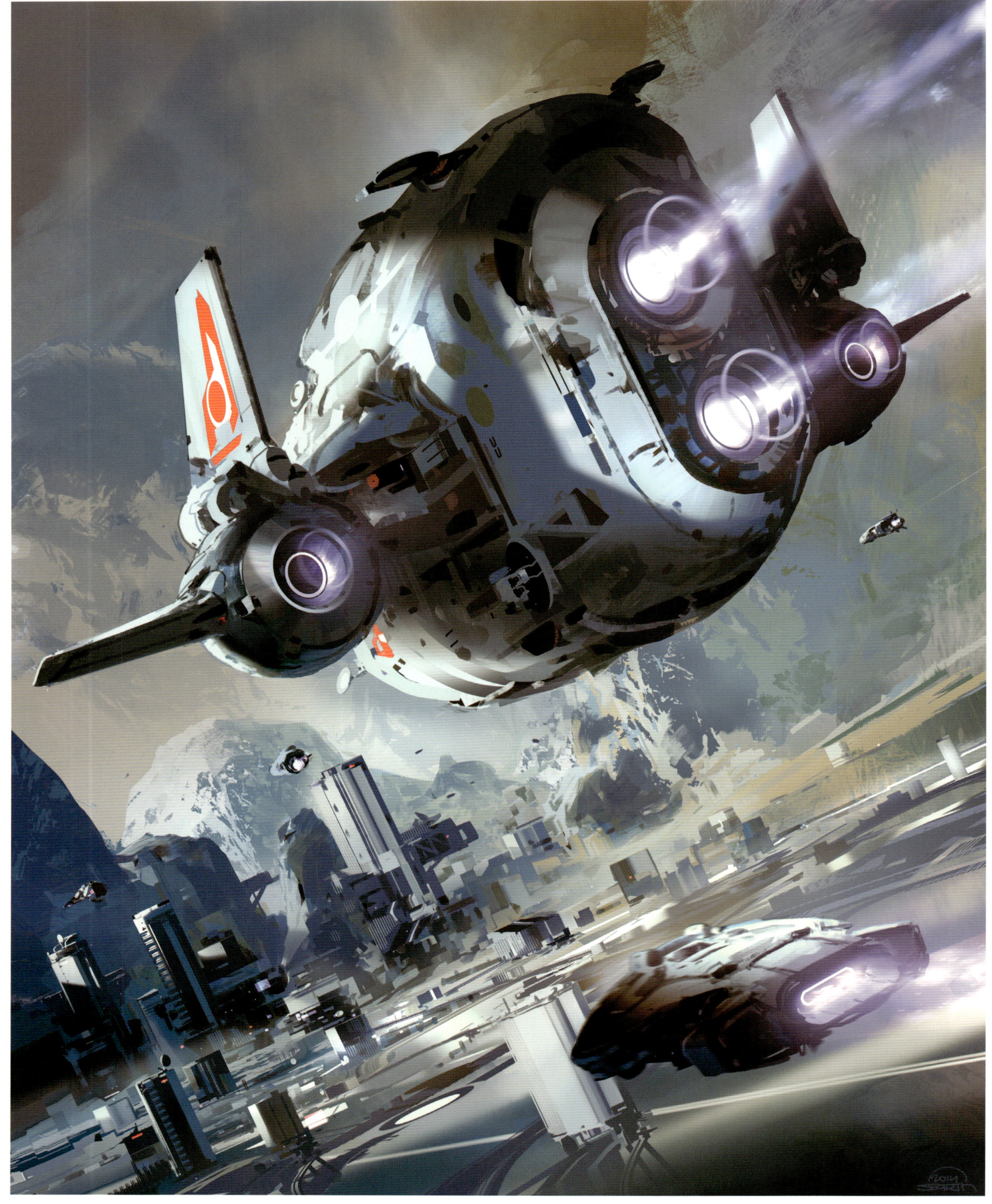

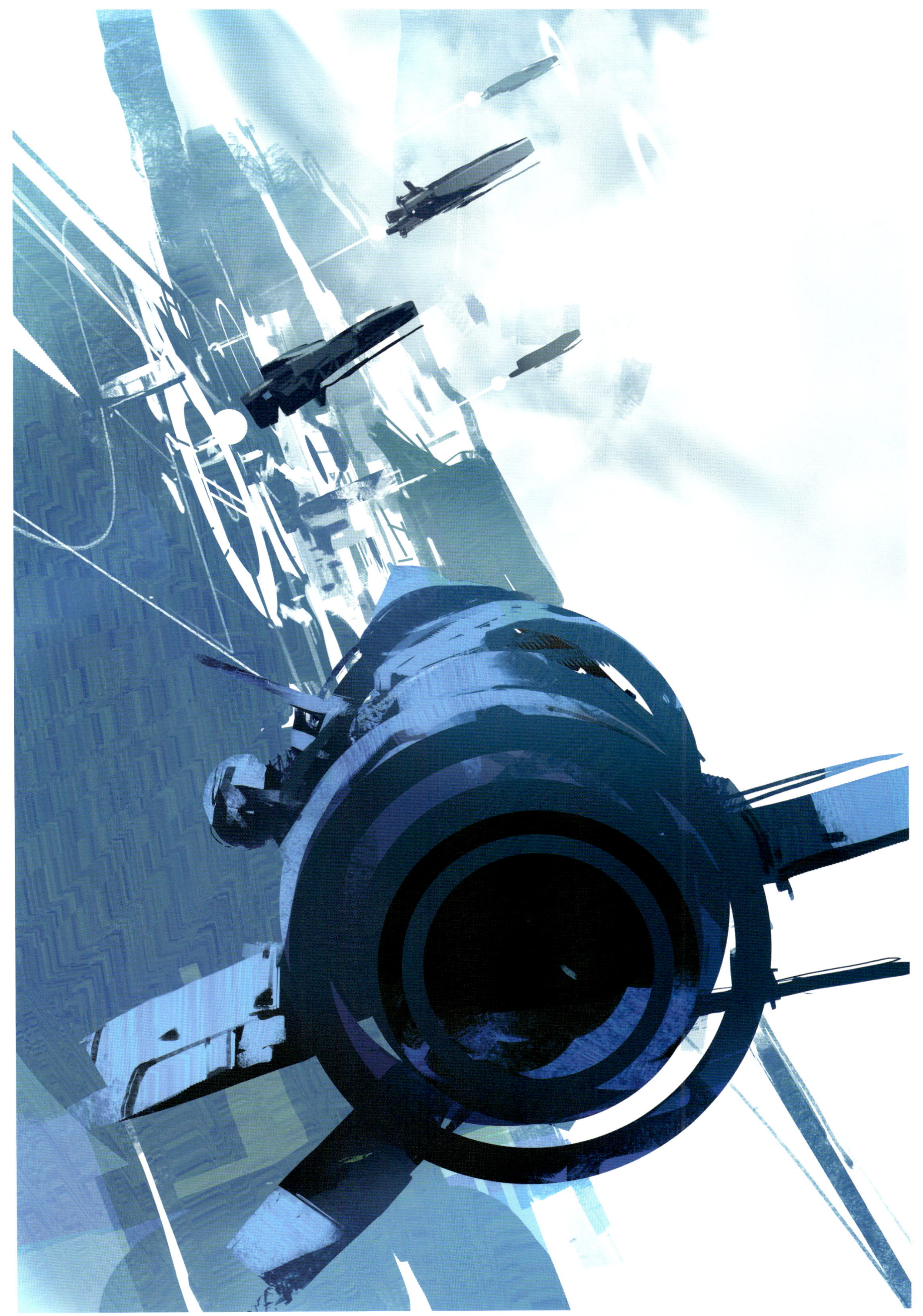

Blue exodus, 2013

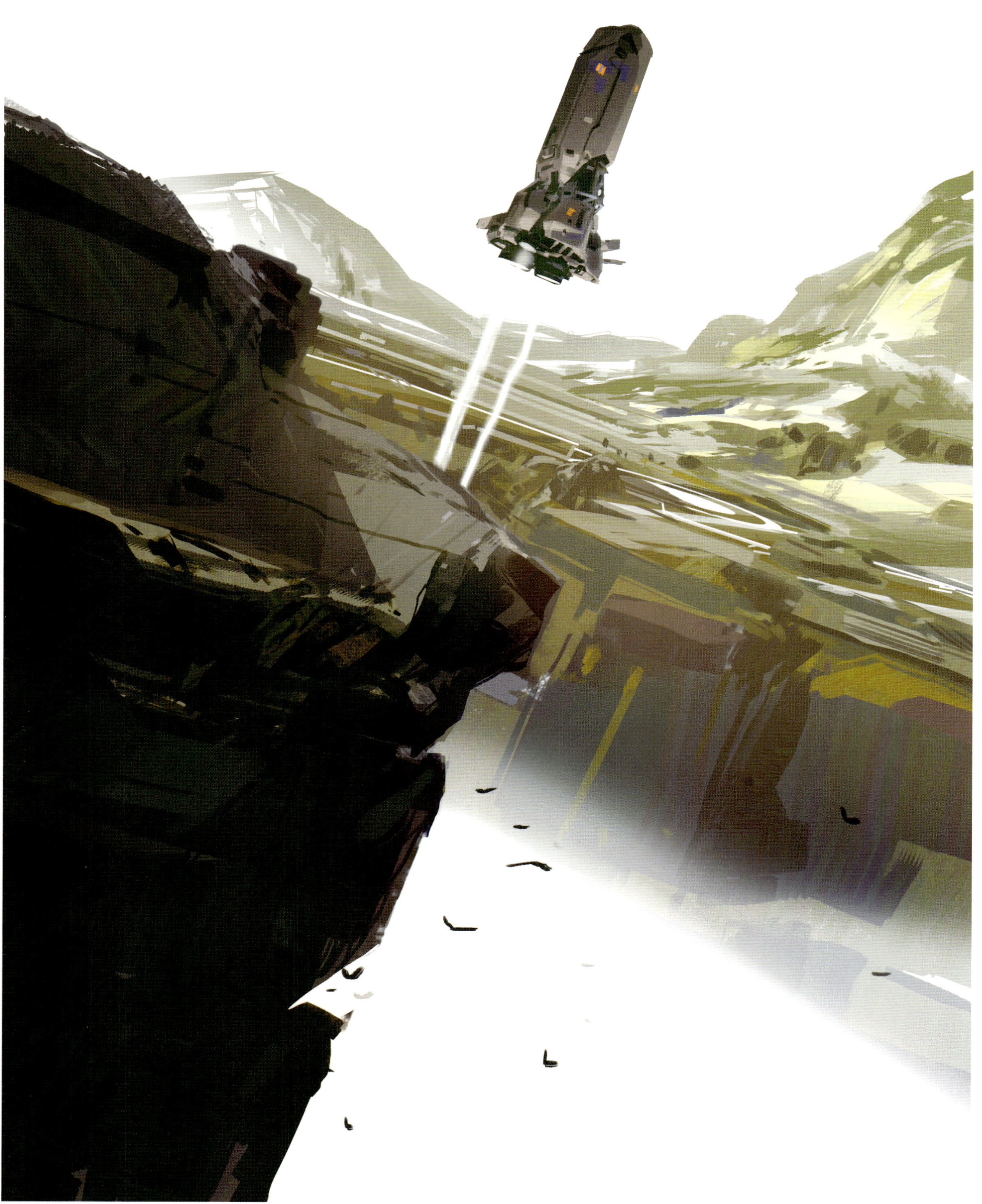

Canyon takeoff, 2013

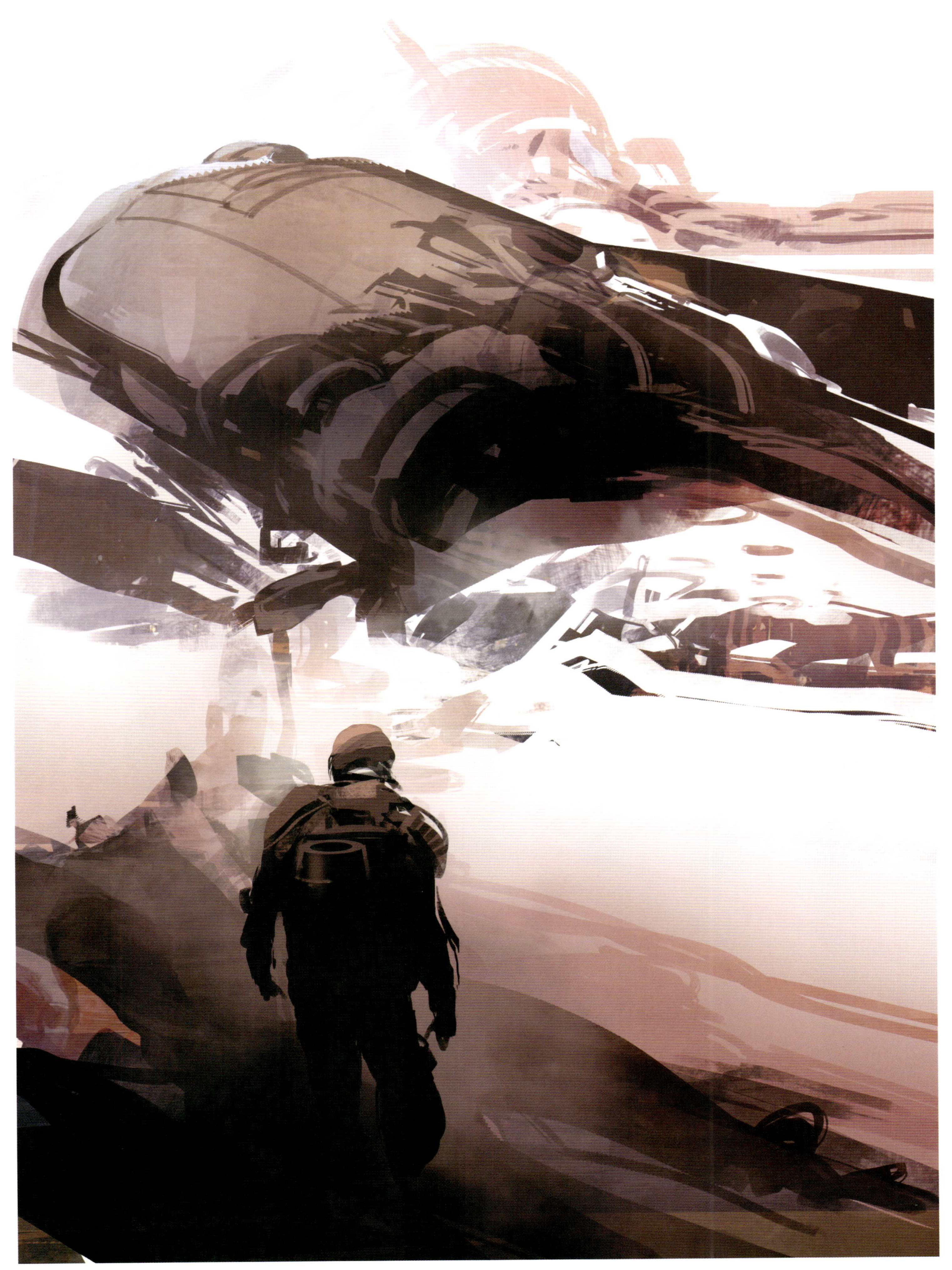

Scavengers, 2013

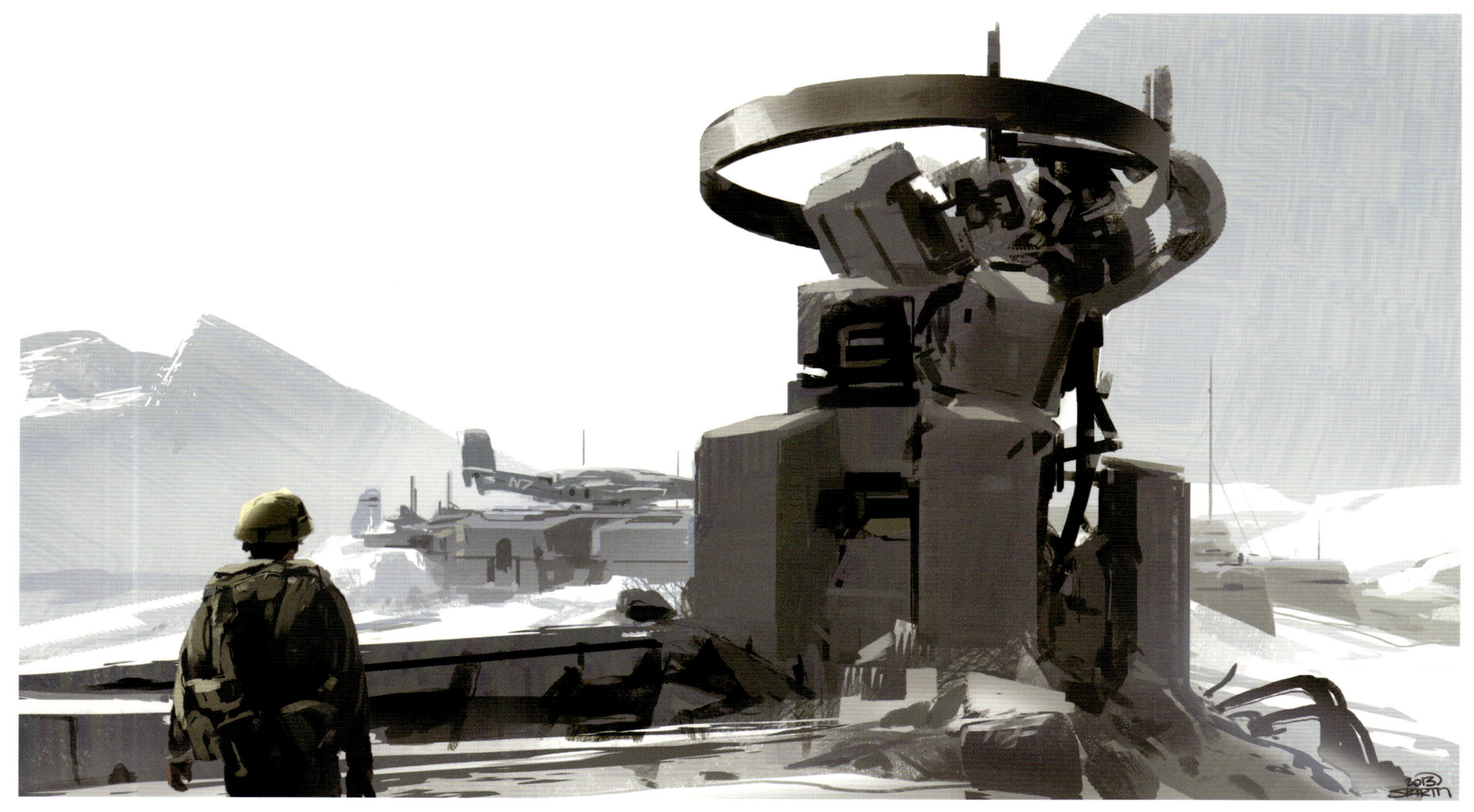

above Unknown machinery, 2013
opposite Desert mech, 2013

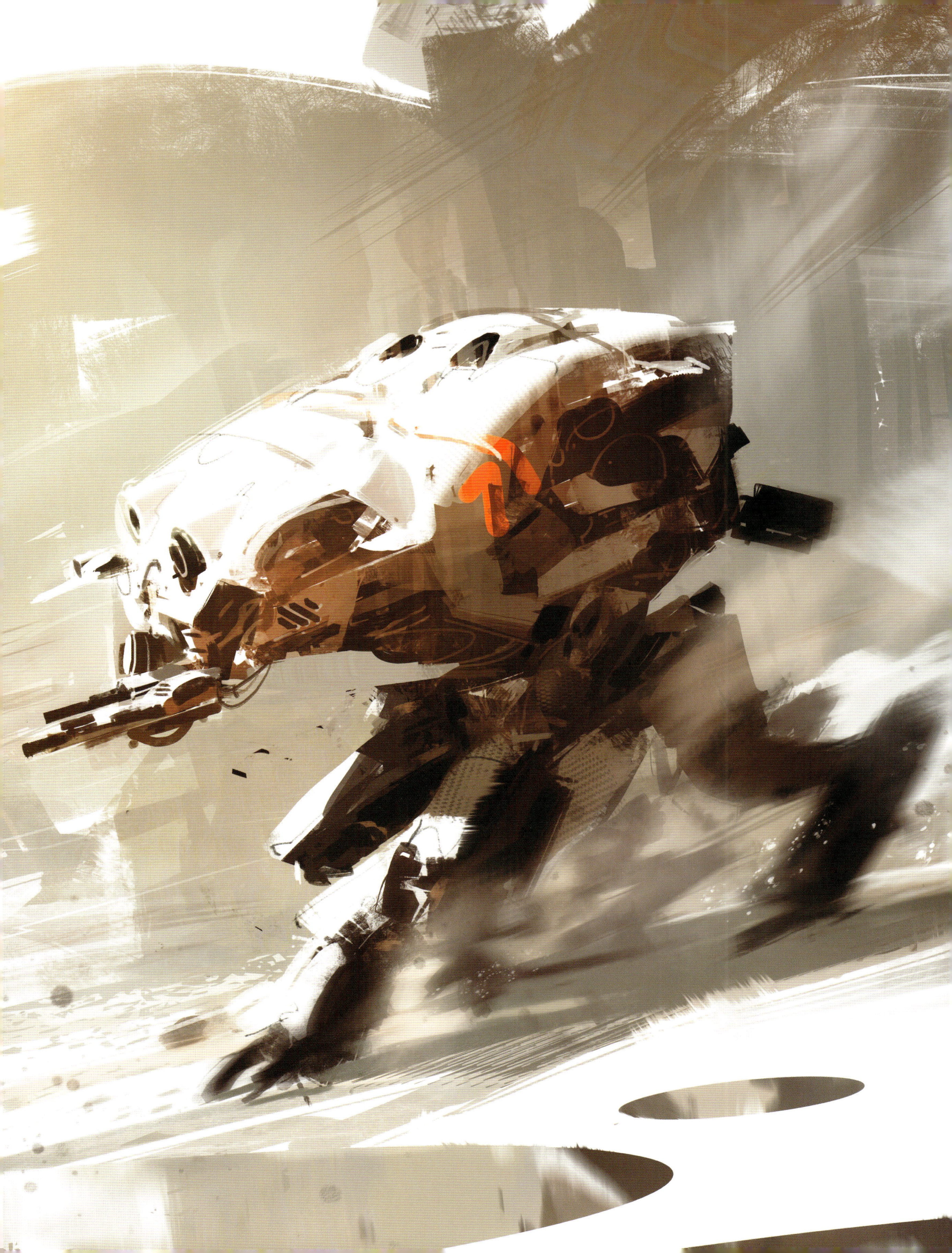

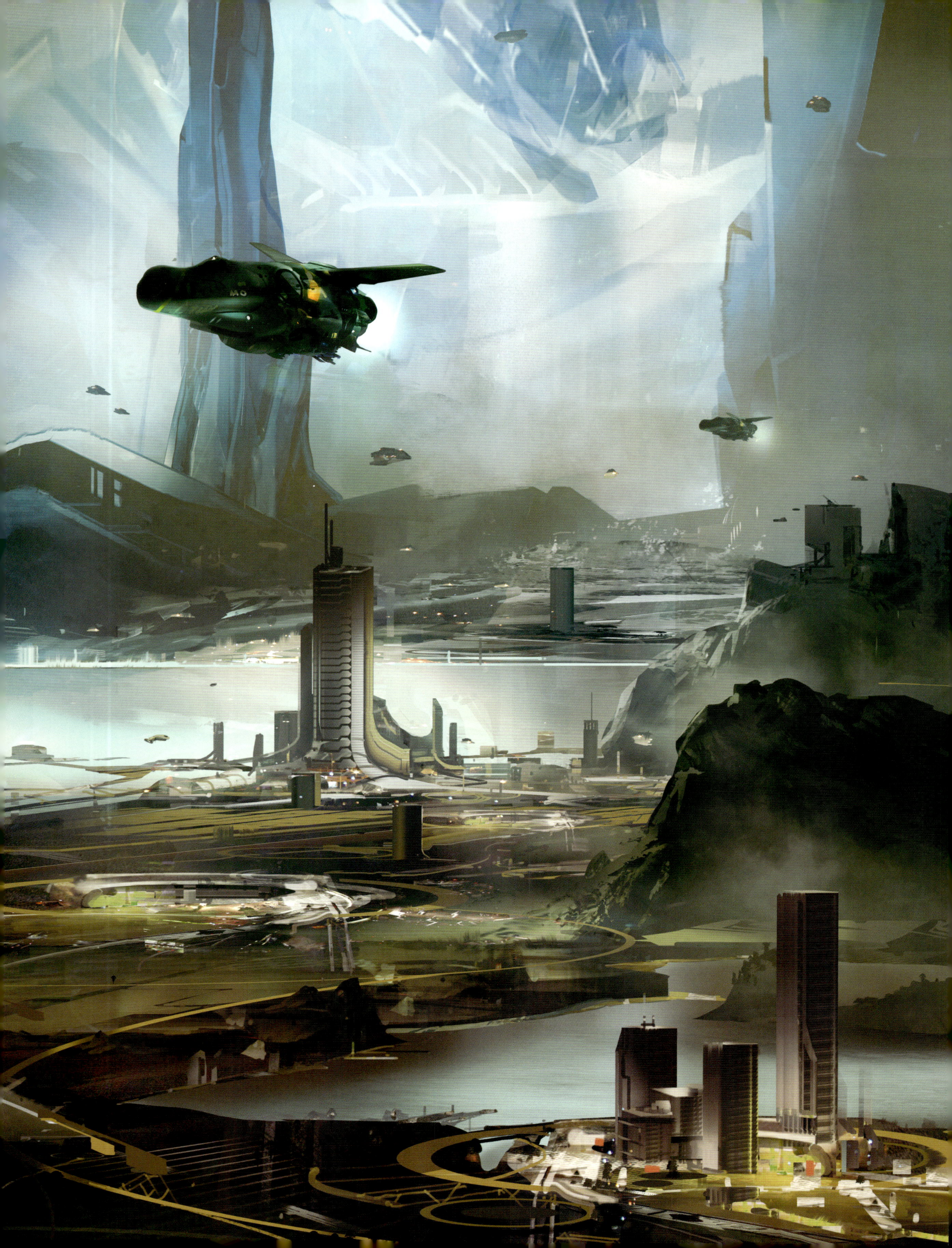

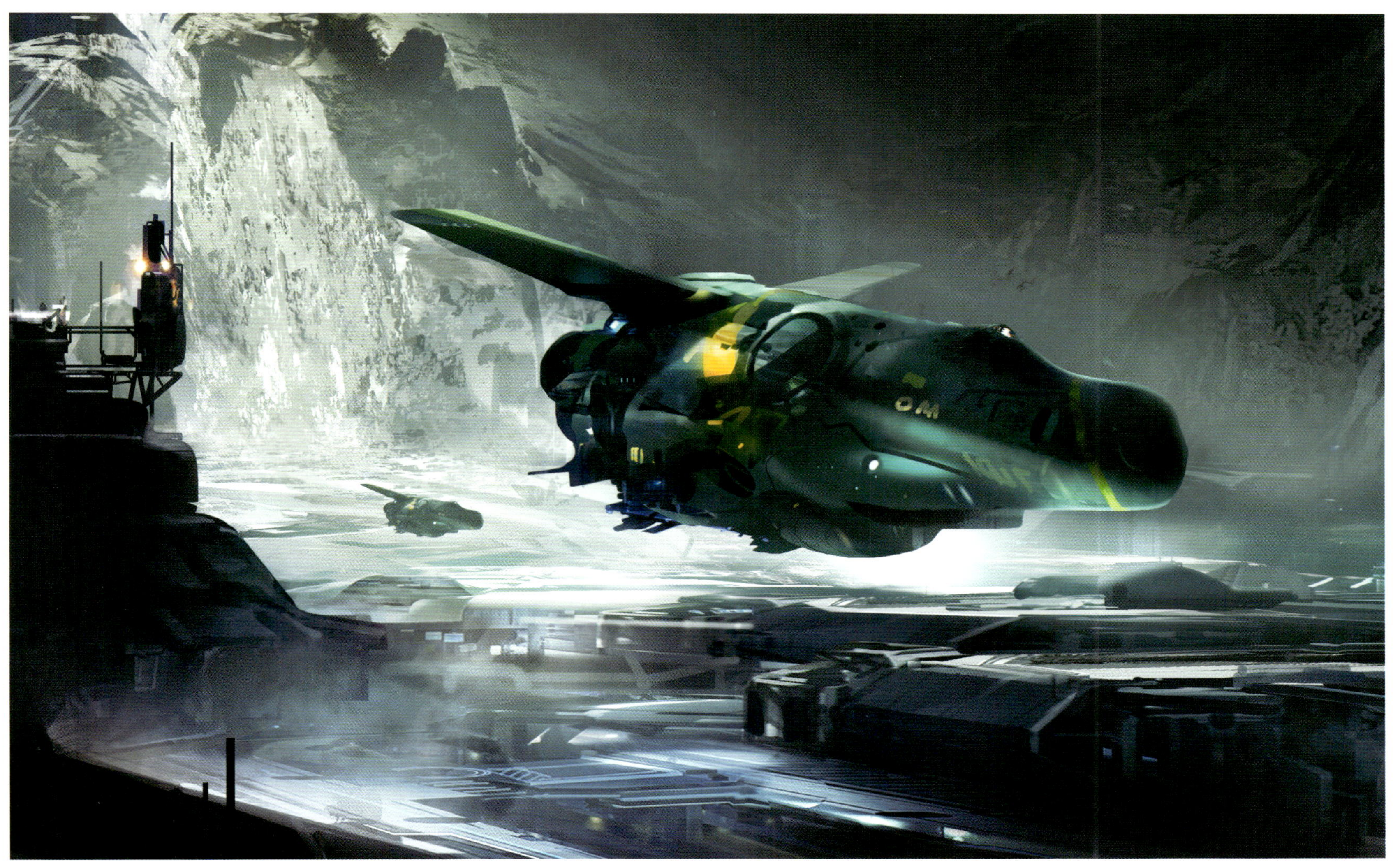

above Alternate cover concept
opposite Book cover, *On the Razor's Edge* by Michael Flynn, 2012

The smart placement of elements within a framed scene is what makes an image successful—rendering comes second.

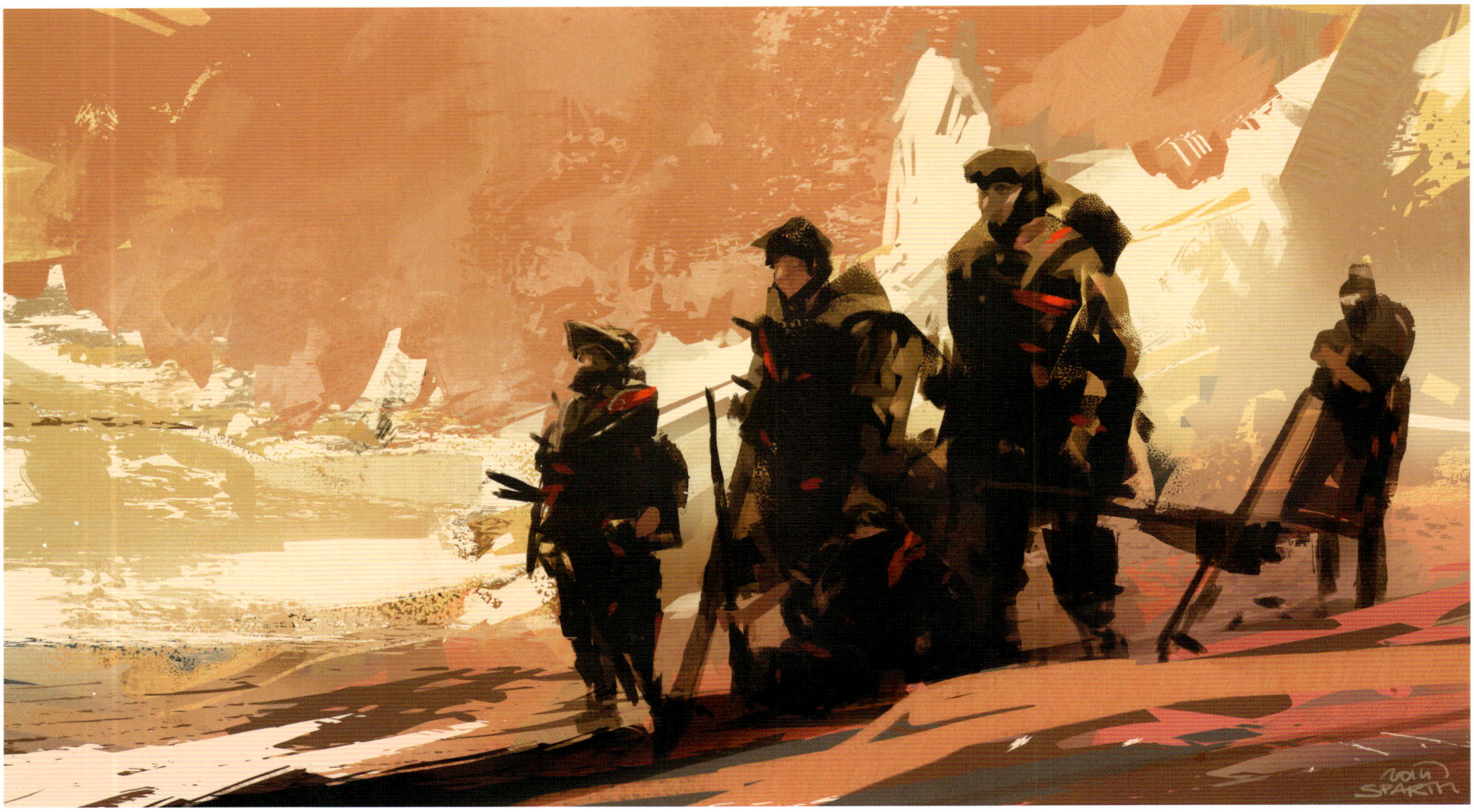

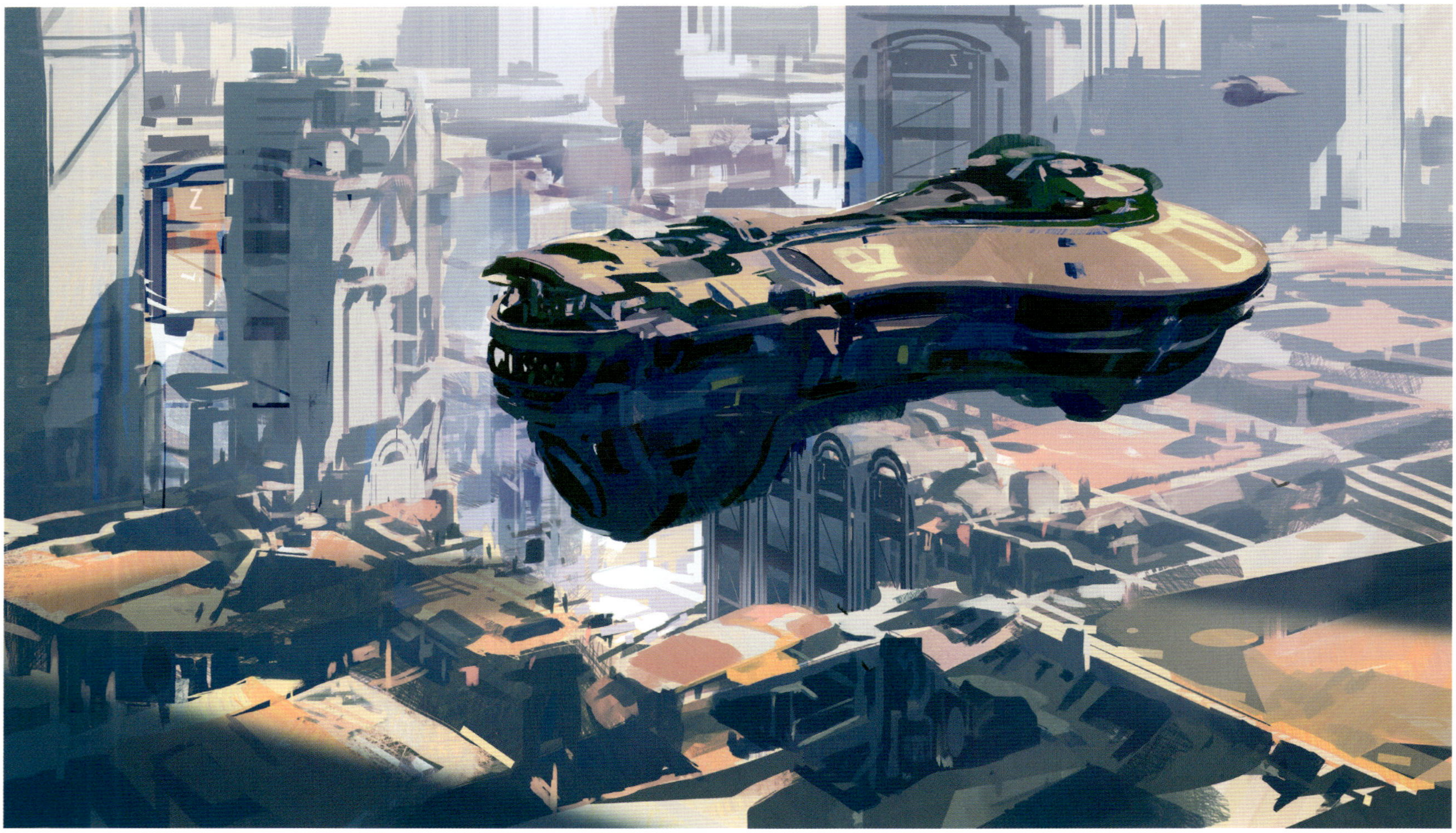

above
Desert men, 2014
Pagoda, 2014

opposite
Book cover, *The Daedalus Incident*
by Michael J. Martinez, 2012

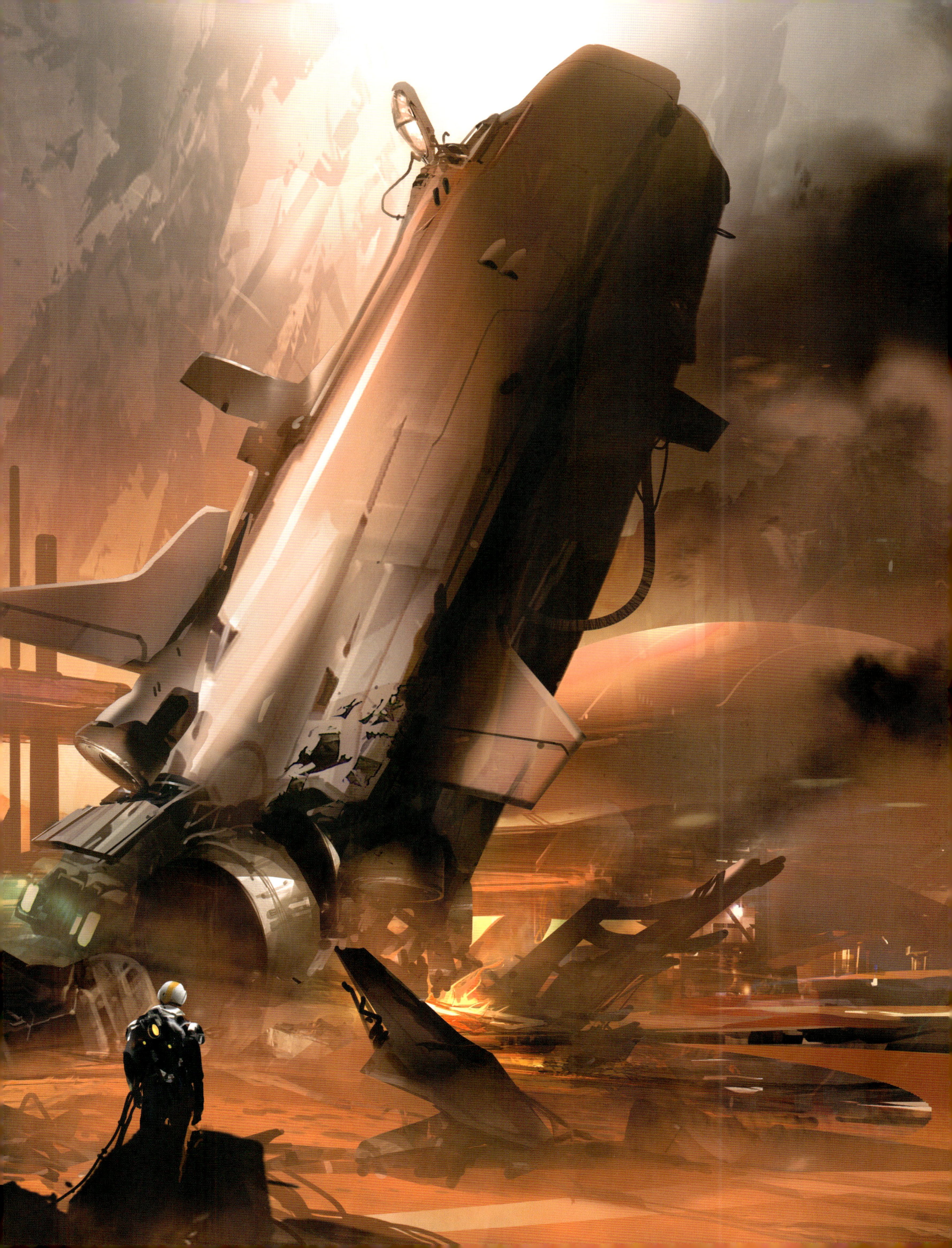

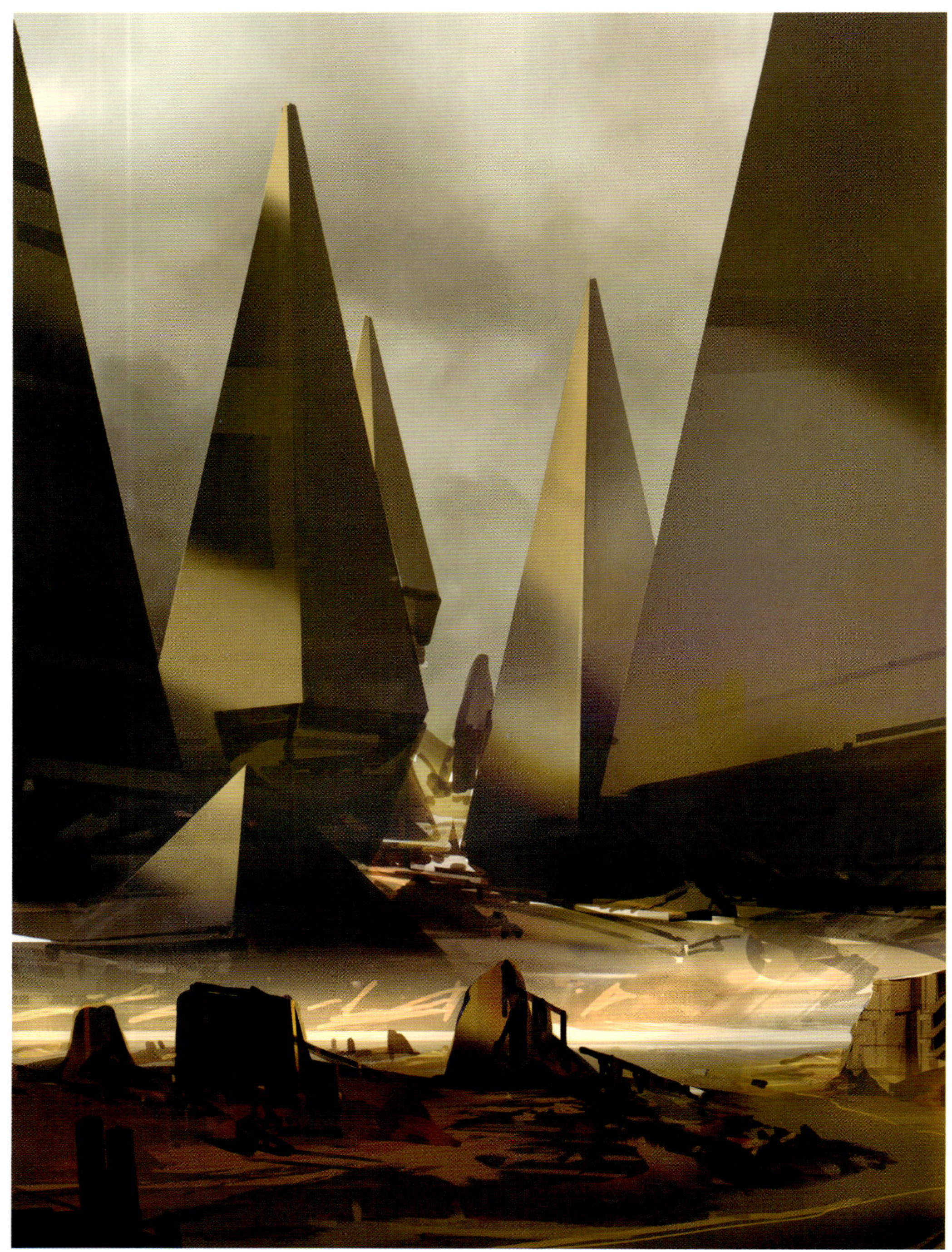

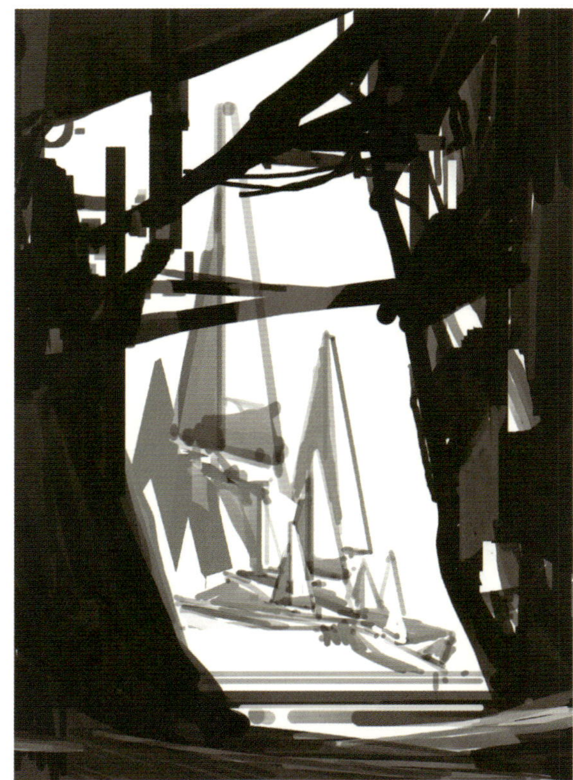

Book cover concepts, *Osiris: Book One of the Osiris Project* by E.J. Swift, 2012

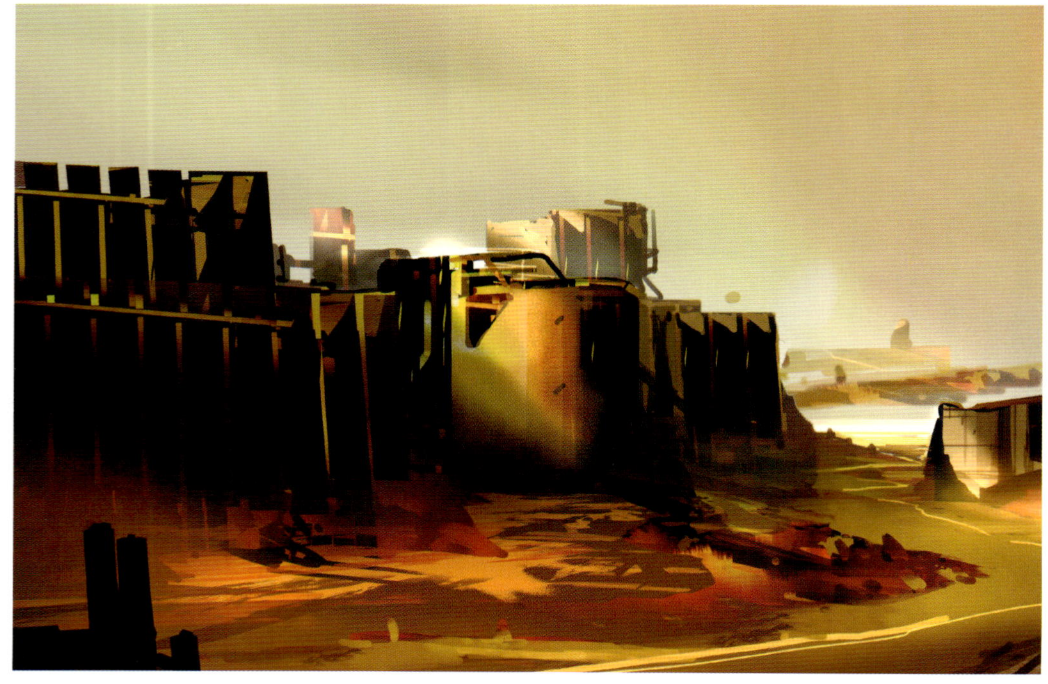

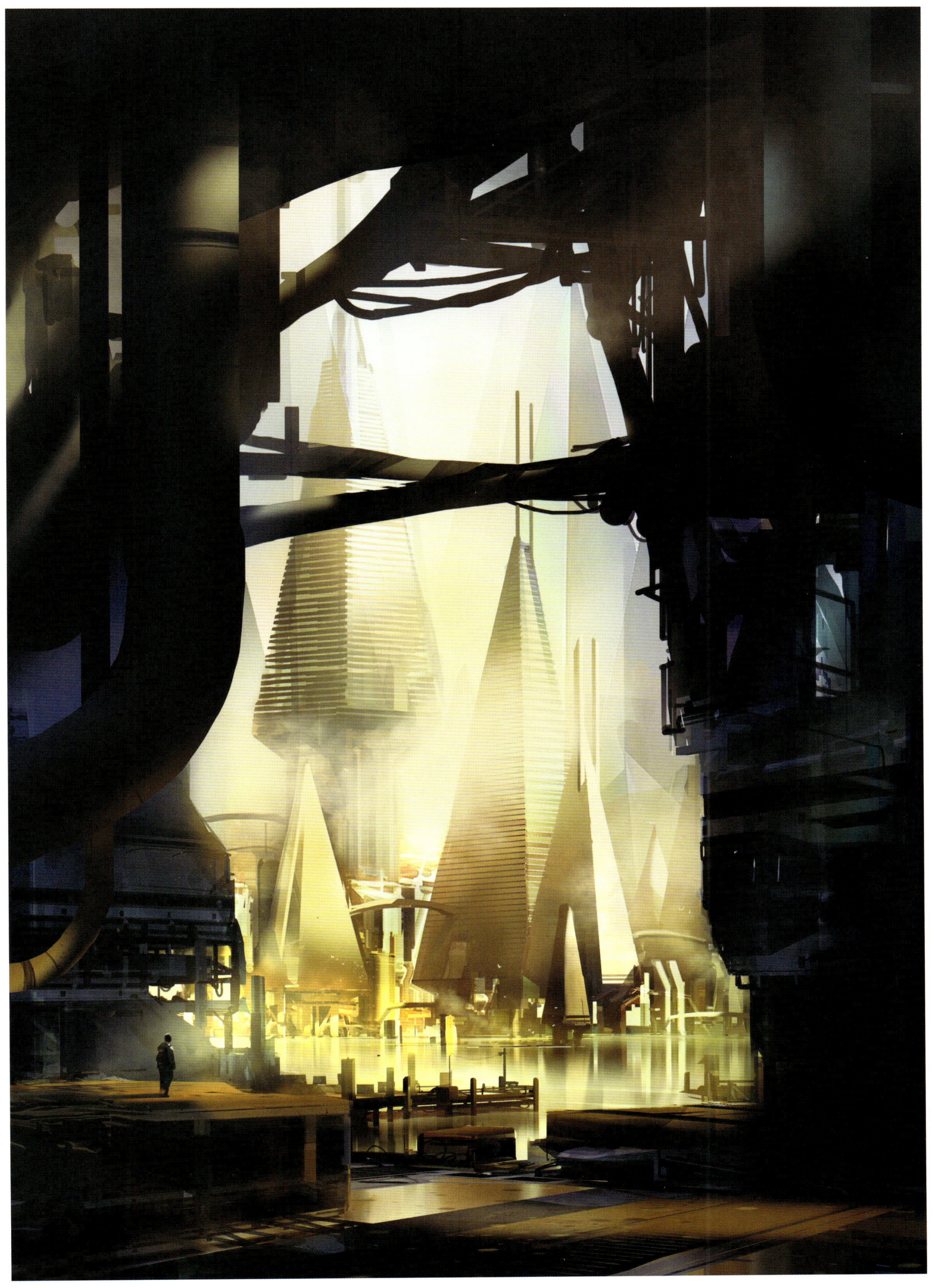

Final book cover, *Osiris: Book One of the Osiris Project* by E.J. Swift, 2012

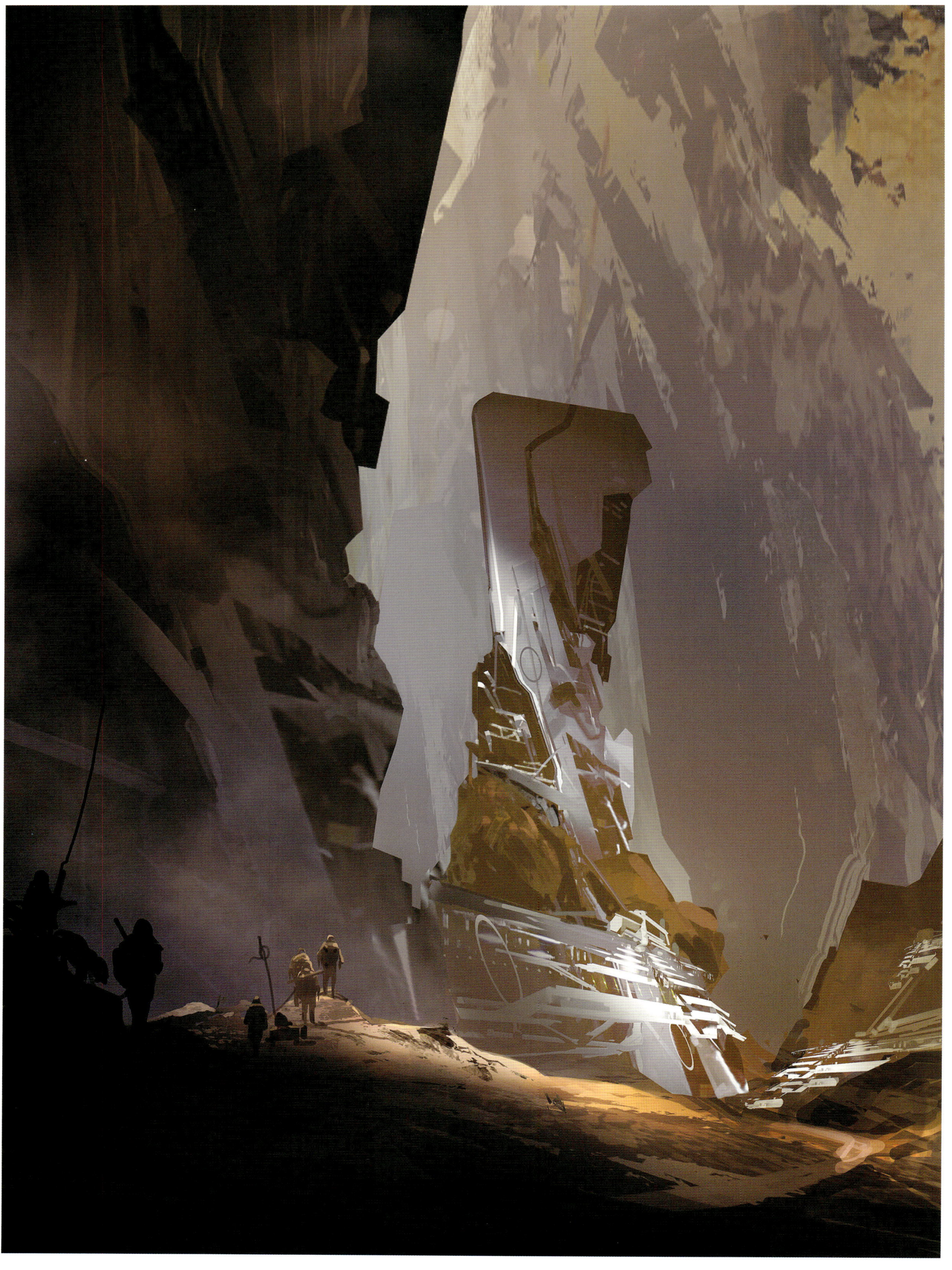

Book cover concept, *Cataveiro: Book Two of the Osiris Project* by E.J. Swift, 2013

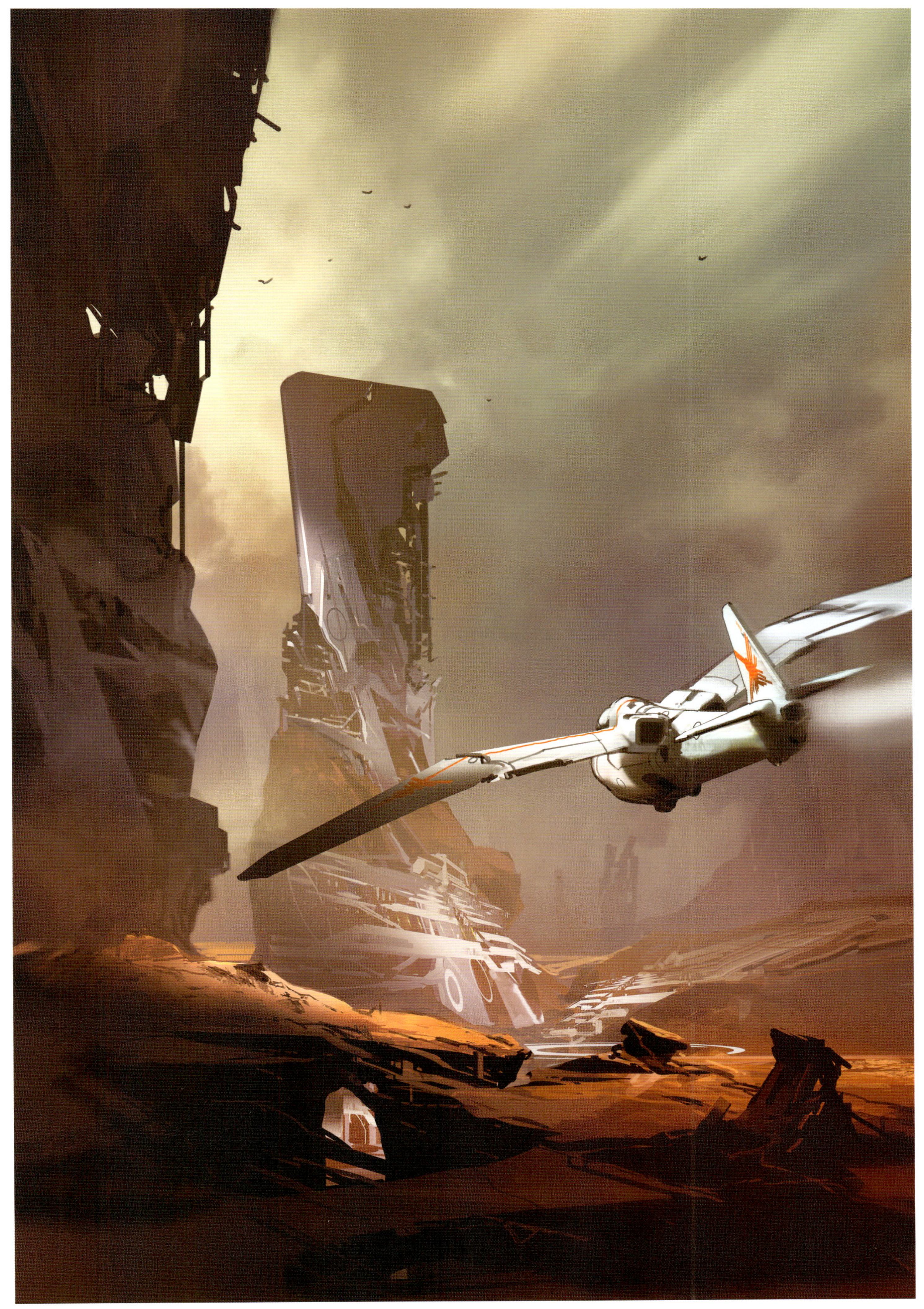

Final book cover, *Cataveiro: Book Two of the Osiris Project* by E.J. Swift, 2013

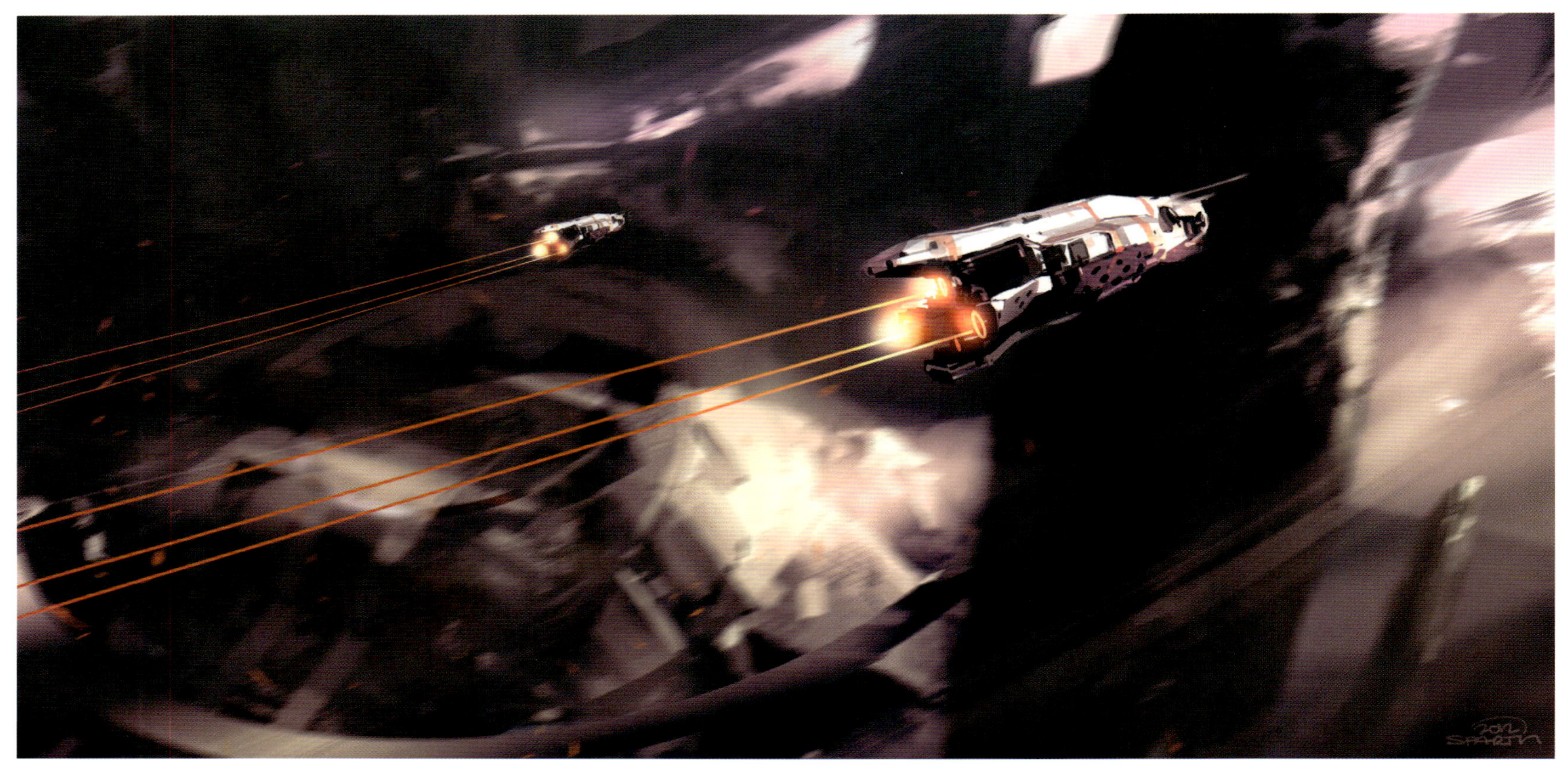

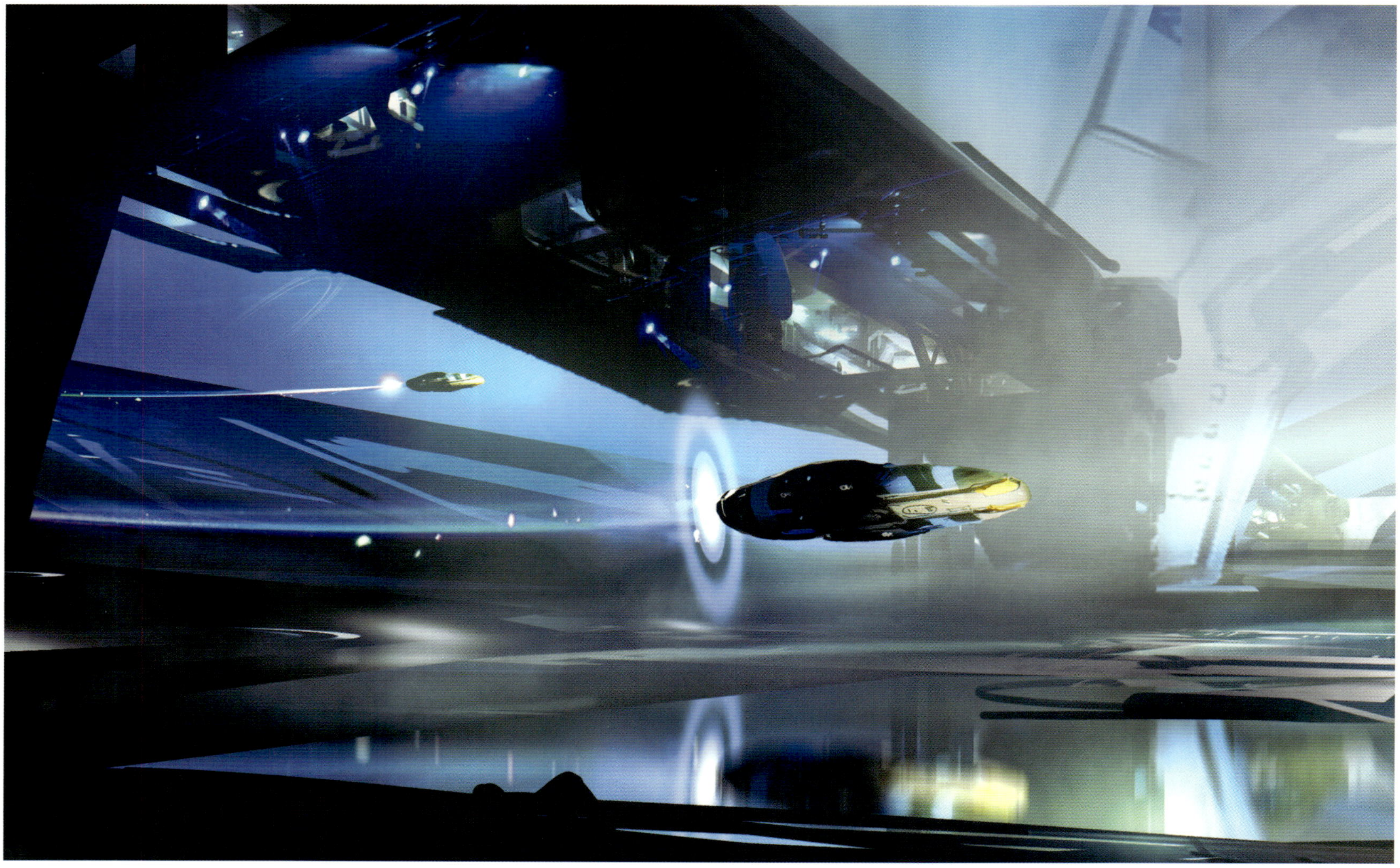

Speedy pinko, 2012
Arche, 2012

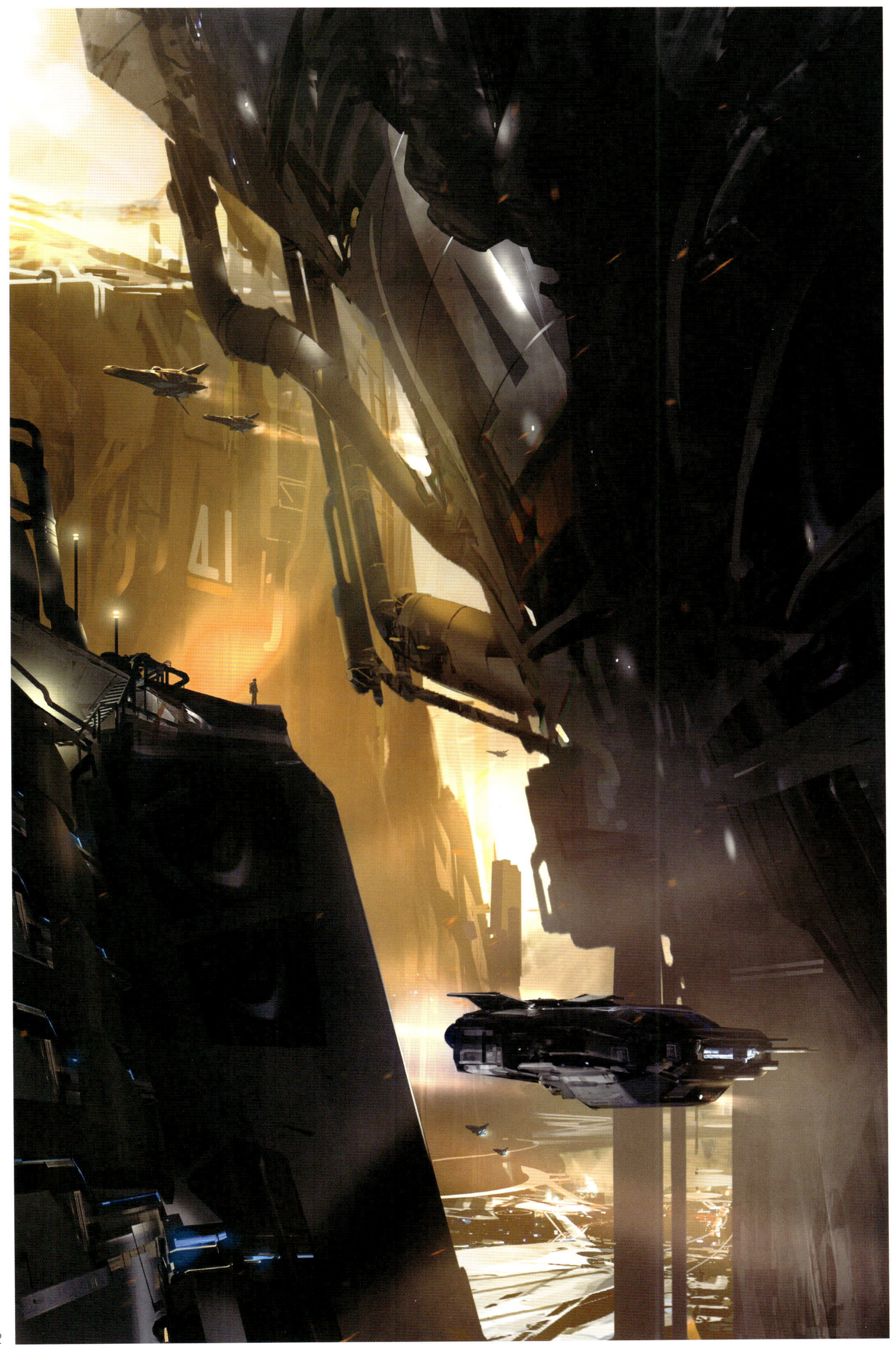

Visions of Mars, 2012

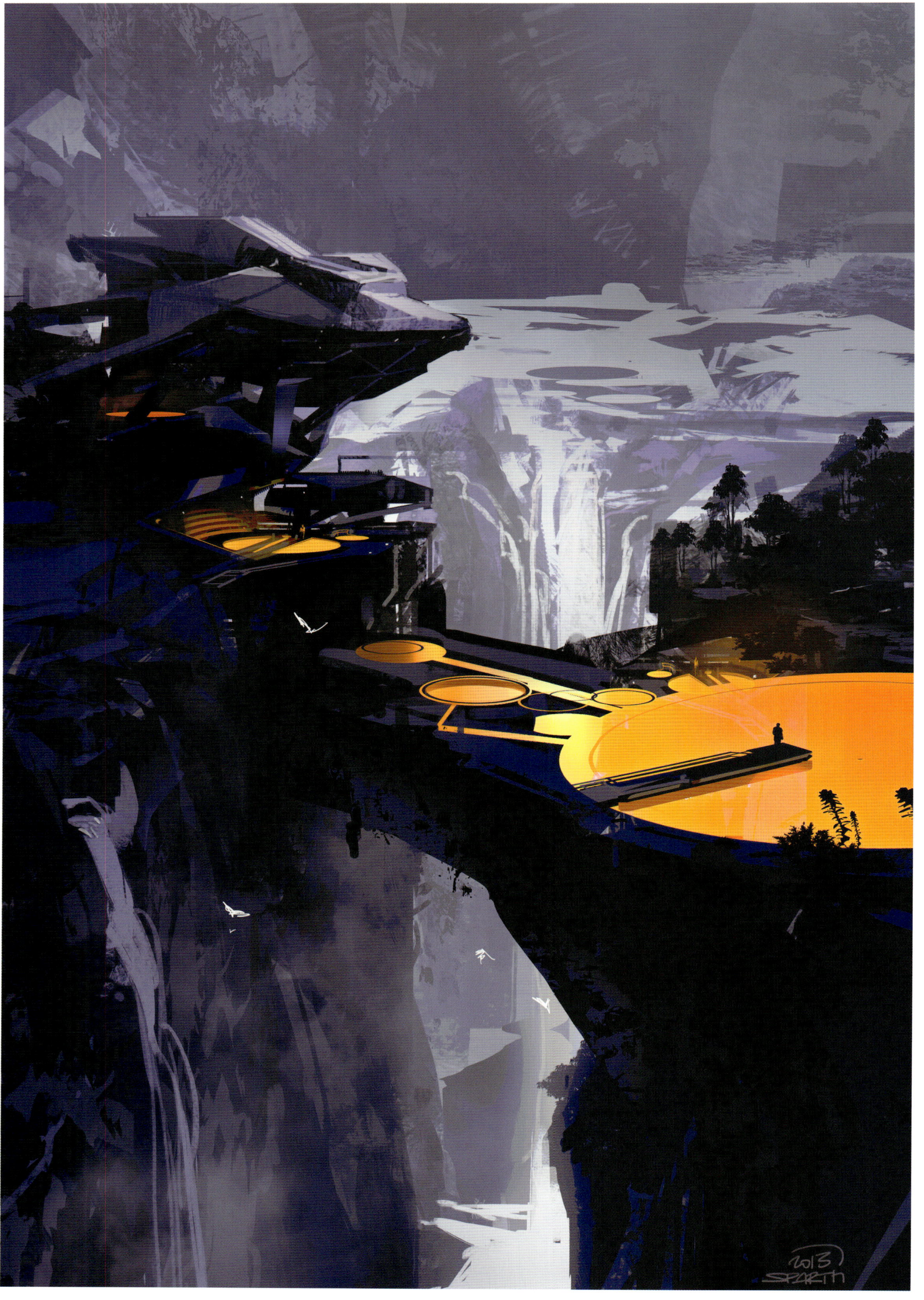

Red pool, 2013

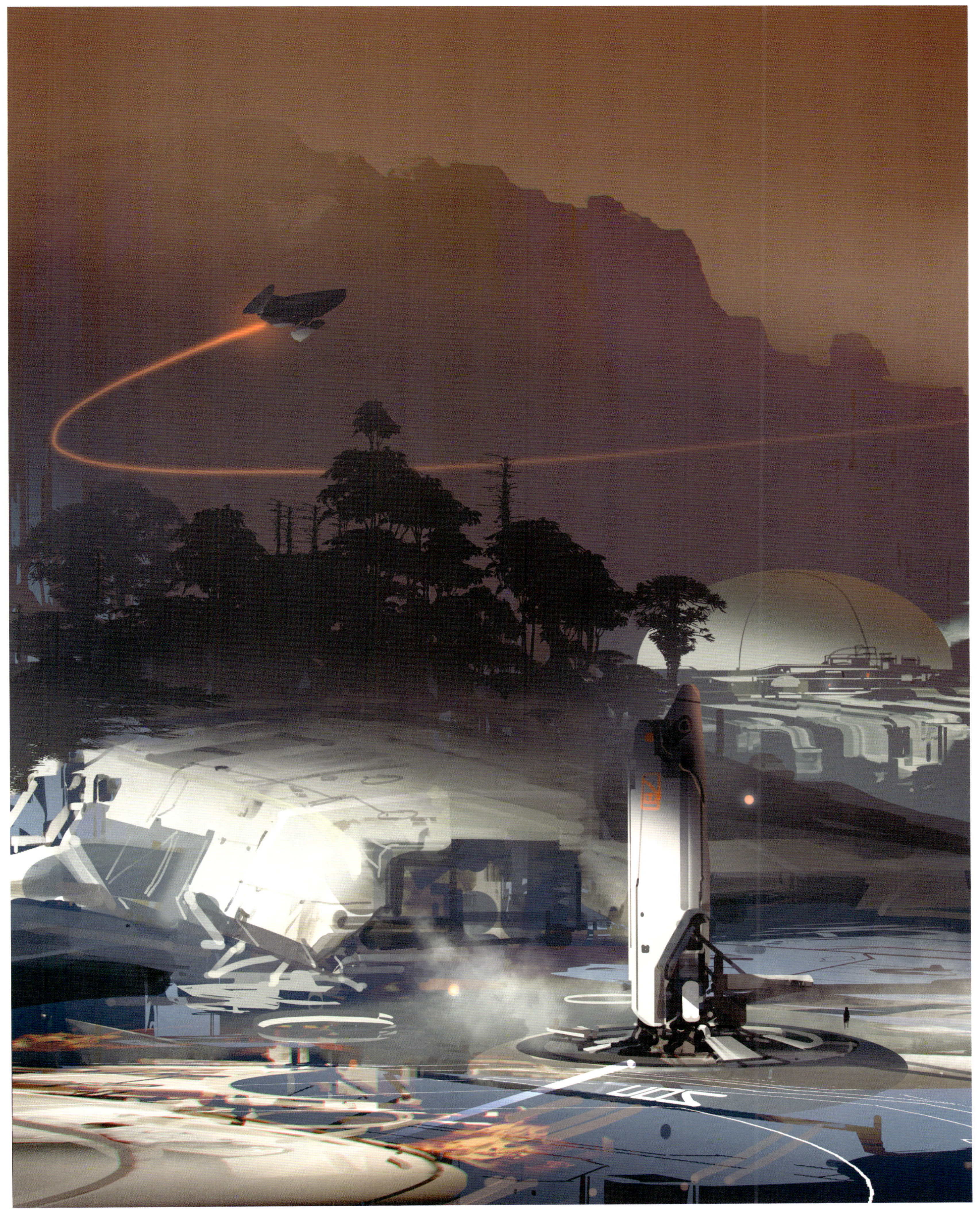

Zou, 2012

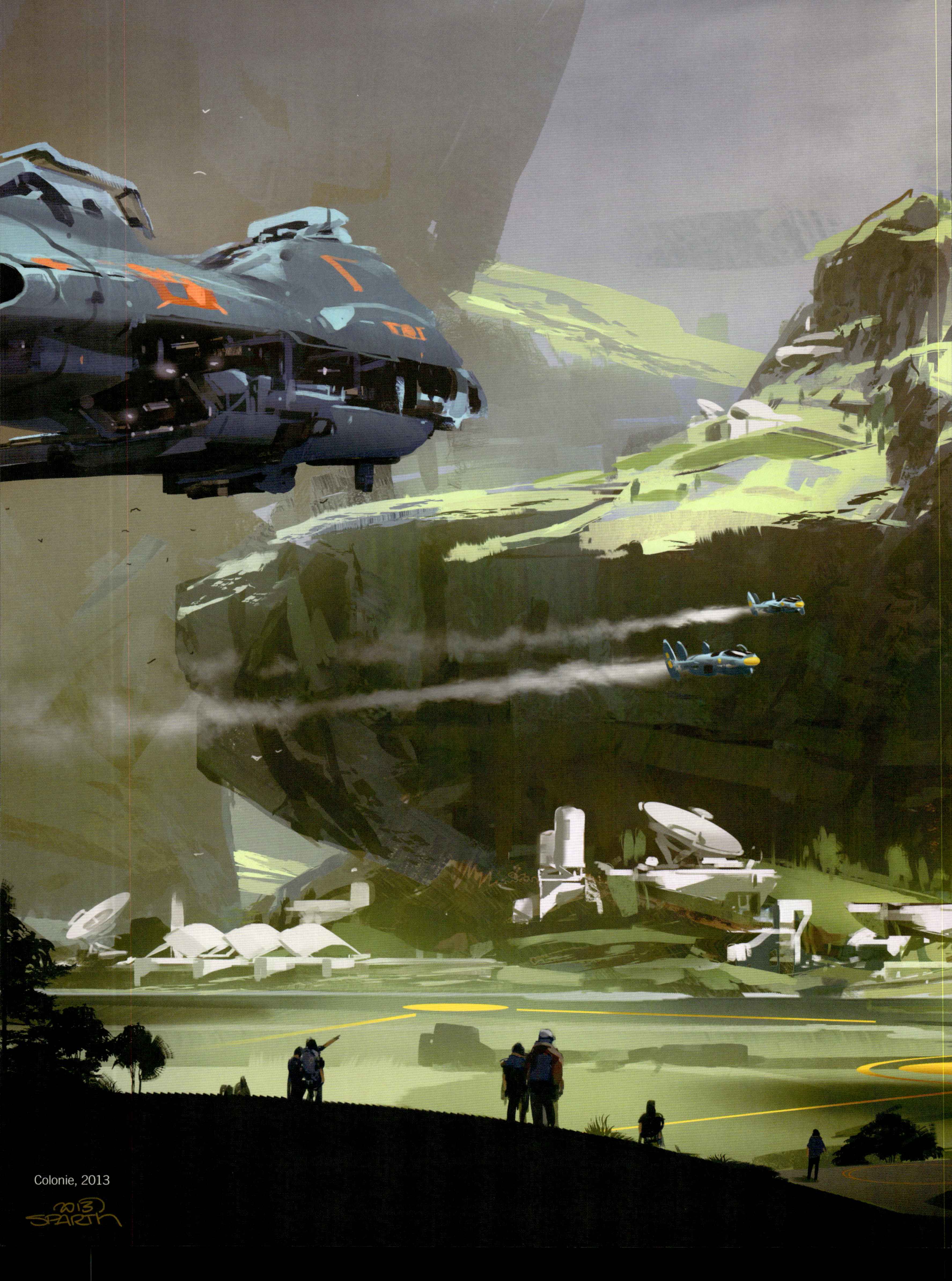

Colonie, 2013

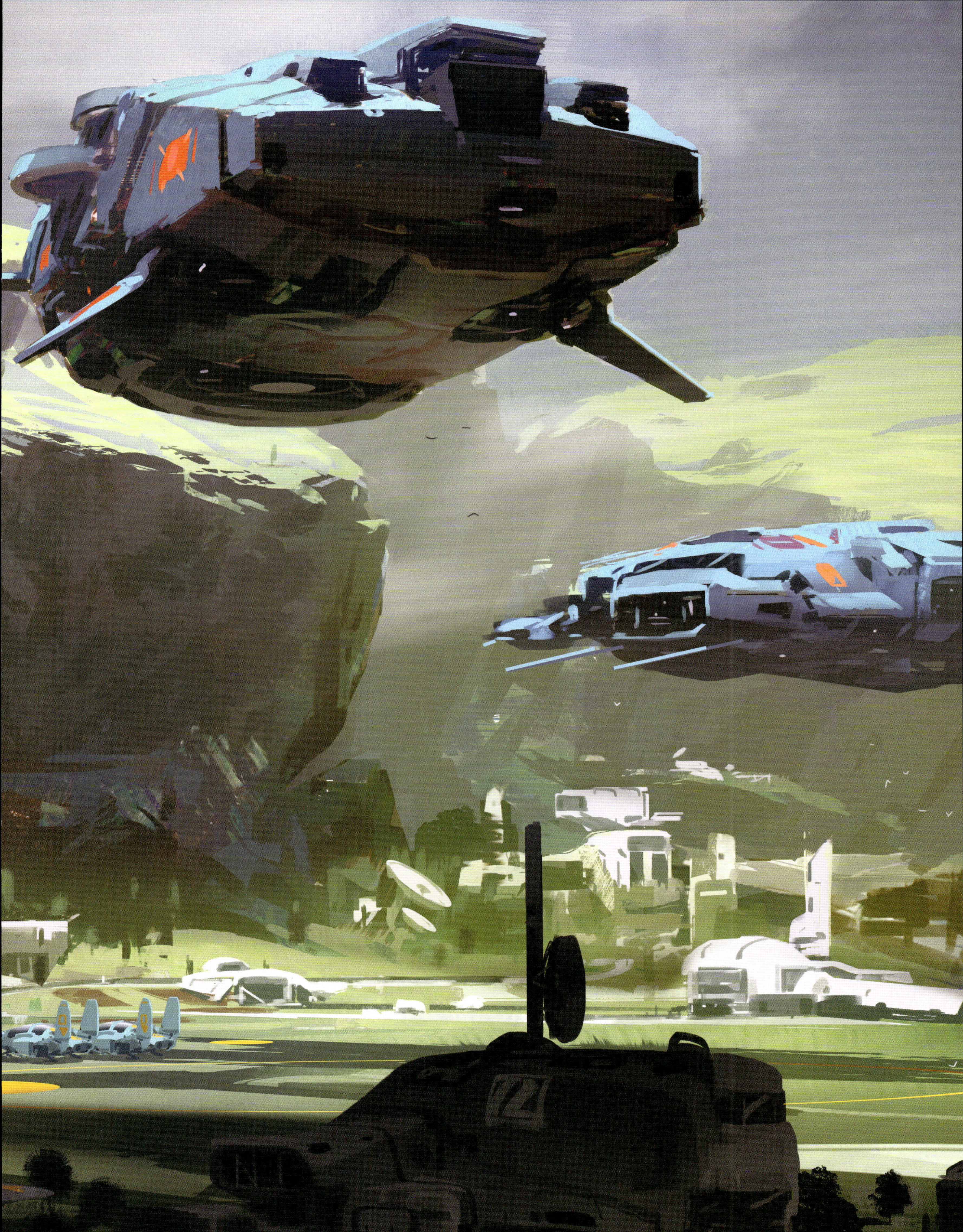

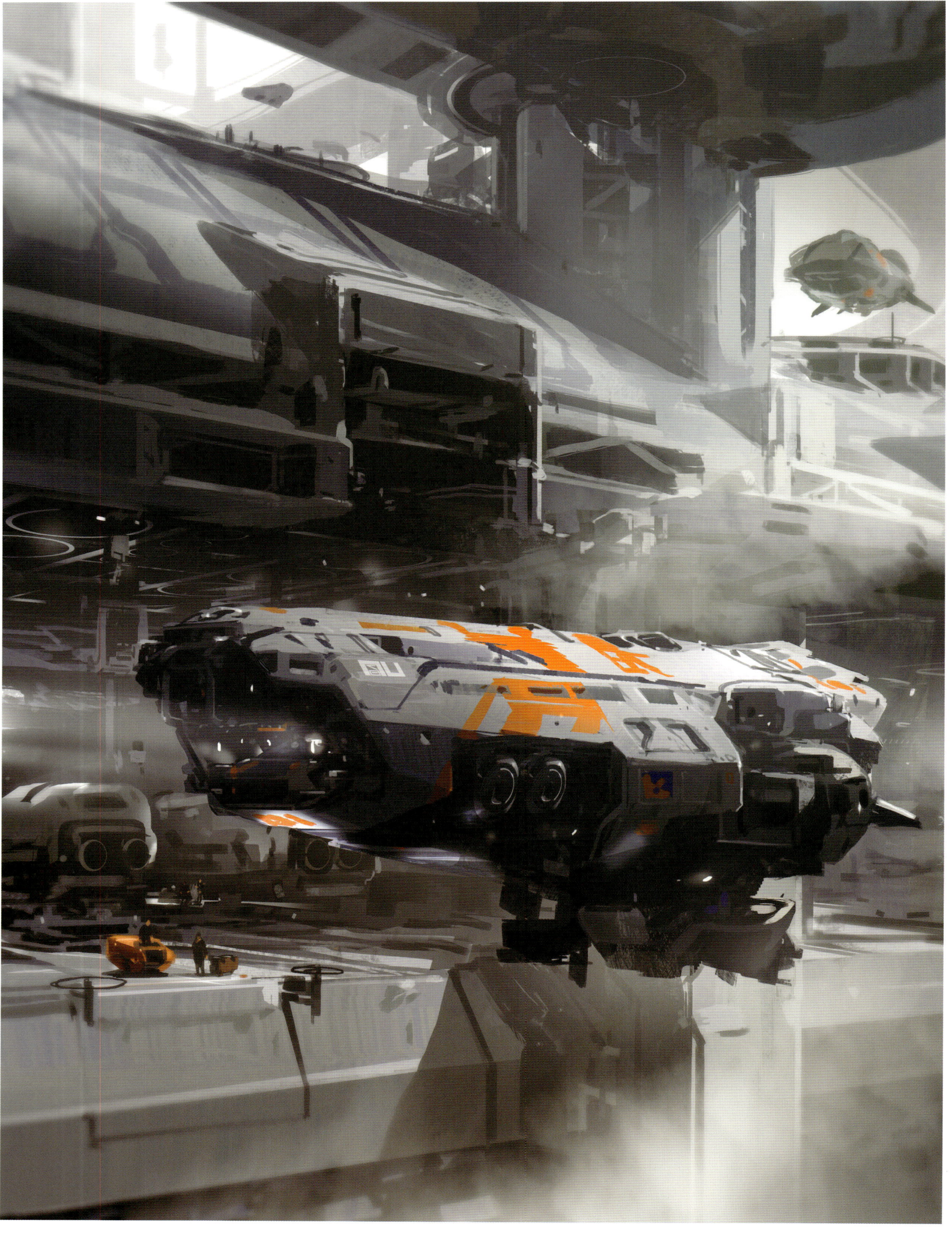

Oceanoship, 2013

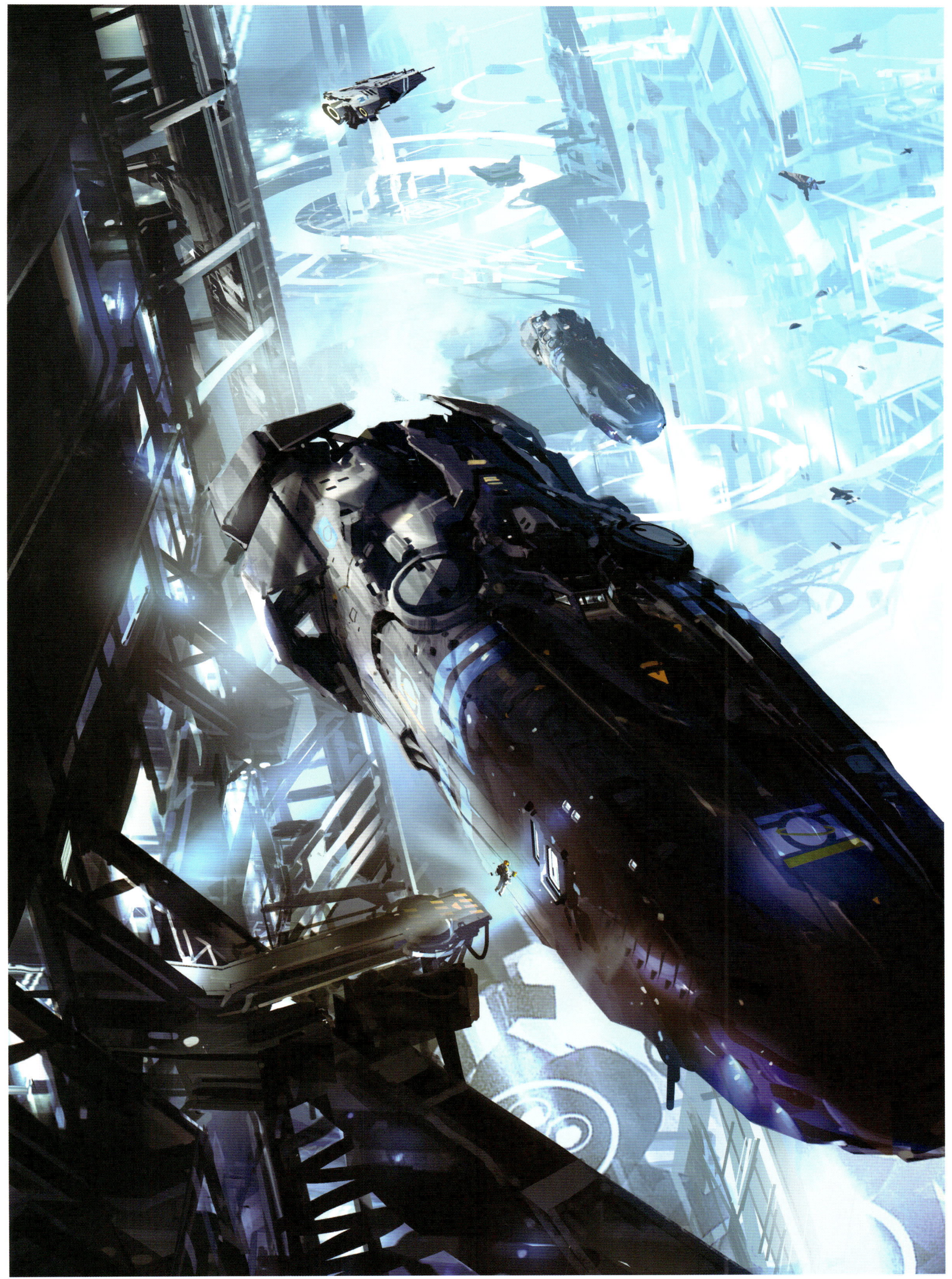

Space transfer, 2013

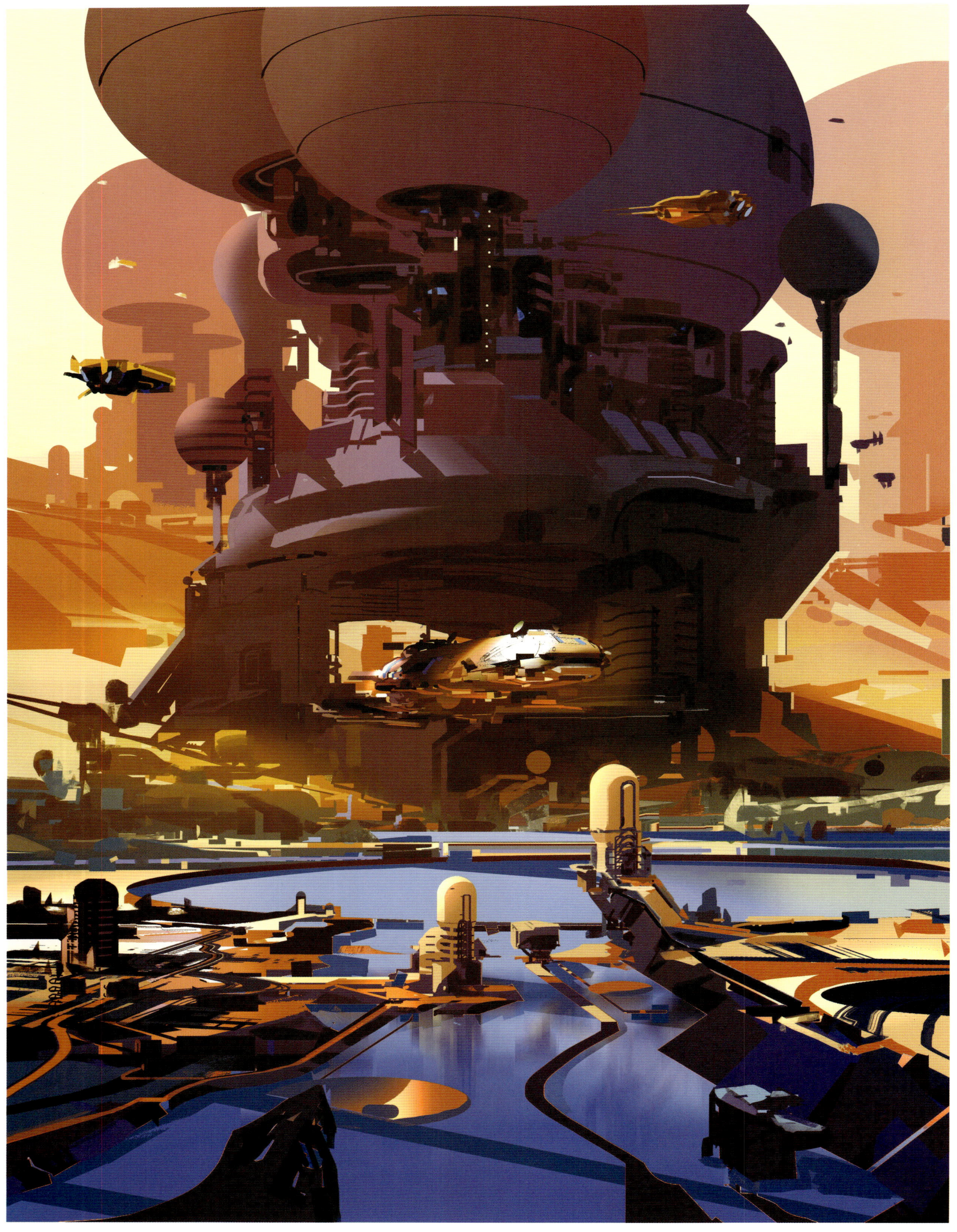

The bay, 2014

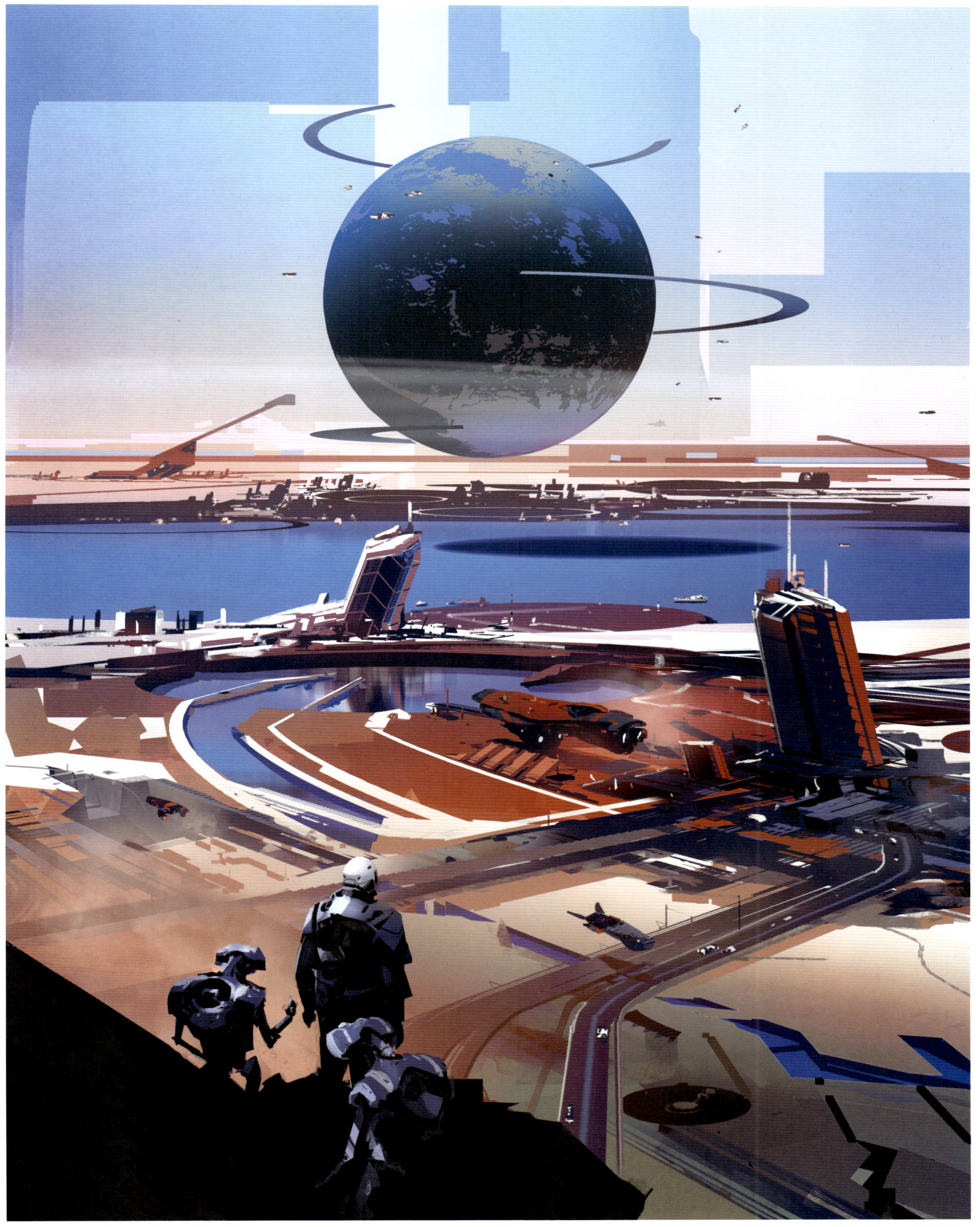

Mini terre, 2013

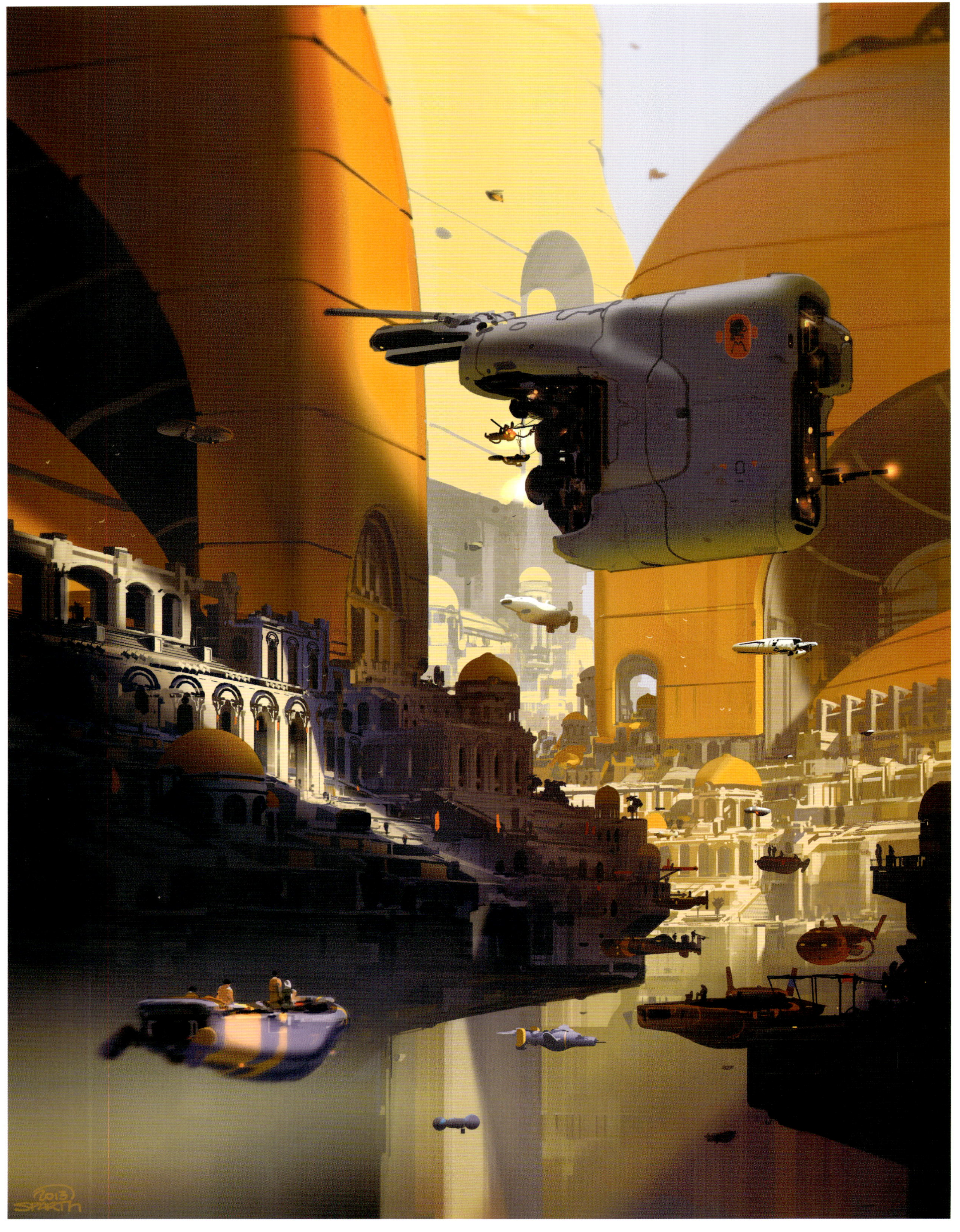

Suspended city, 2013

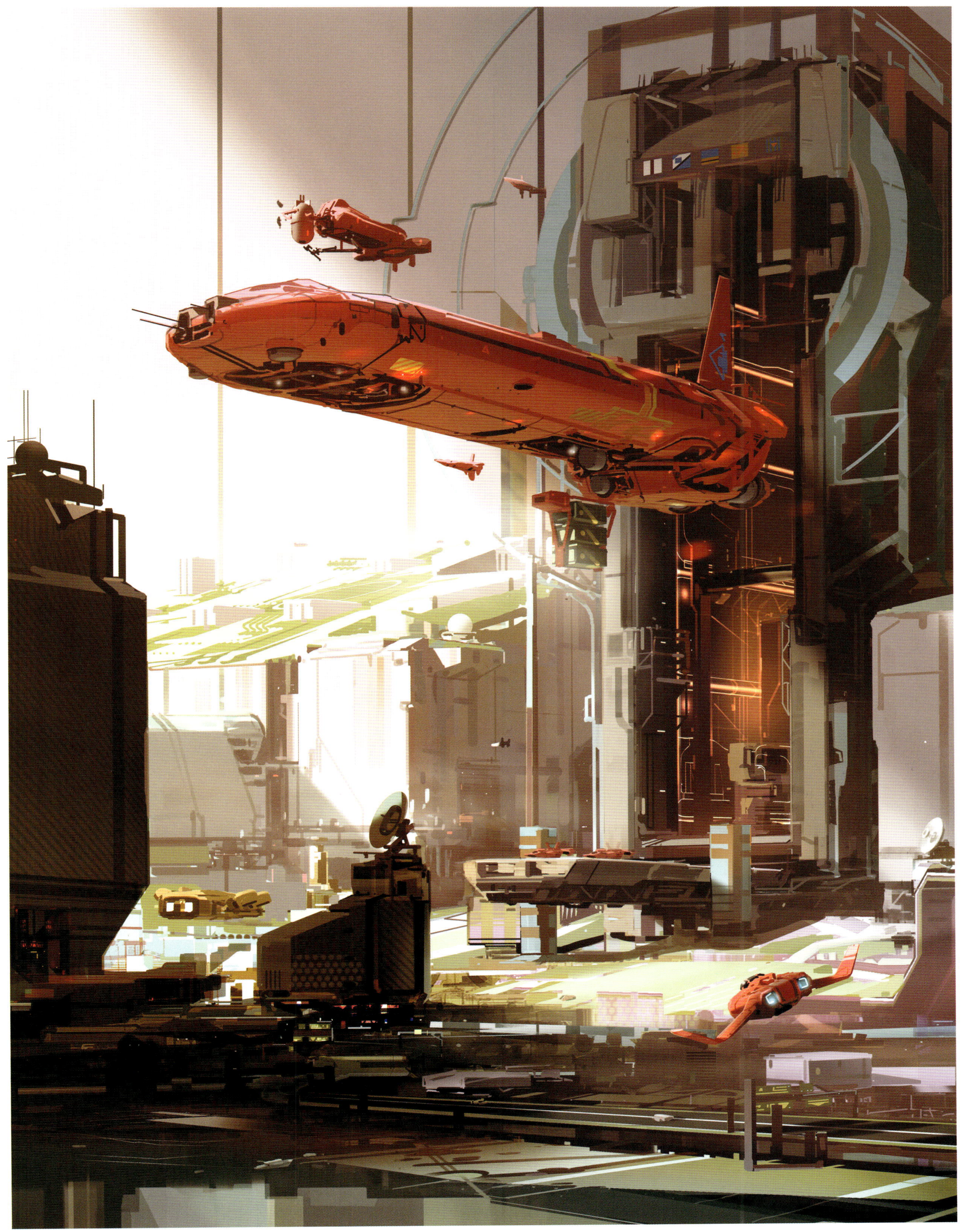

Assemblage, 2013

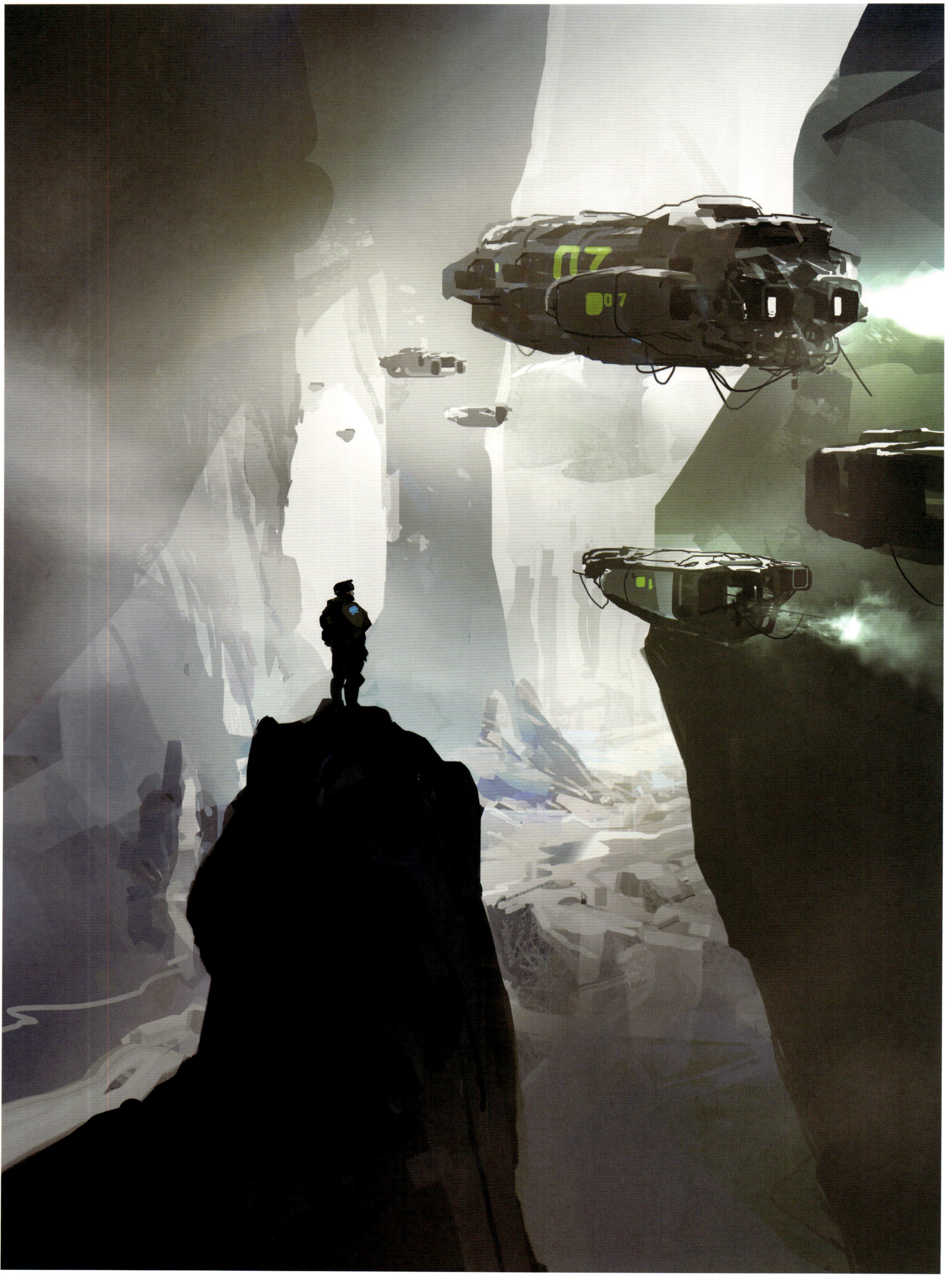

Armada, 2012

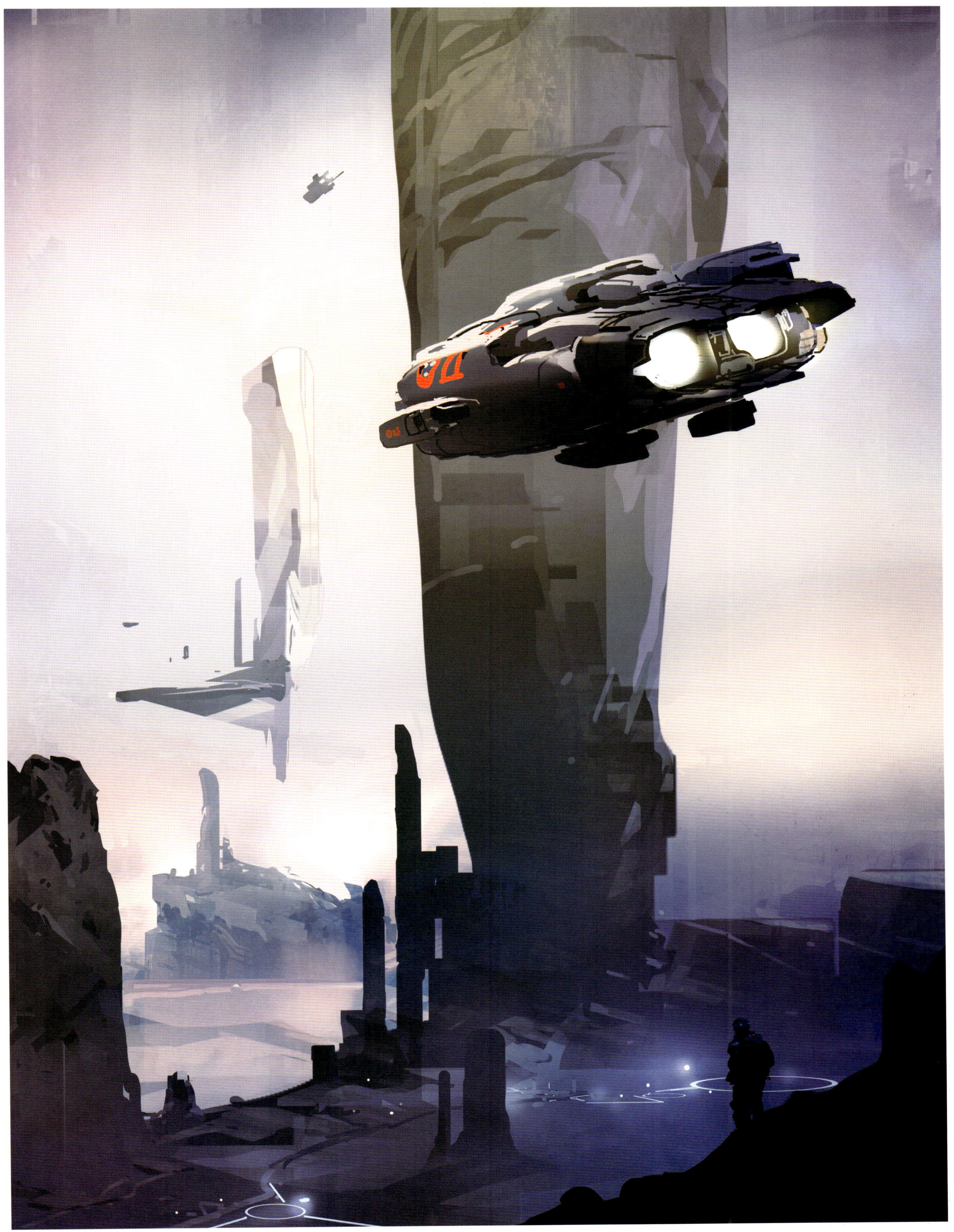

Monomonde, 2012

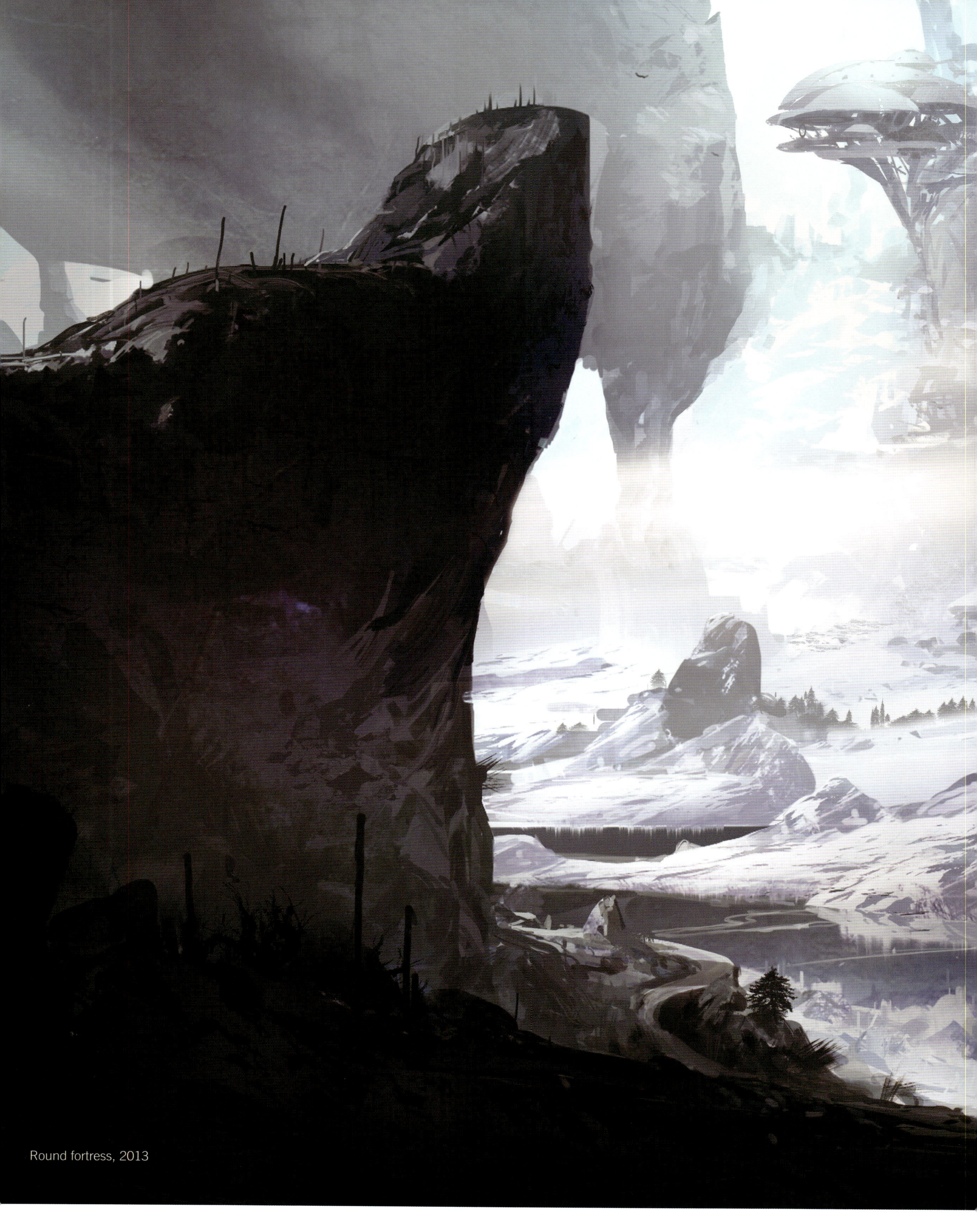

Round fortress, 2013

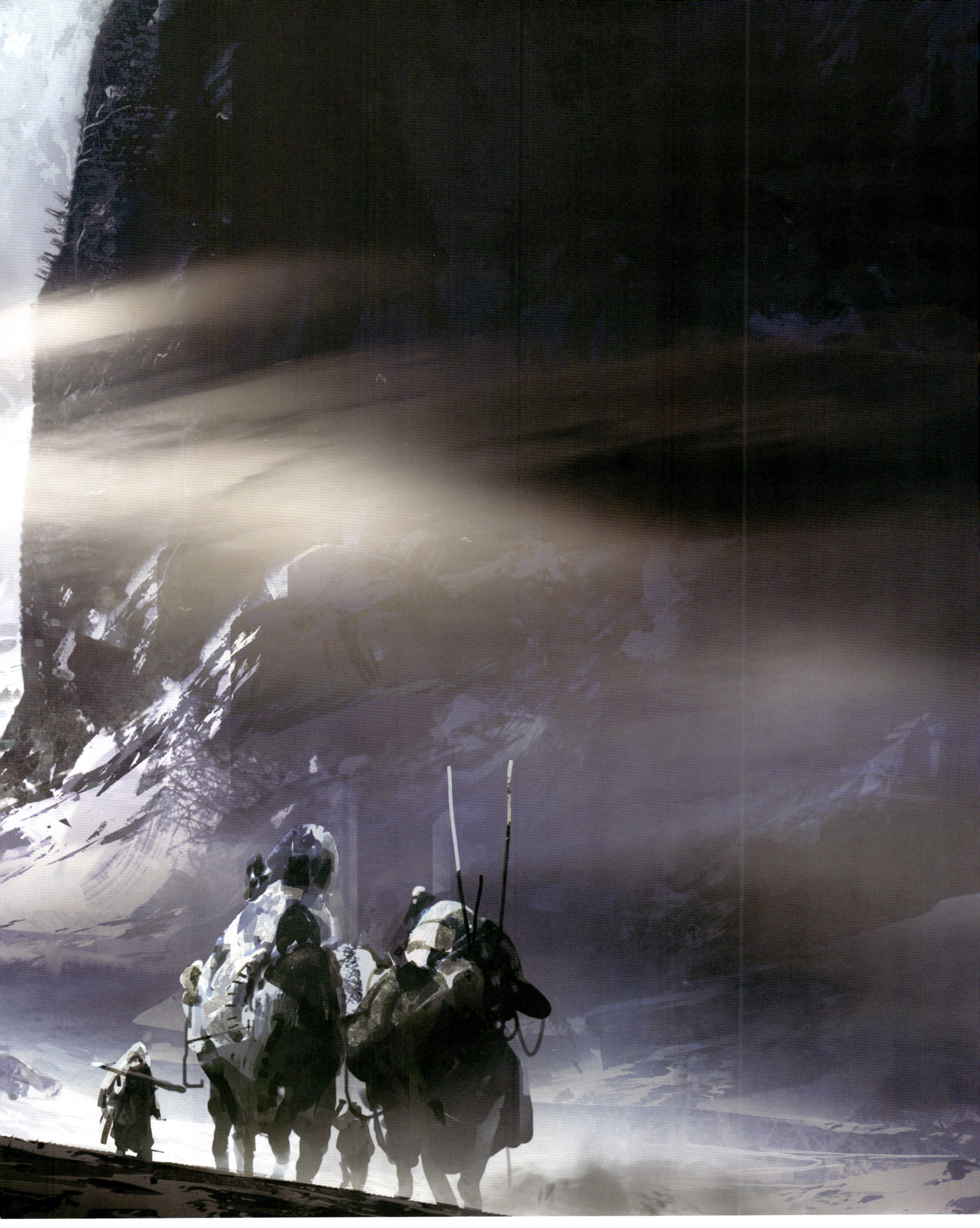

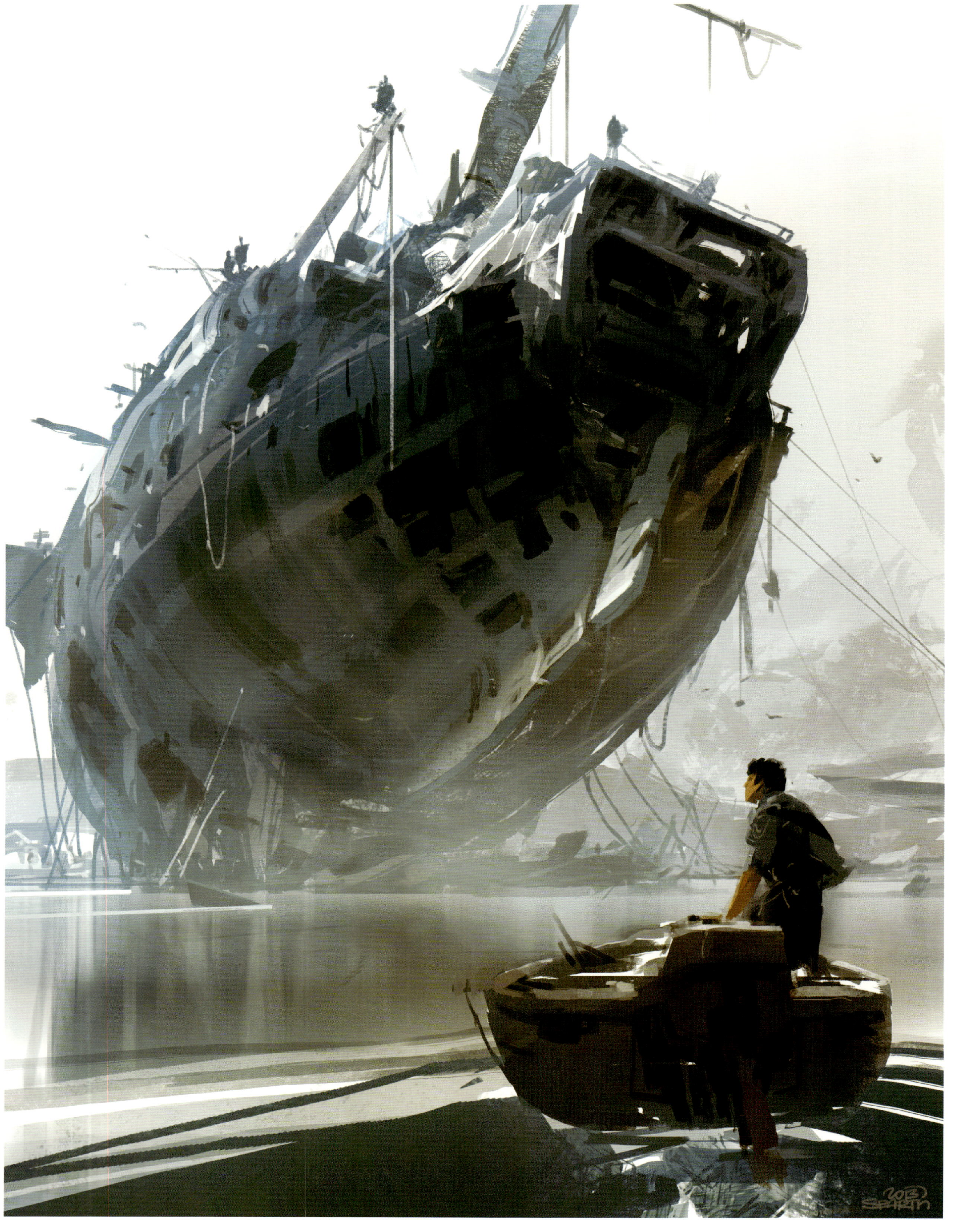

Epave, 2013

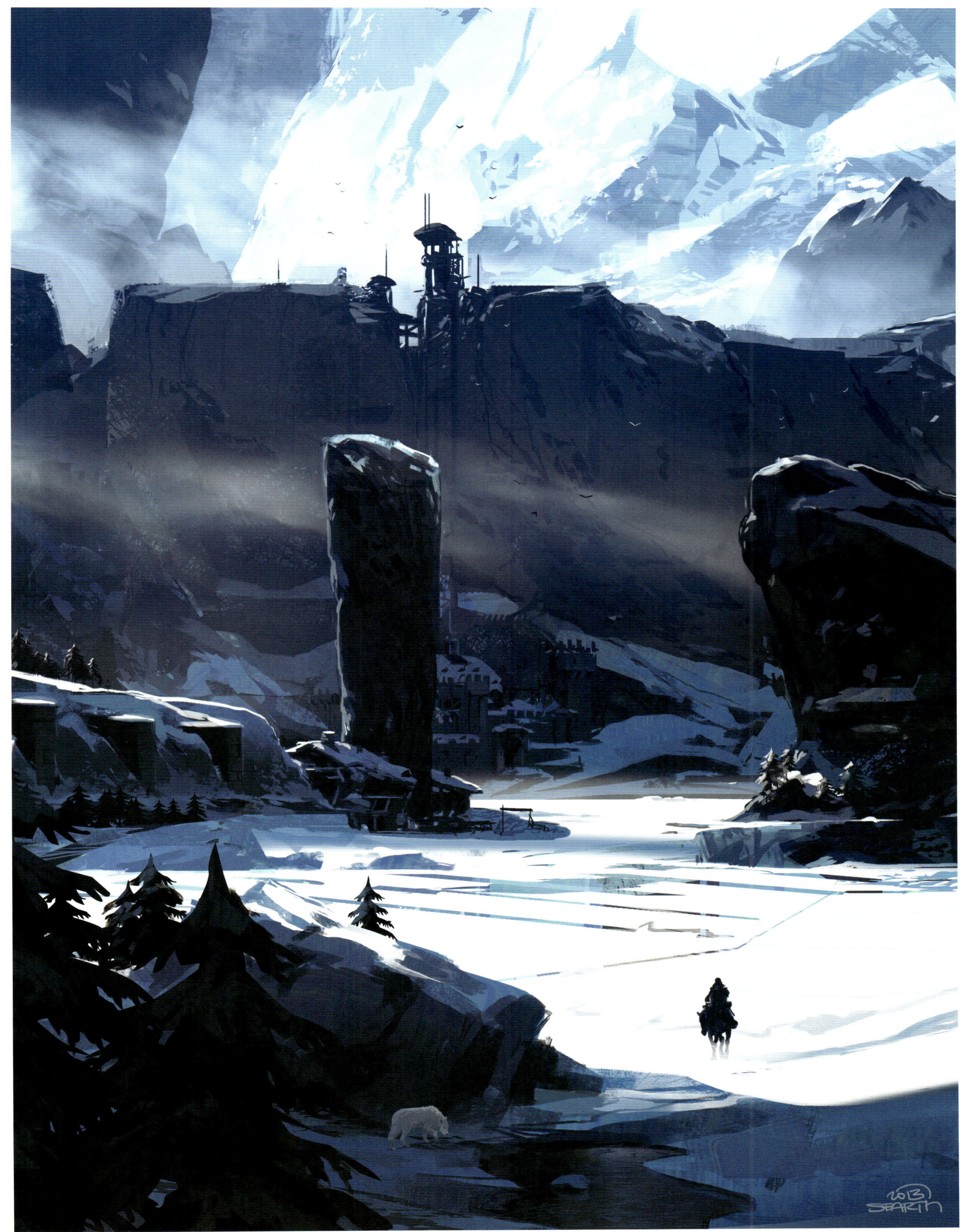

Tribute to *Game of Thrones* by George R.R. Martin, 2013

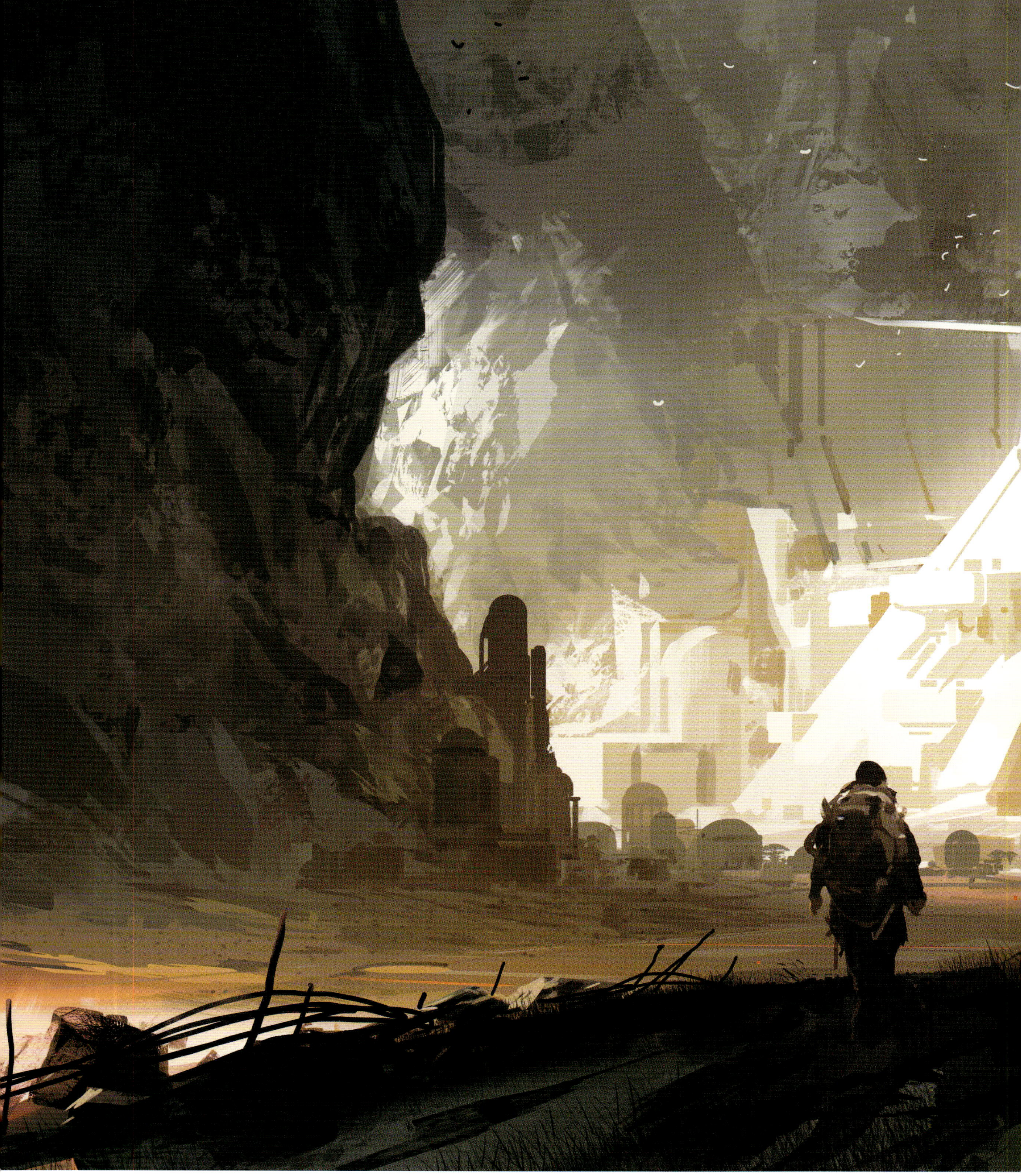

Le temple, 2014

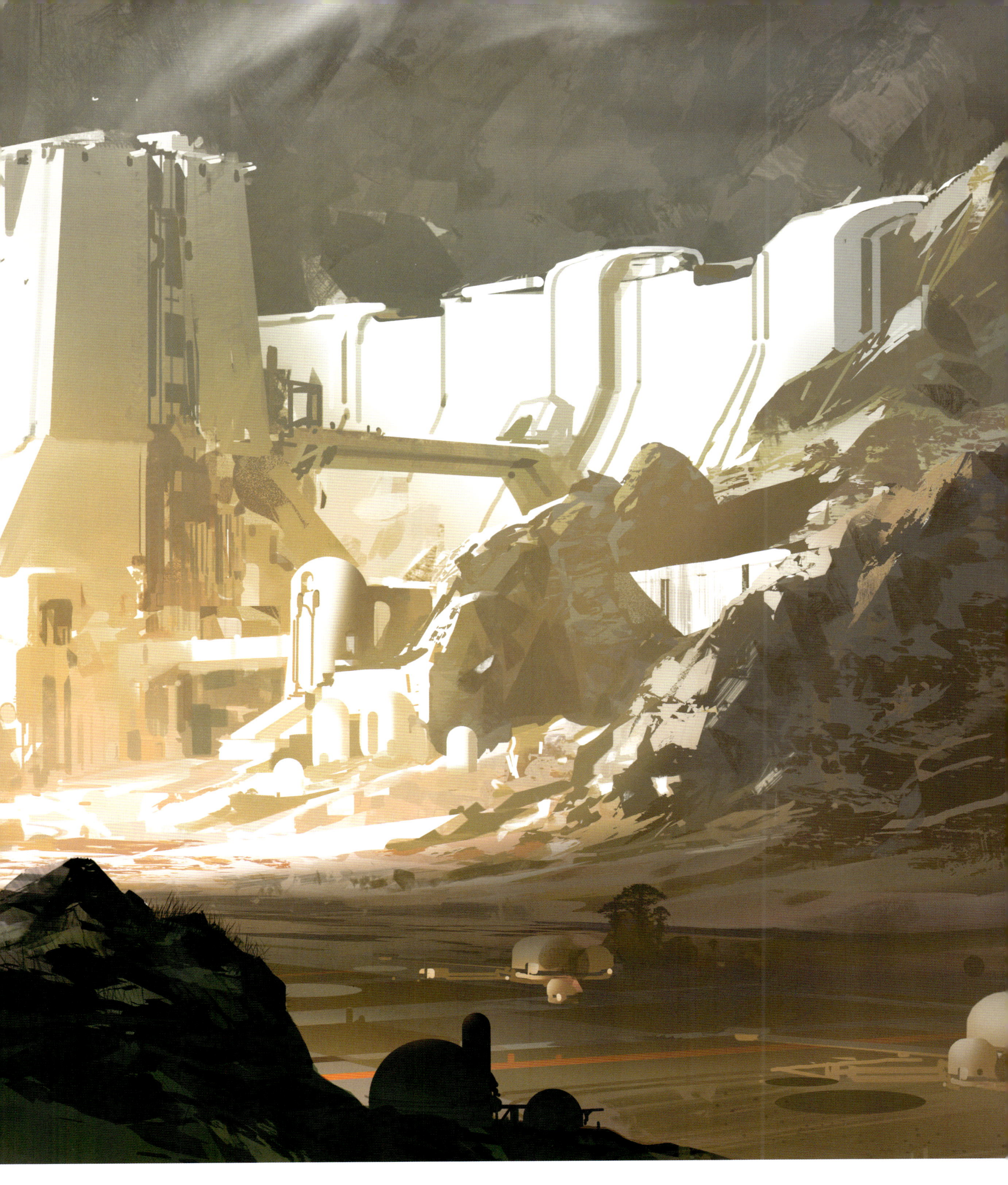

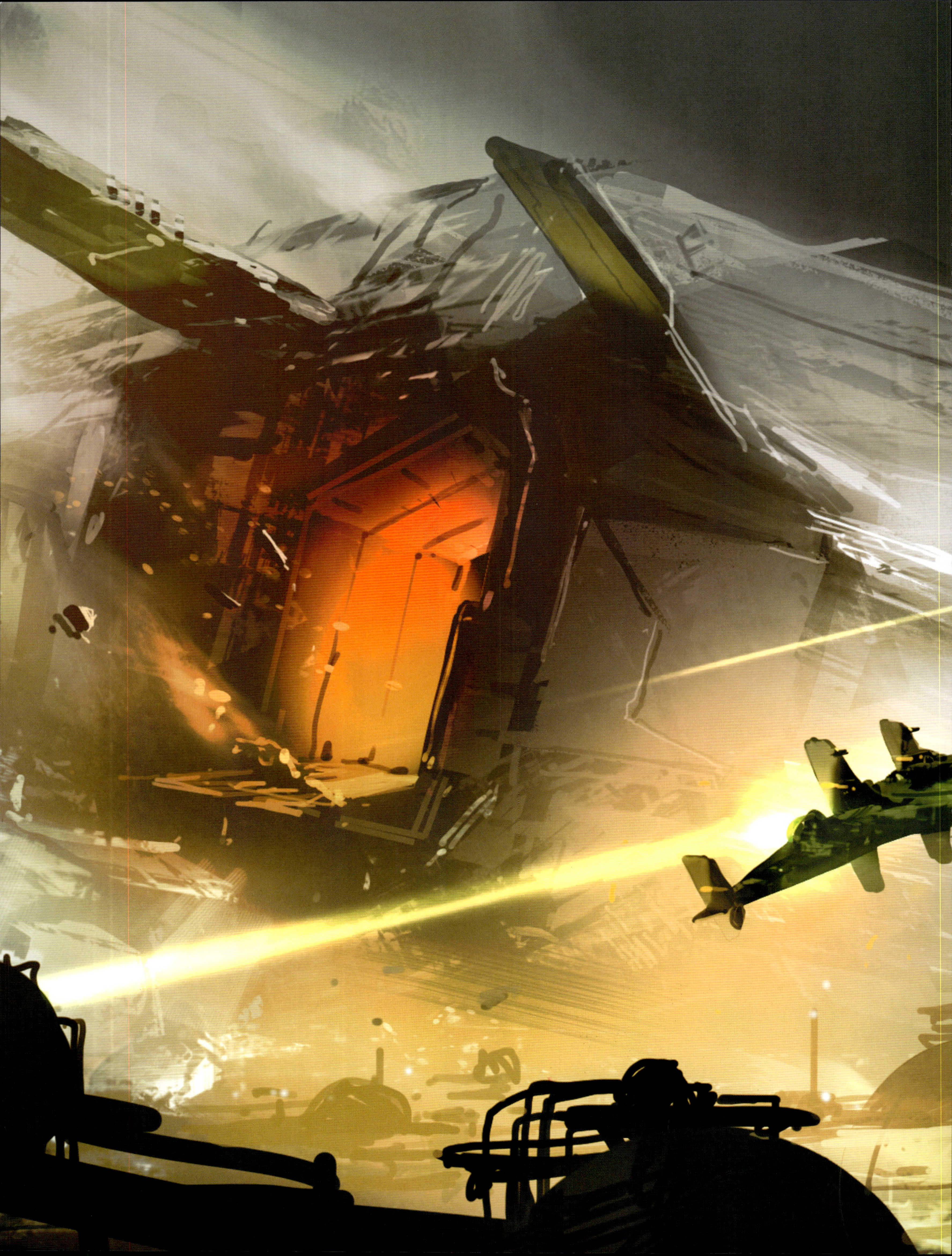

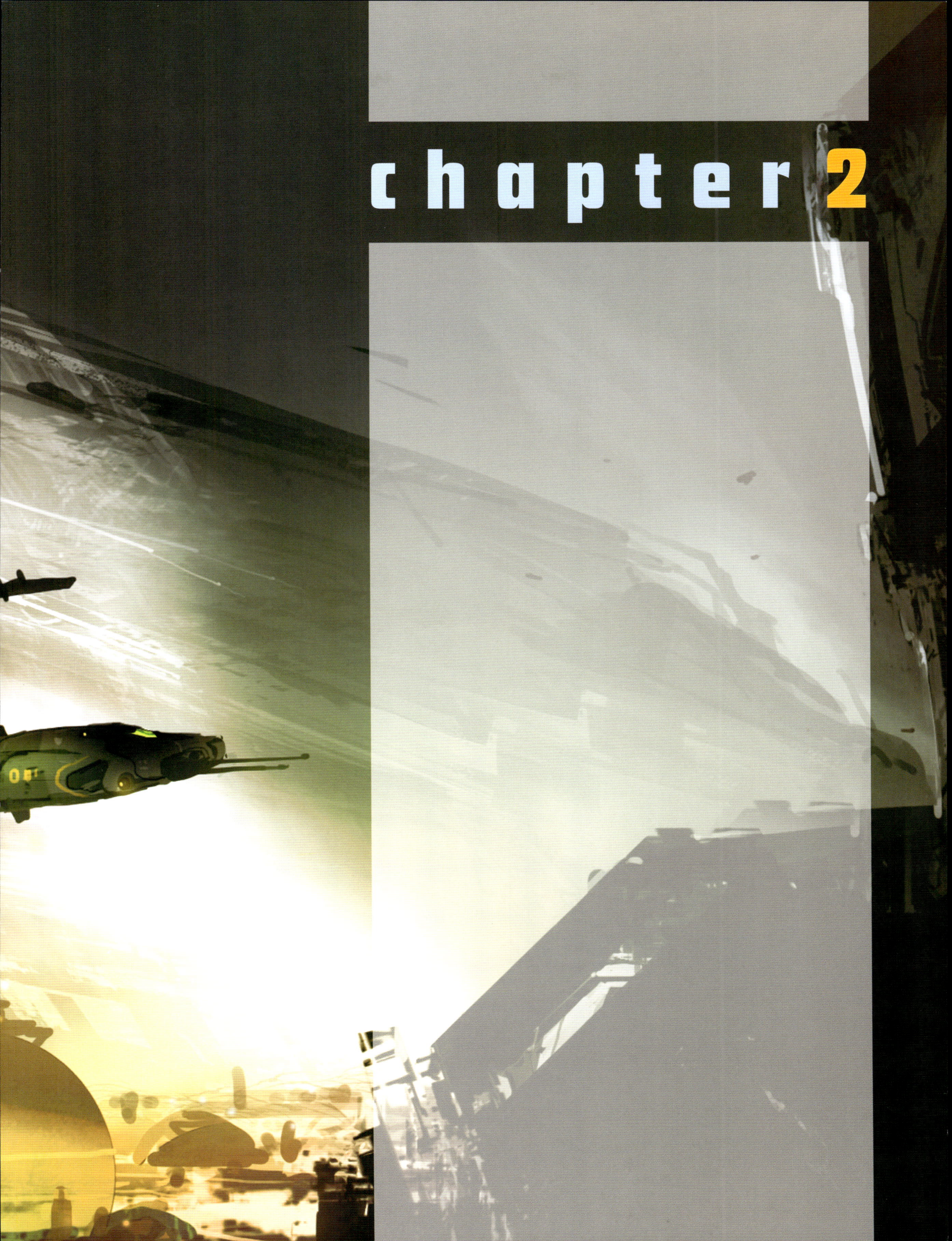

chapter 2

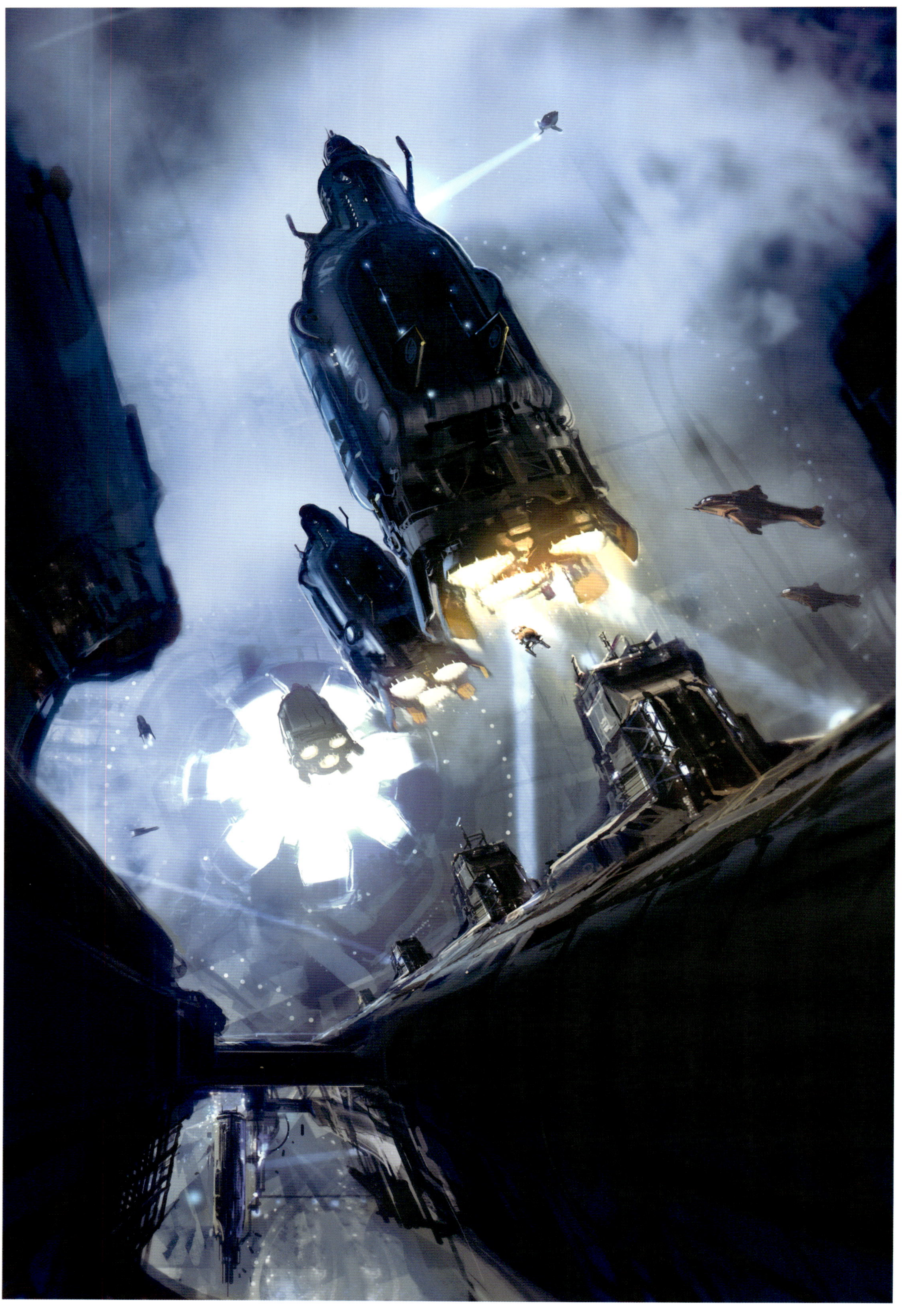

Halo 4 promotional concept, 2010

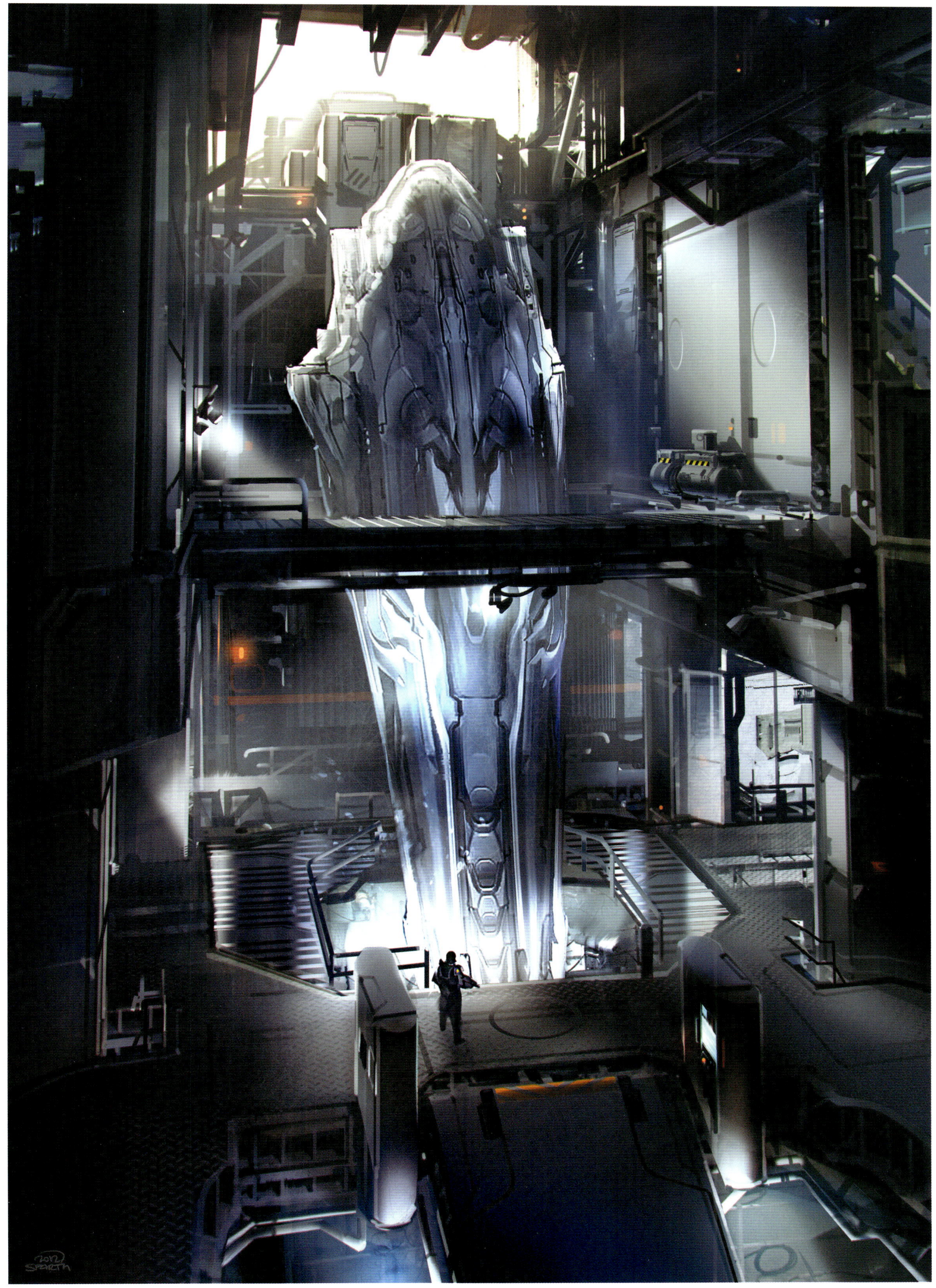

Halo 4 multiplayer map concept, 2012

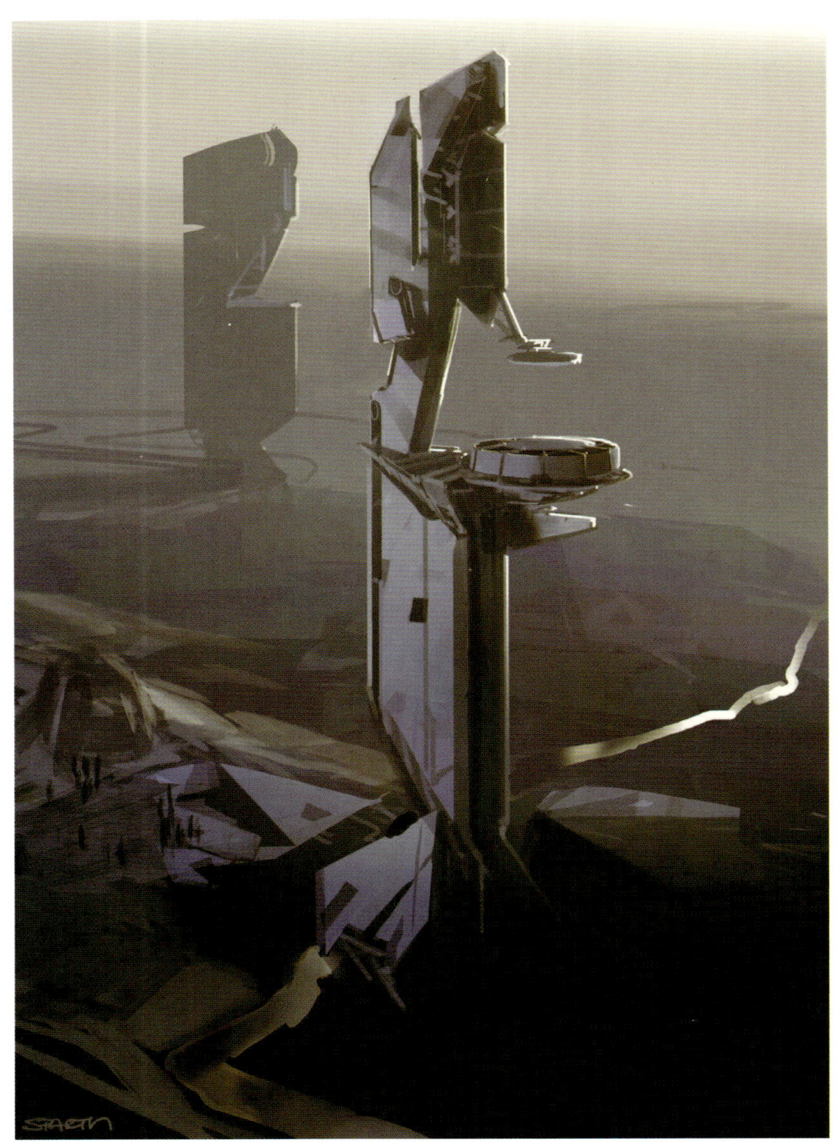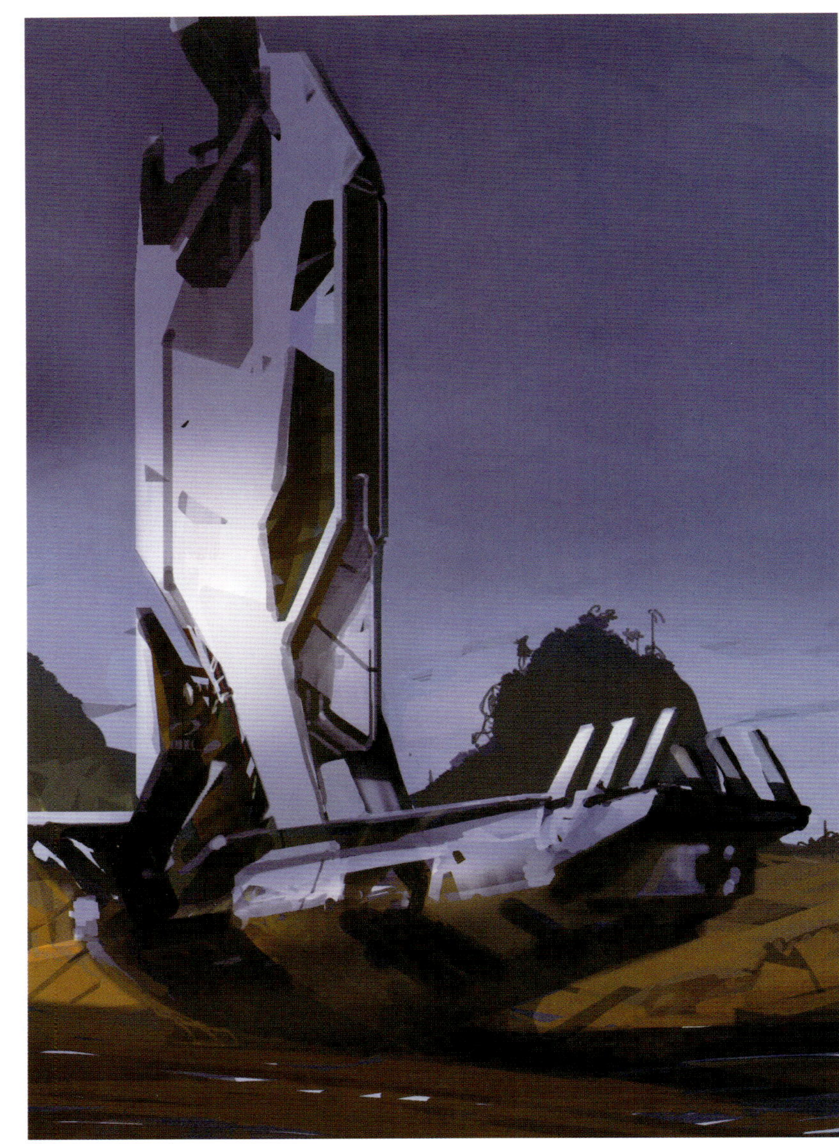

Halo 4 Forerunner research, 2010

In a game like Halo**, you're always on your guard to avoid enemies and incoming surprises.**

It's the same for design: a constant yet intentionally broken rhythm for anything Forerunner encapsulates—the feeling of otherness, abnormality, and weirdness.

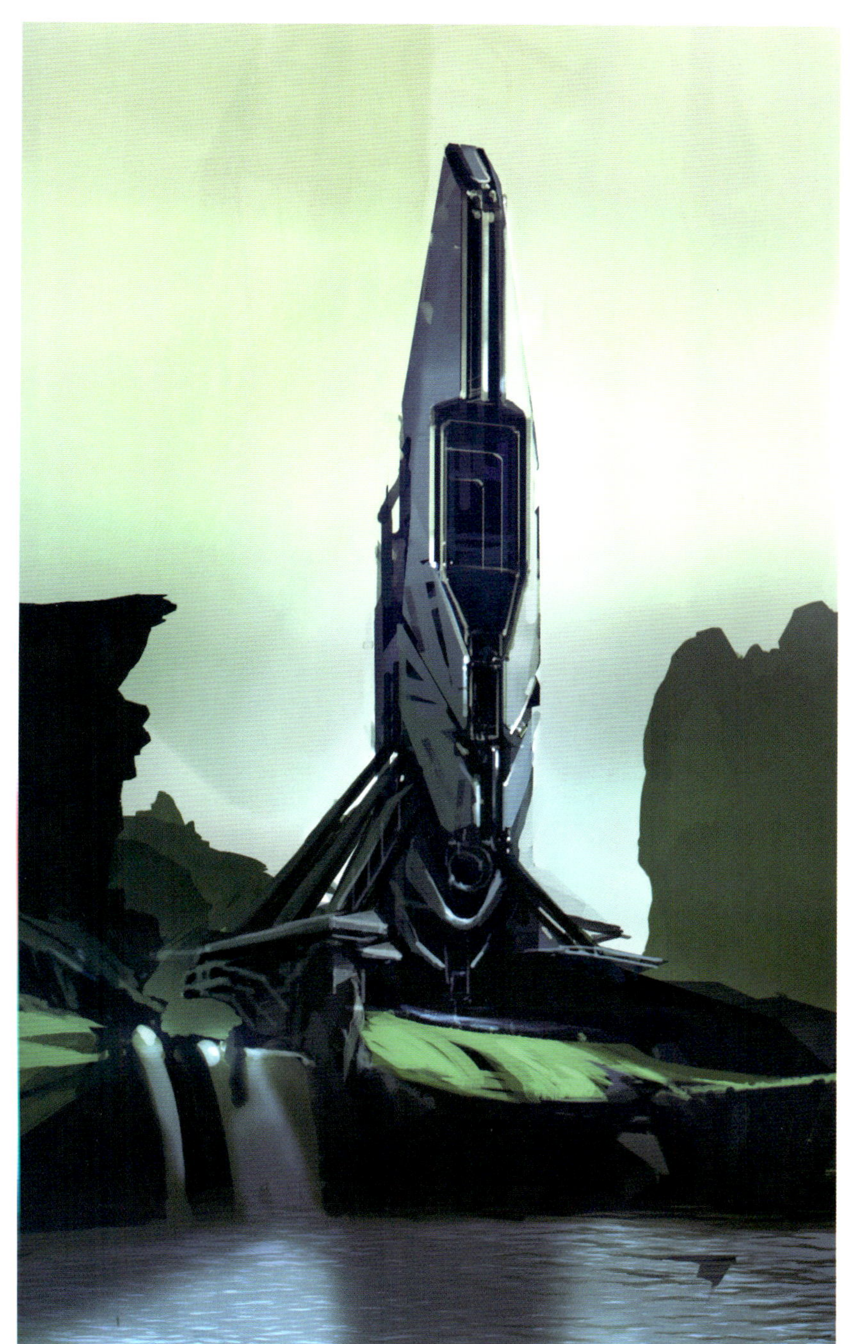
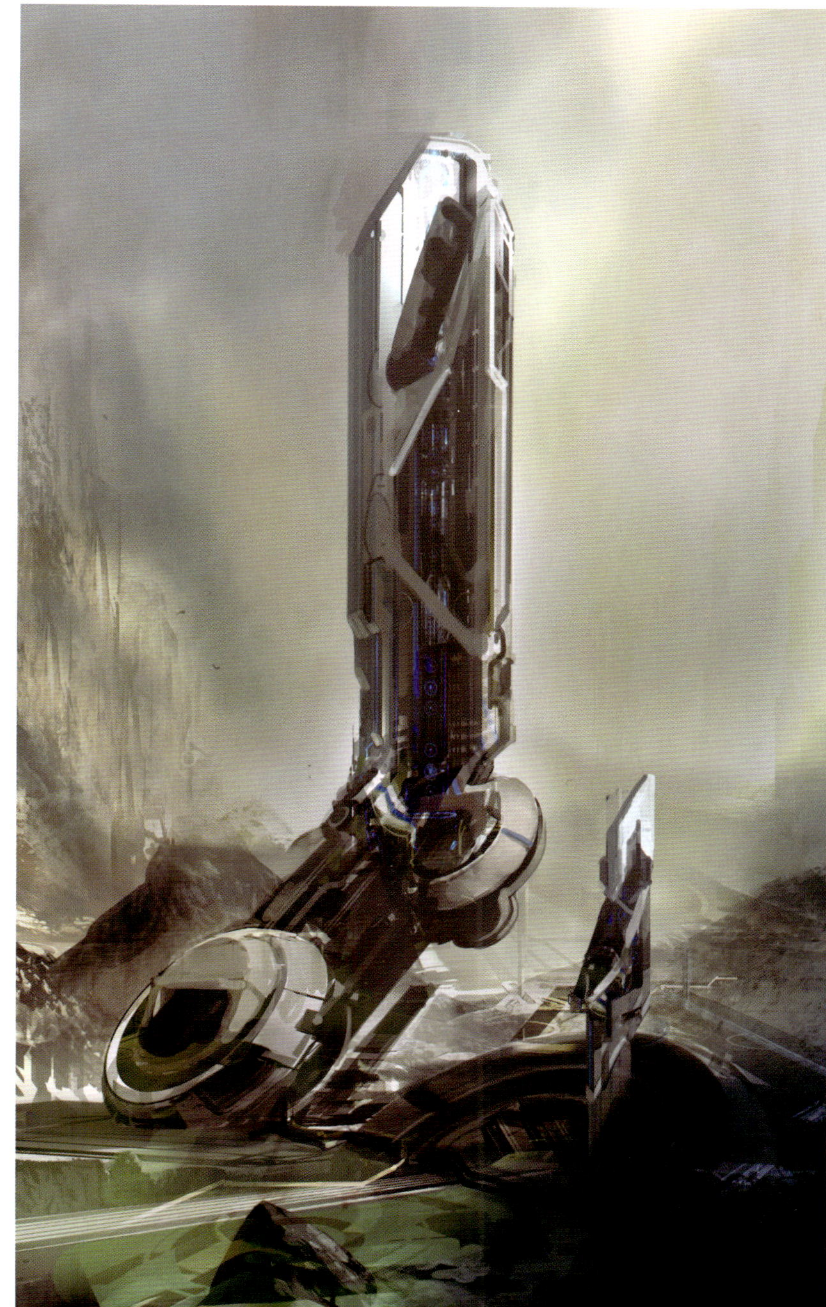
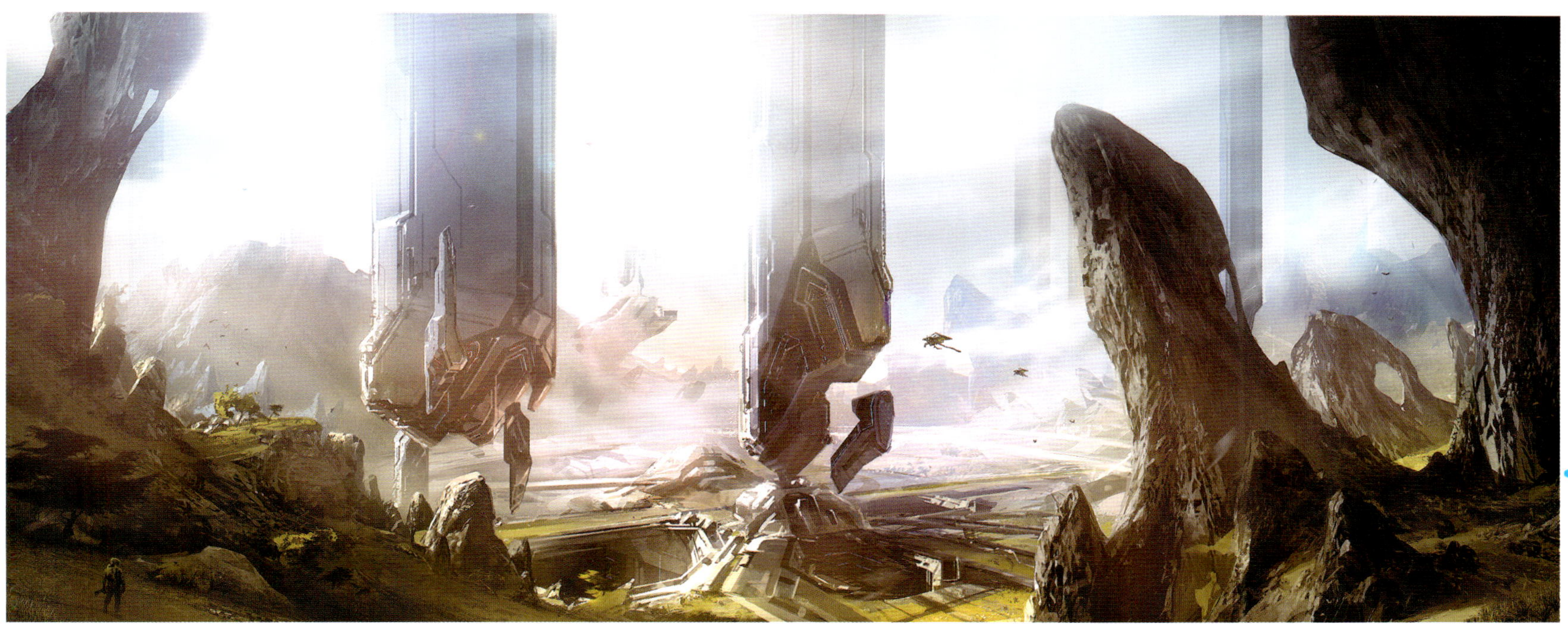

Halo 4 preproduction concept art, 2010

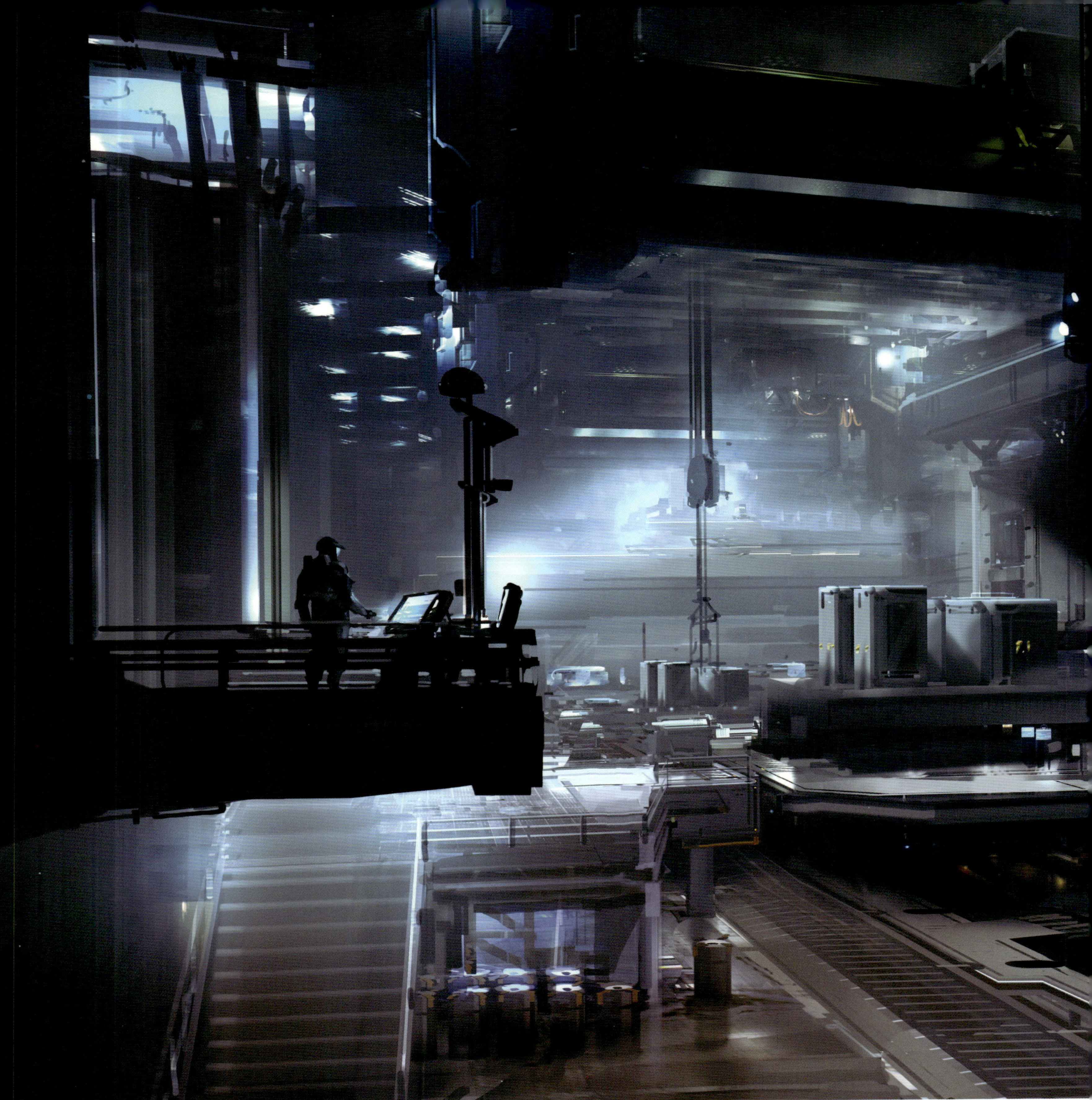

Halo 4 UNSC *Infinity* bay concept, 2010
Initial sketch by Jihoon Kim

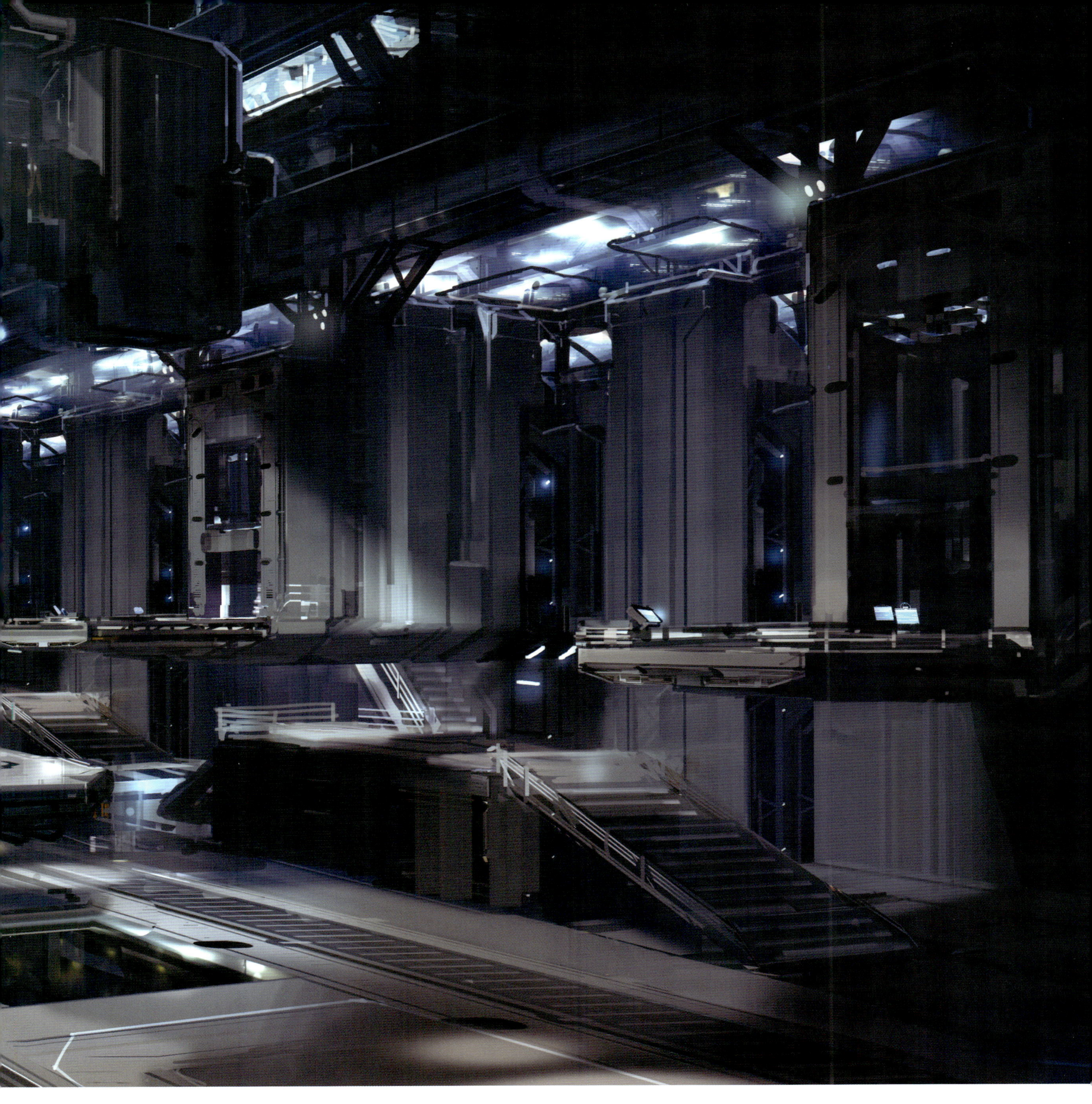

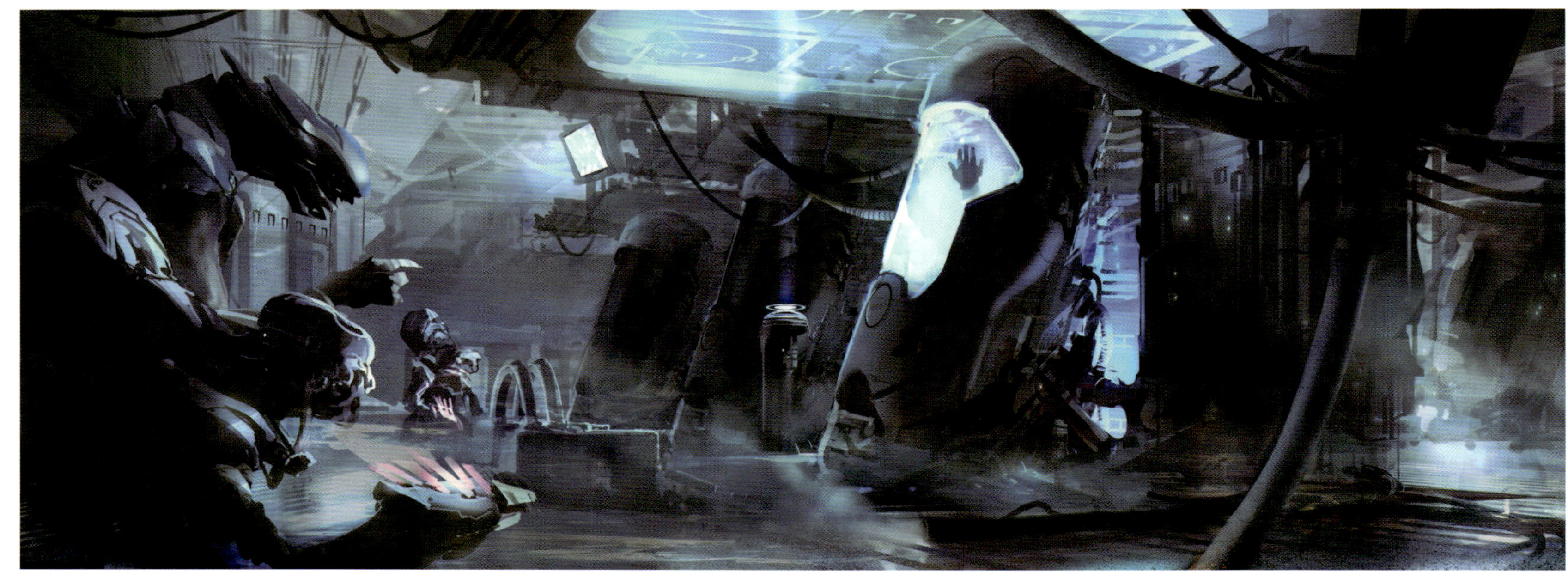

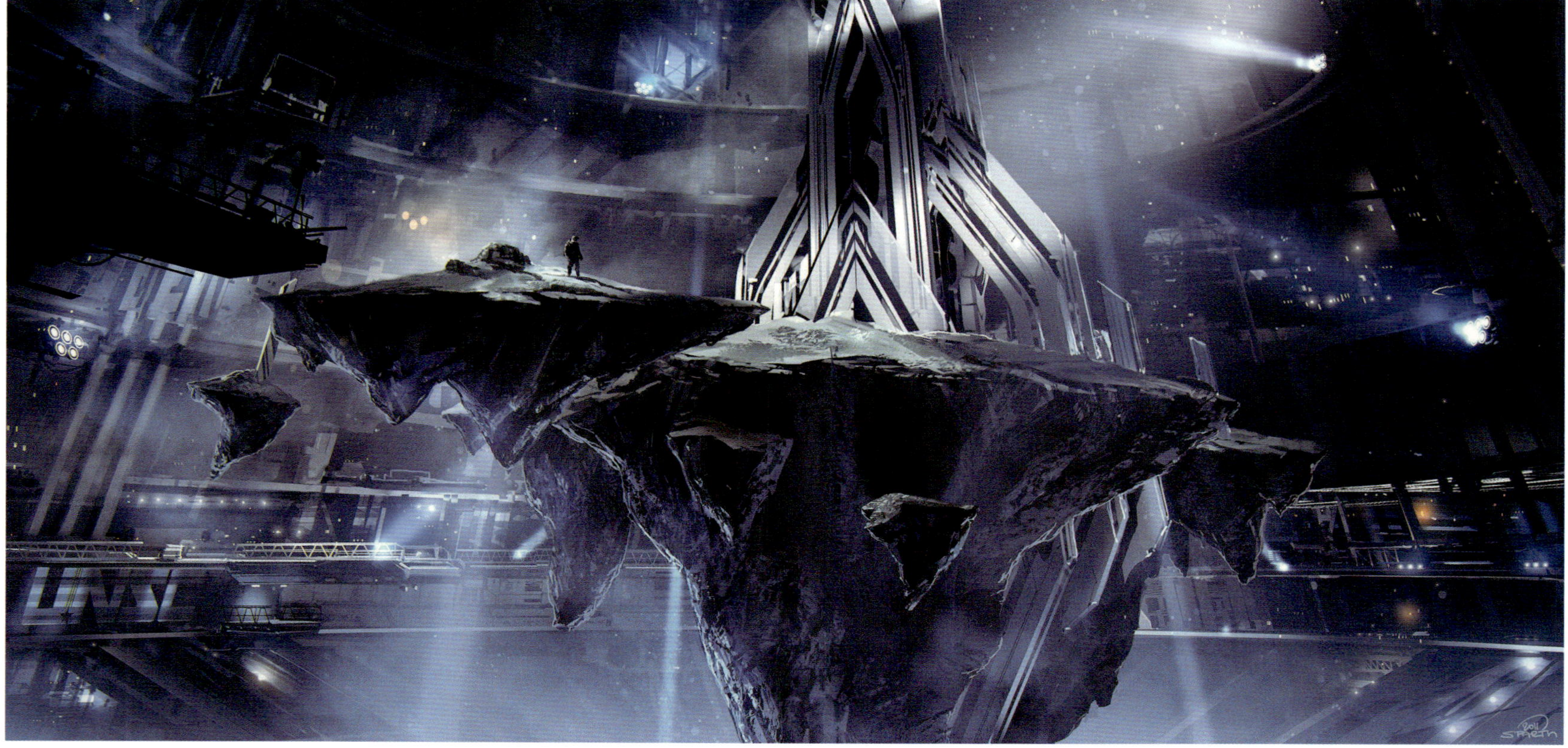

Halo 4 cryotube, 2010
Halo 4 Artifact concept, 2010

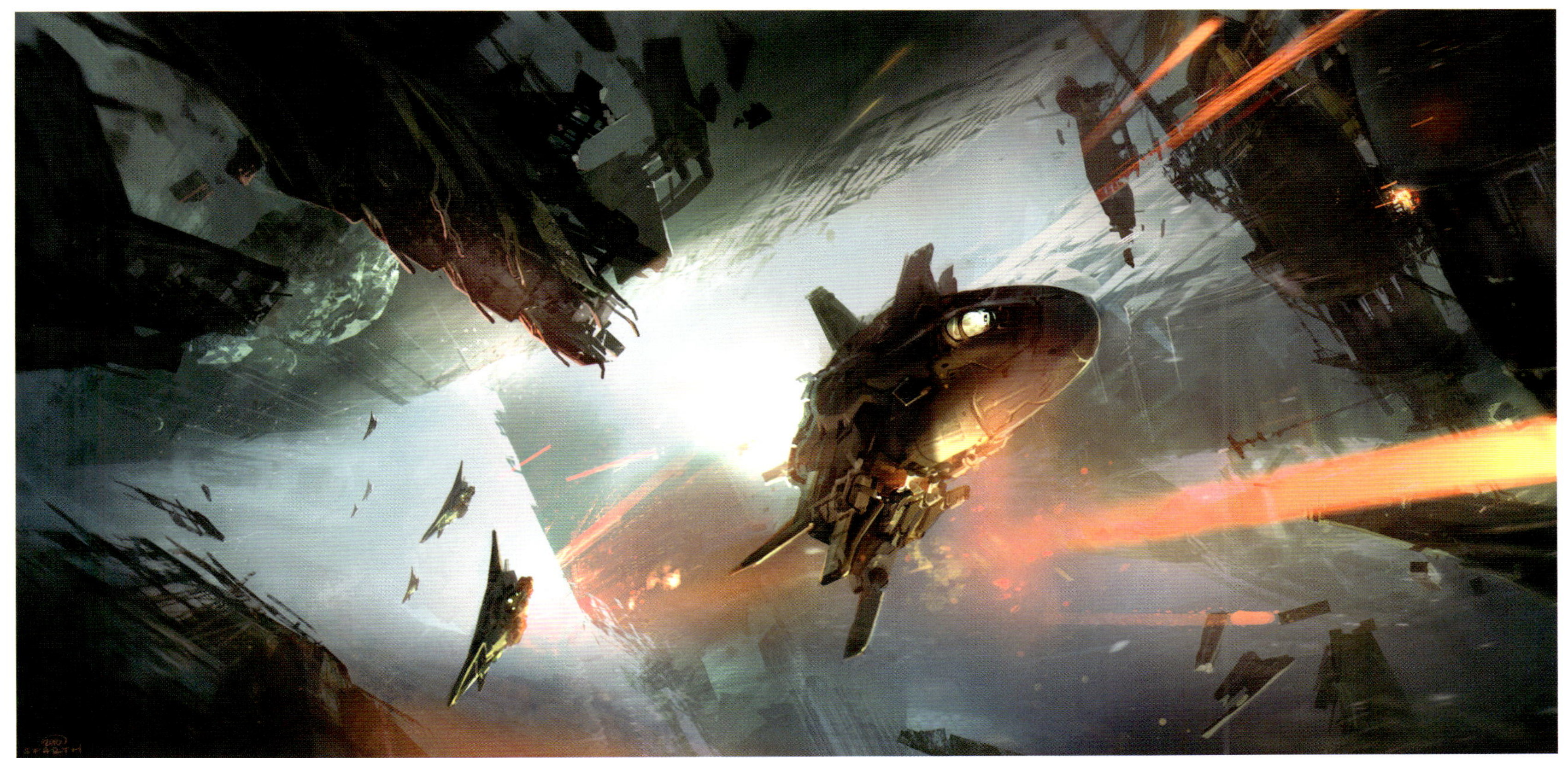

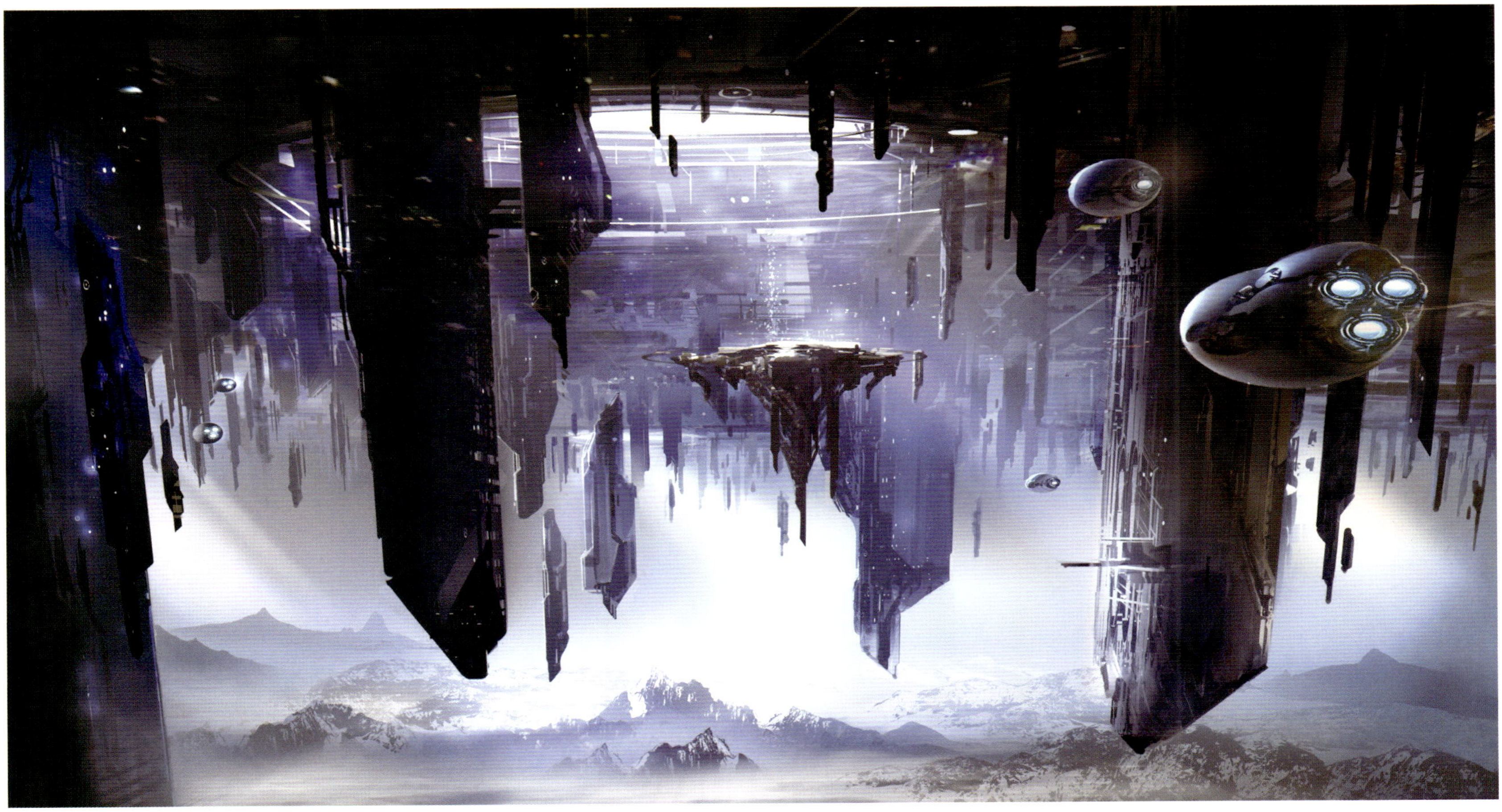

Halo 4 concept art, 2010
Halo 4 concept art, 2011

pages 56–57 Comic book covers
Halo: Escalation, #6 and #7, 2013

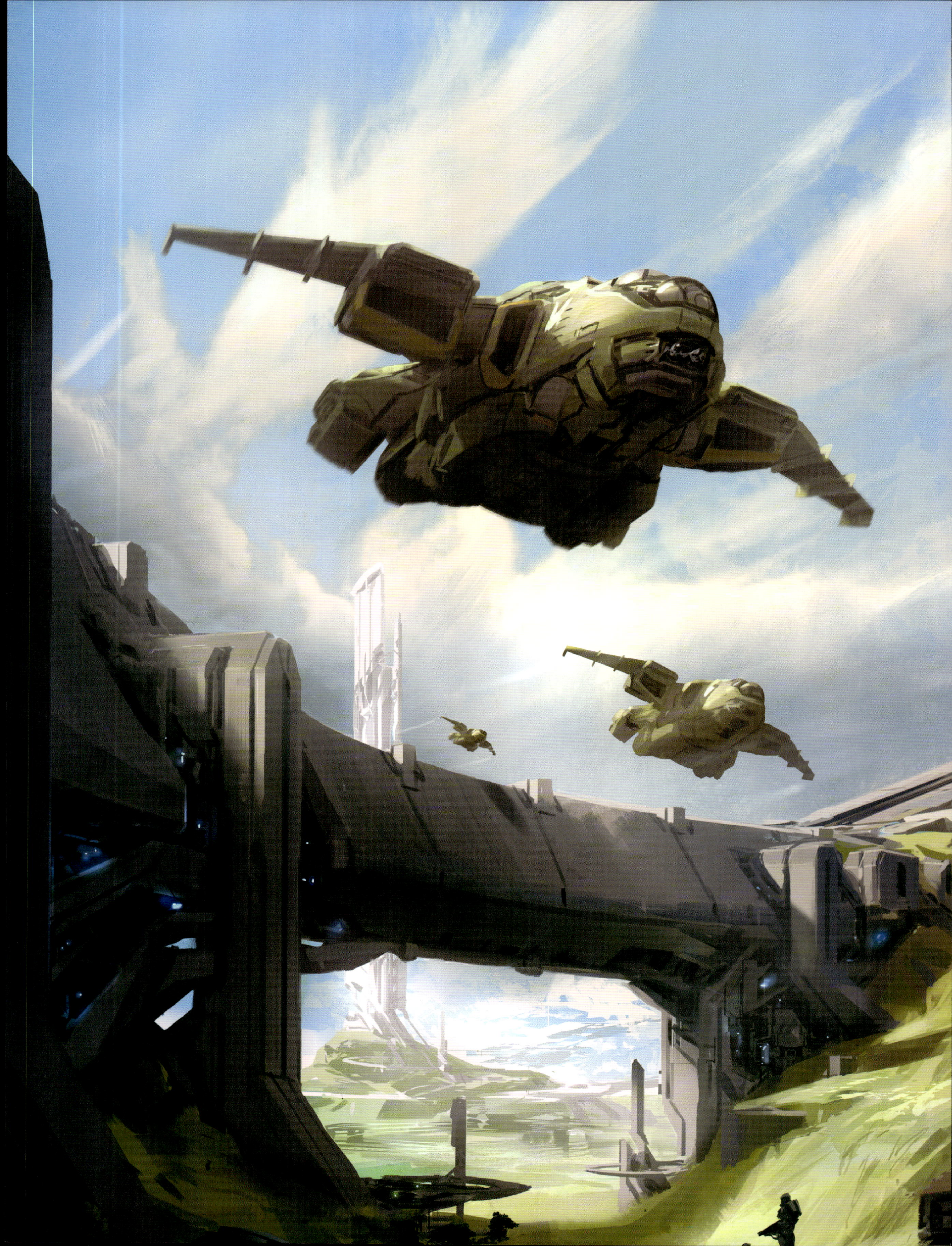

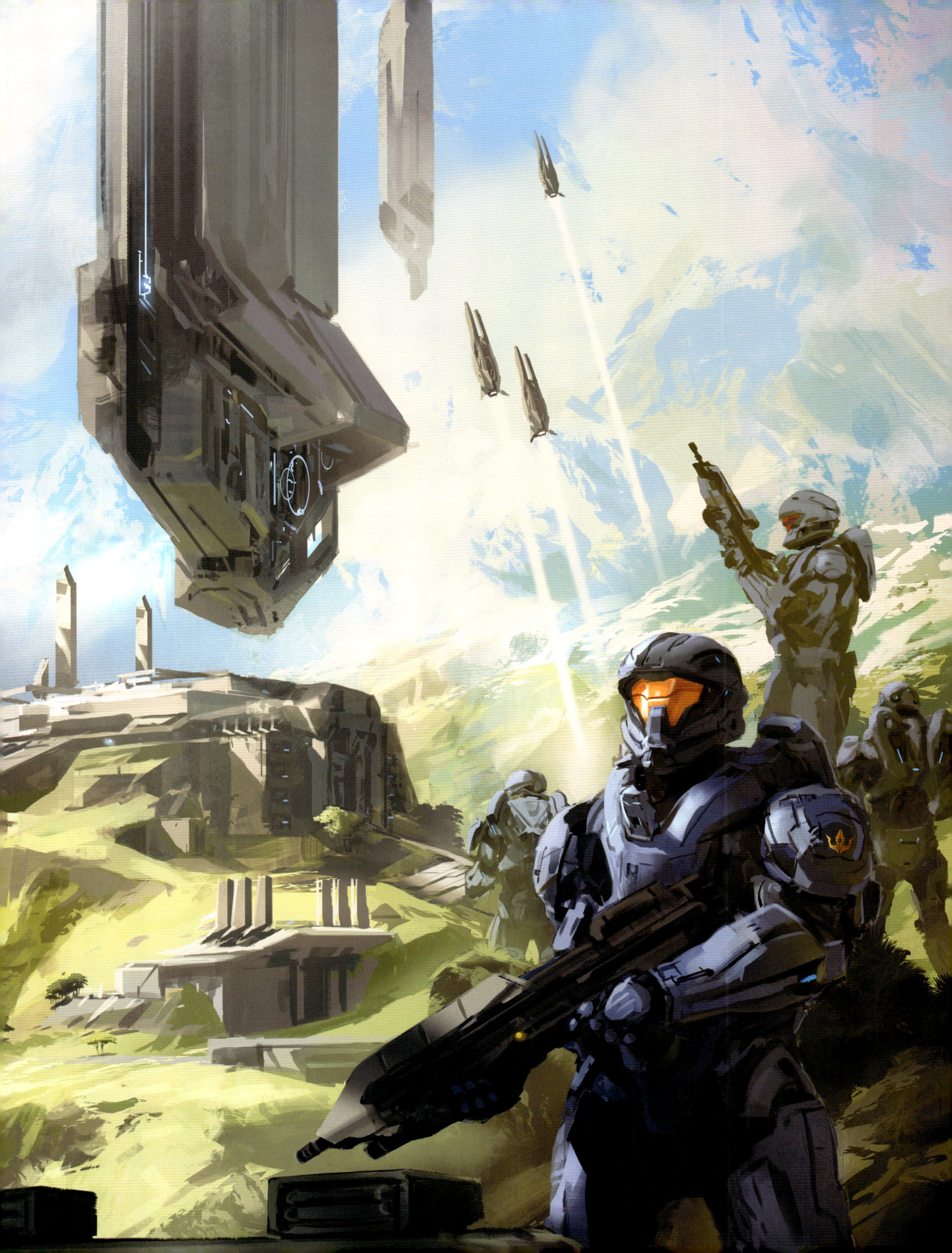

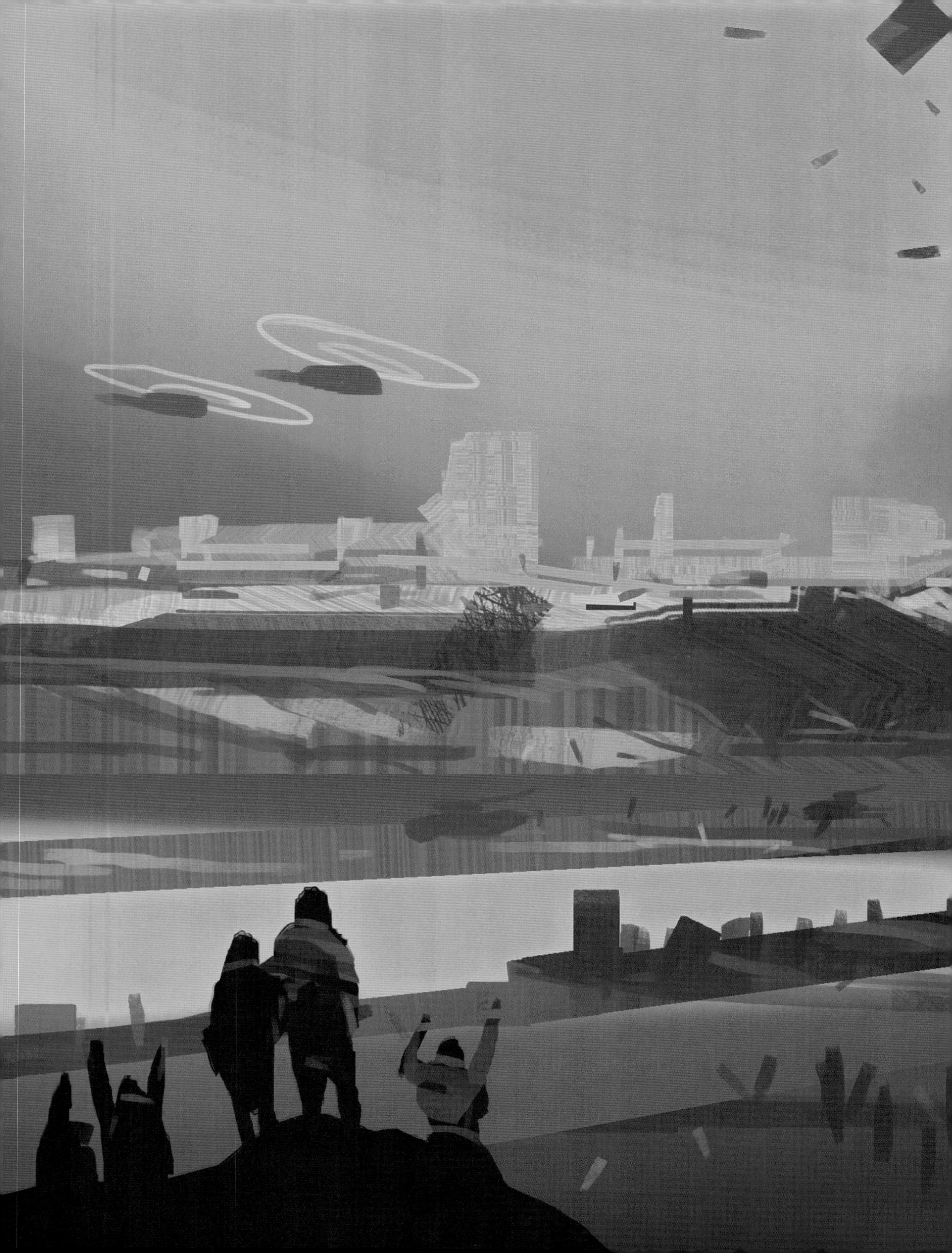

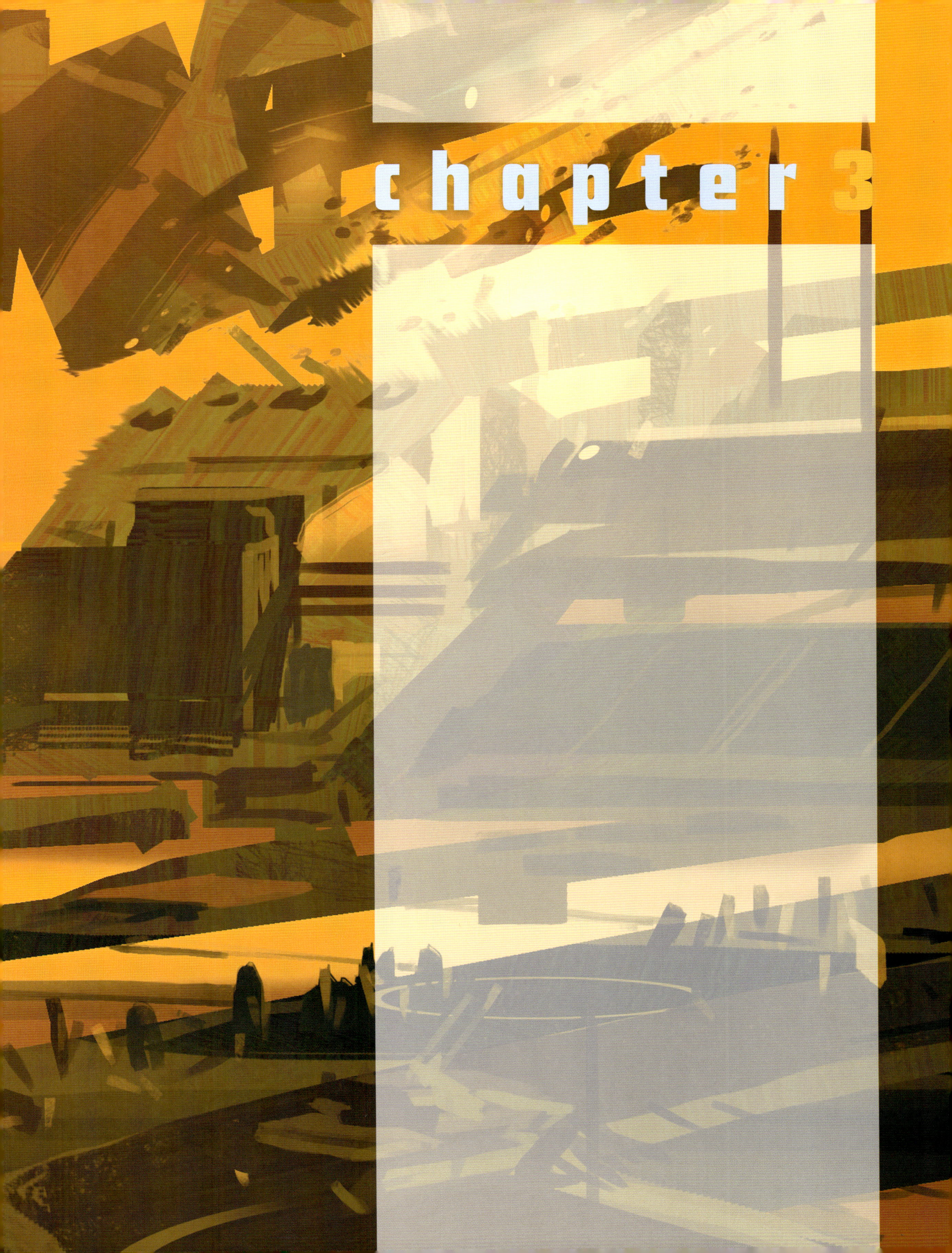

chapter 3

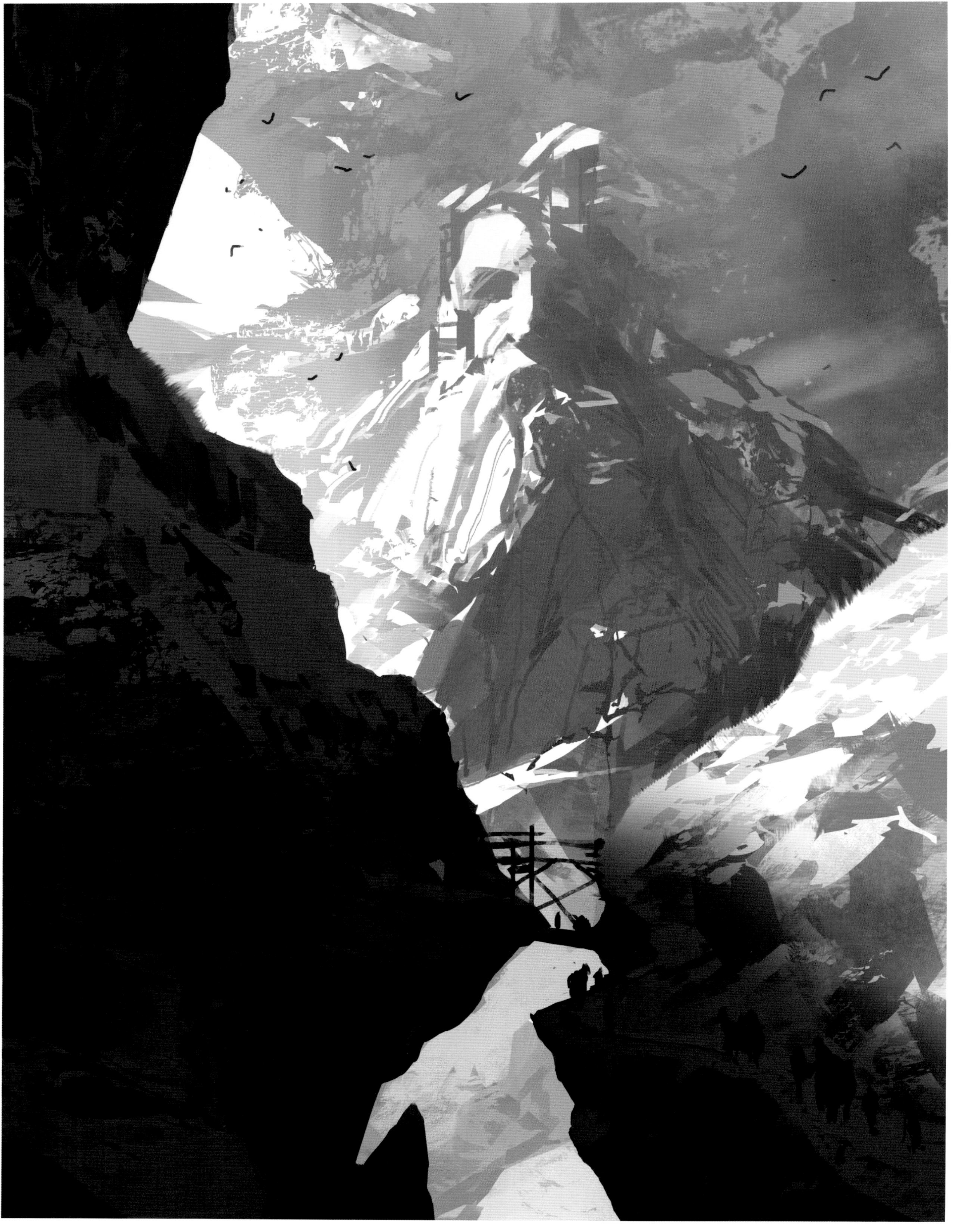

God of winter, 2013

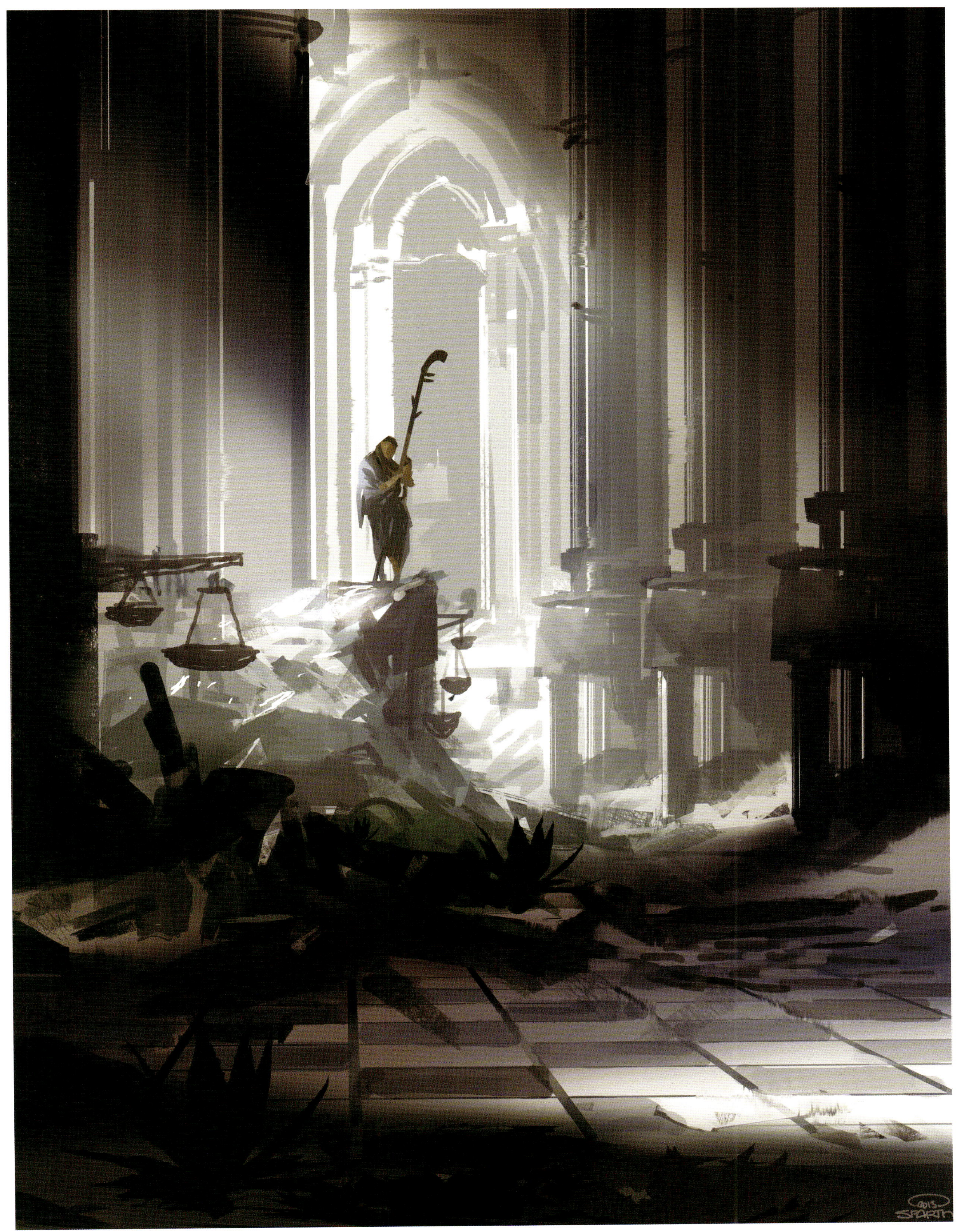

Prophet, 2013

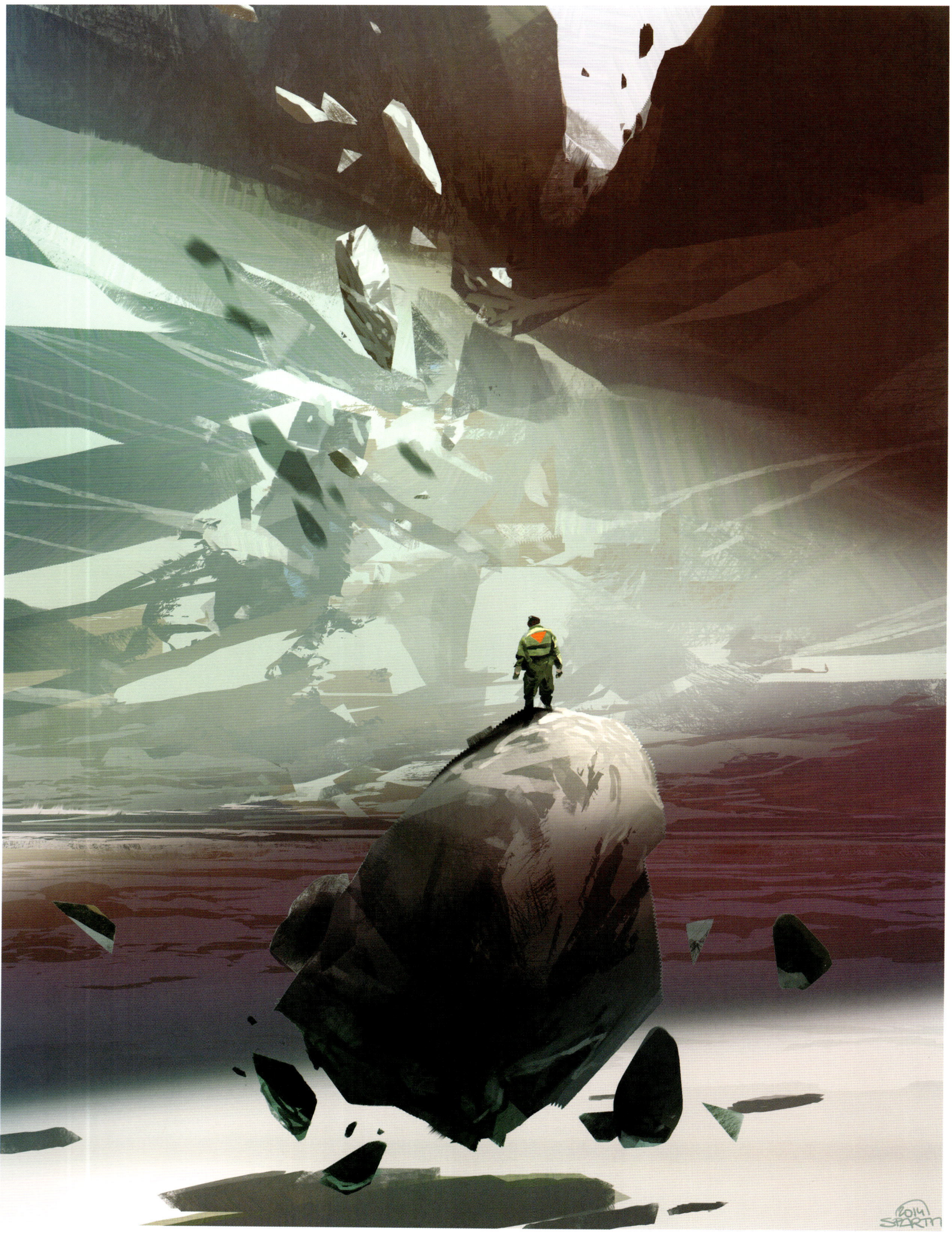

Master of sands, 2014

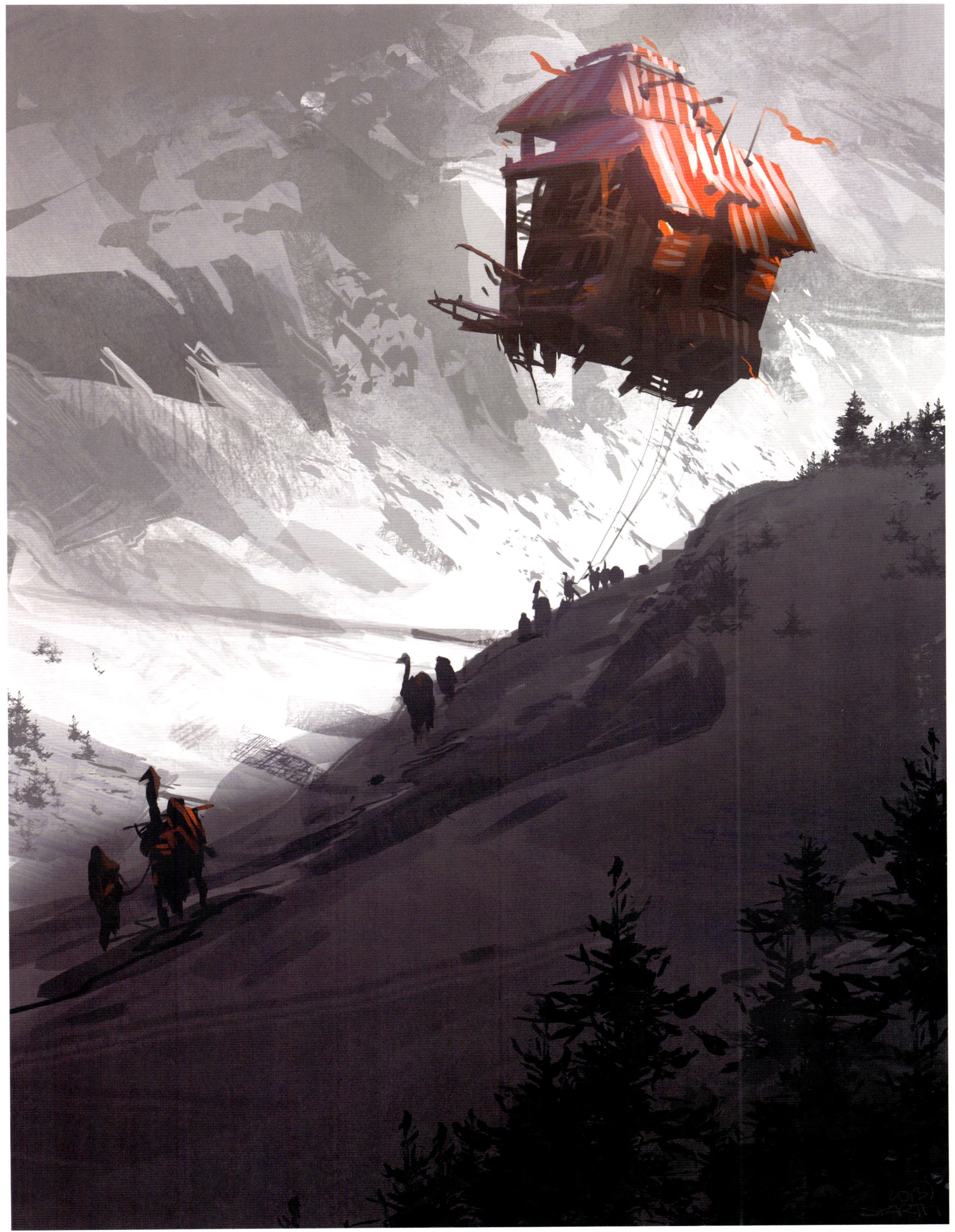

Flying house, 2013

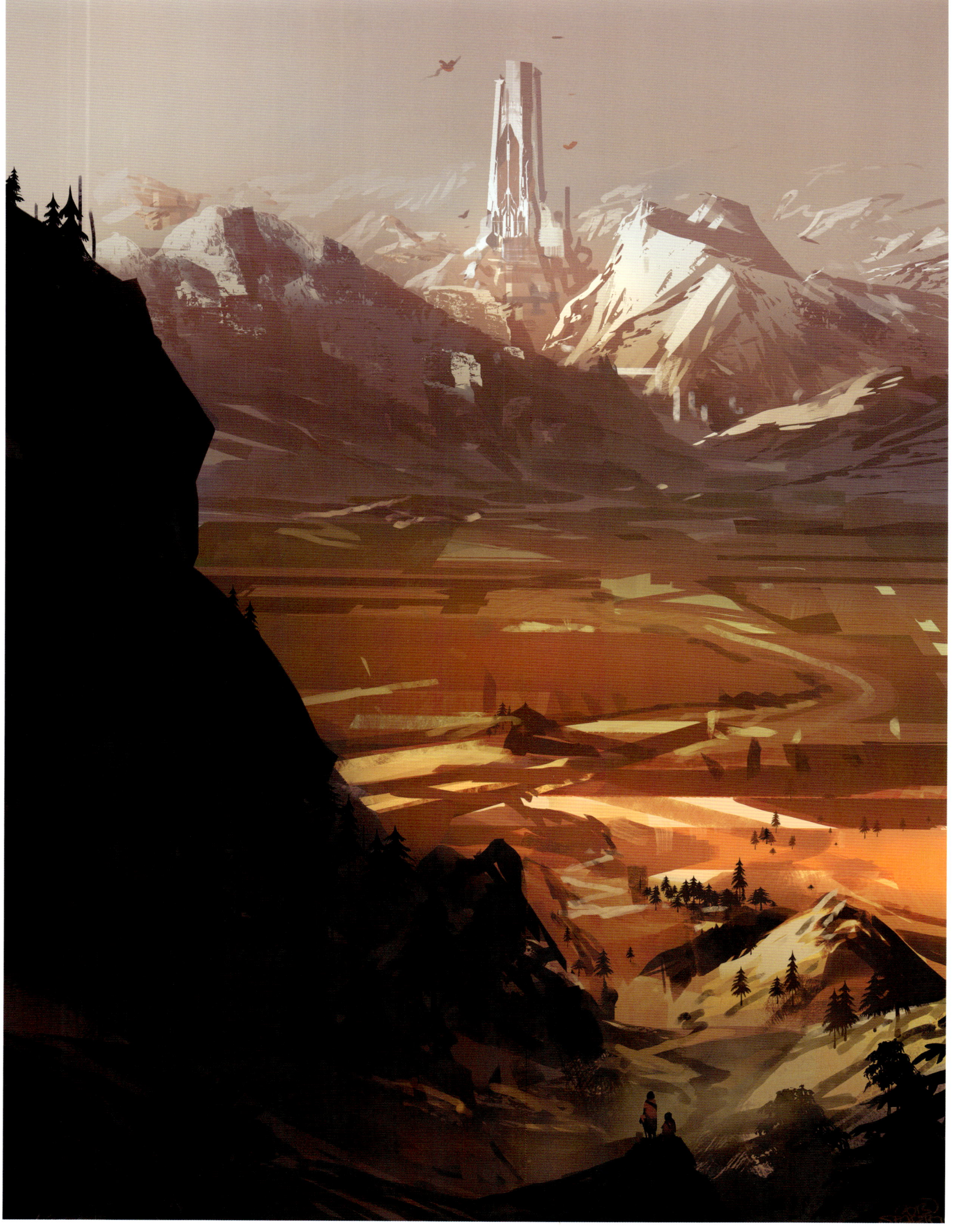

Mordor, 2013

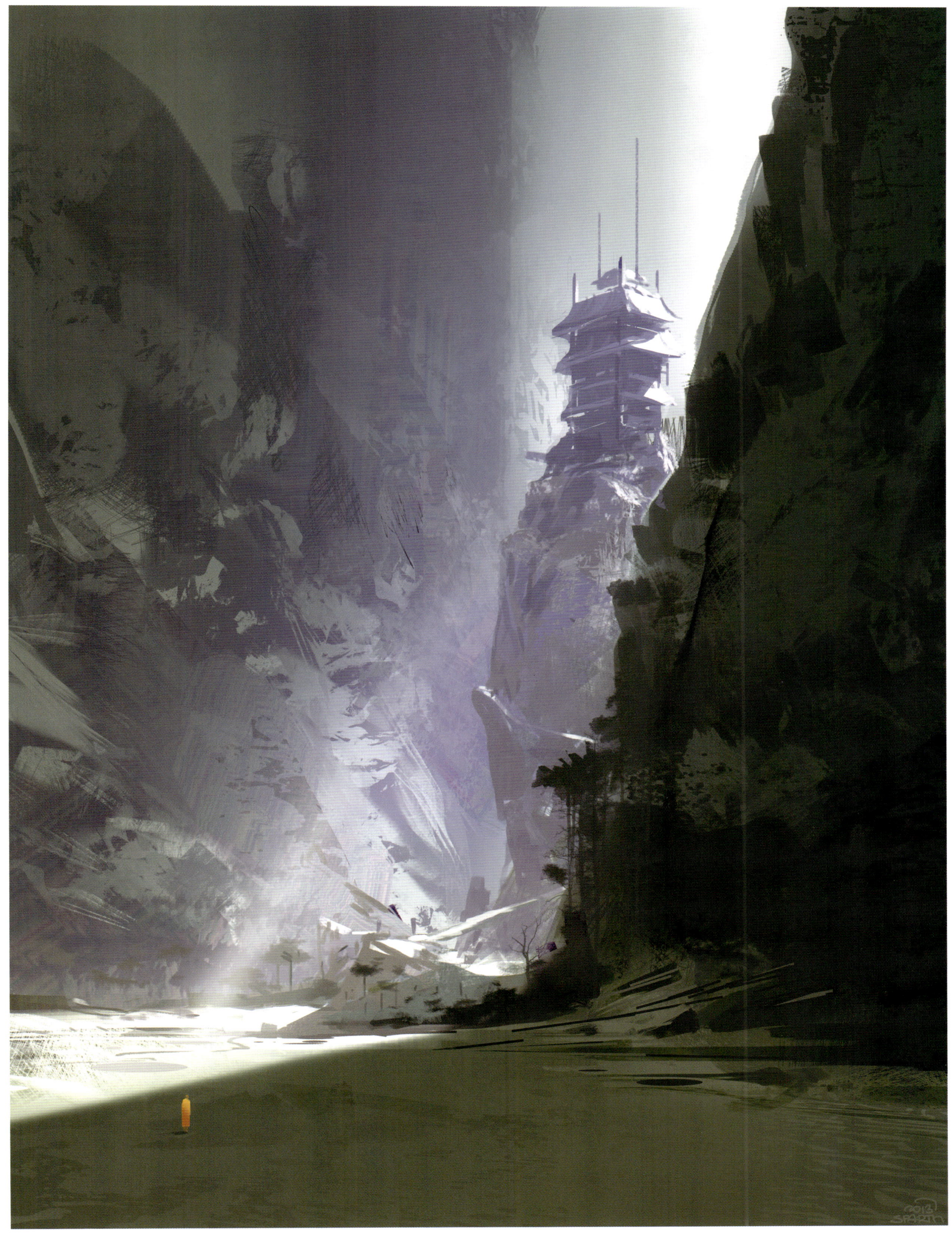
Meditation, 2013

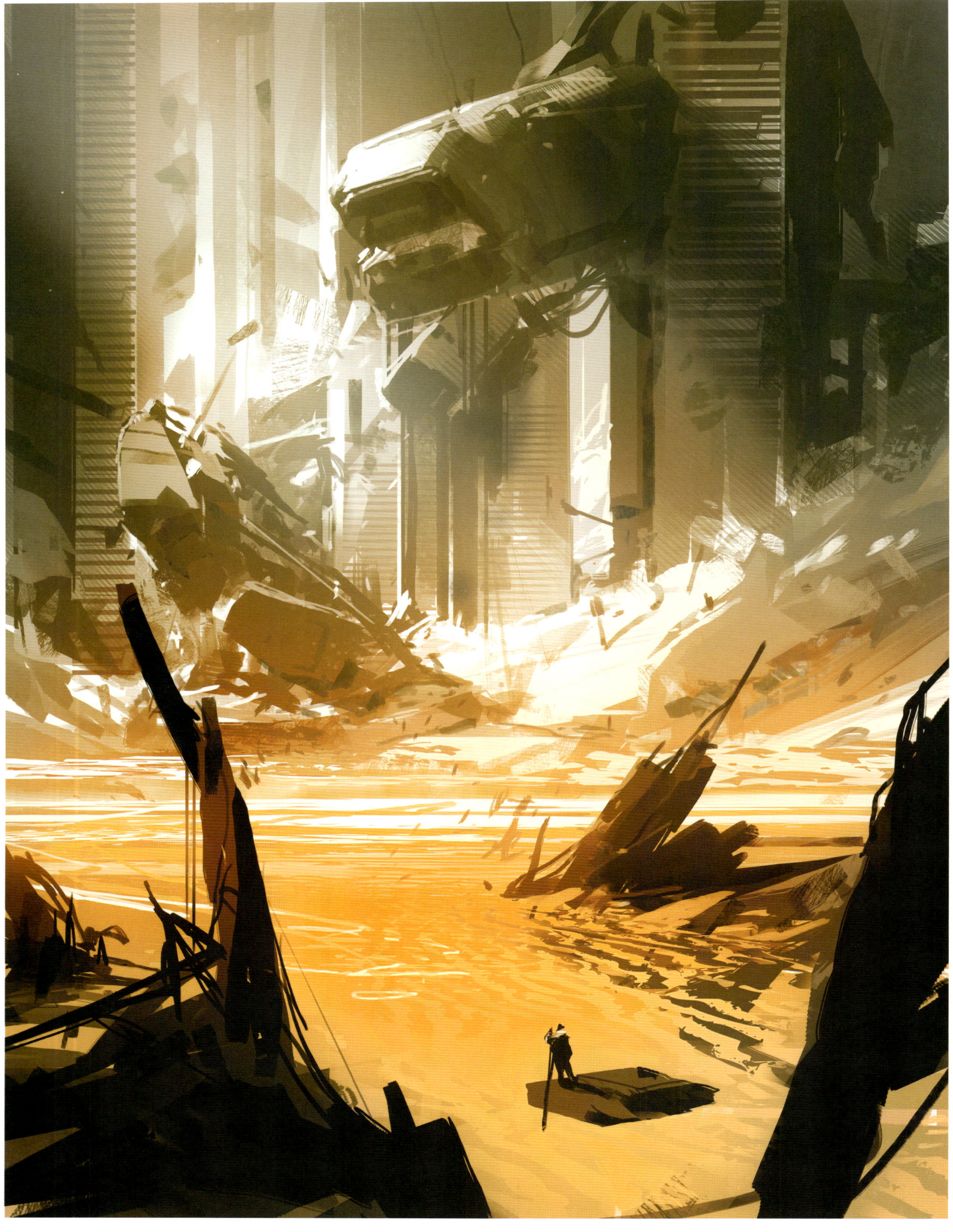

Dying world, 2013

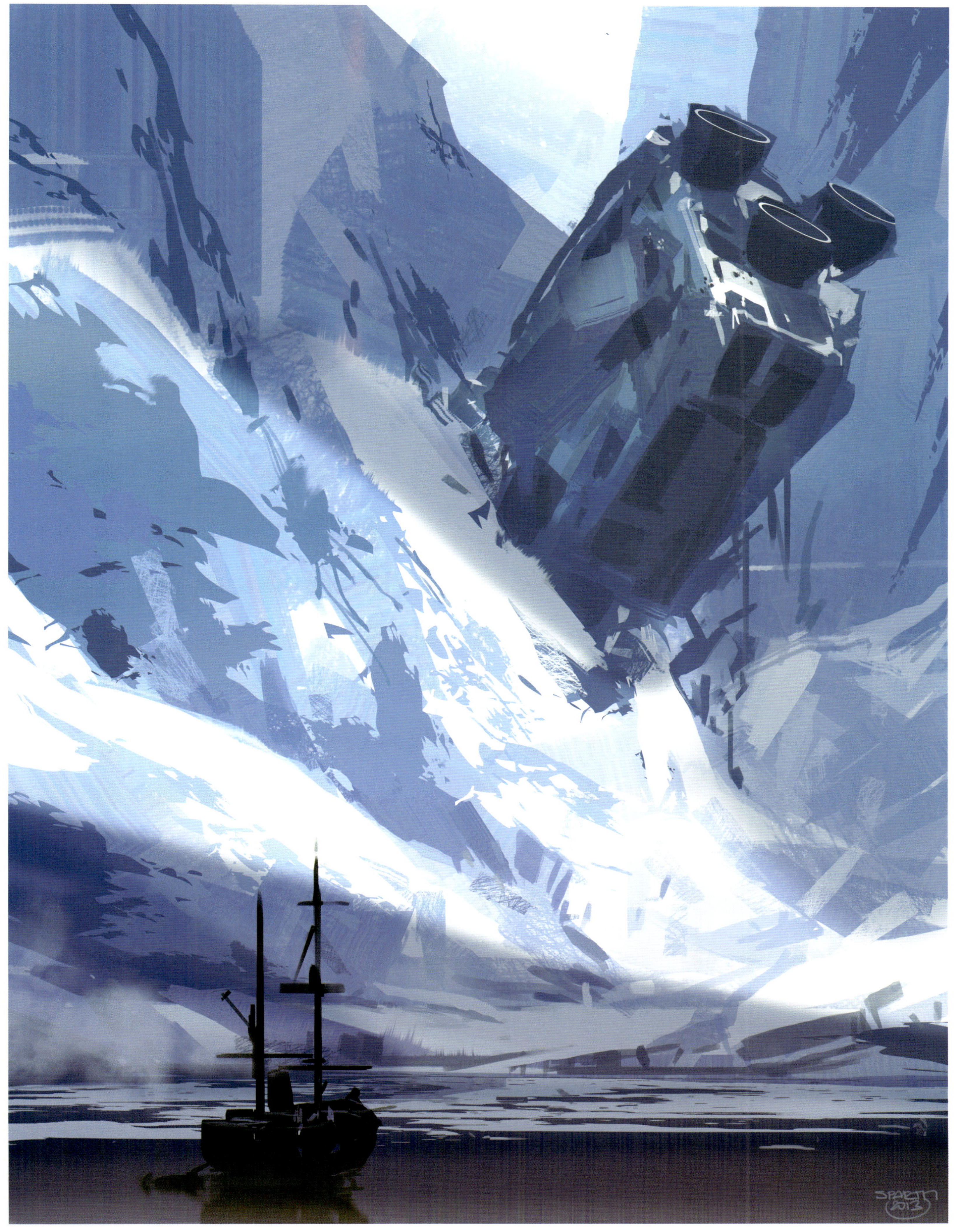

Discovery, 2013

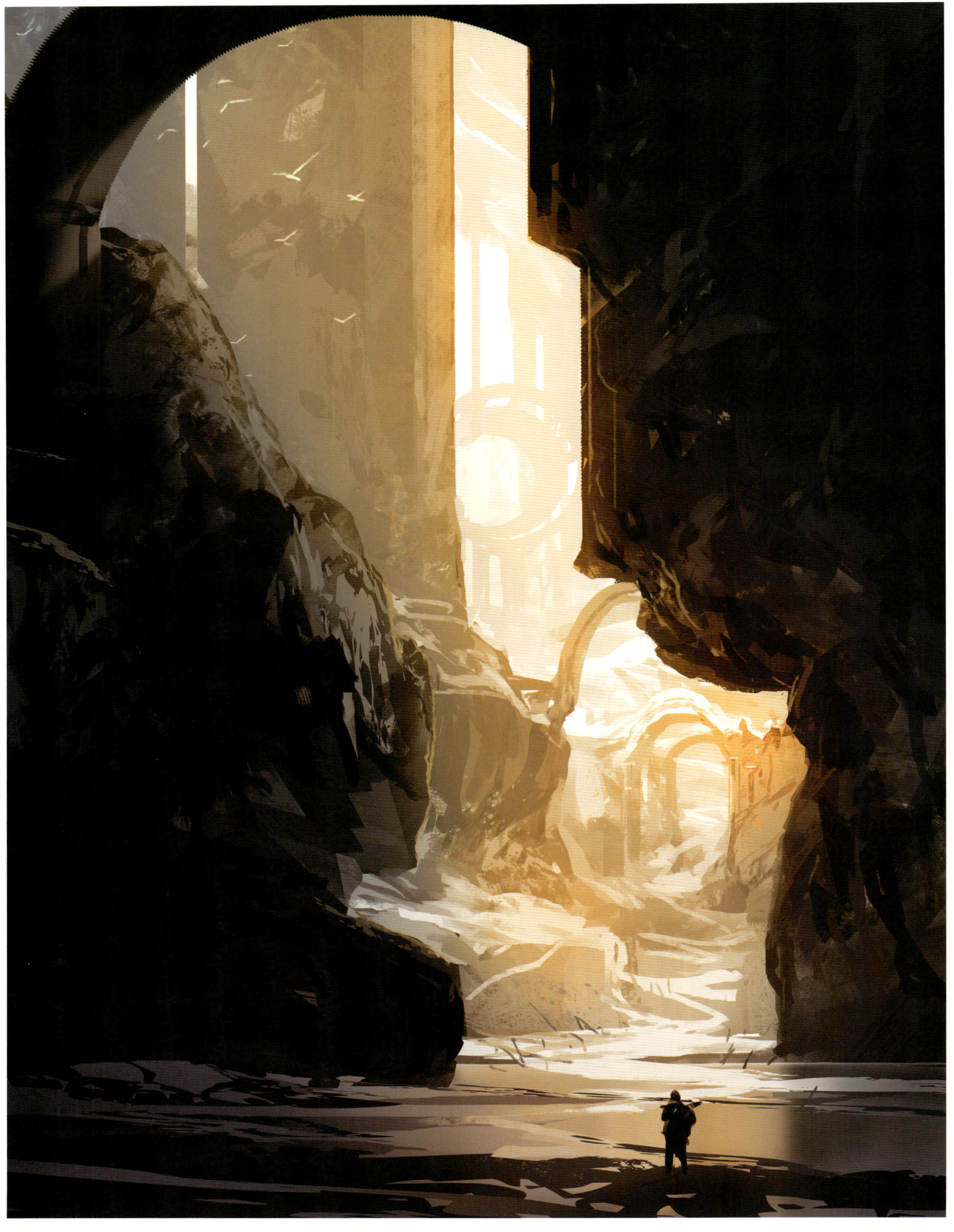

Undiscovered cave, 2013

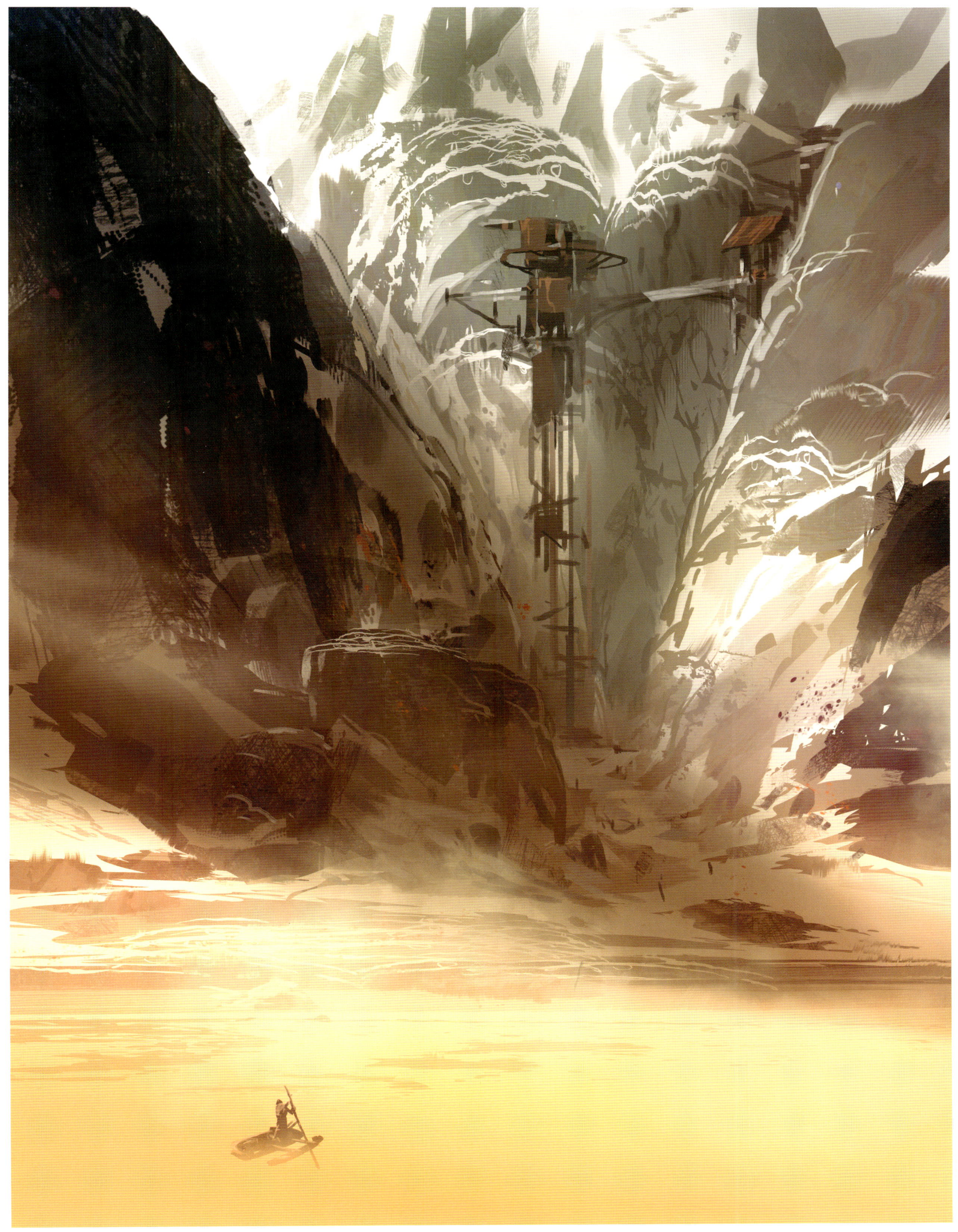

Inside the volcano, 2013

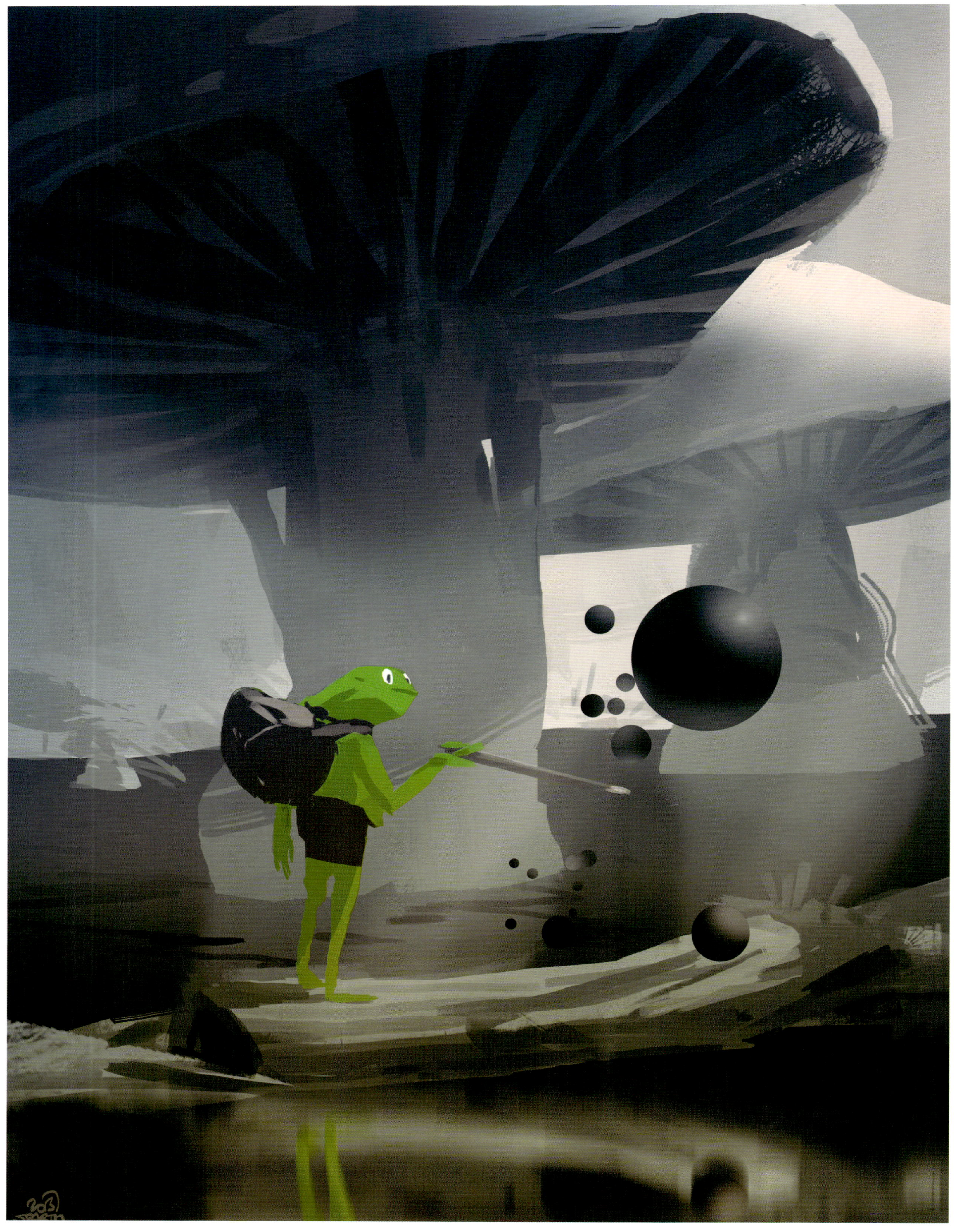

Deadly goo, 2013

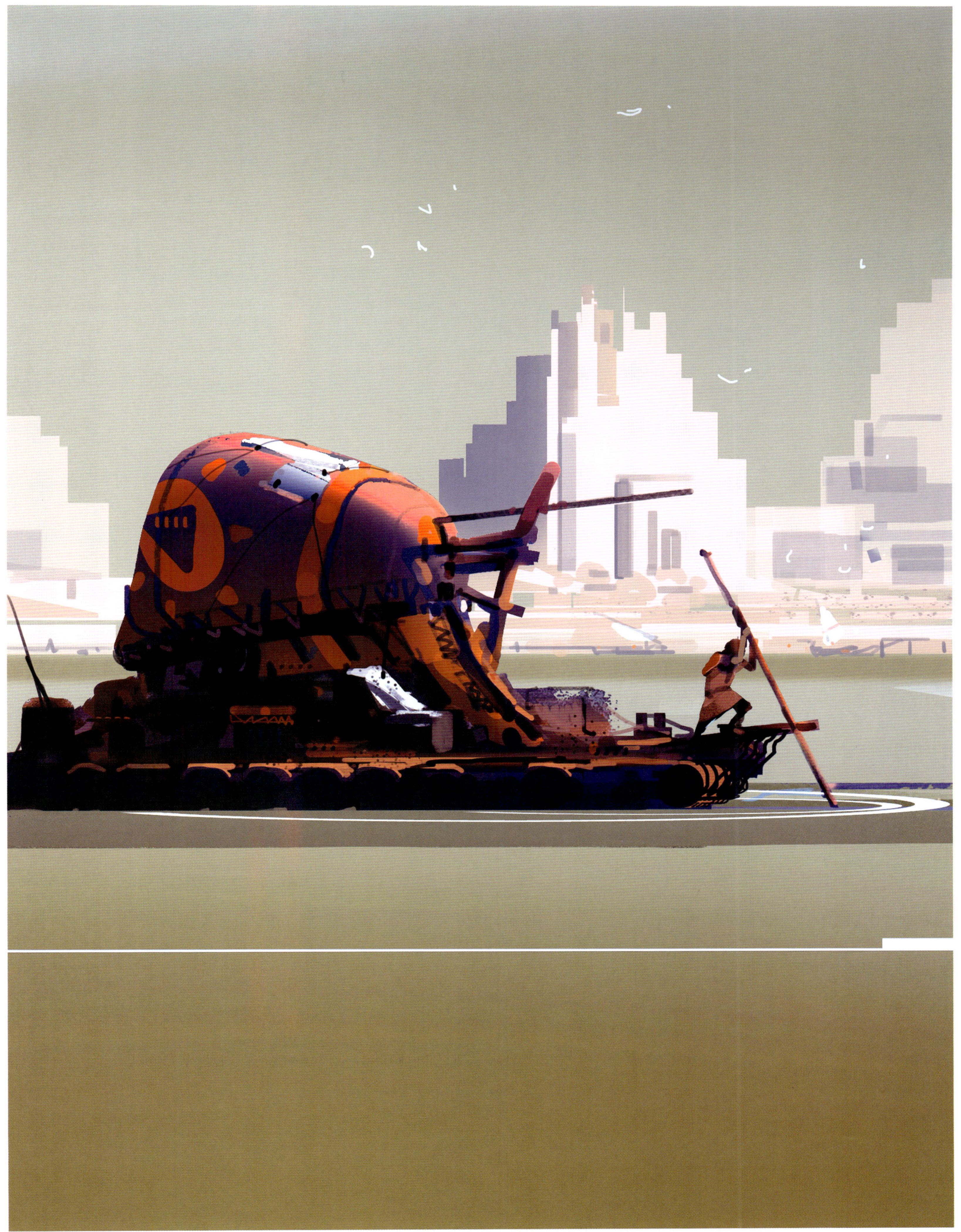

Boathouse, 2013

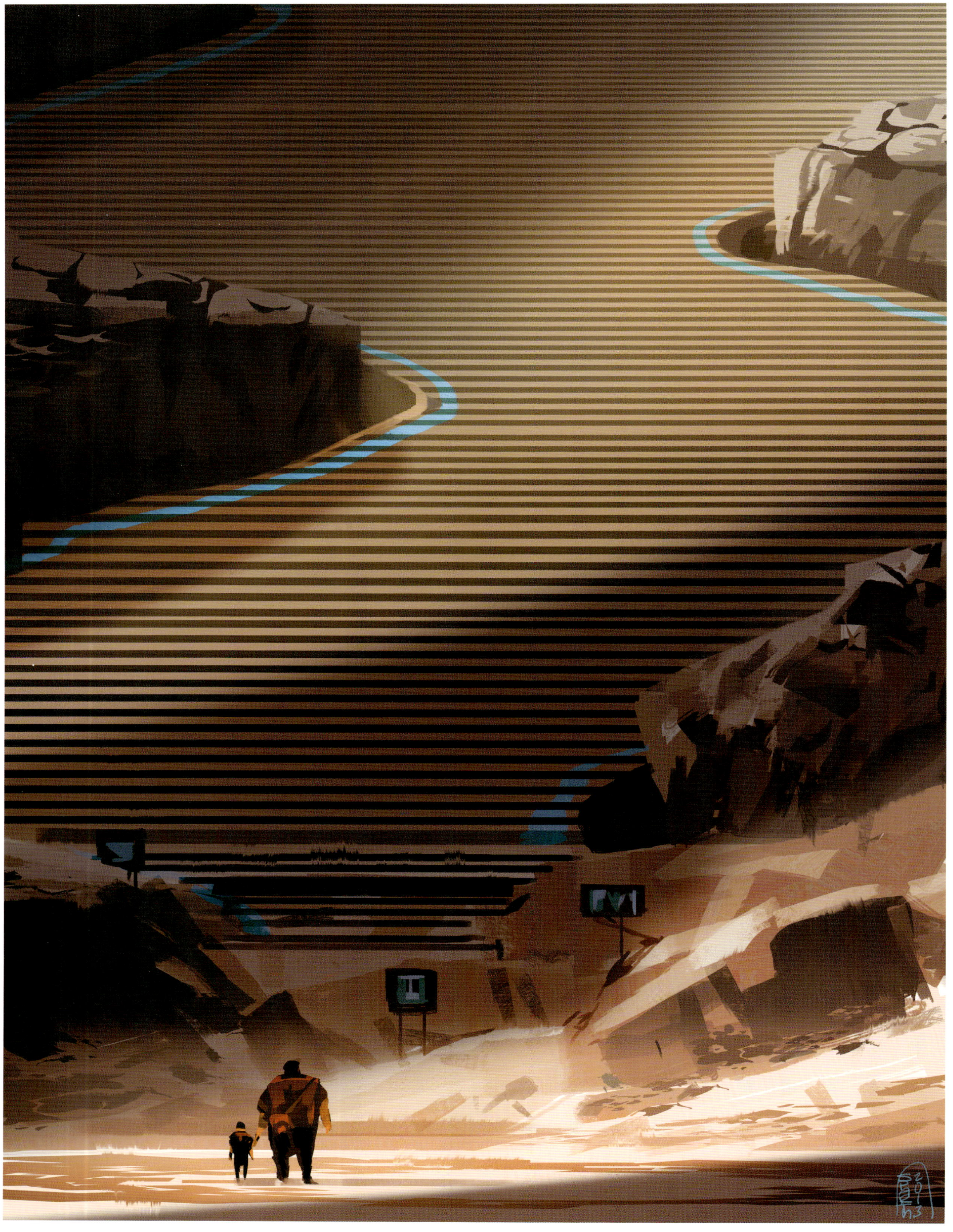

Giant staircase, 2013

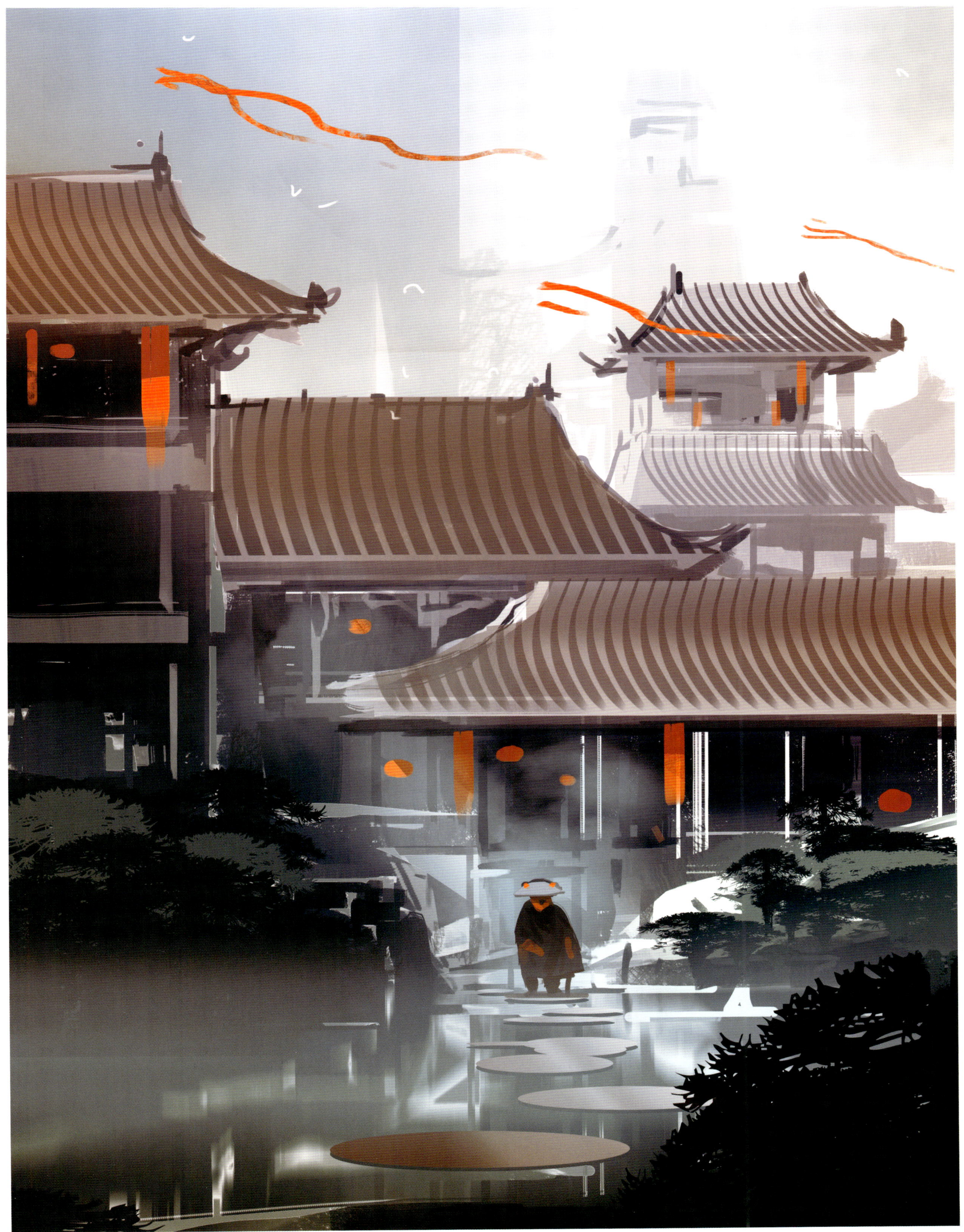

Red panda village, 2013

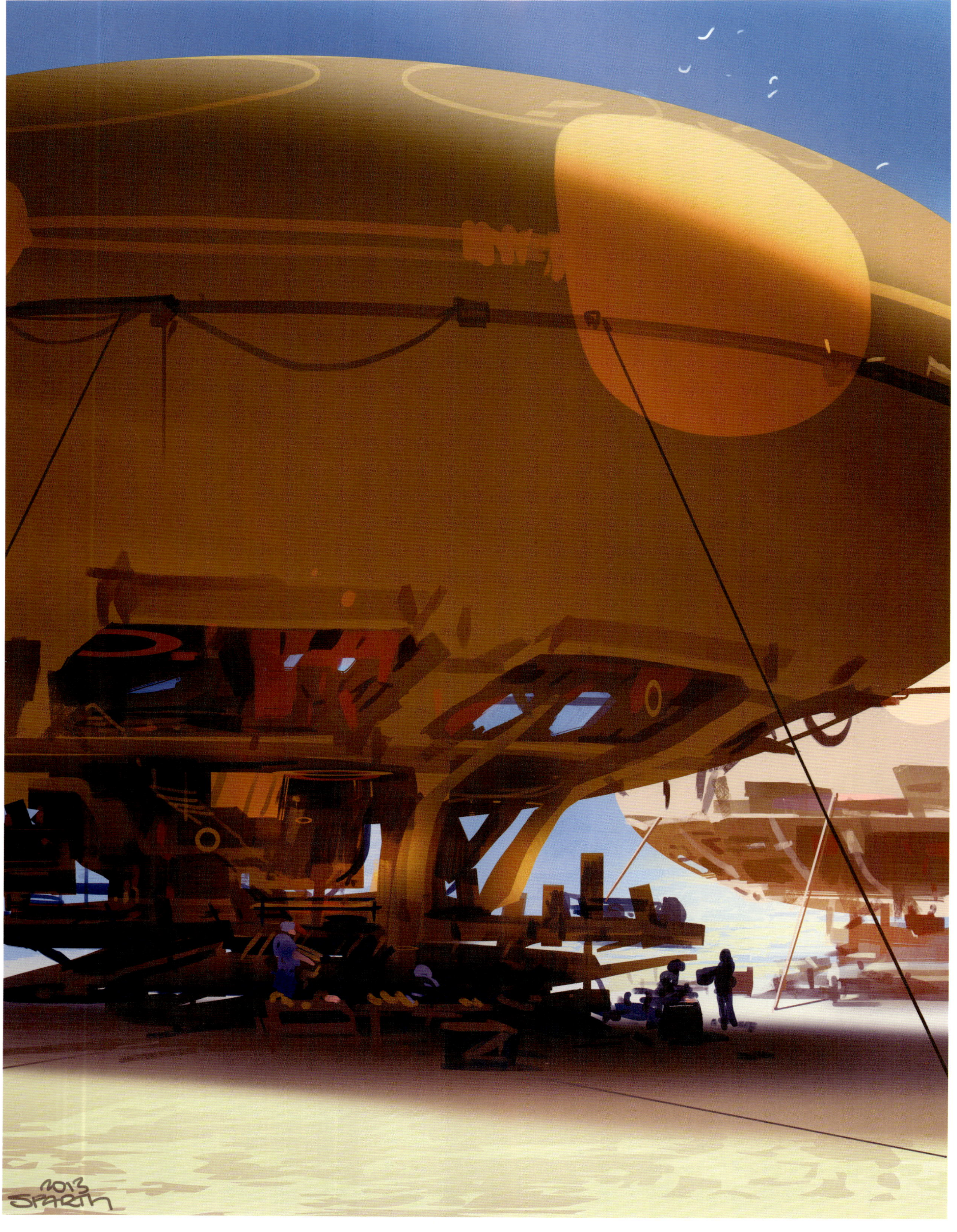

Market day I, 2013

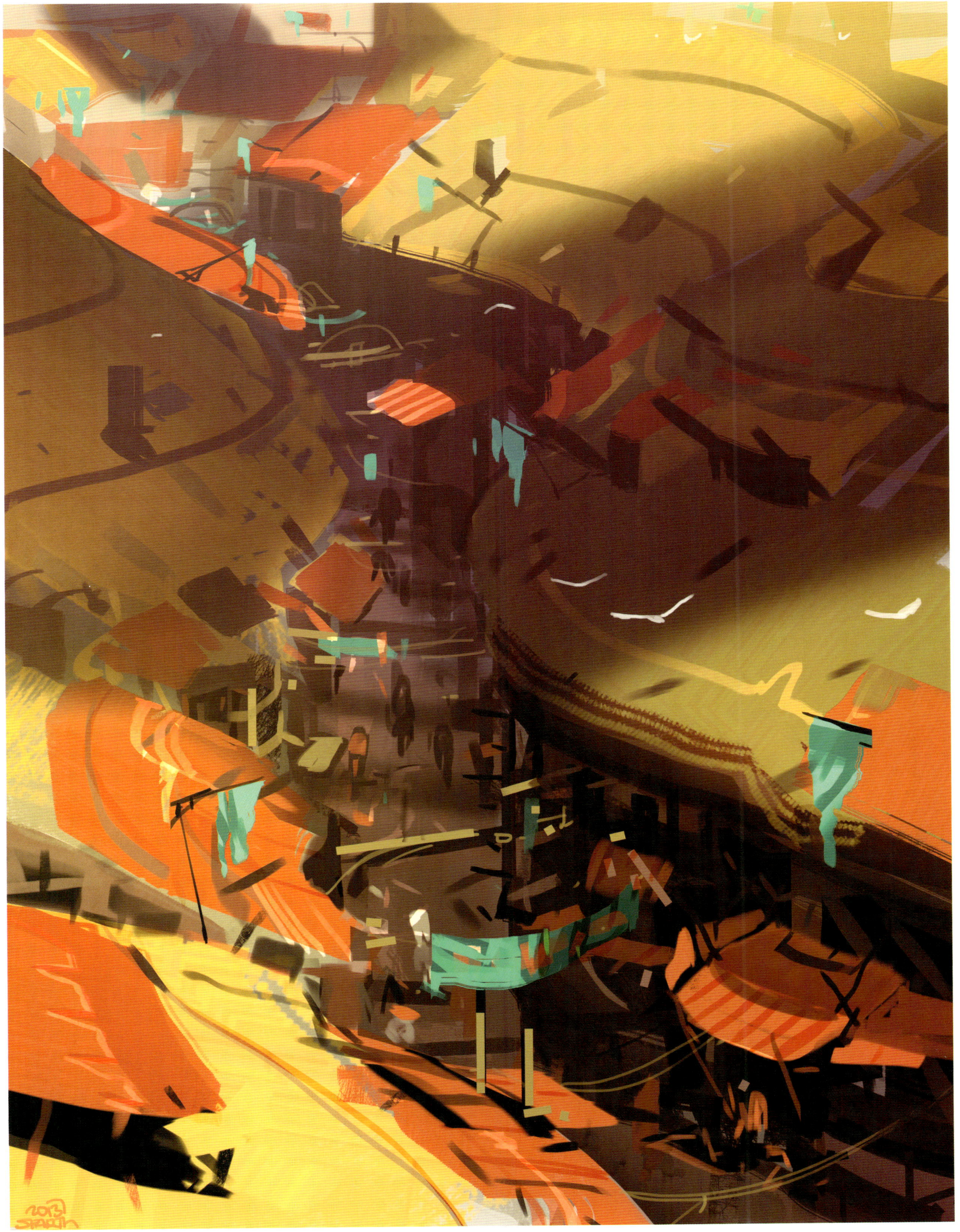

Market day II, 2013

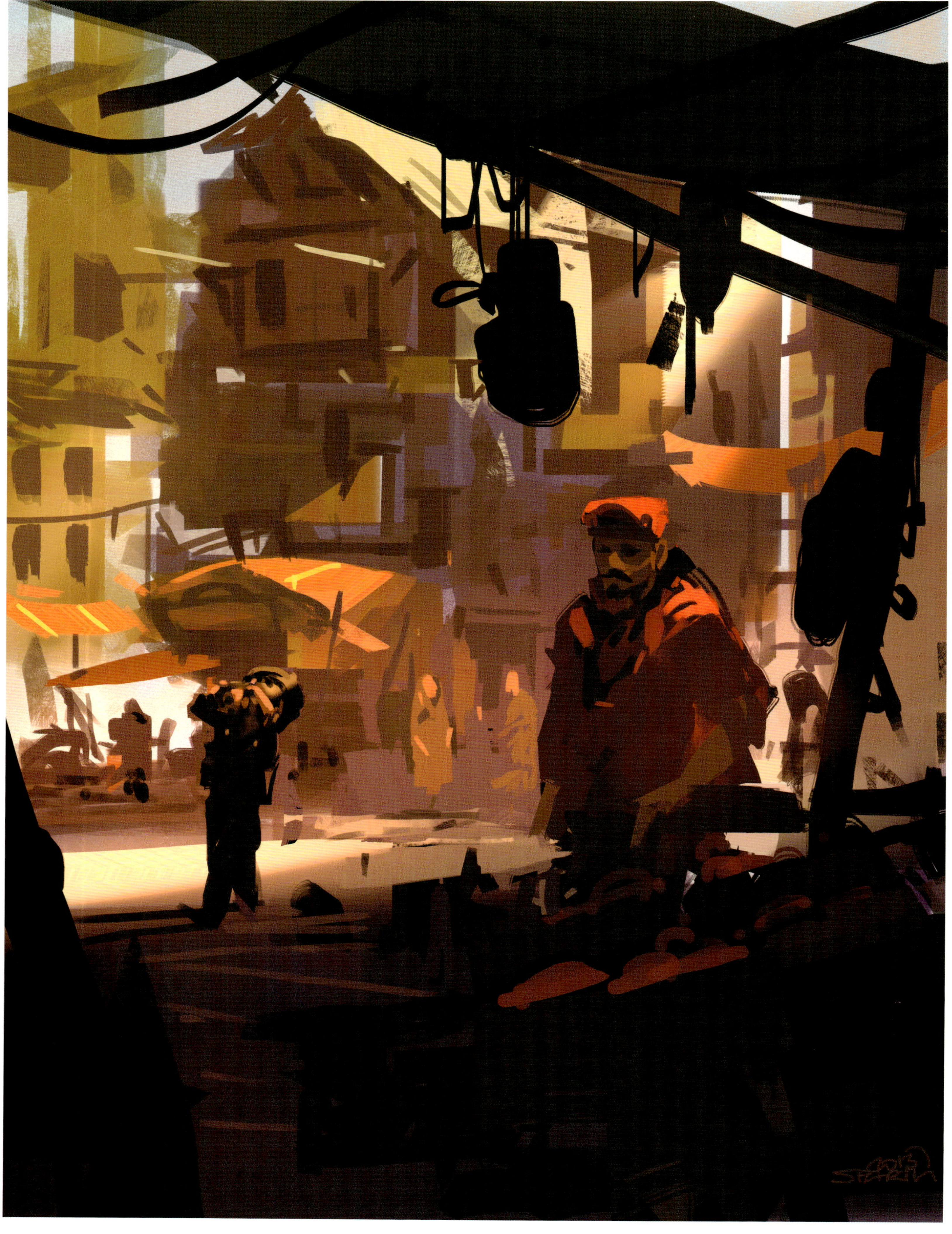

Market day III, 2013

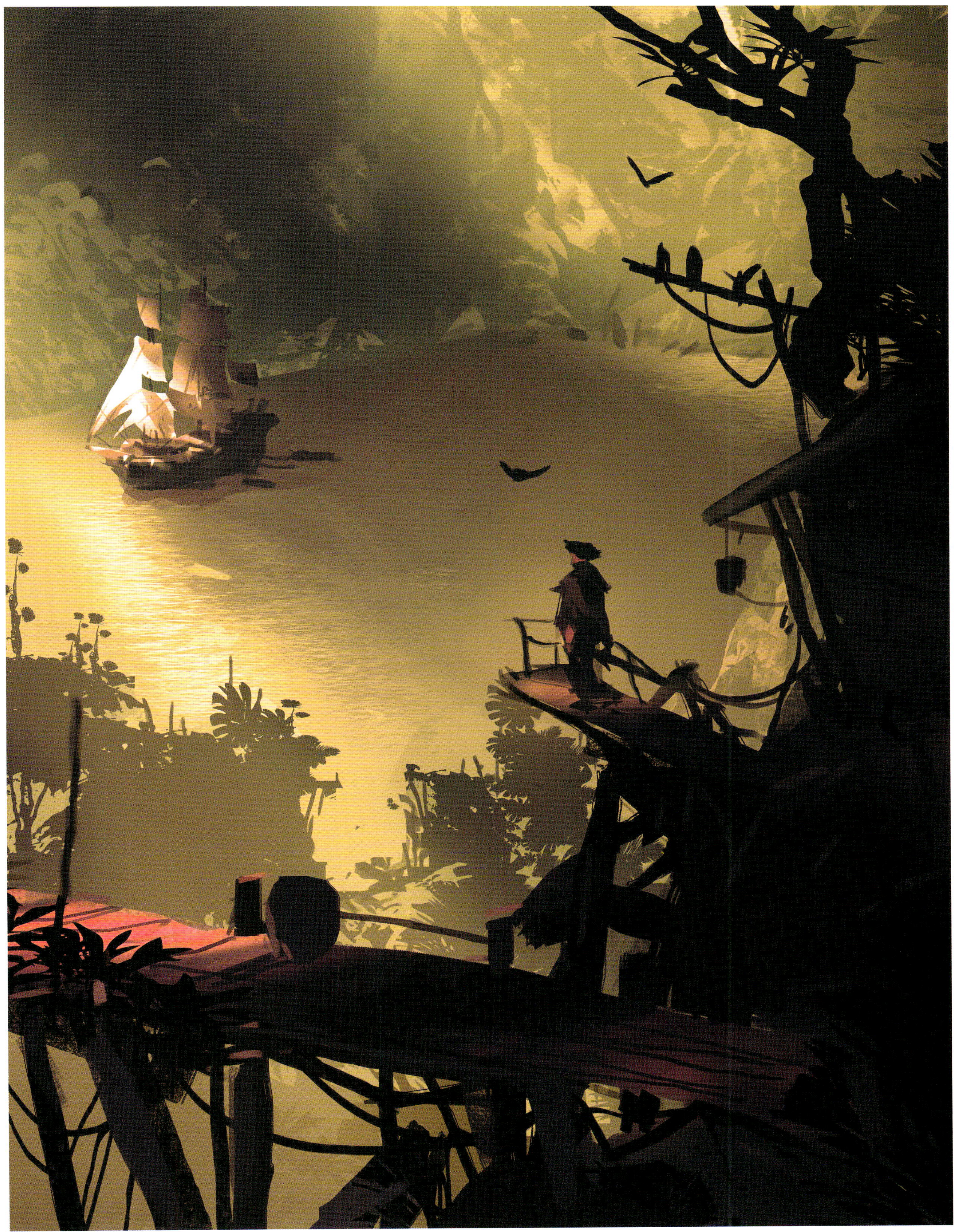

Pirate outlook, 2013

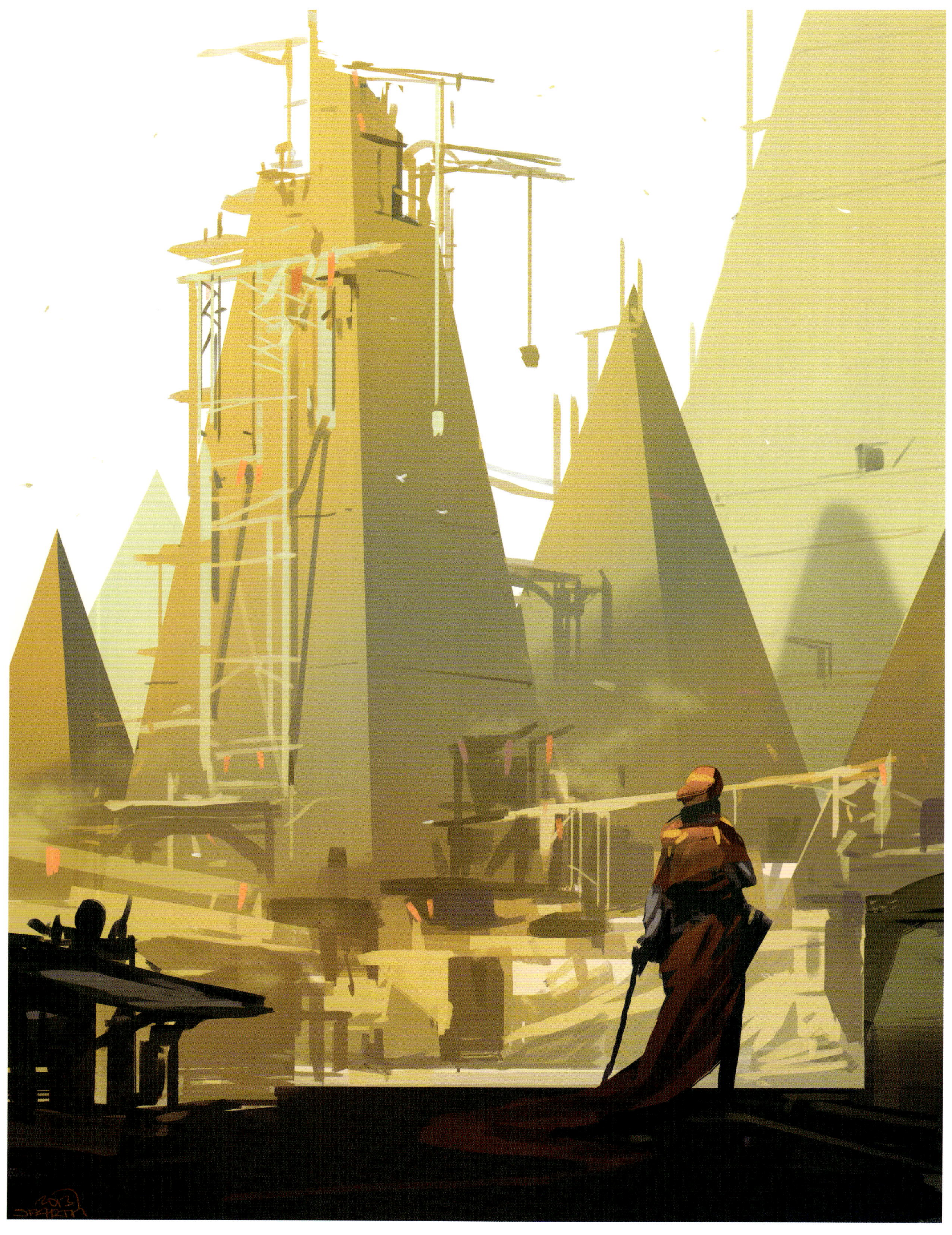

Pyramid lord, 2013

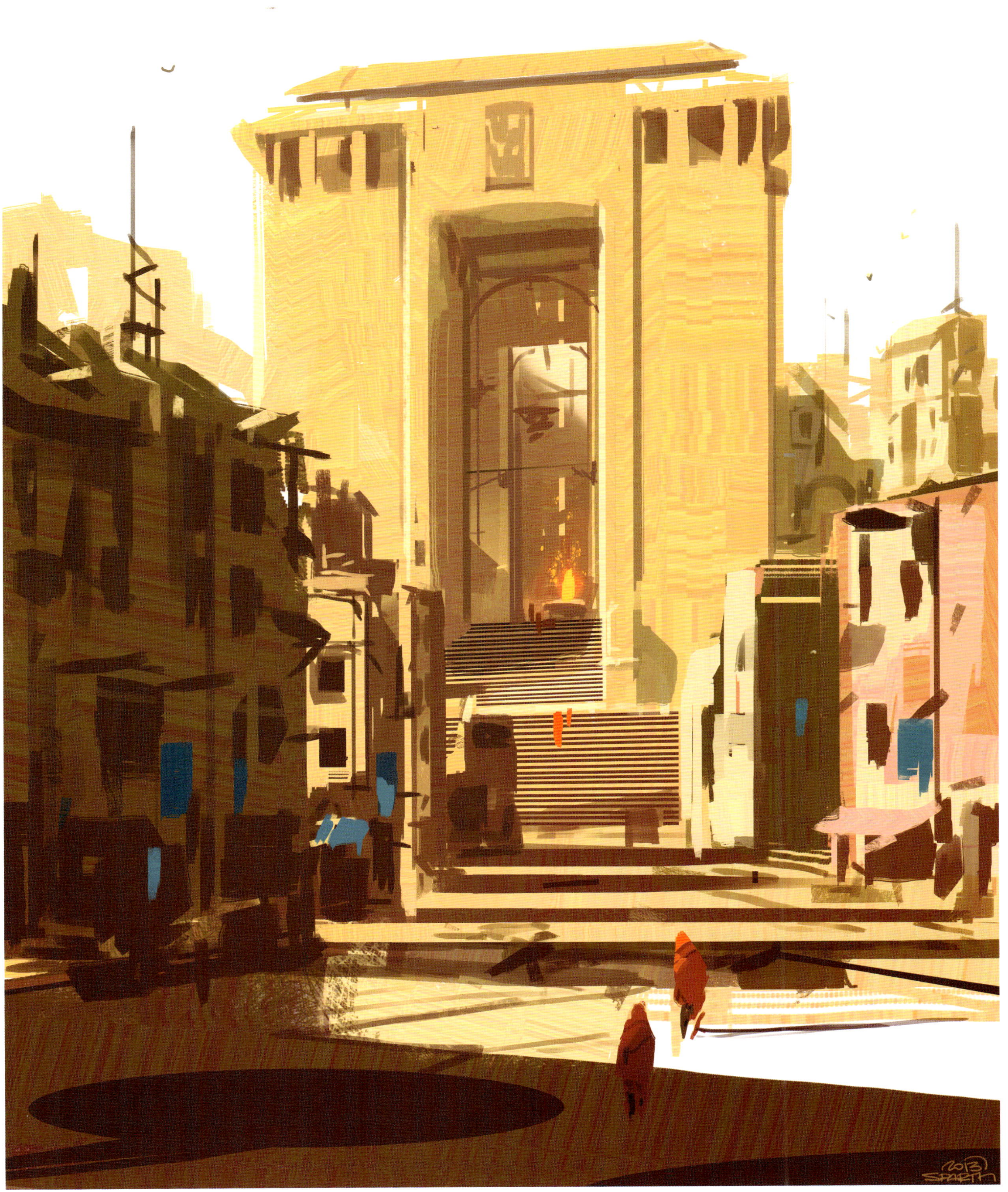

Fire temple, 2013

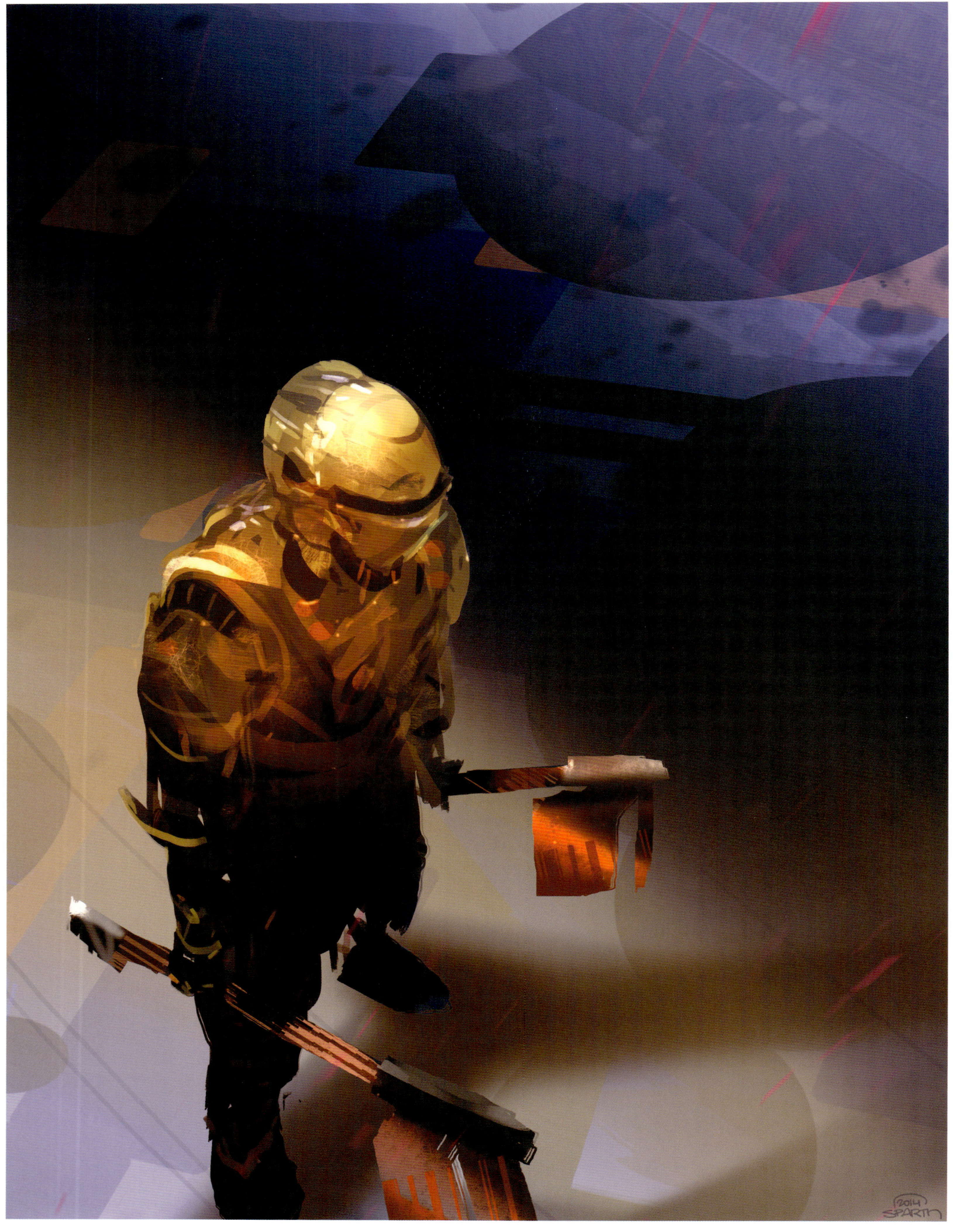

Axeman, 2013

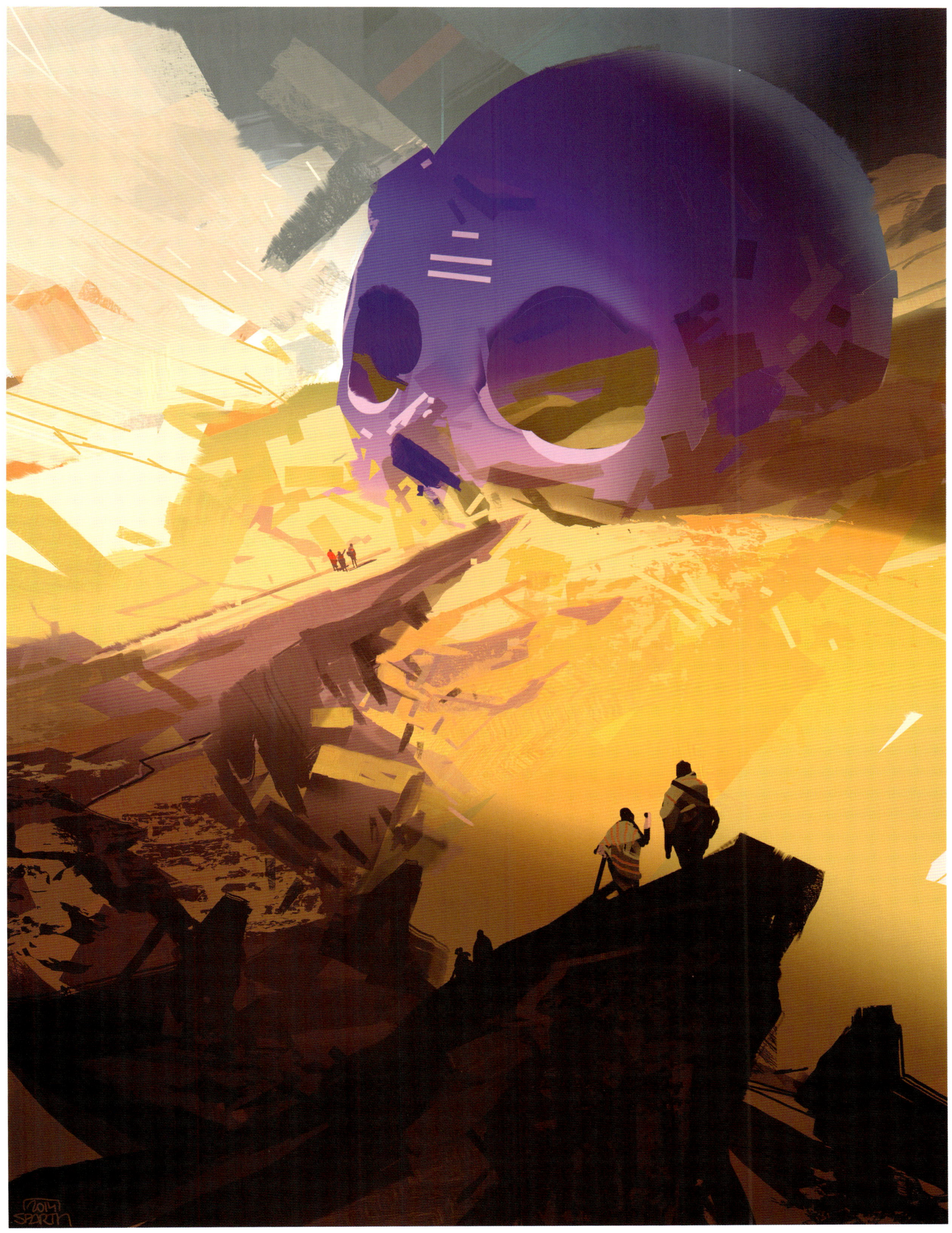

Buried blue skull, 2014

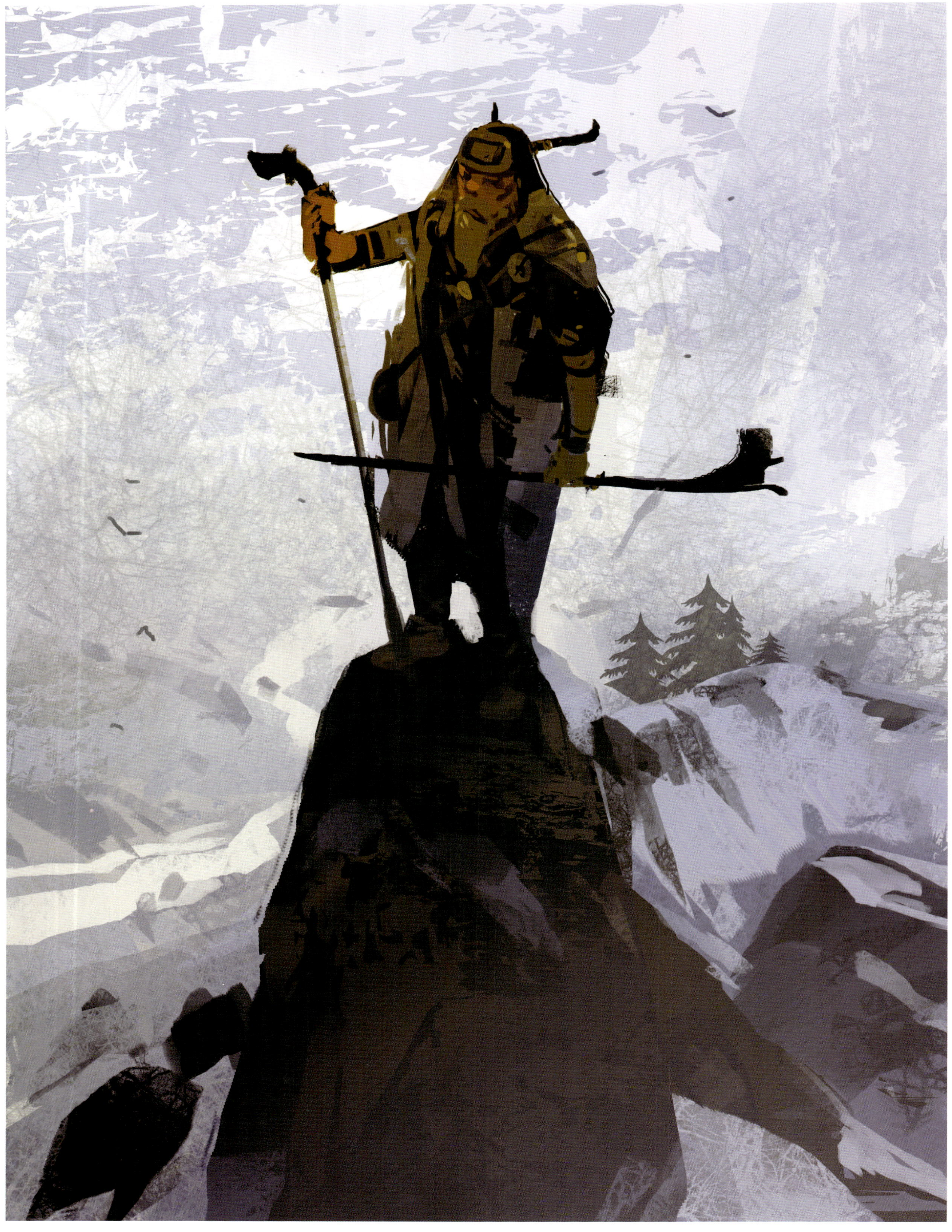

Dwarf warlock, 2013

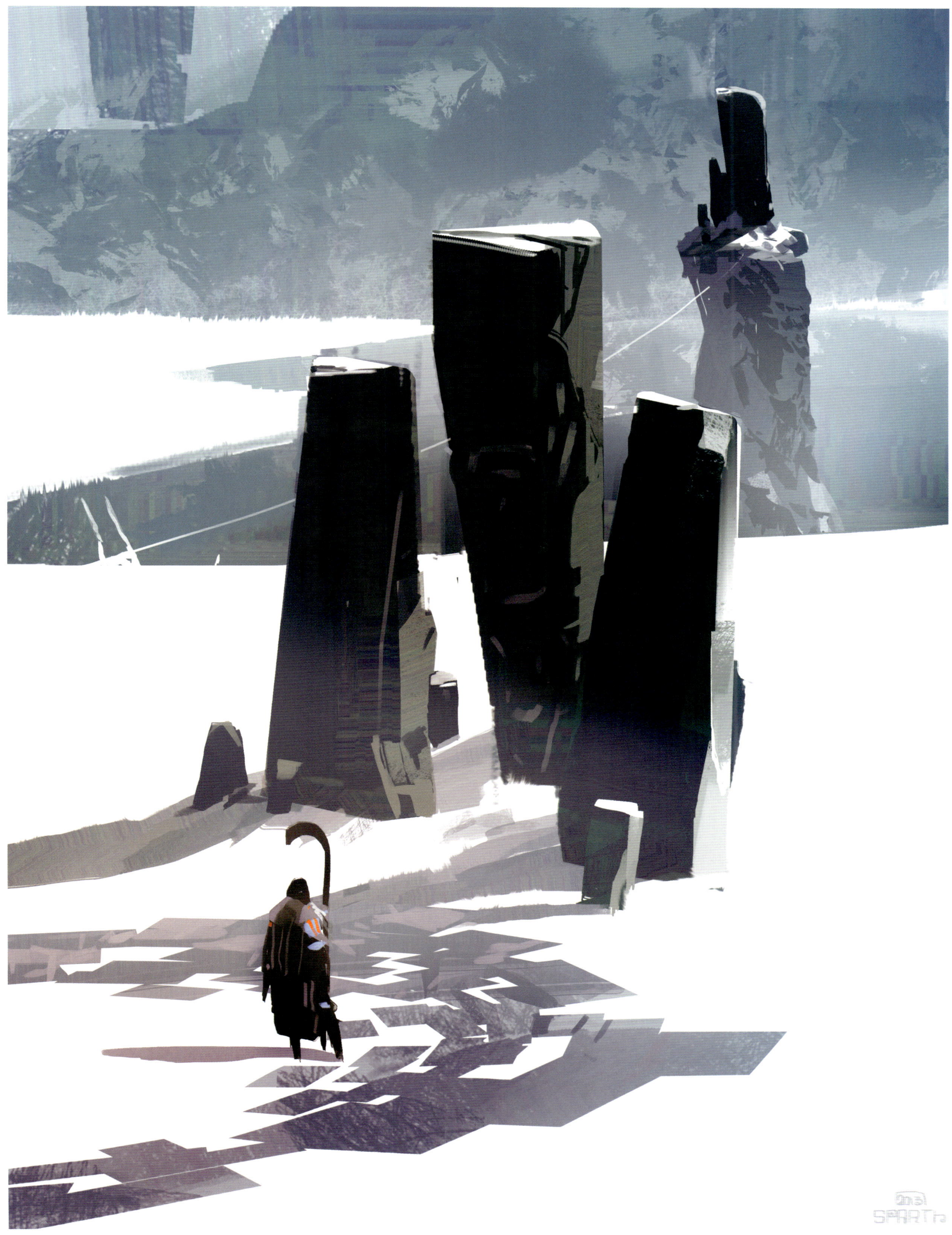

Tomb guardian, 2013

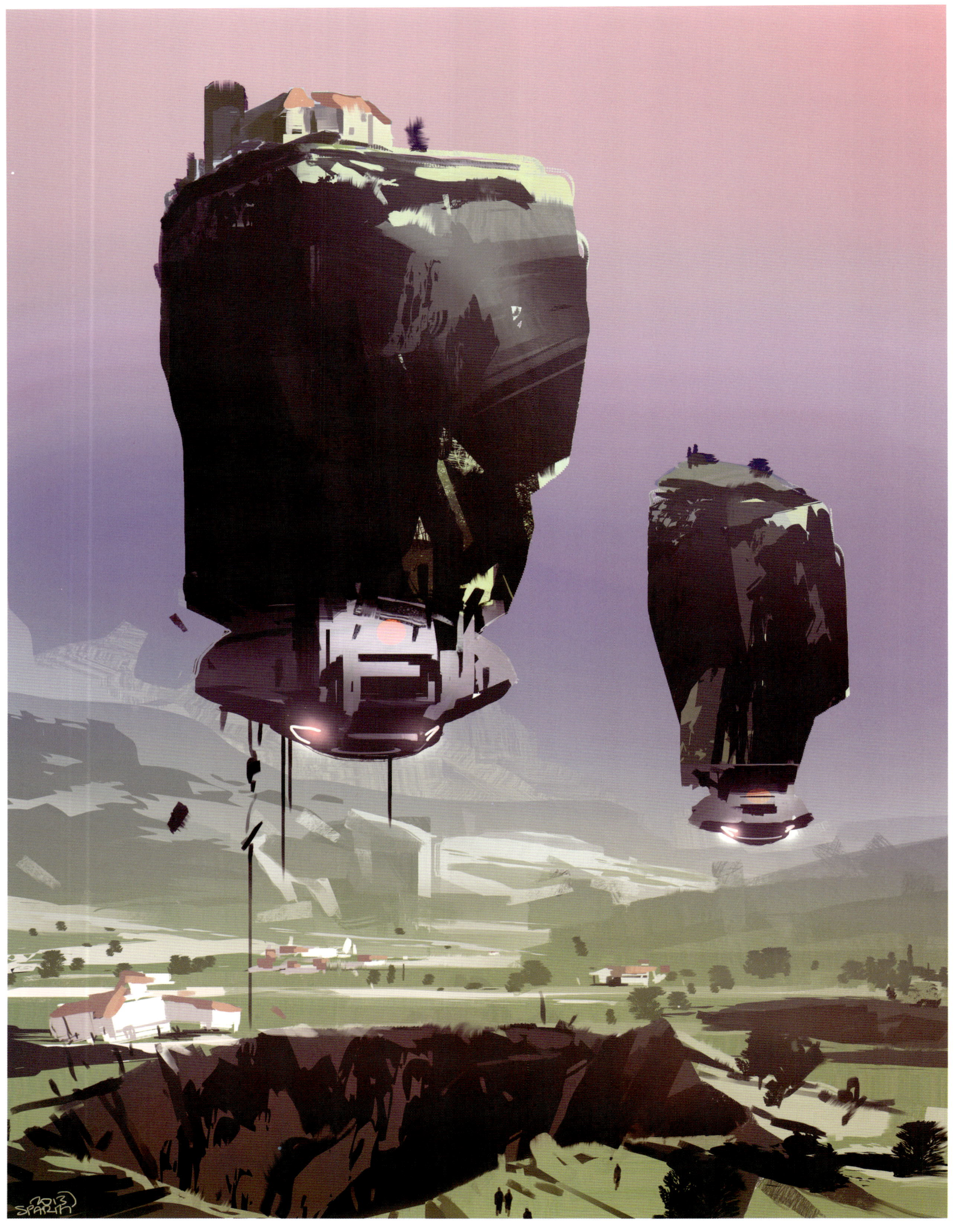

Strange encounter, 2013

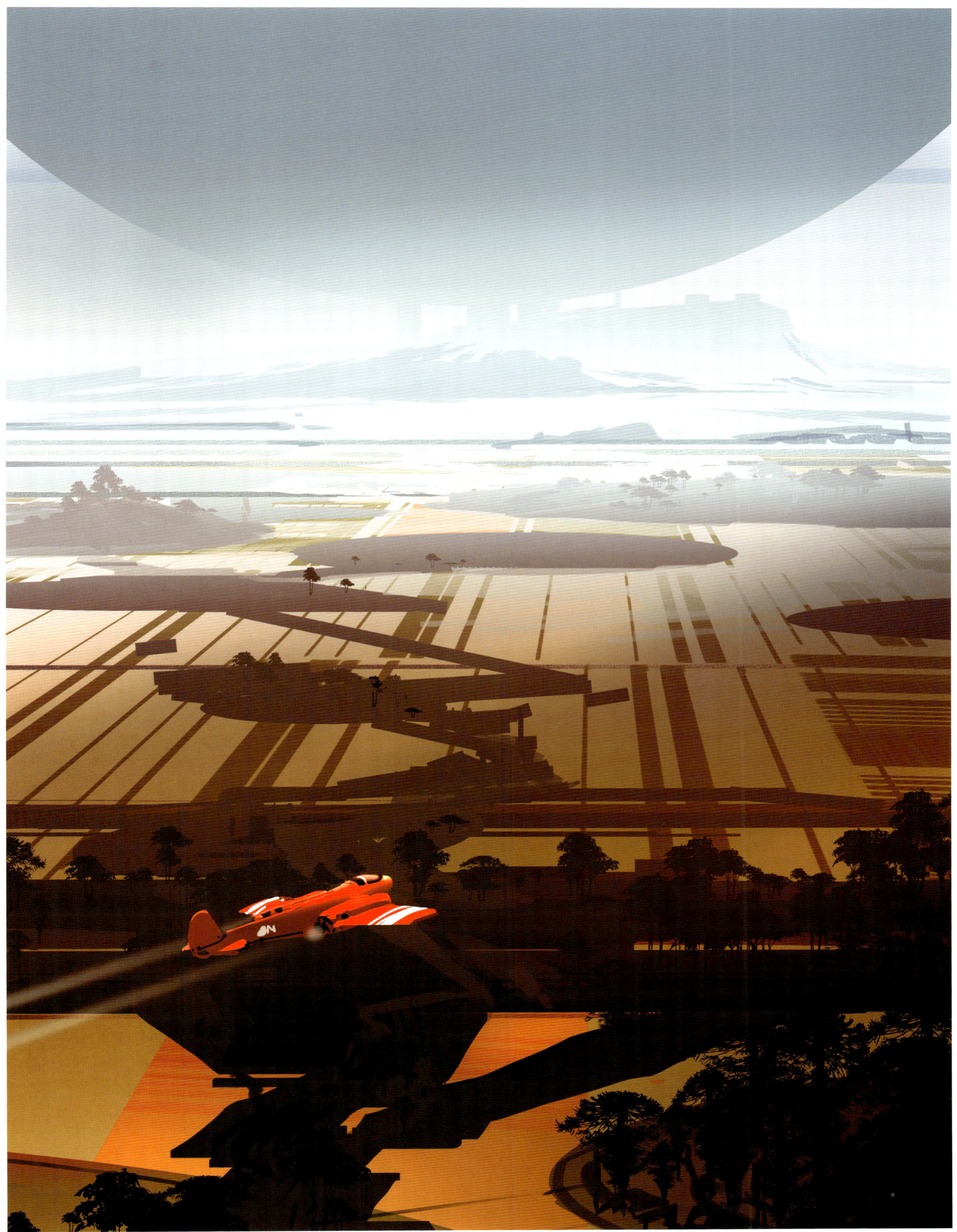

Into the marshland, 2013

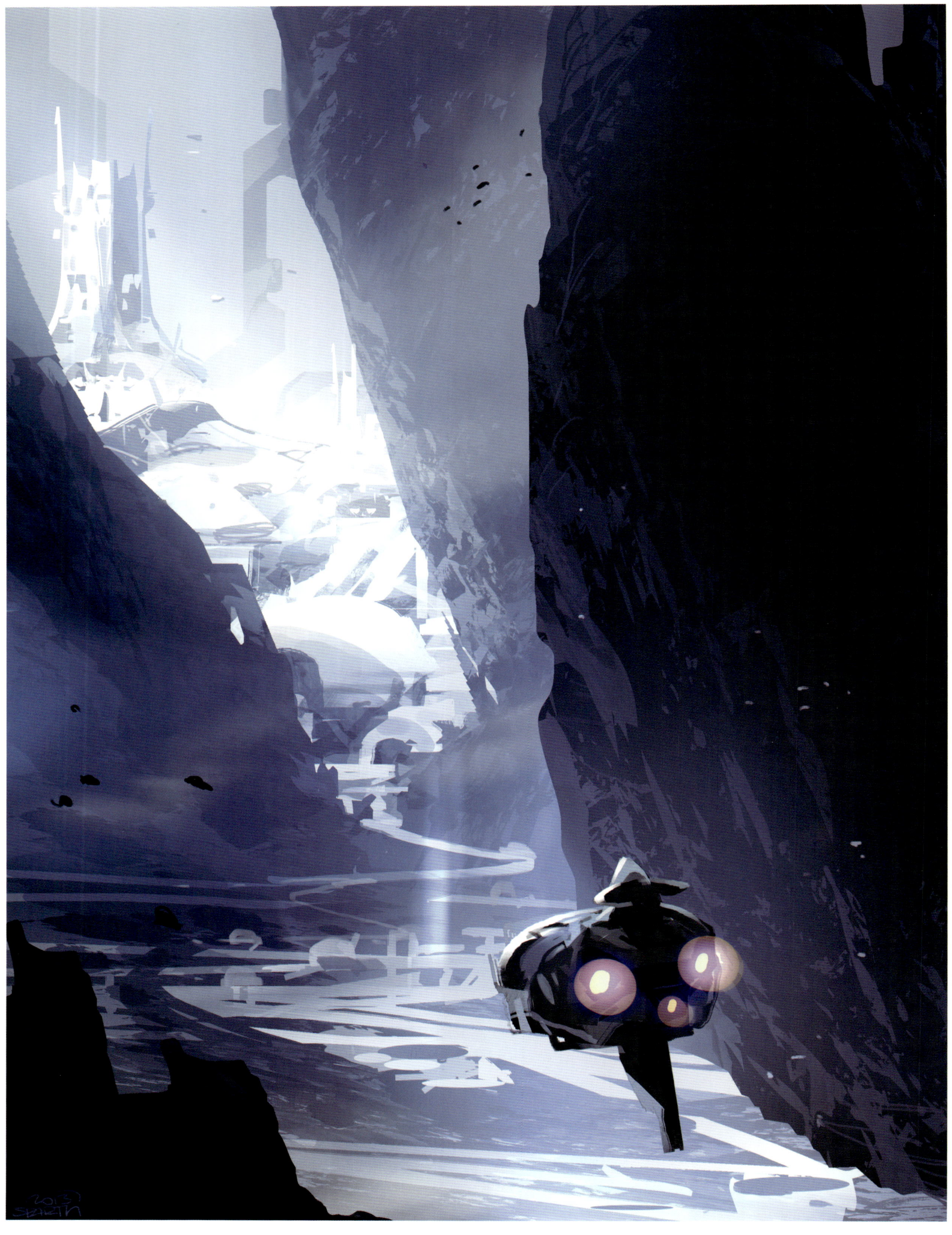

Underground kingdom, 2013

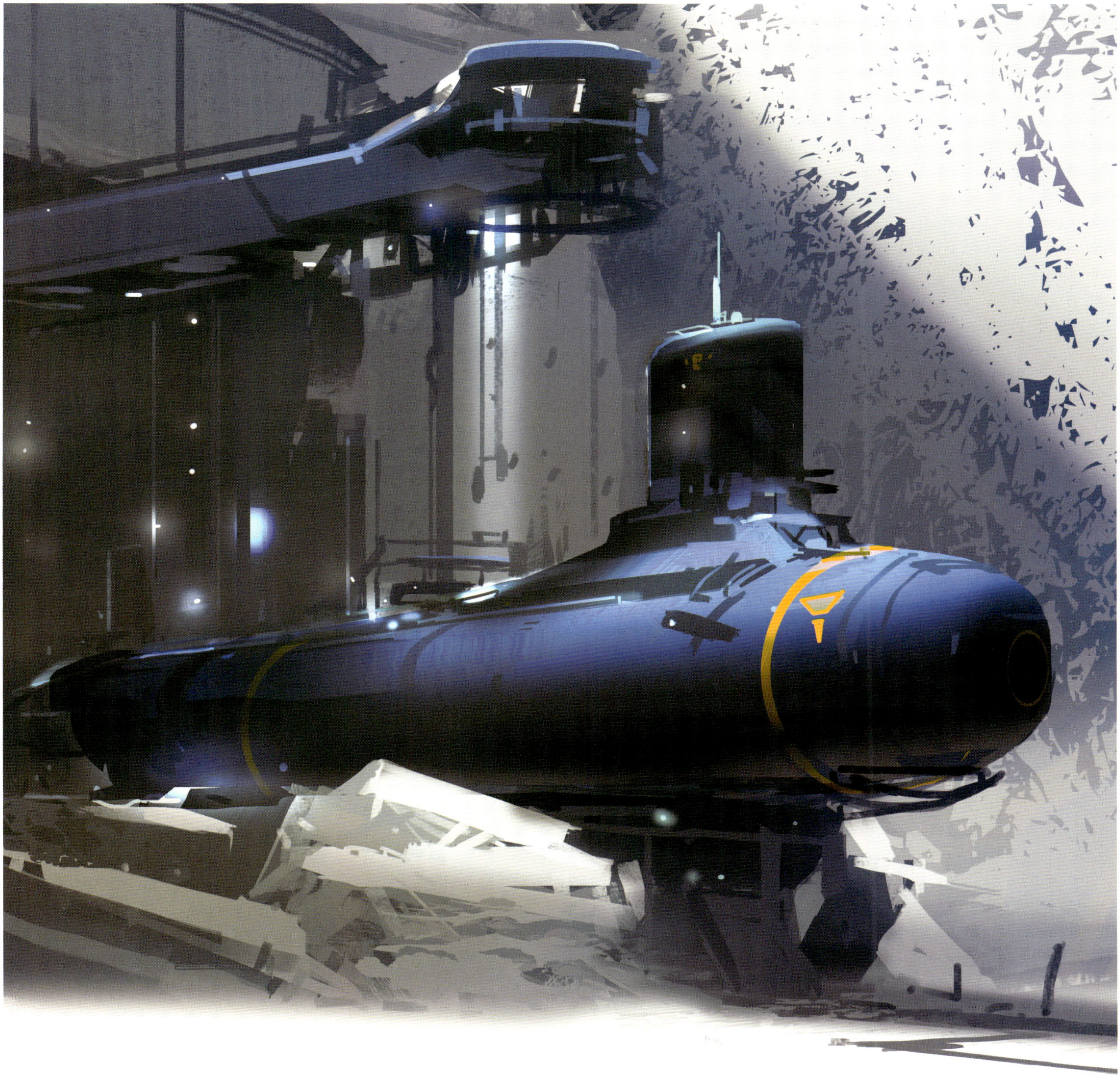

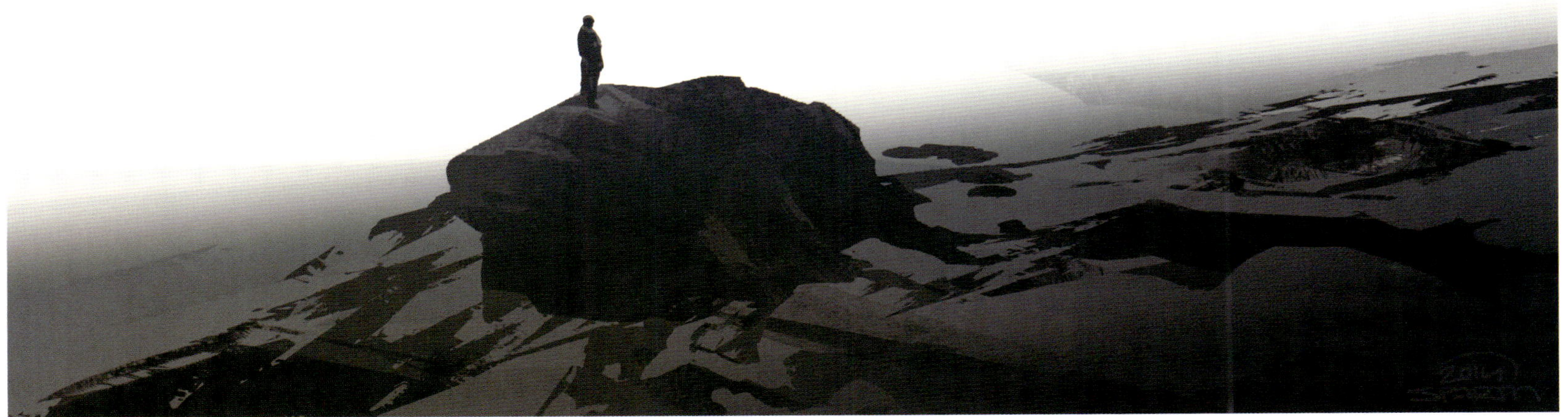

Arctic sub, 2014

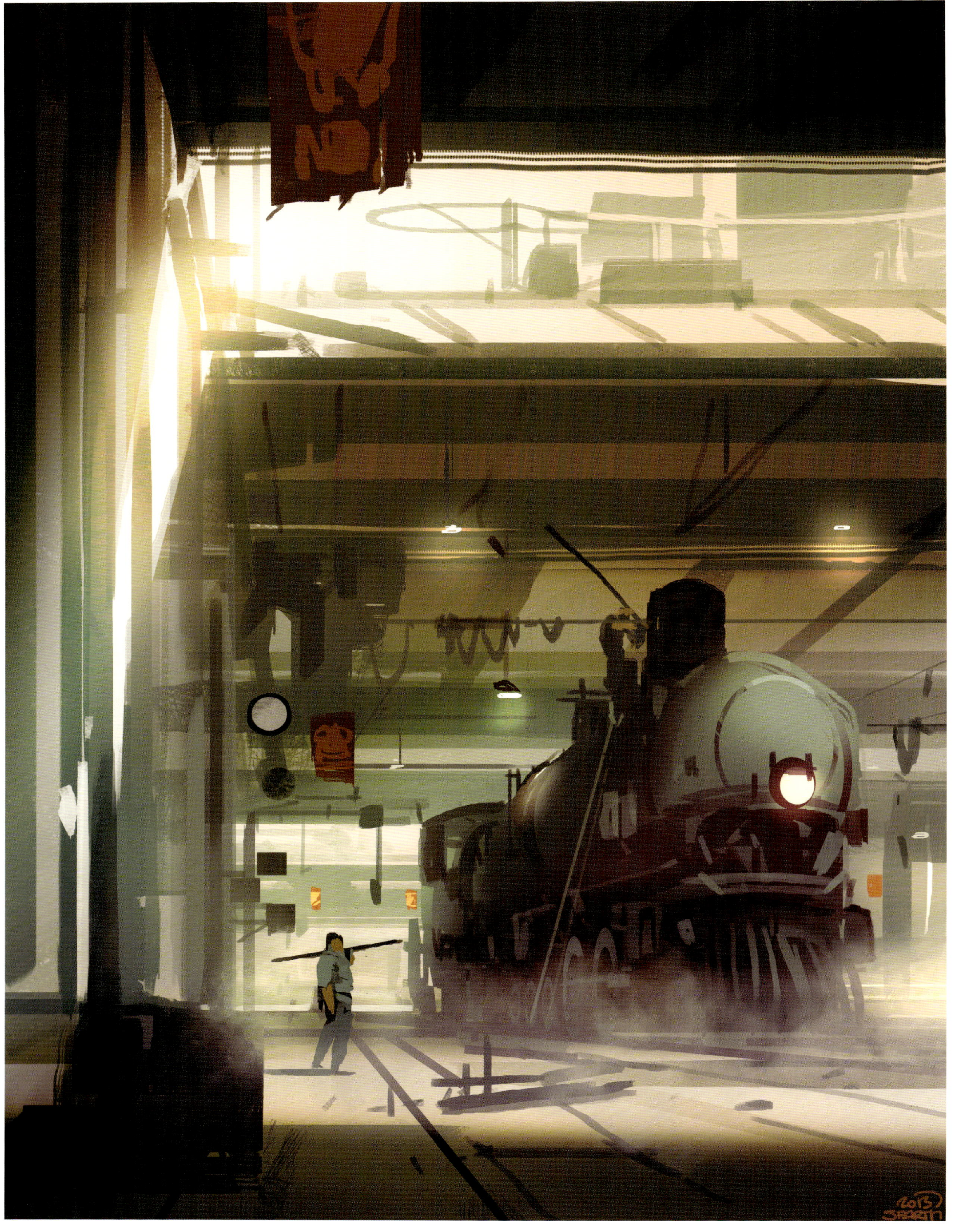

Hangar, 2013

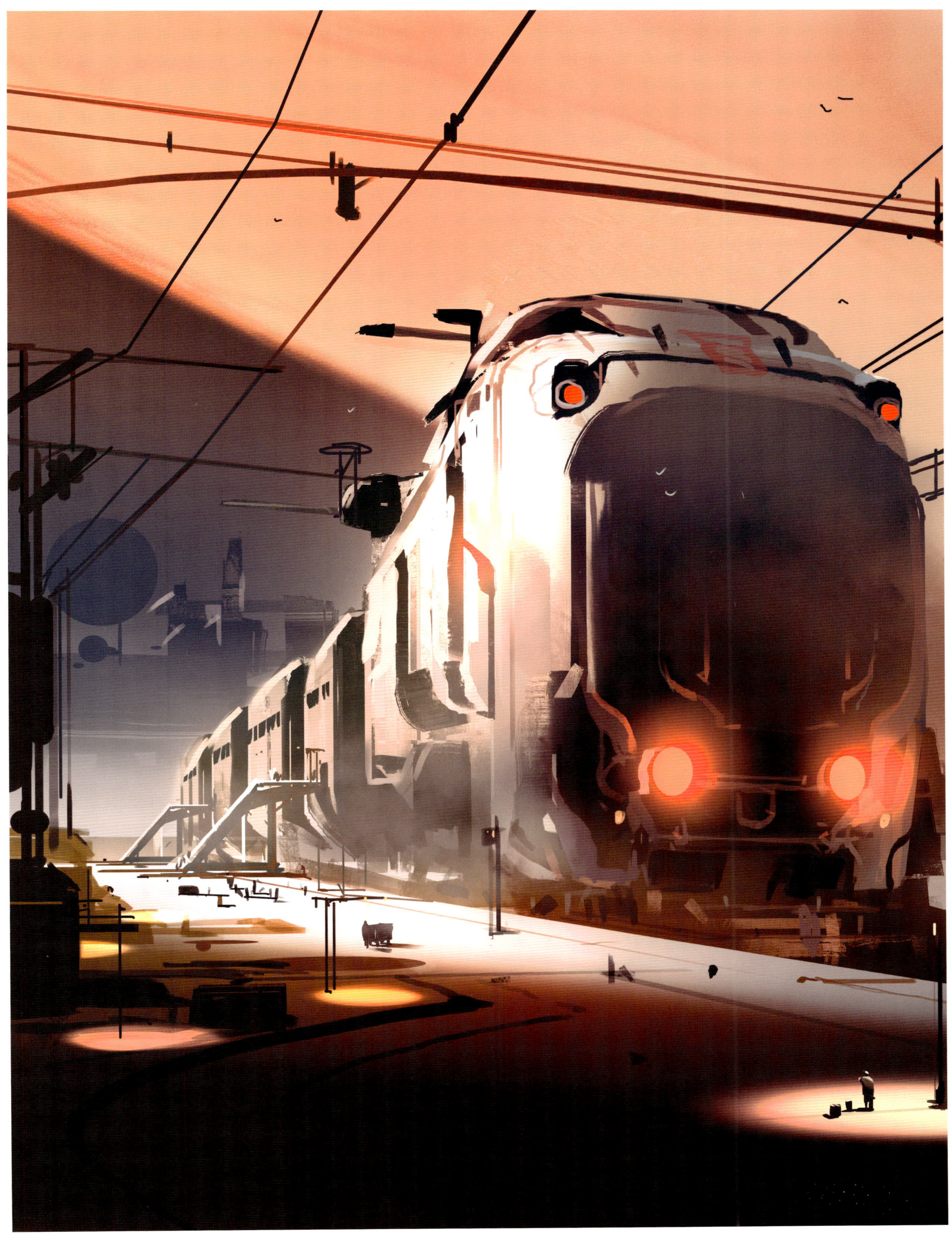

Really, really big train, 2013

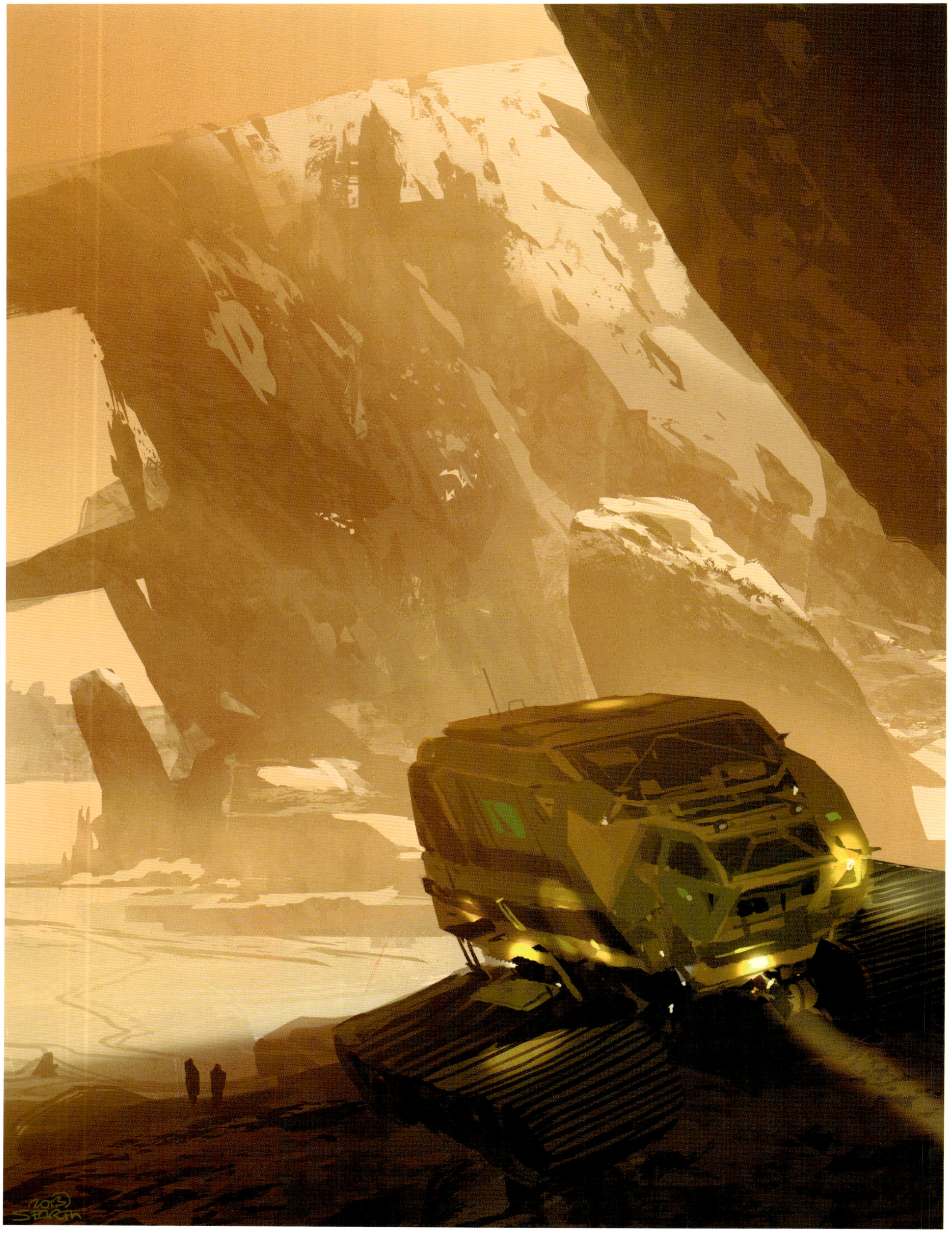

Sandstorm, 2013

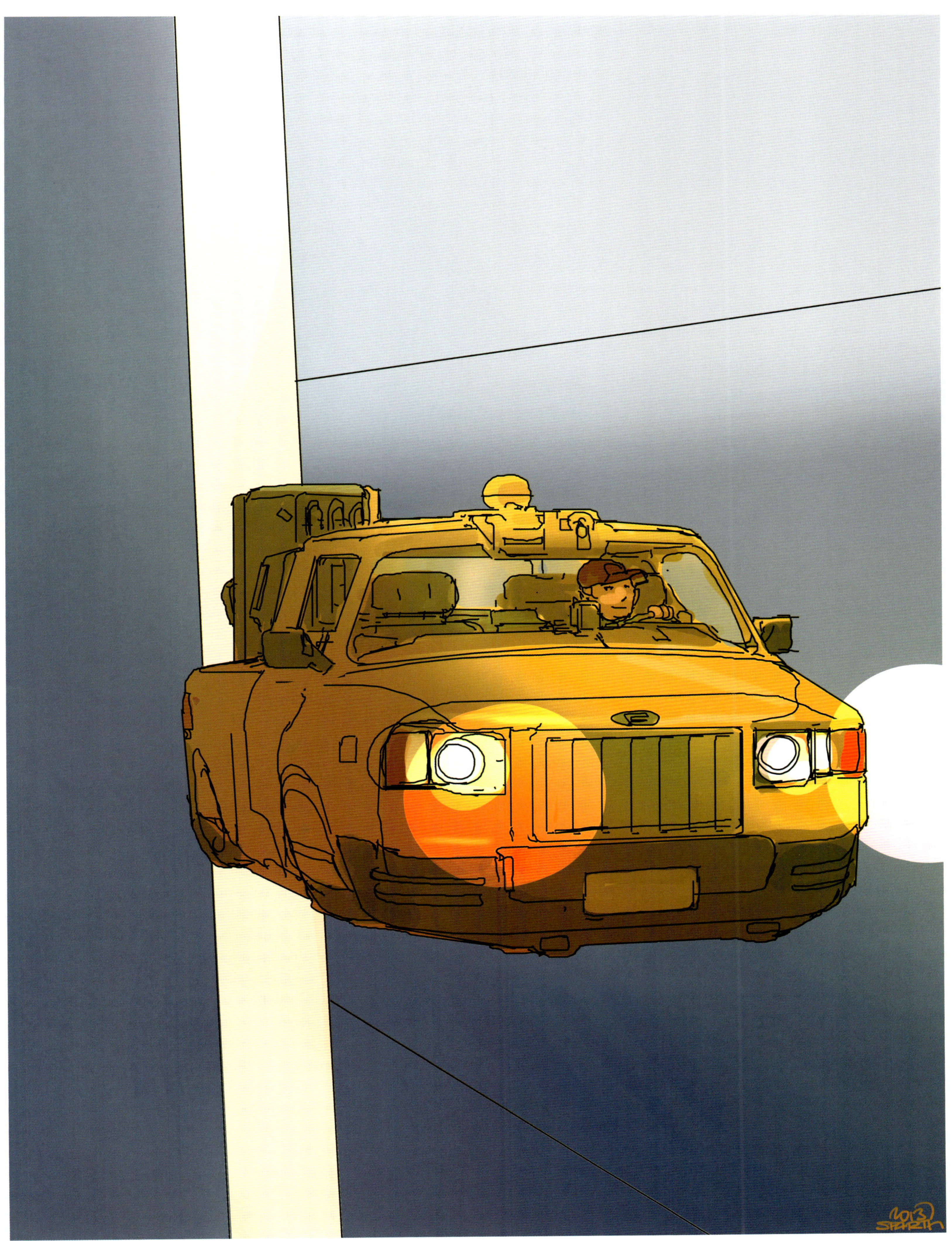

Future truck, 2013

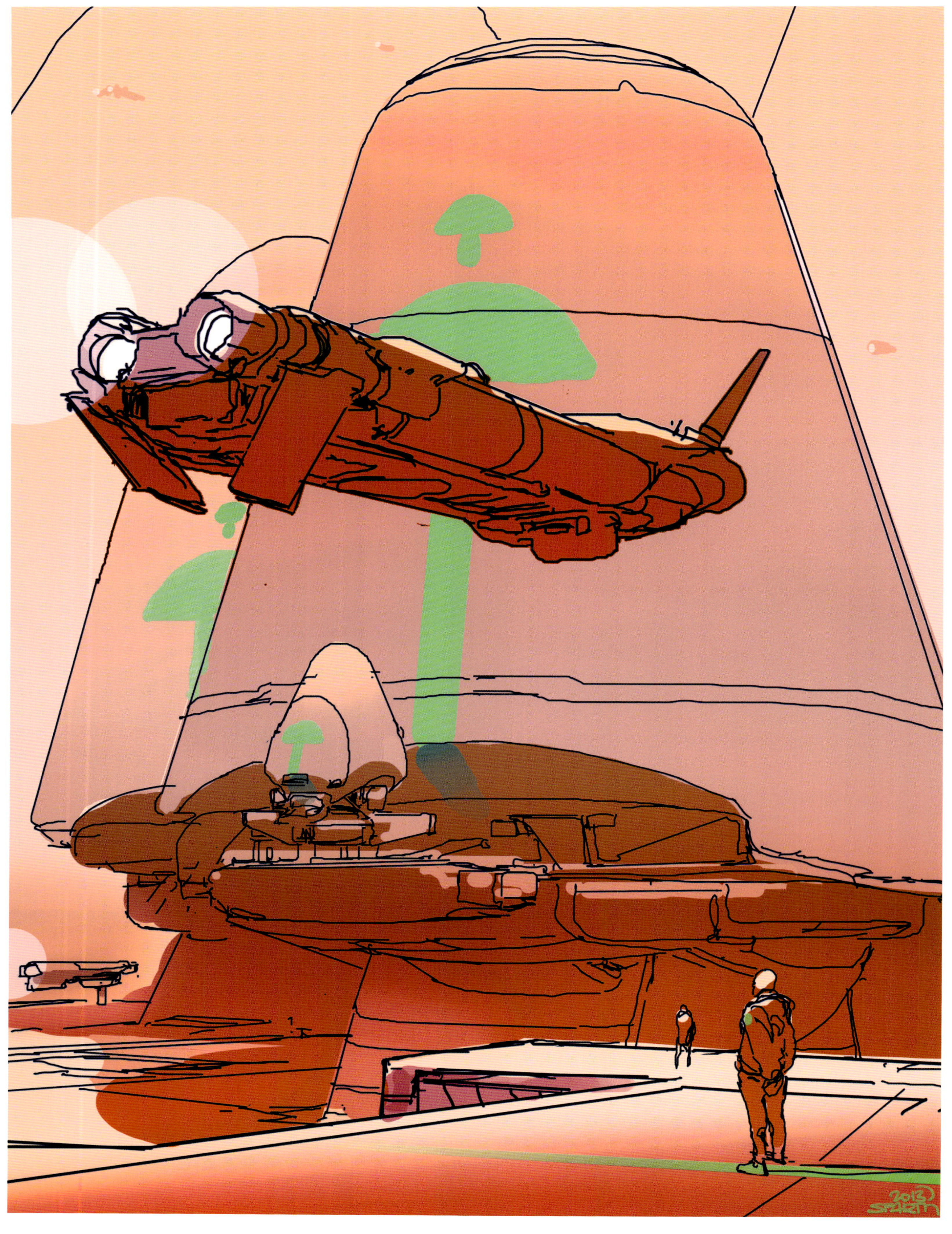

Mushroom statue, 2013

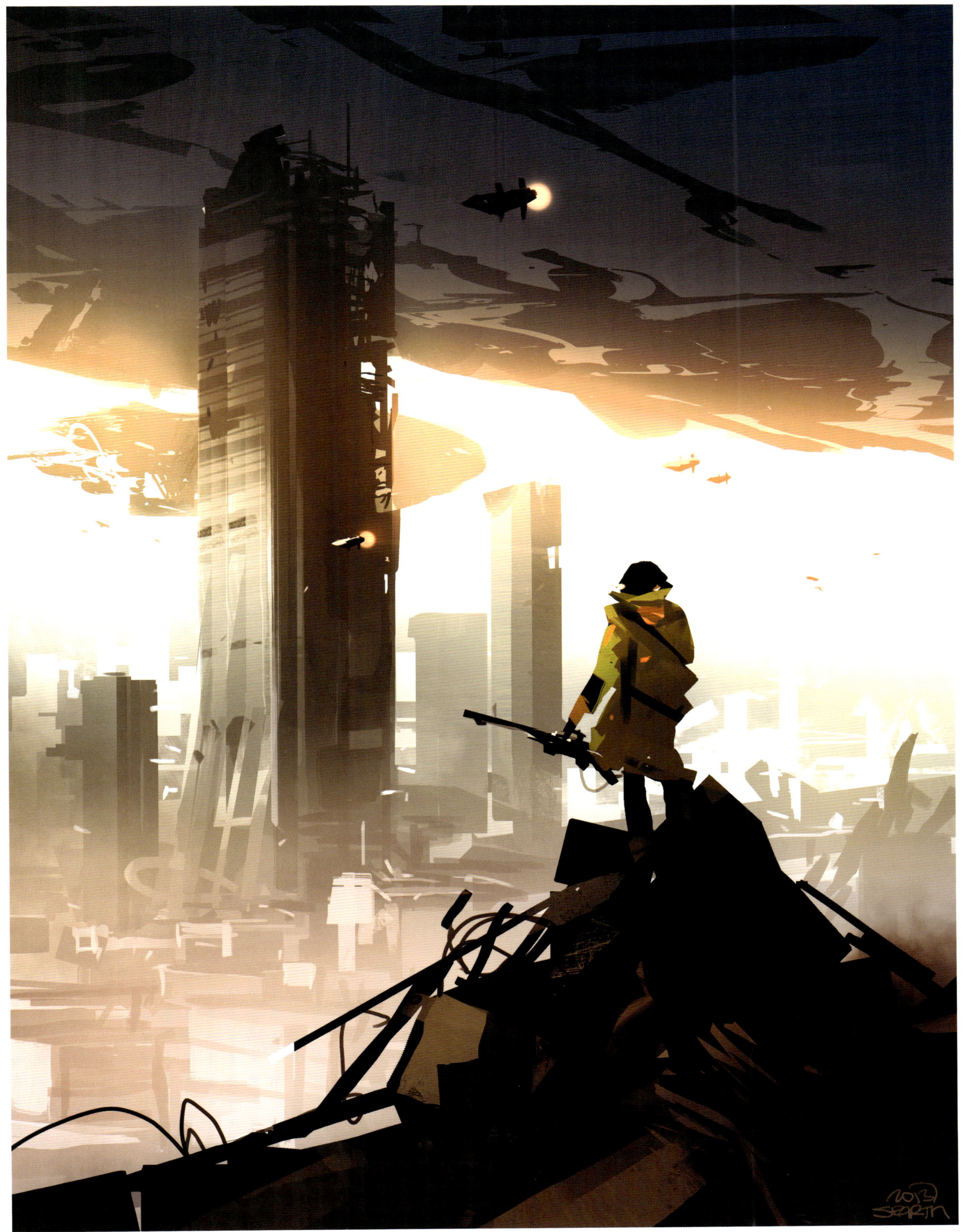

Space invaders I, 2013

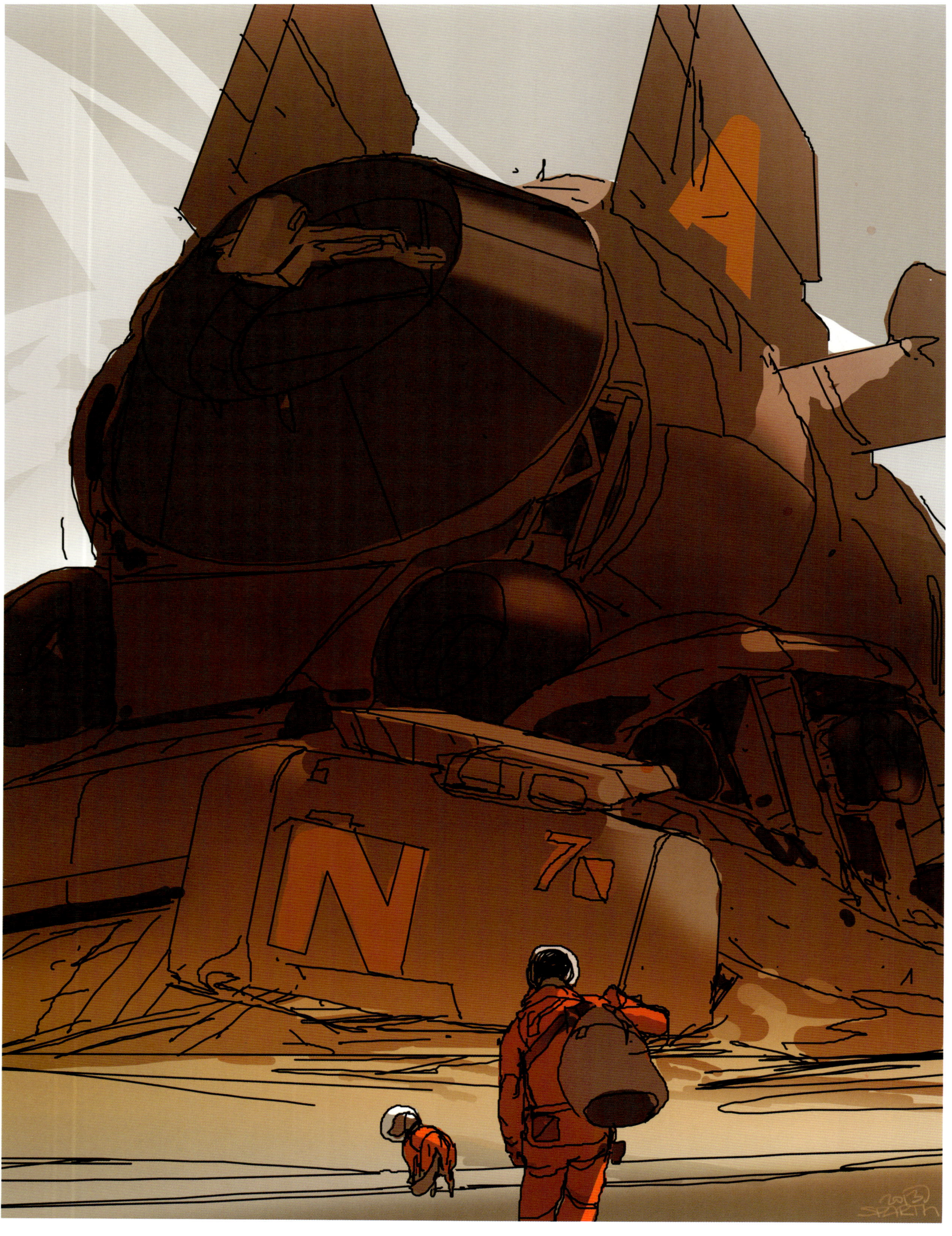

Hidden treasure, 2013

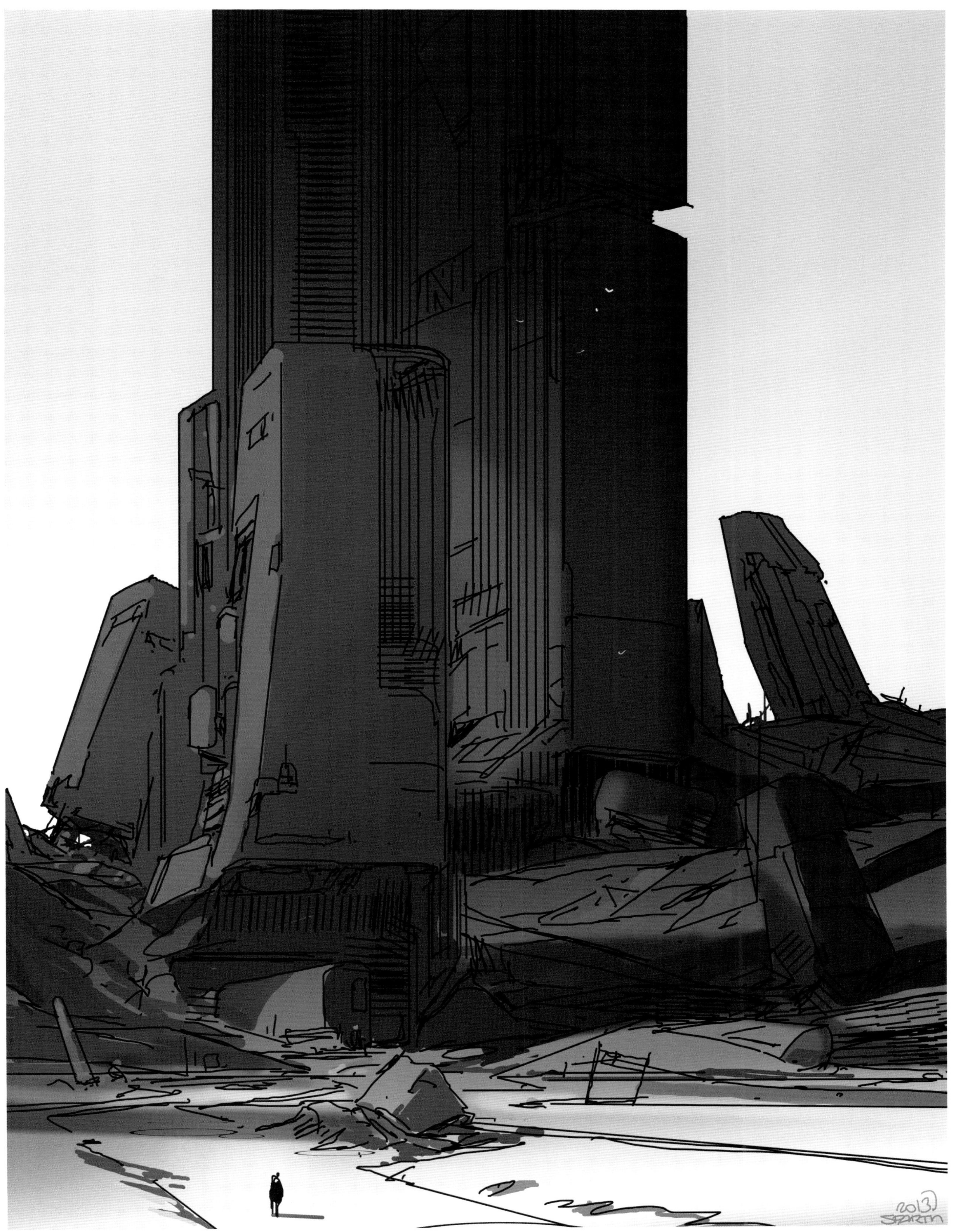

Man-made landscape, 2013

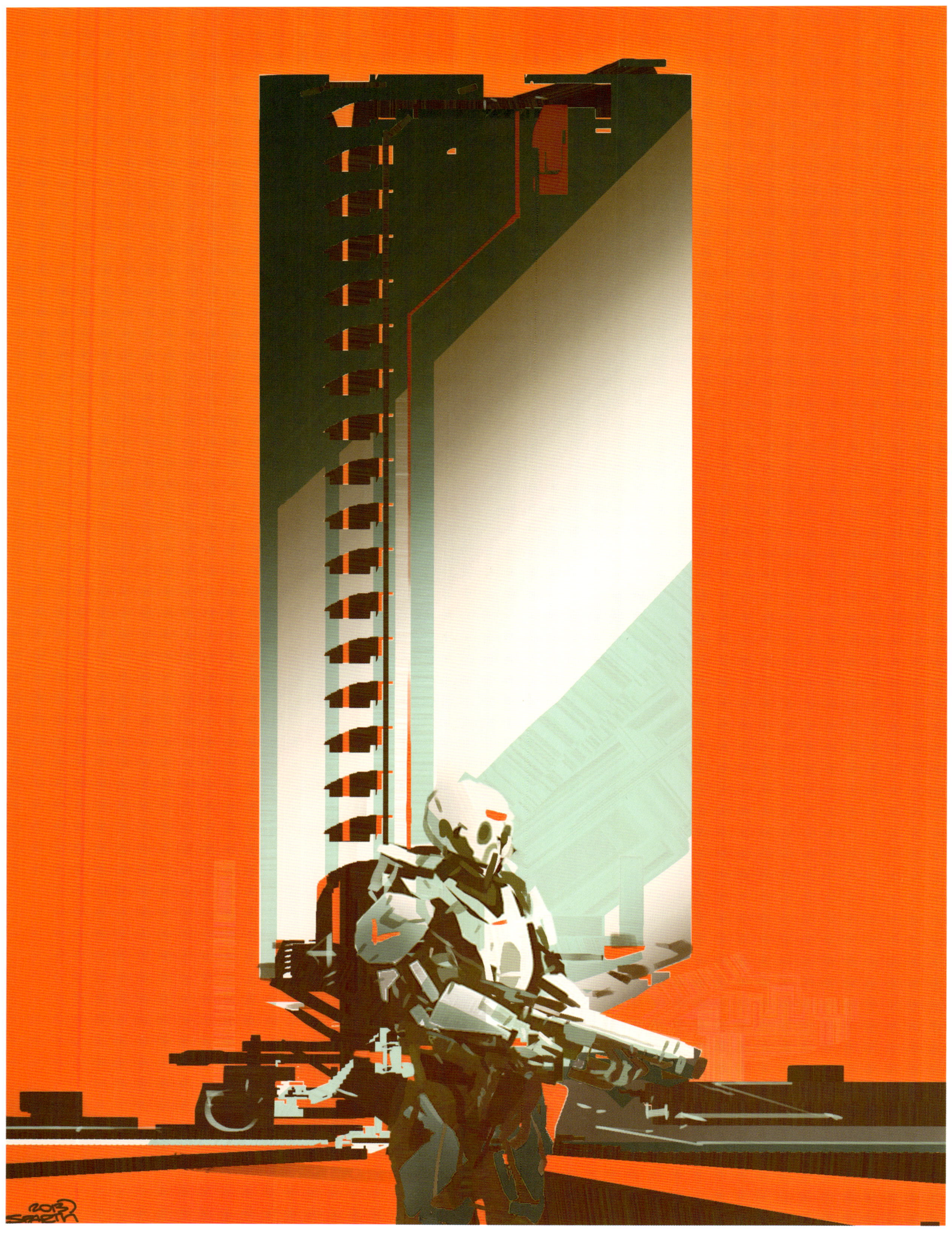

White armor, 2013

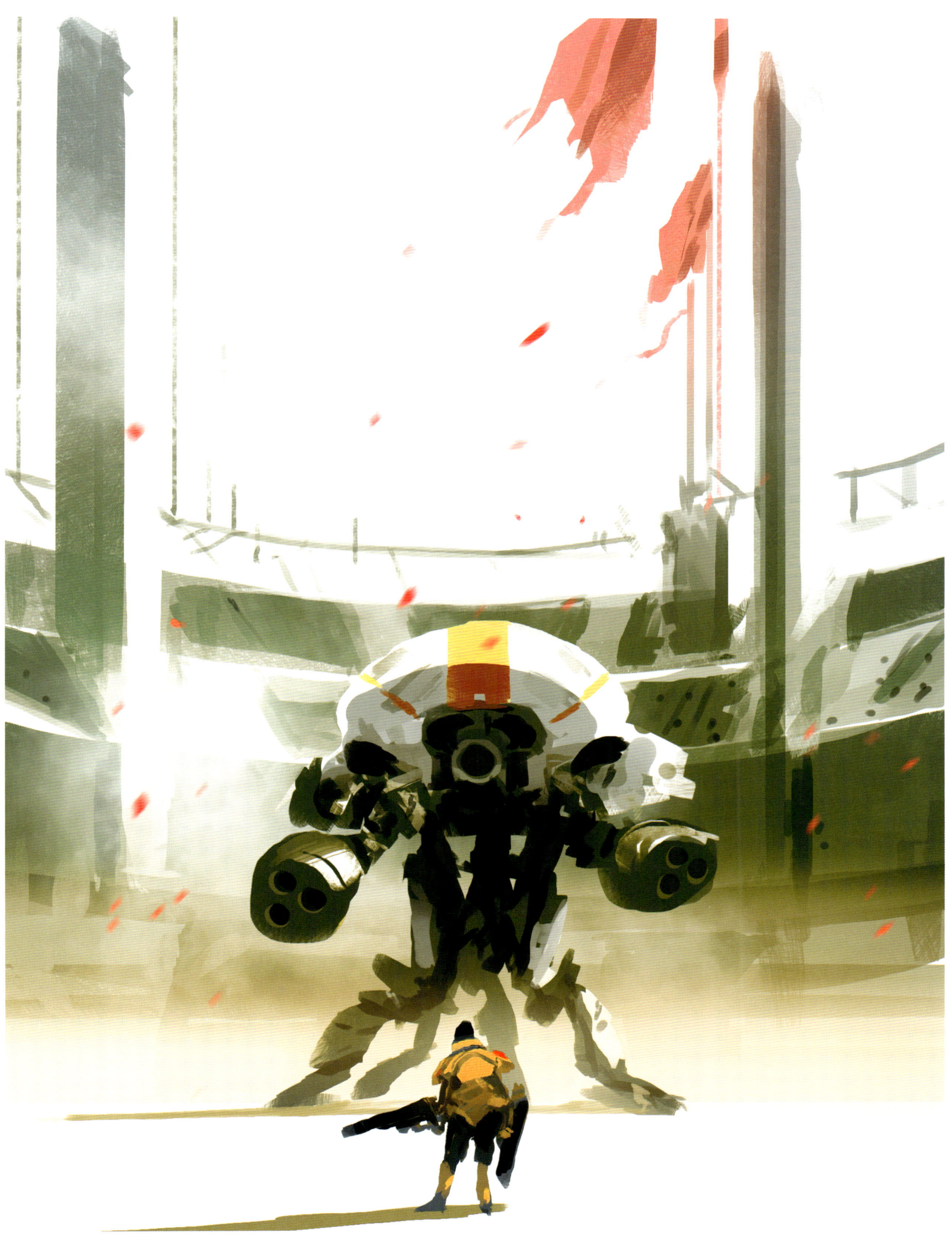

Modern arena, 2013

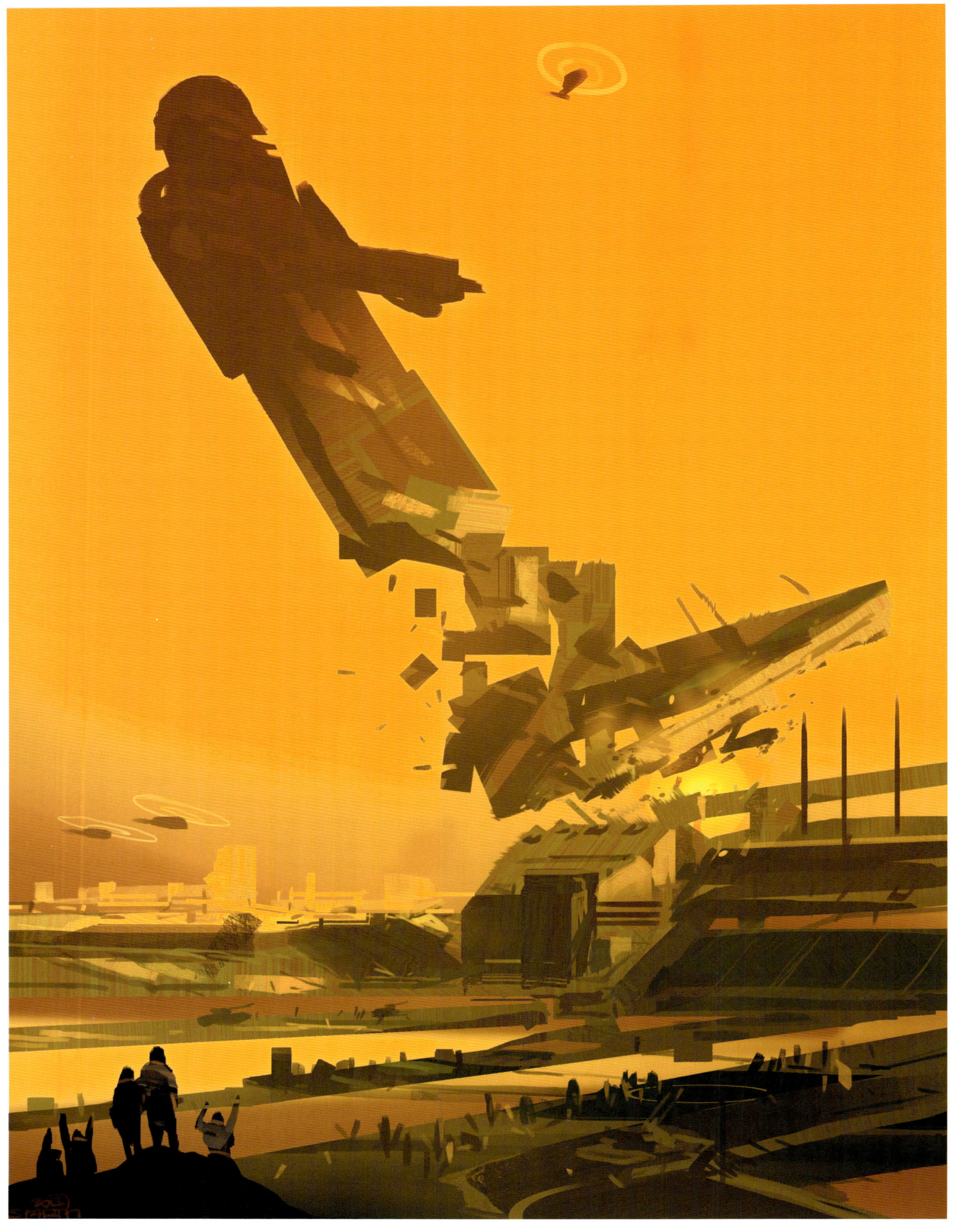

Destruction of a statue, 2013

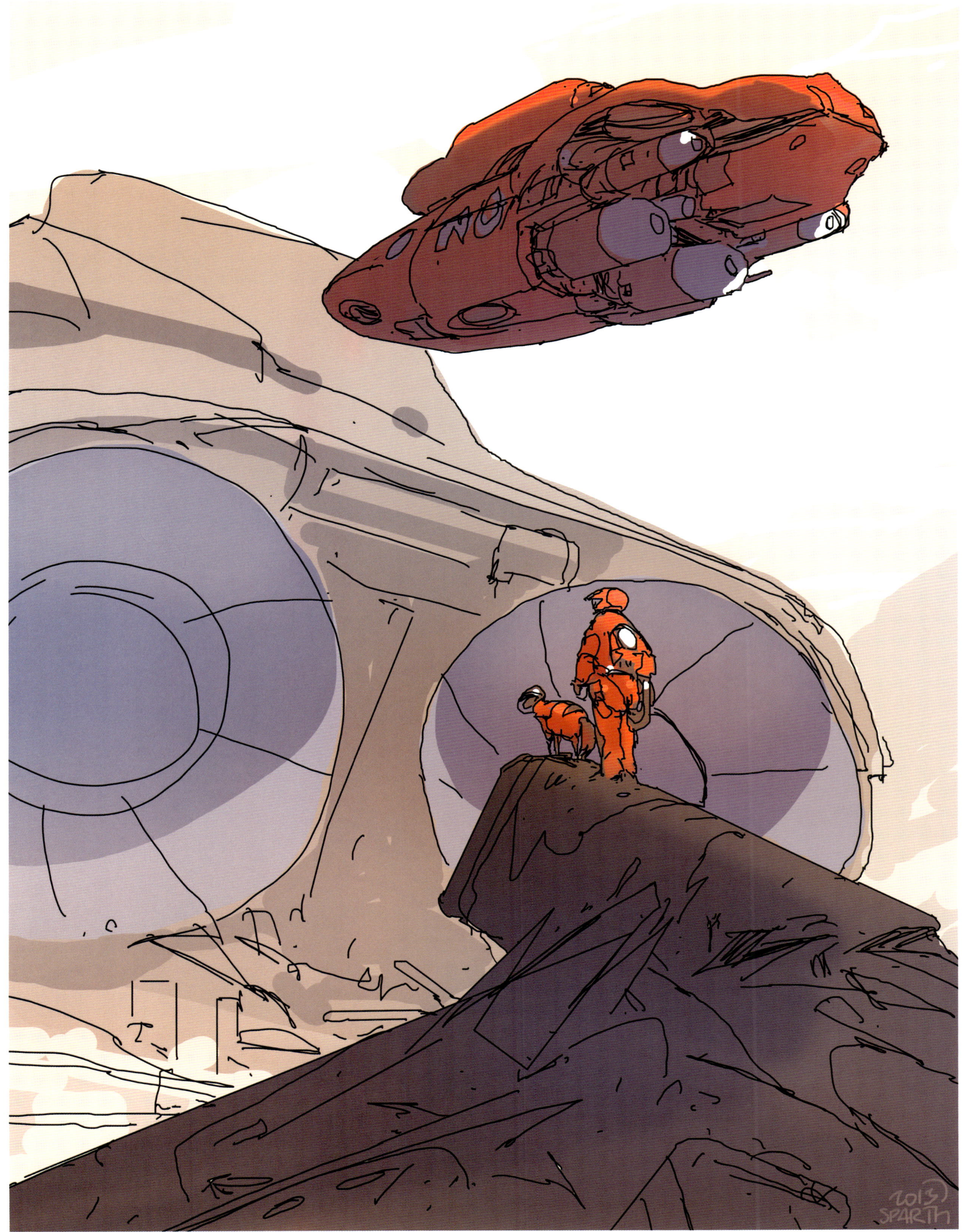

Space invaders II, 2013

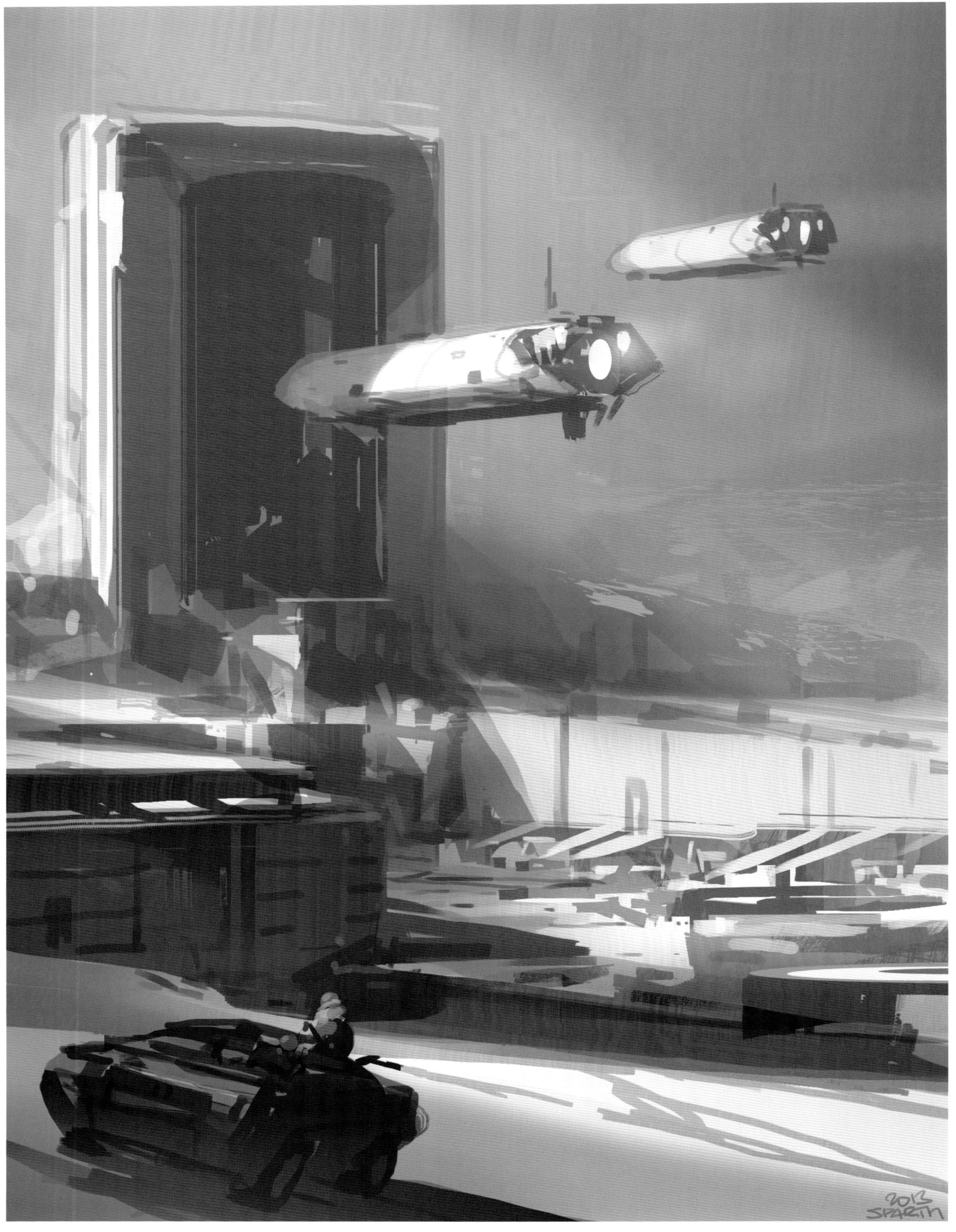

Dark portals, 2013

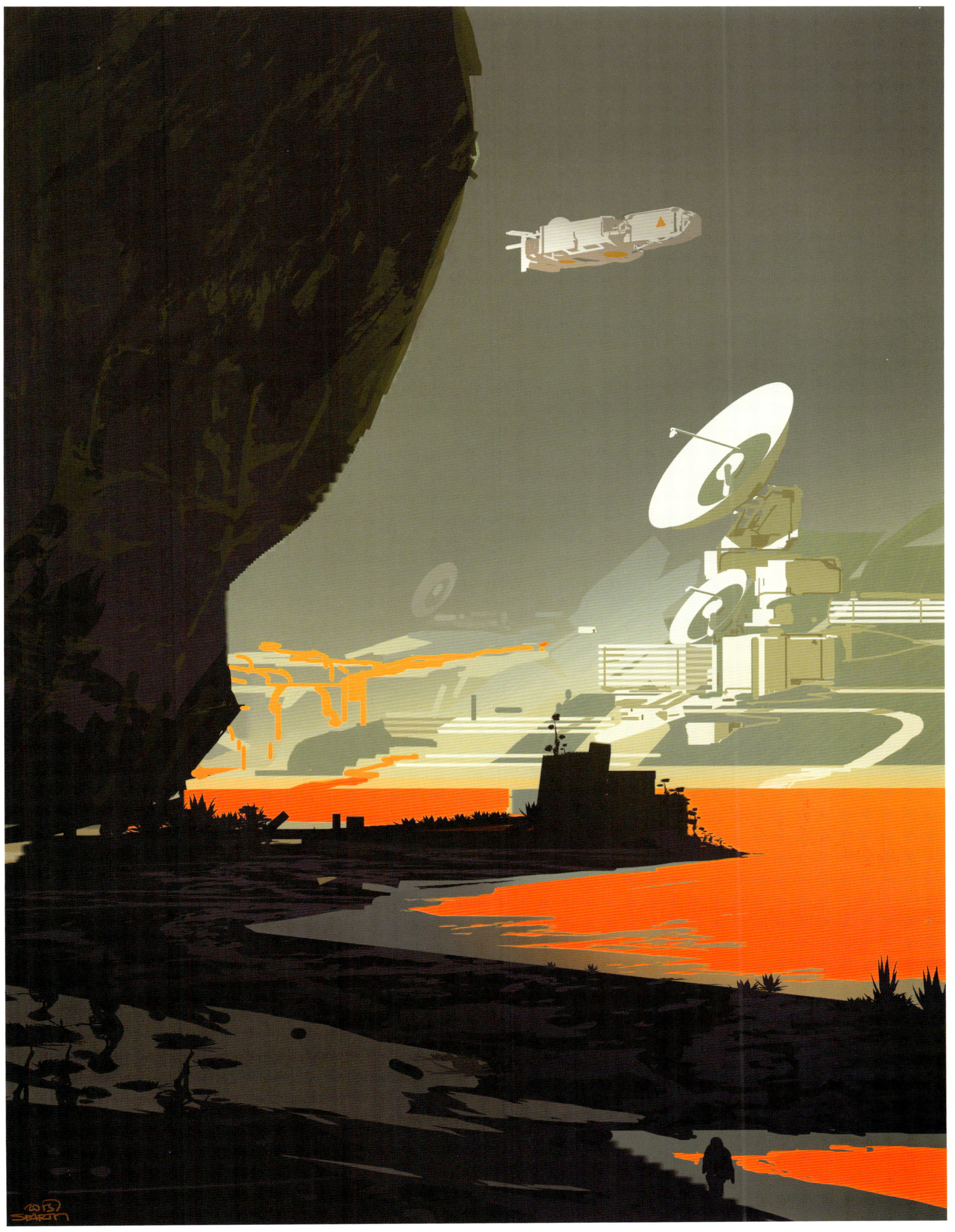

Fire river, 2013

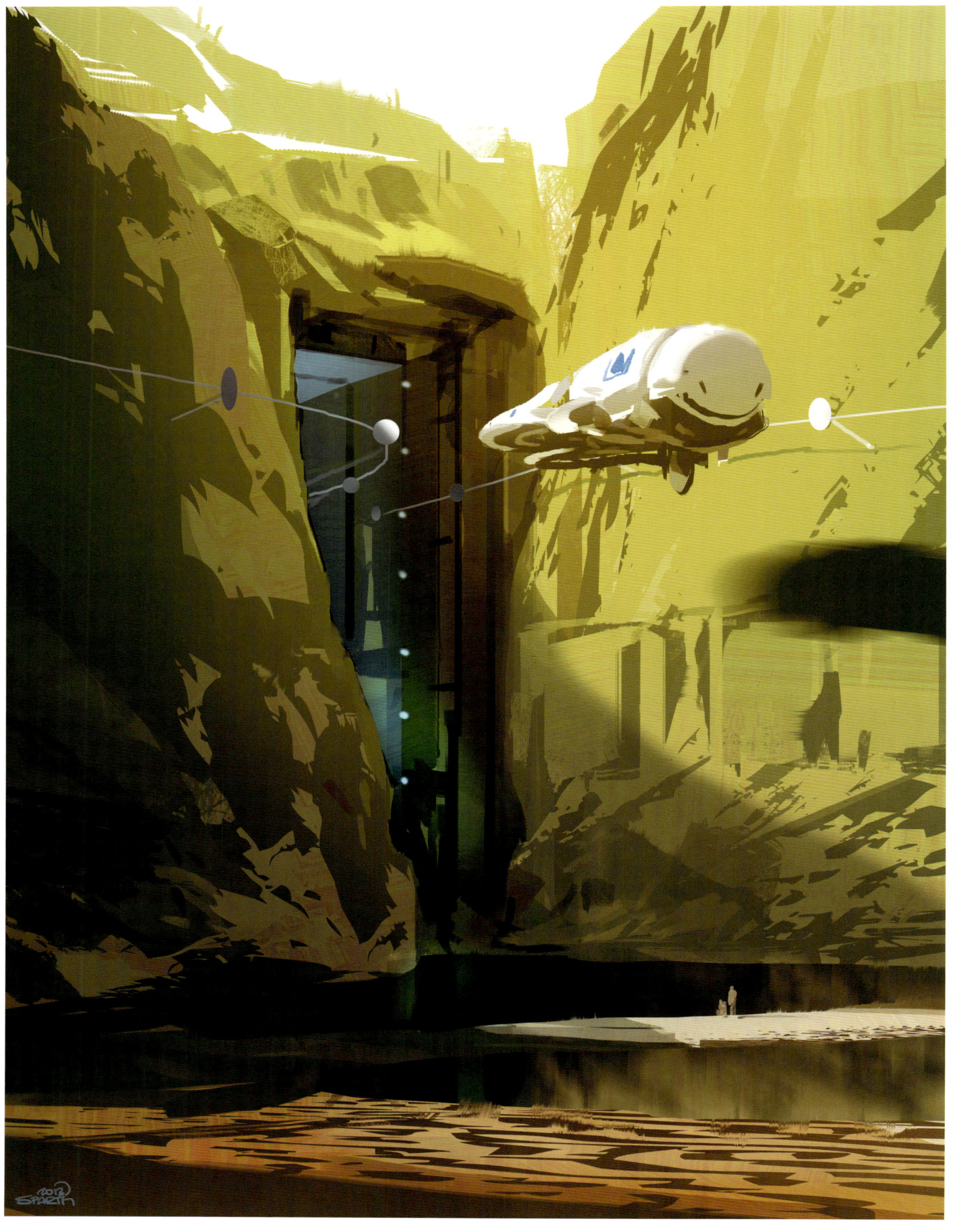

Tunnel entrance, 2013

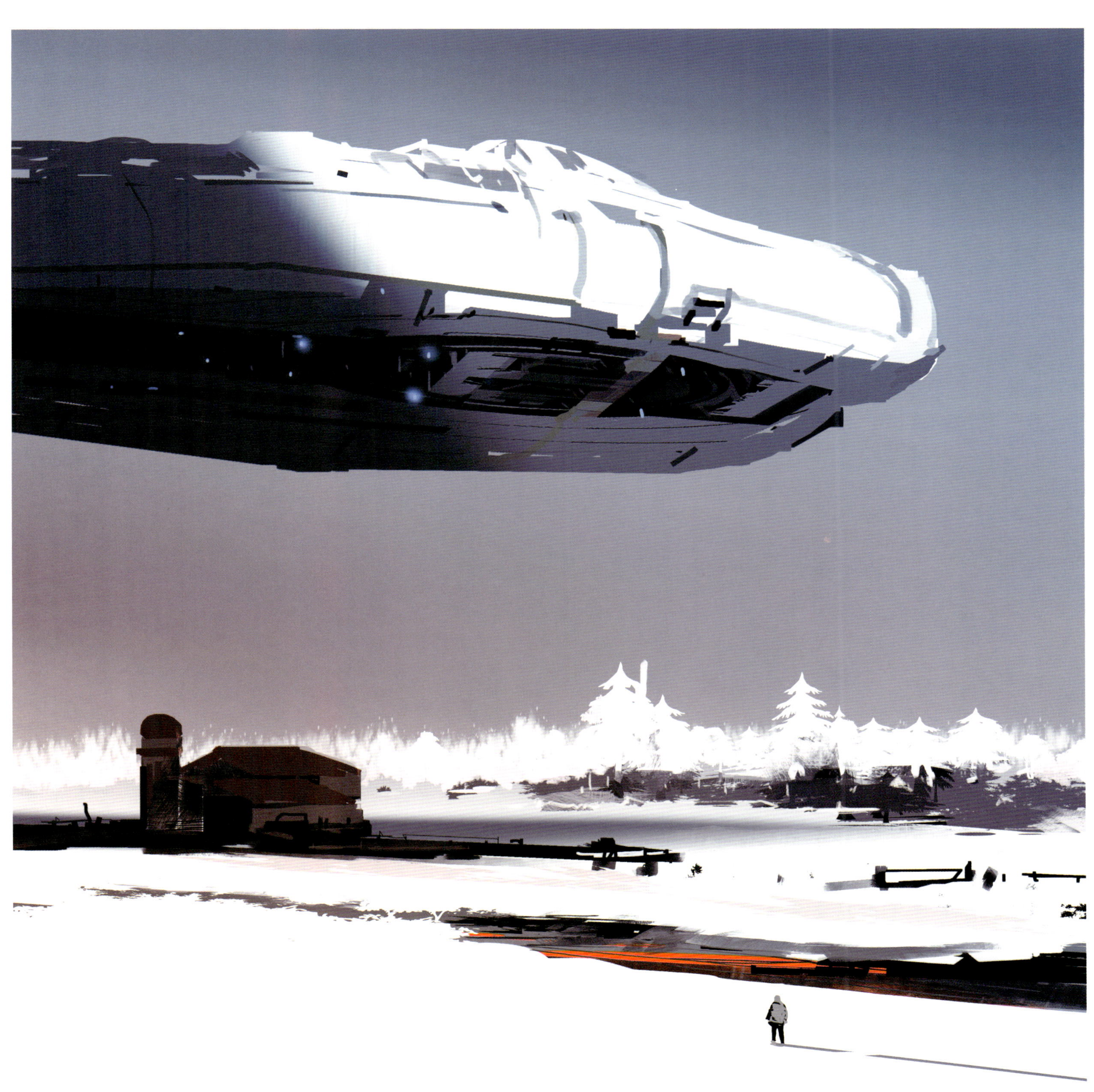

White forest, 2013

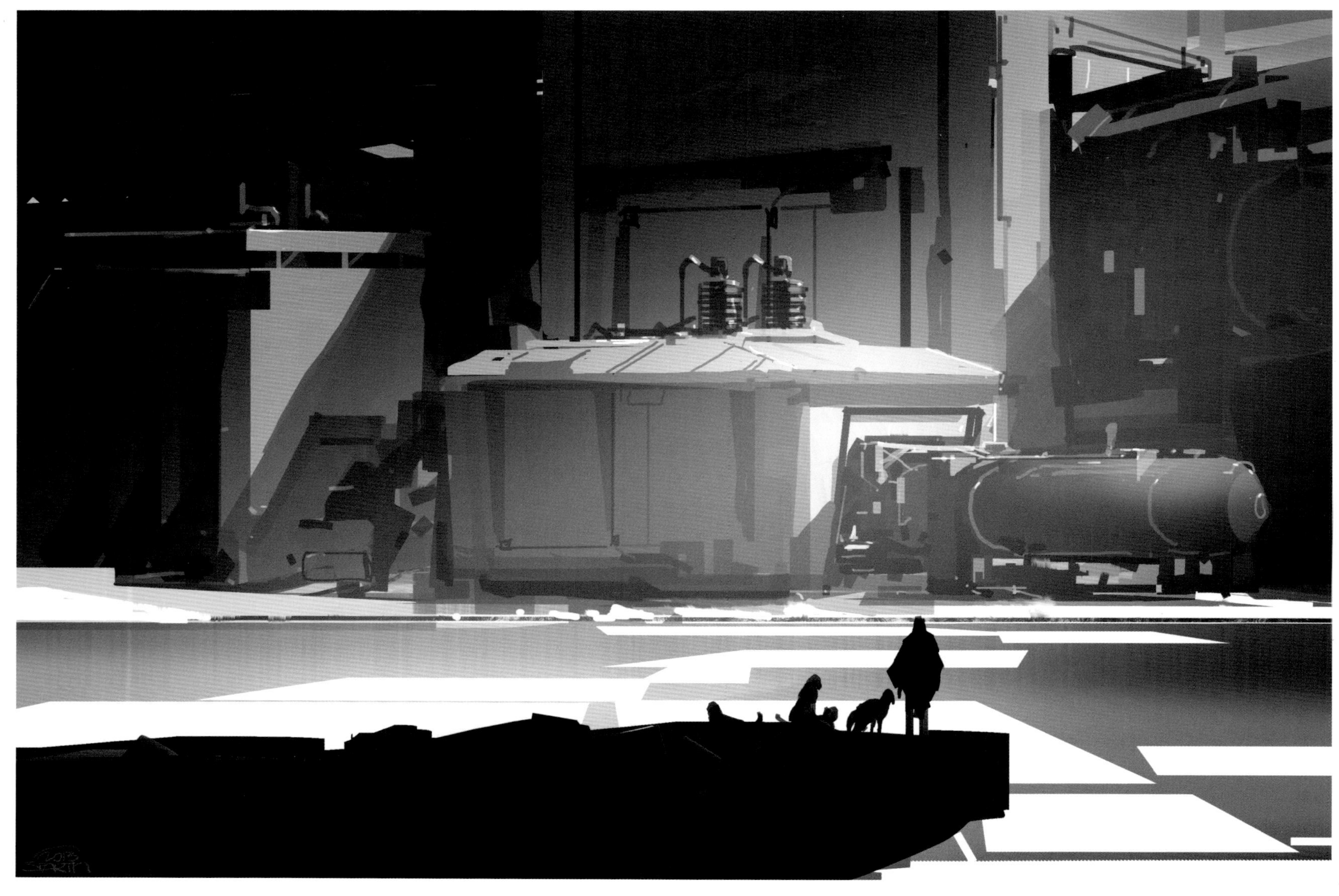

When you work within a 30-minute time frame, you have to lock the composition in your mind first before it reaches the canvas. What prevails is your ability to put a very simple, abstract idea into concrete shapes.

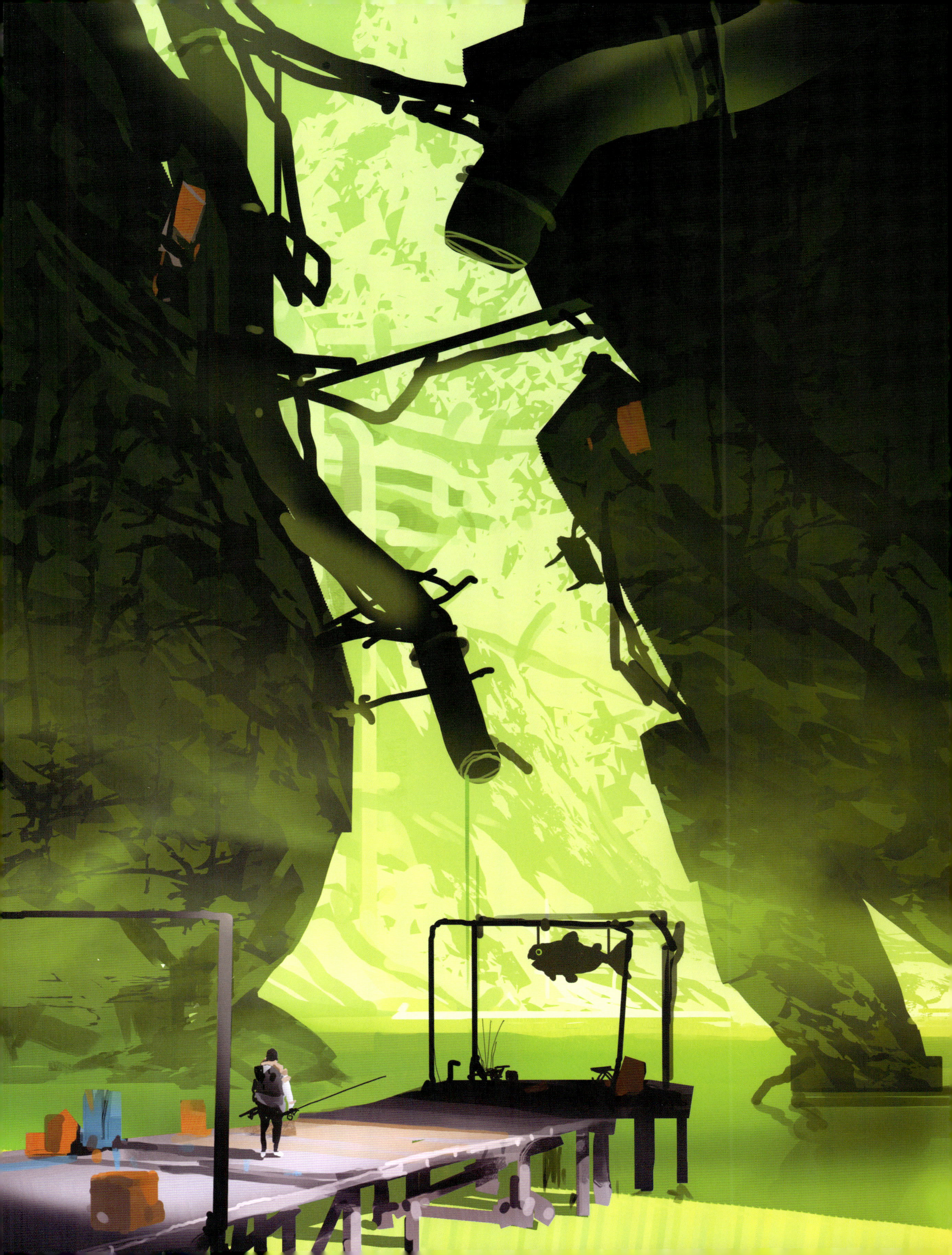

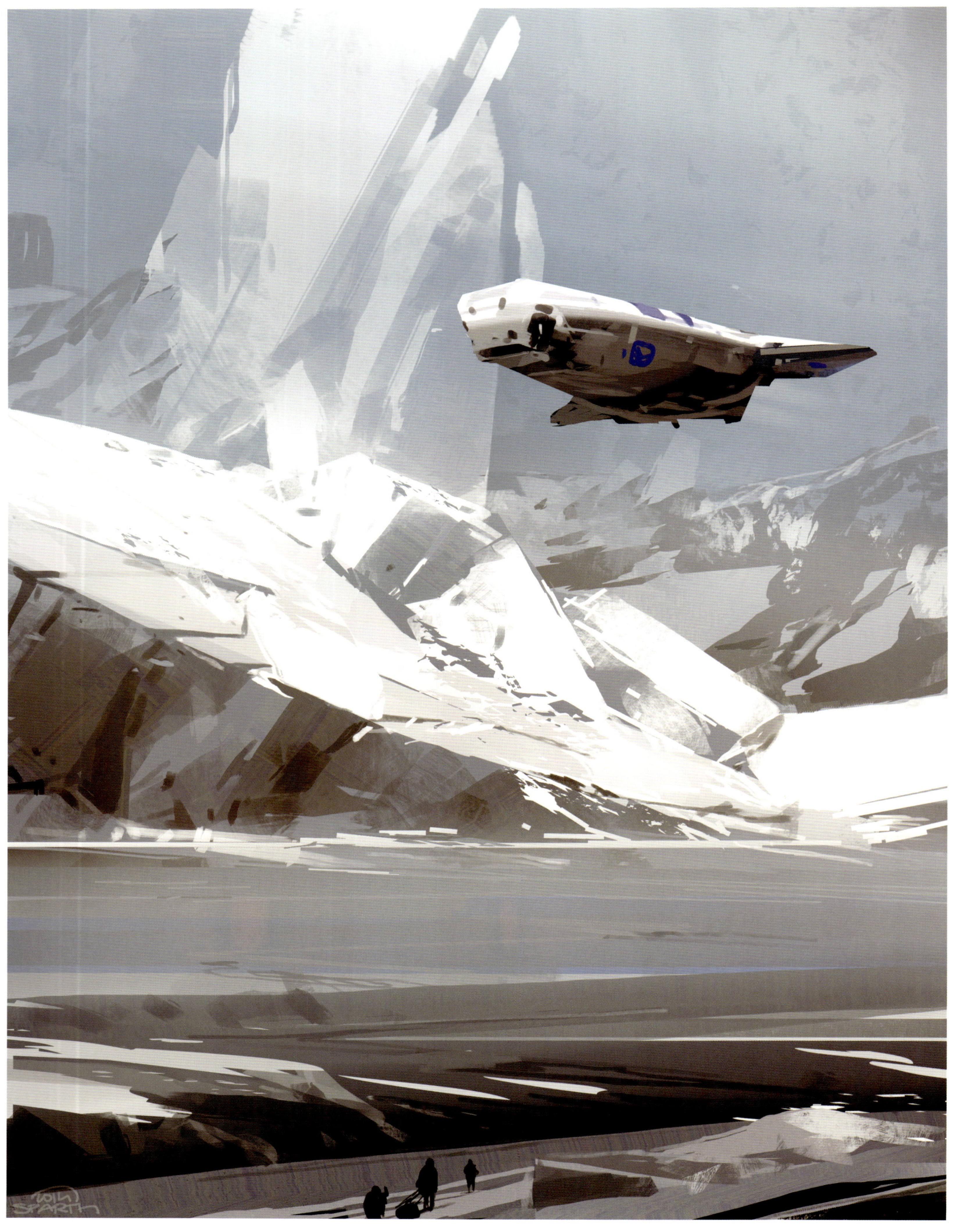

Ice storm, 2014

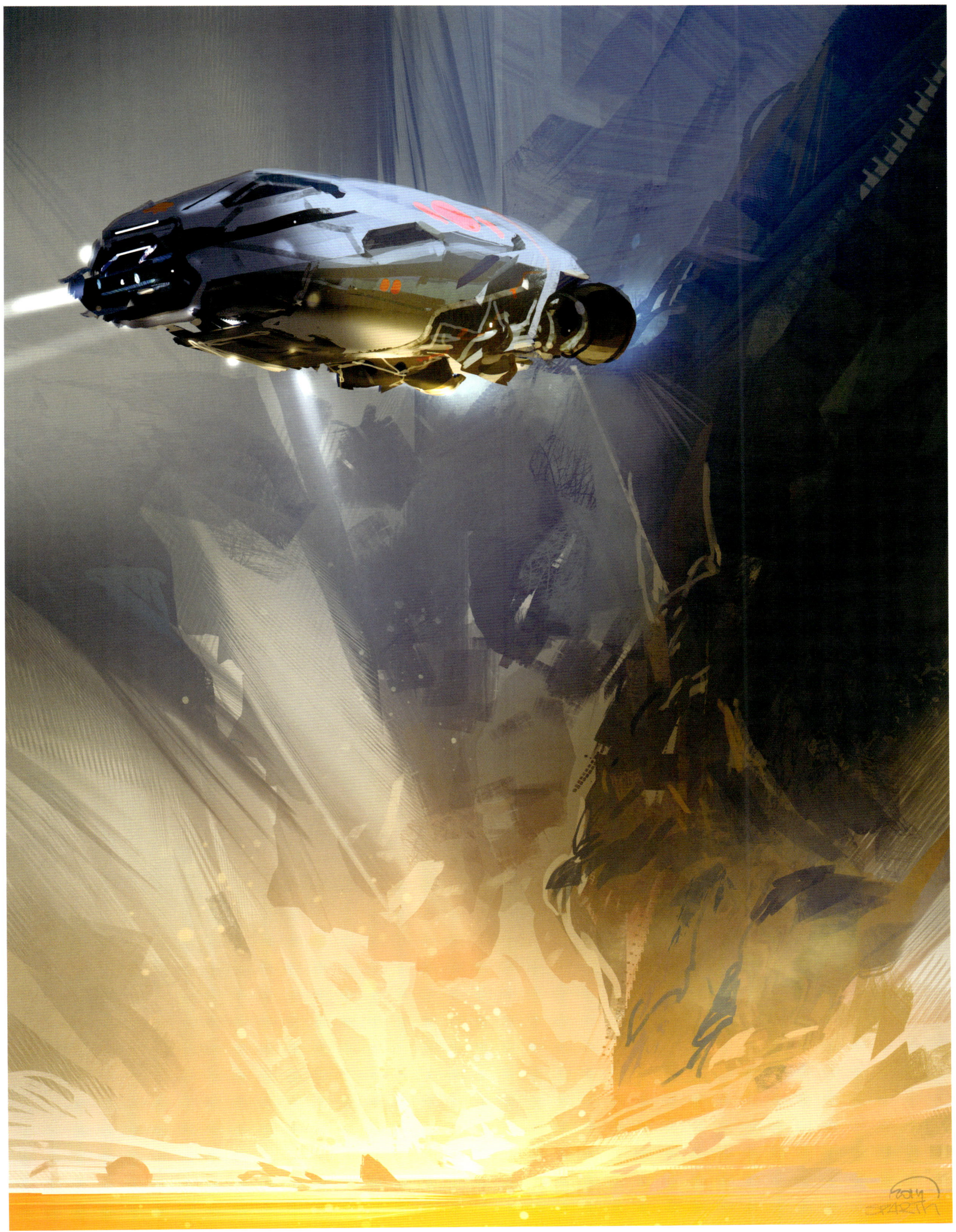

Lava spaceship, 2014

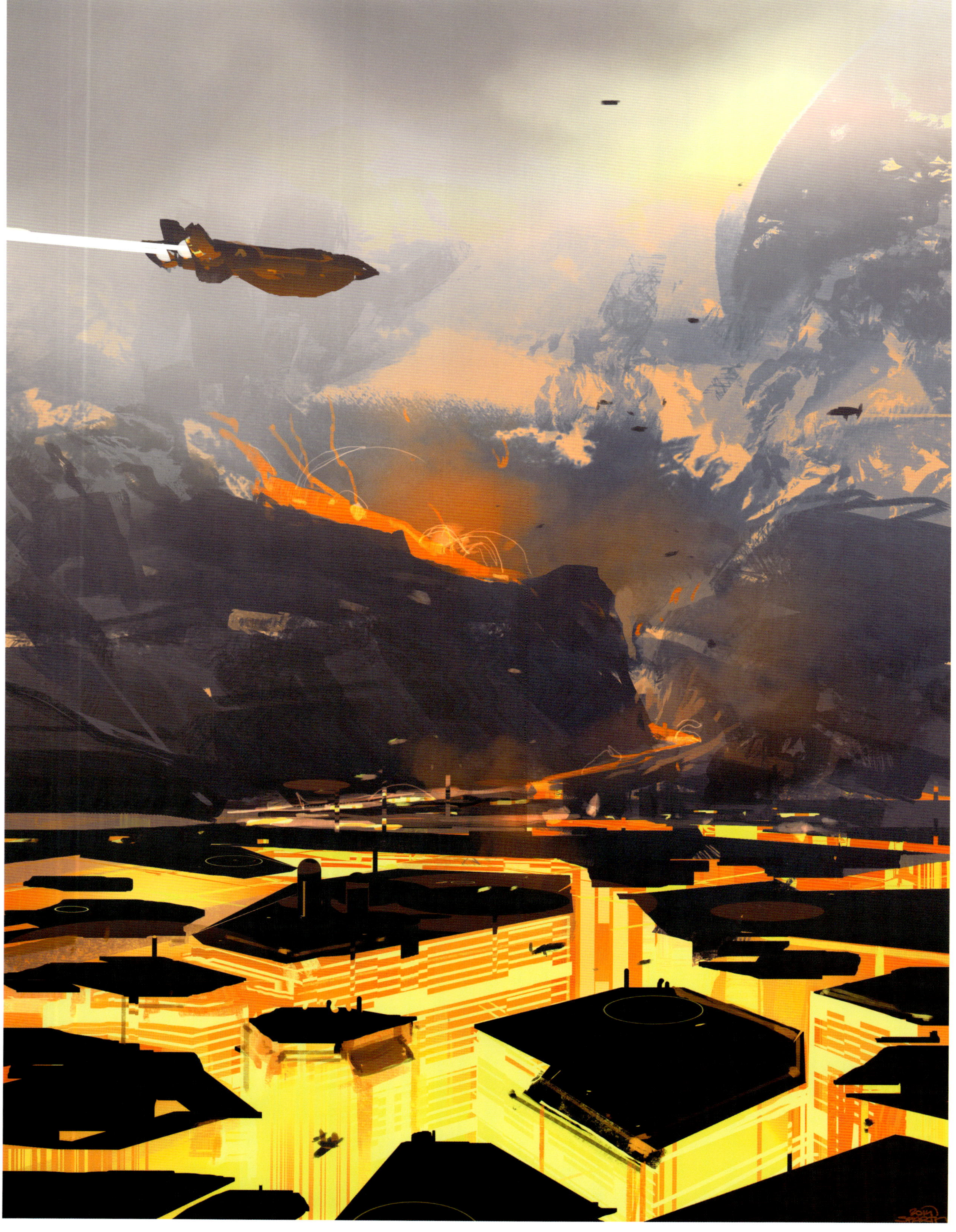

Volcano city, 2014

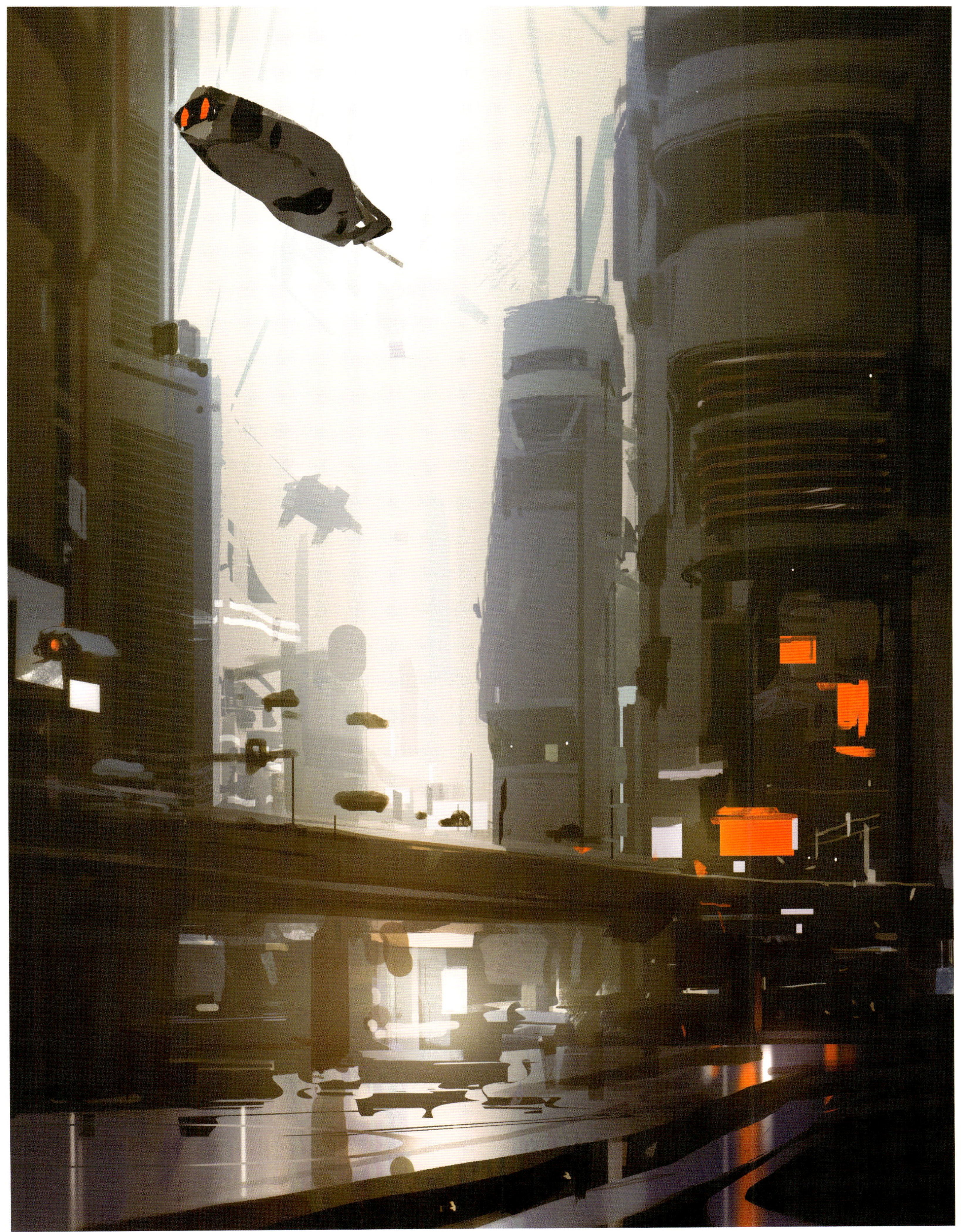

Rainy city, 2014

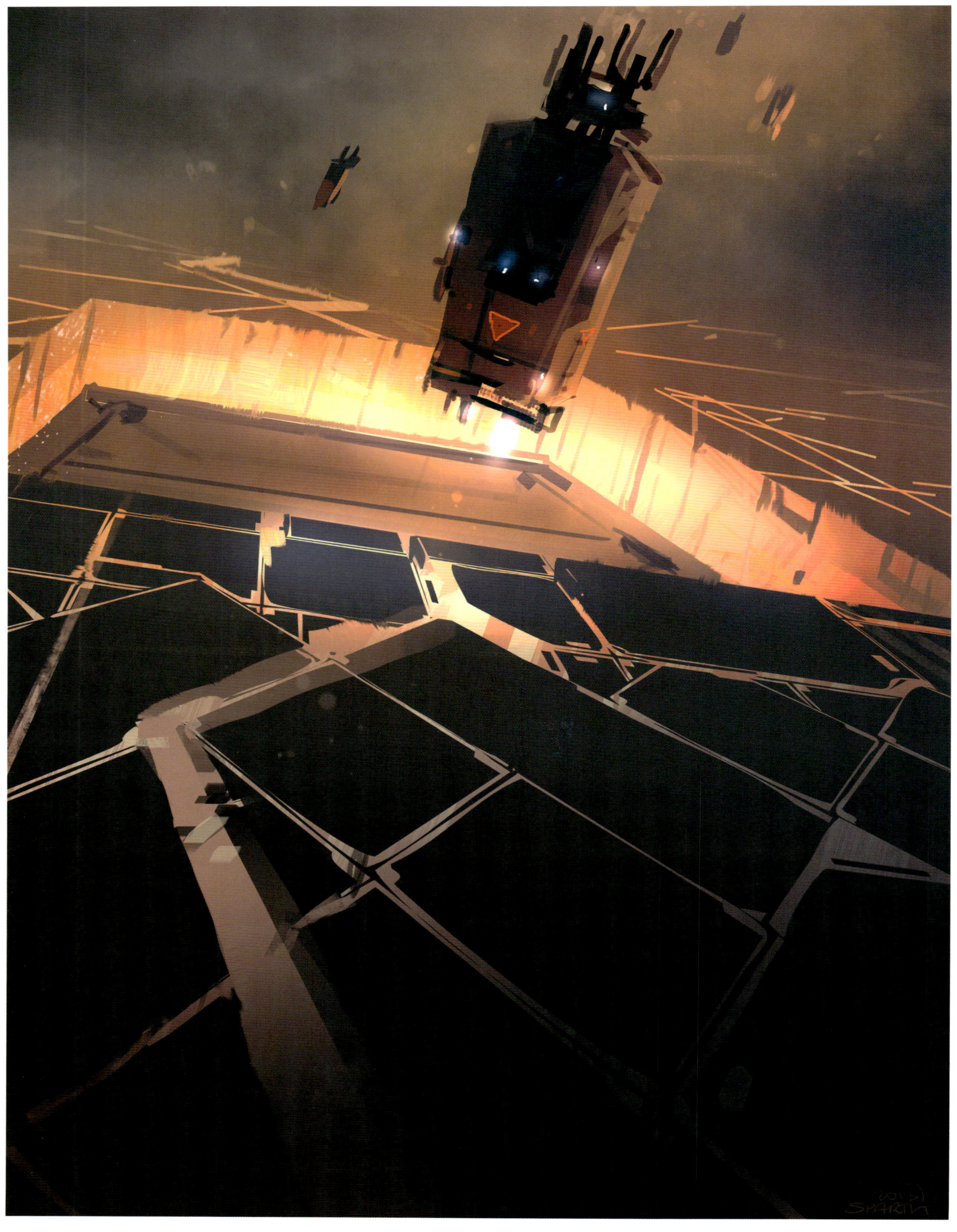

Melting door, 2013

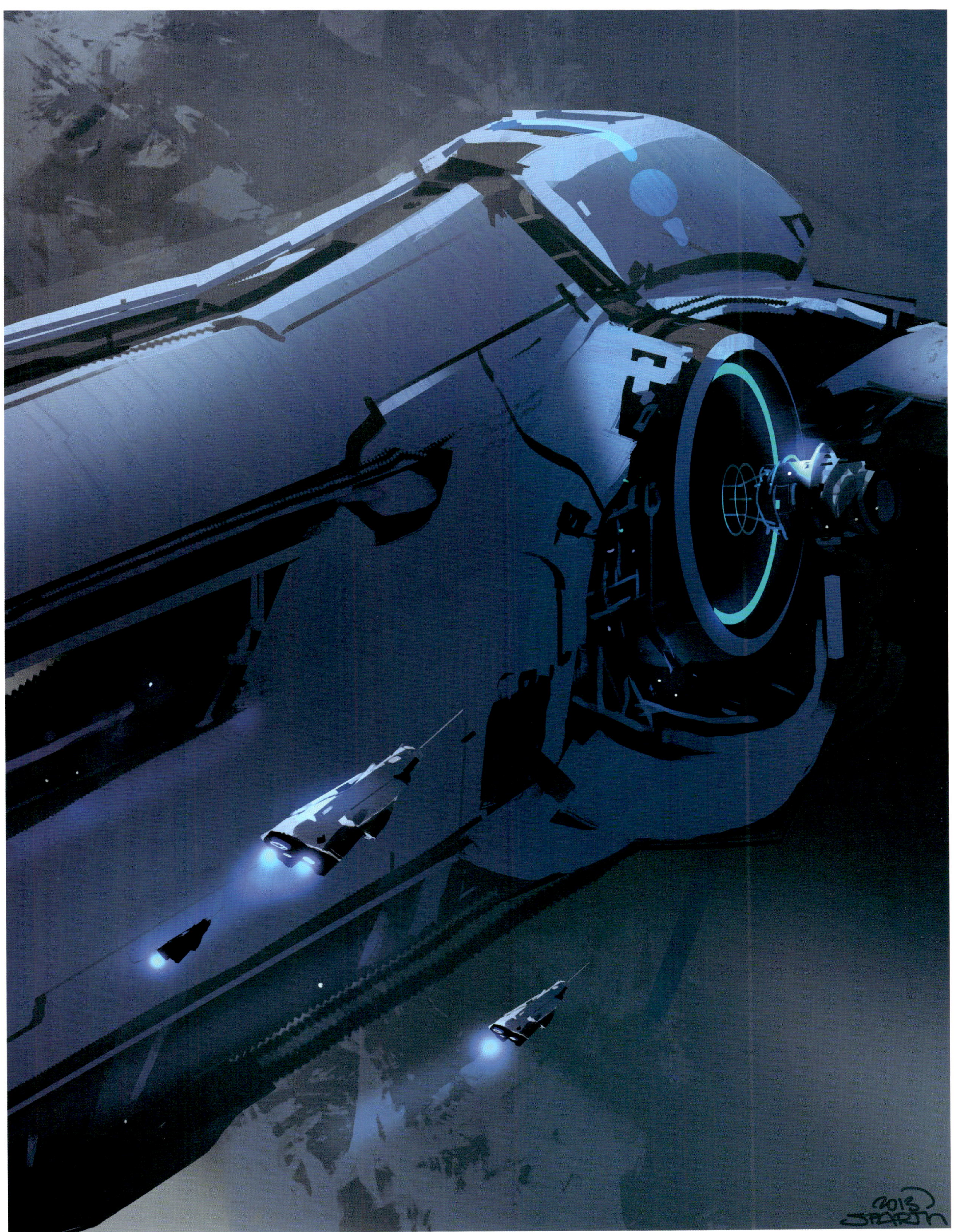

Stardrive maintenance, 2013

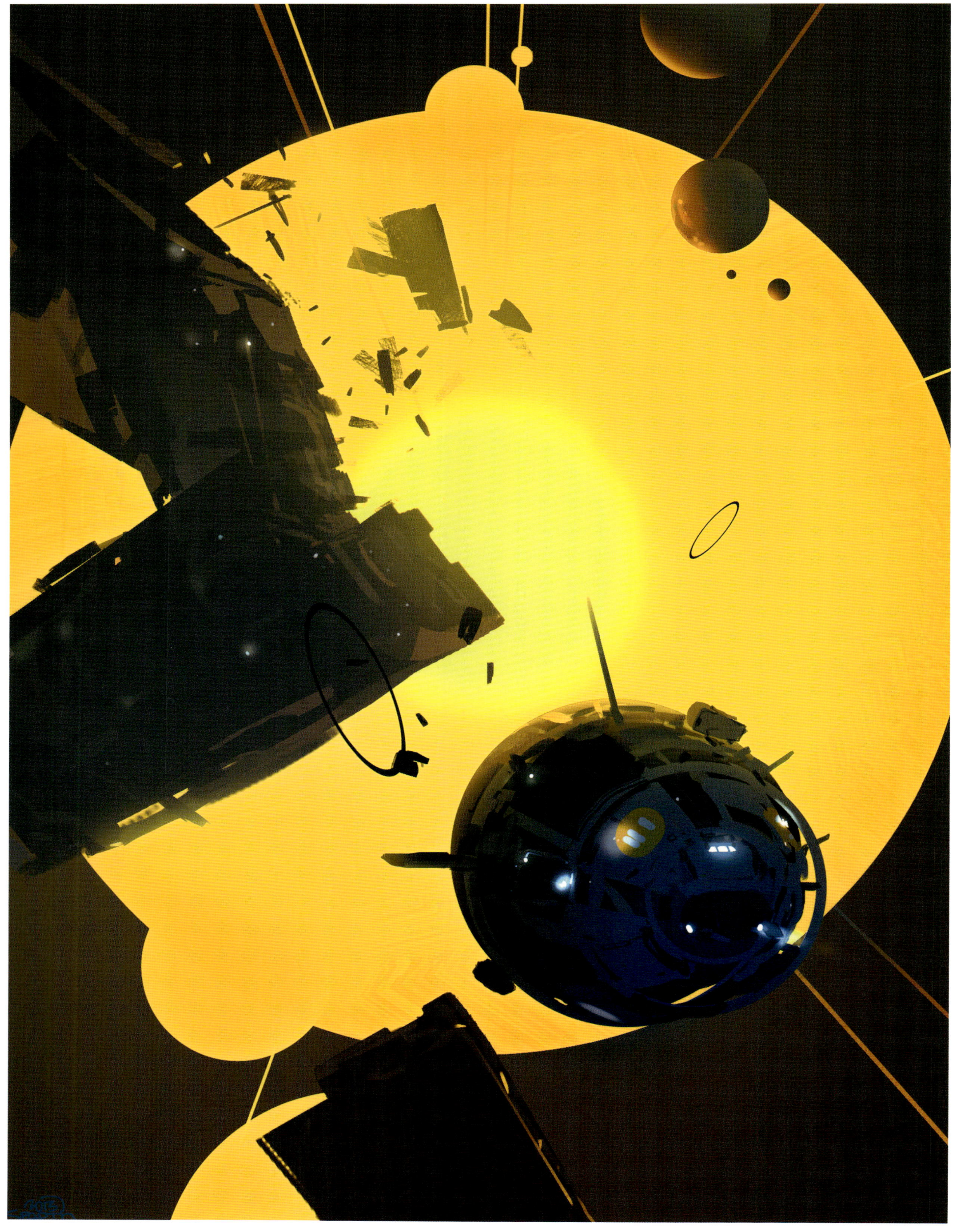

Supernova, 2013

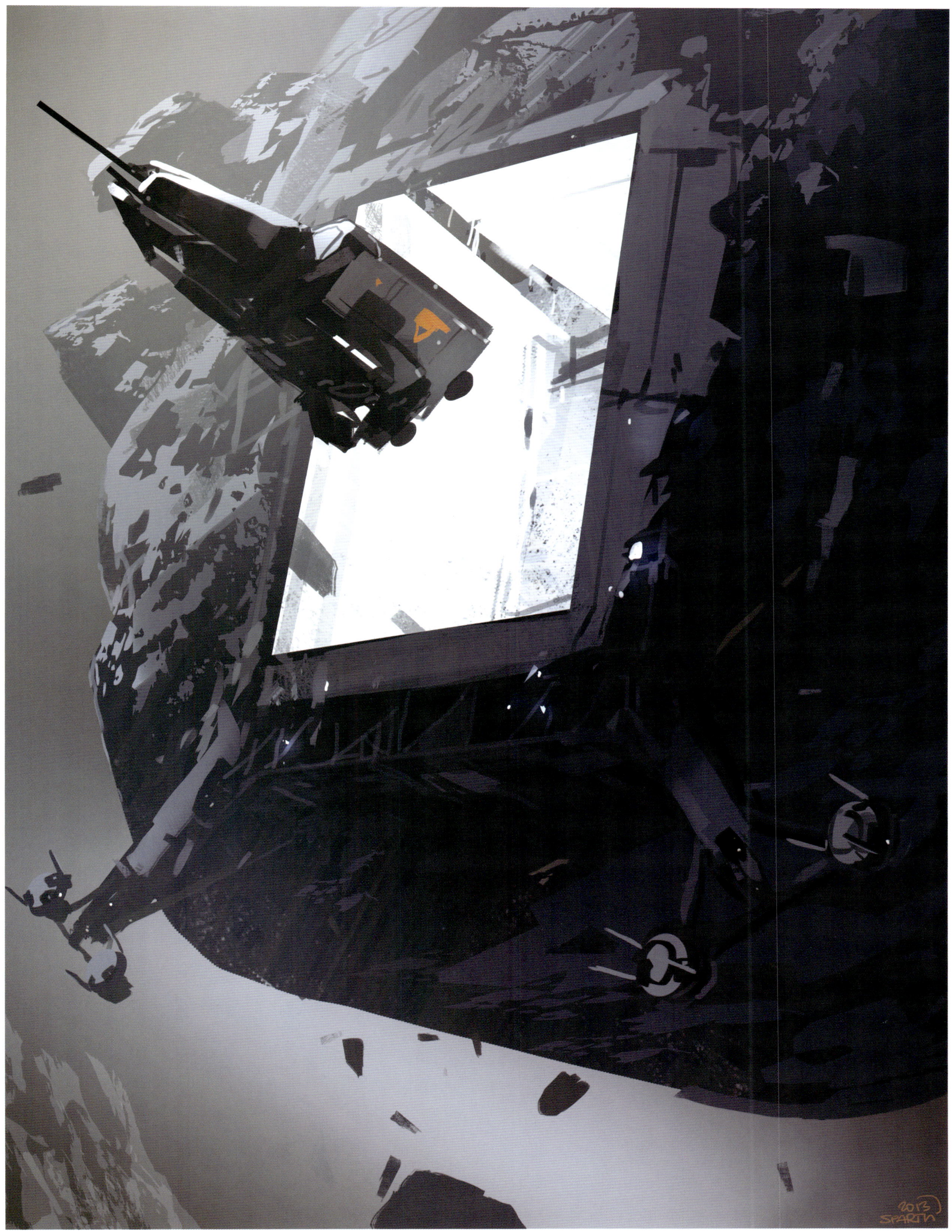

Defense turrets, 2013

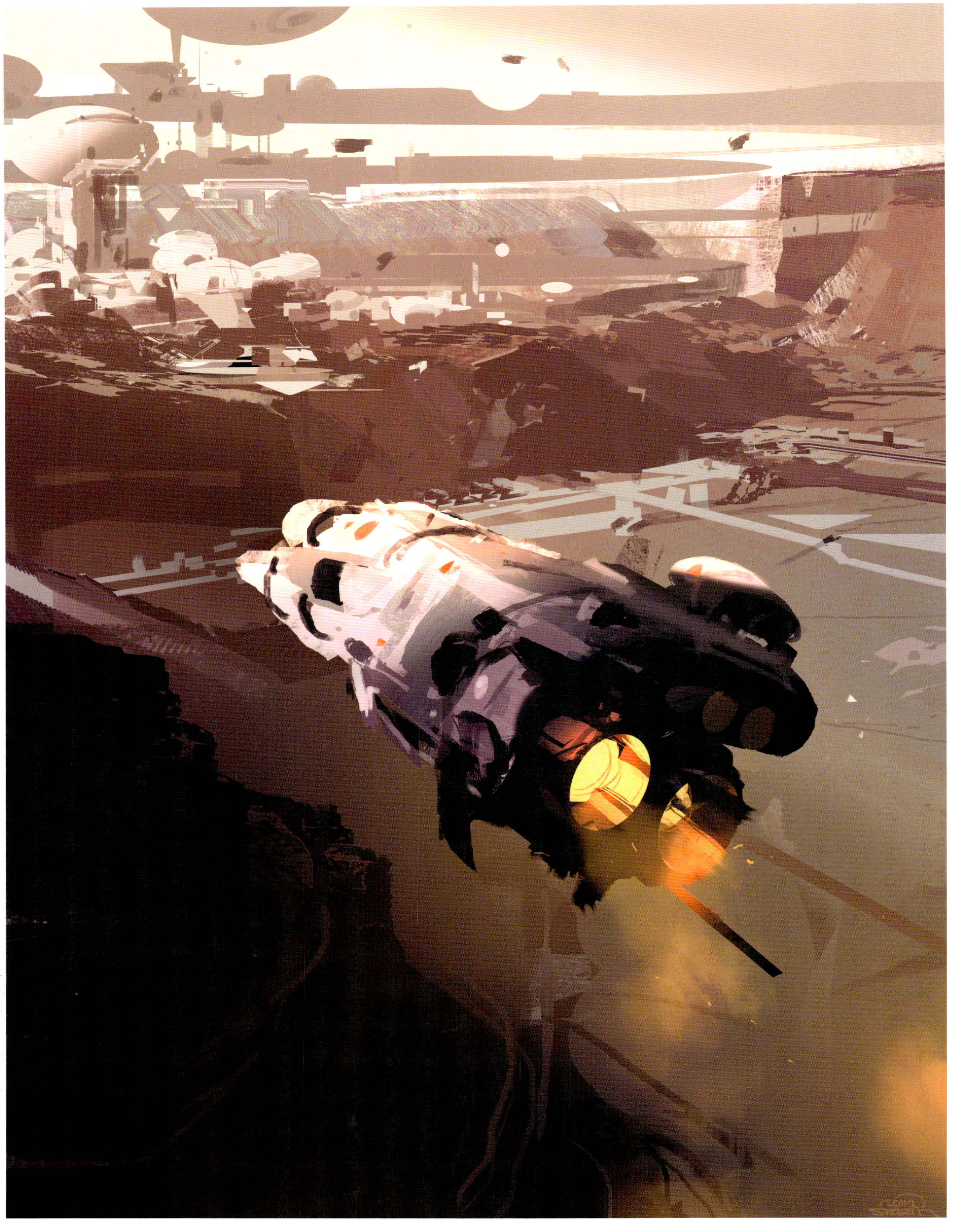

Burnout, 2014

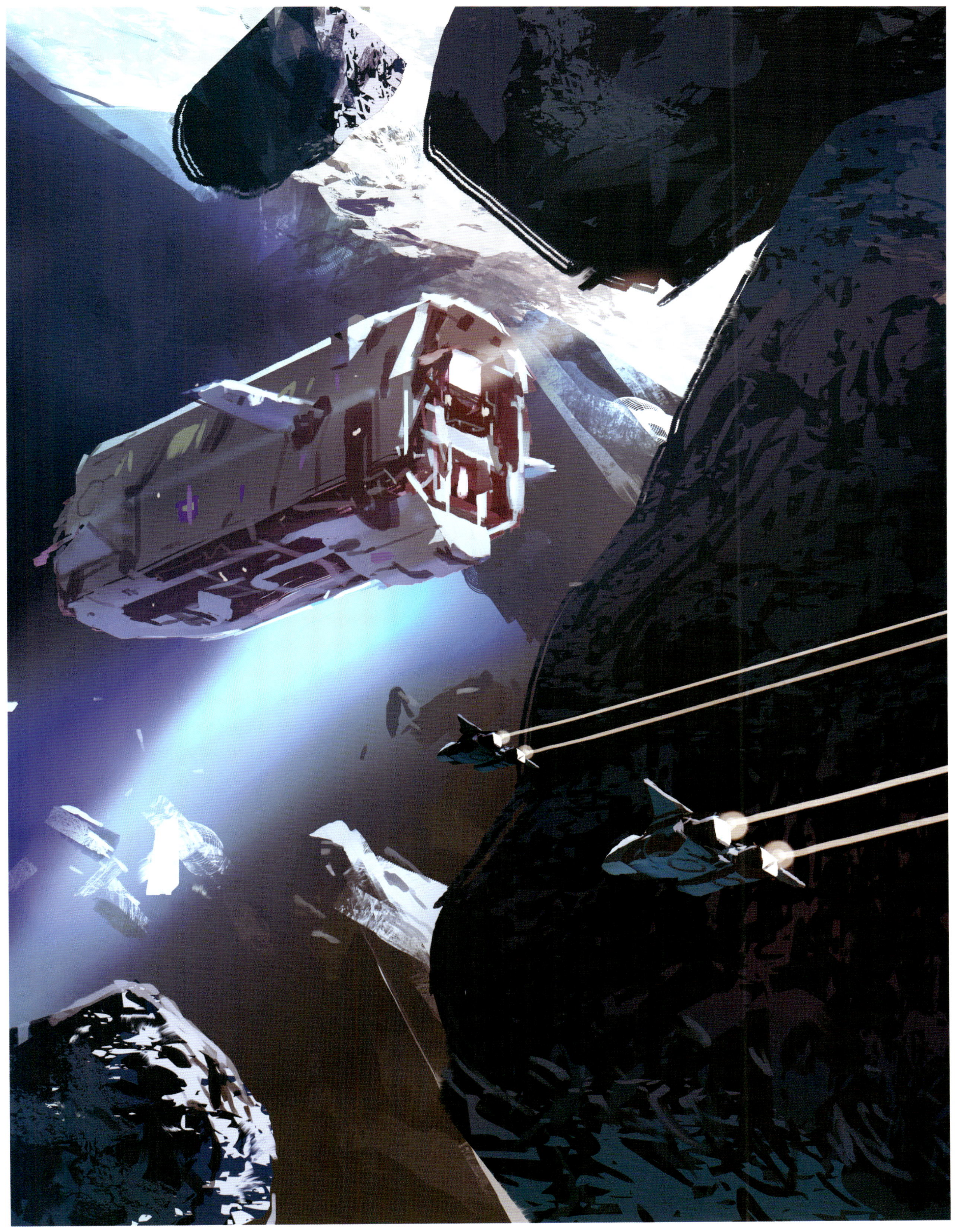

Pirate lookout, 2013

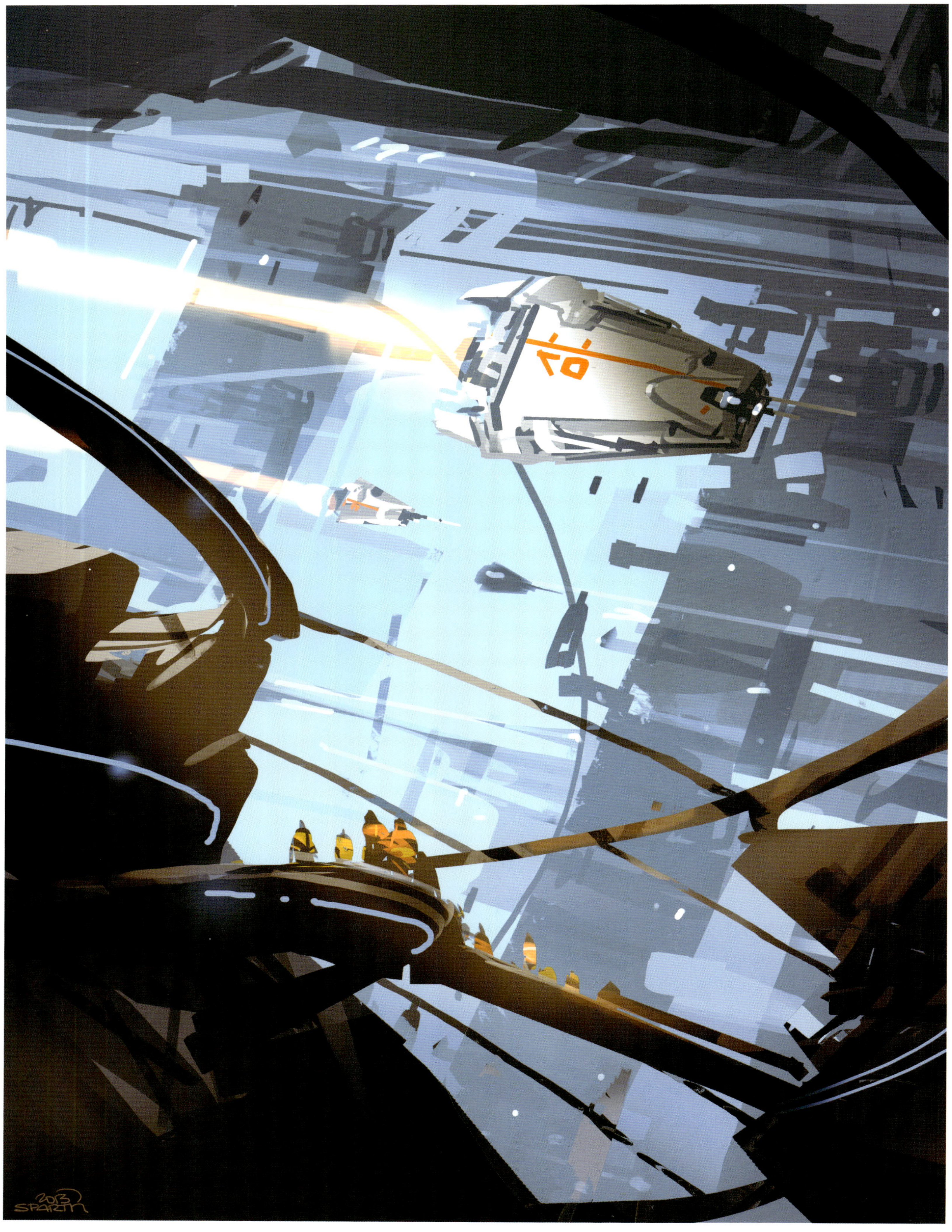

Extreme racing, 2013

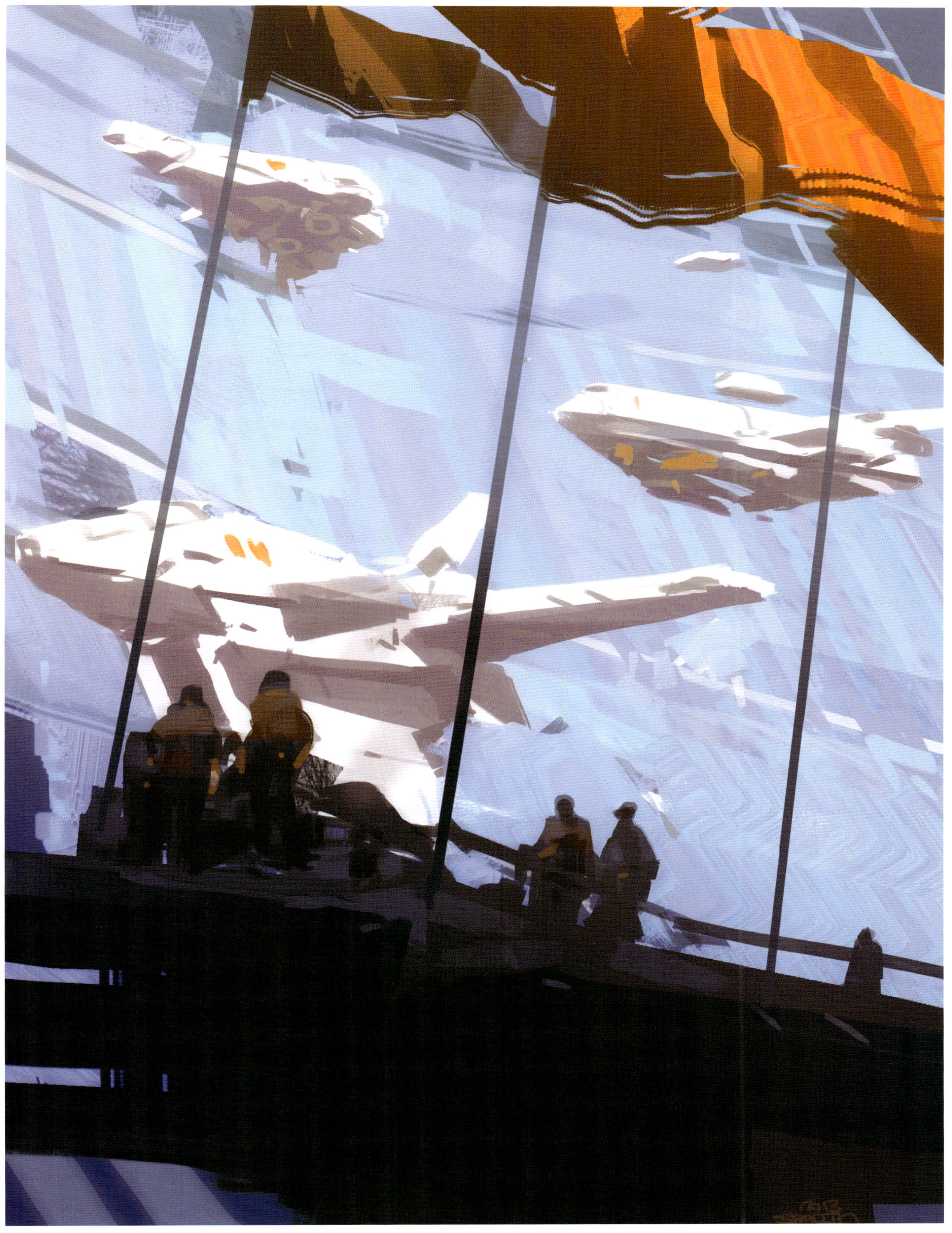

Space race, 2013

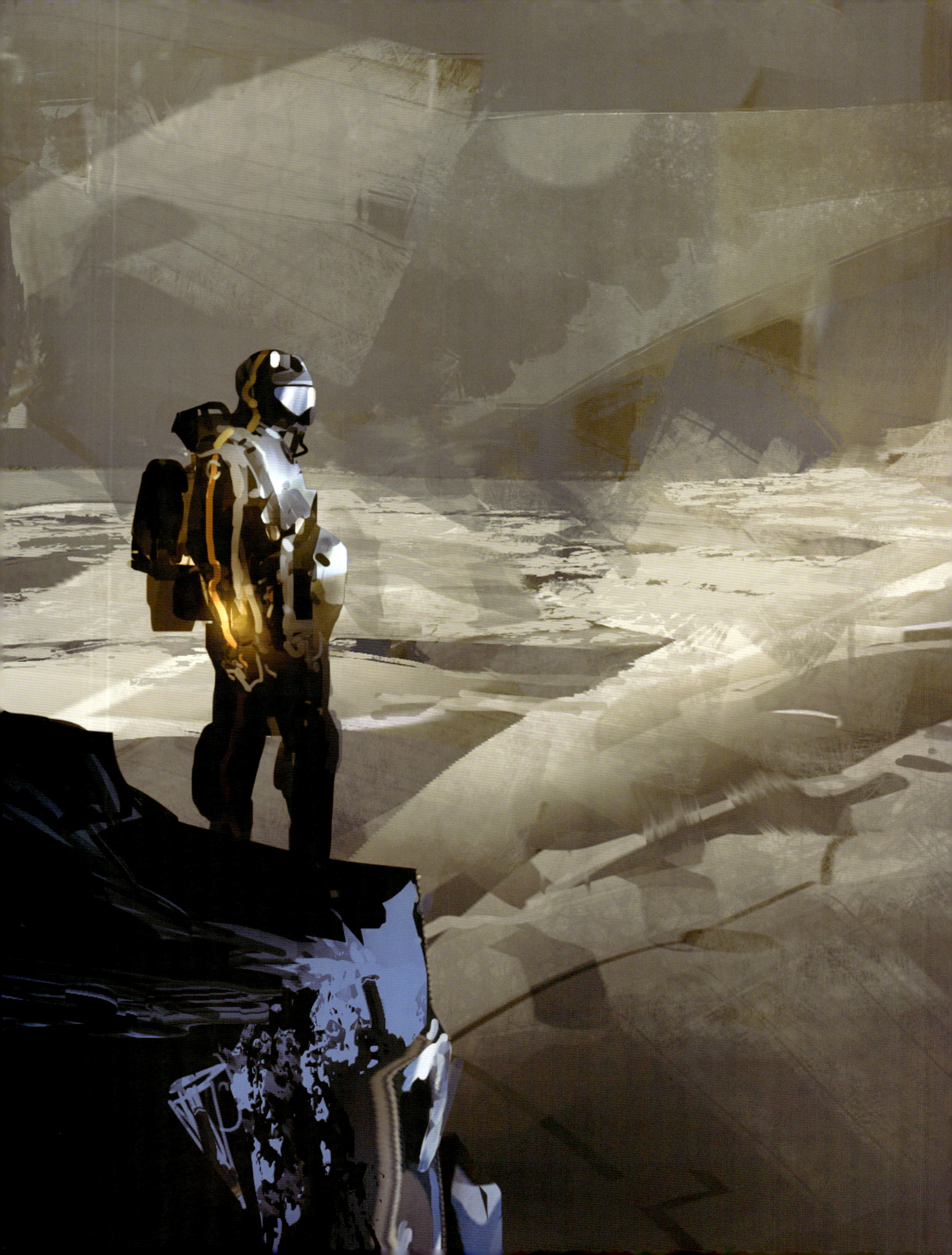

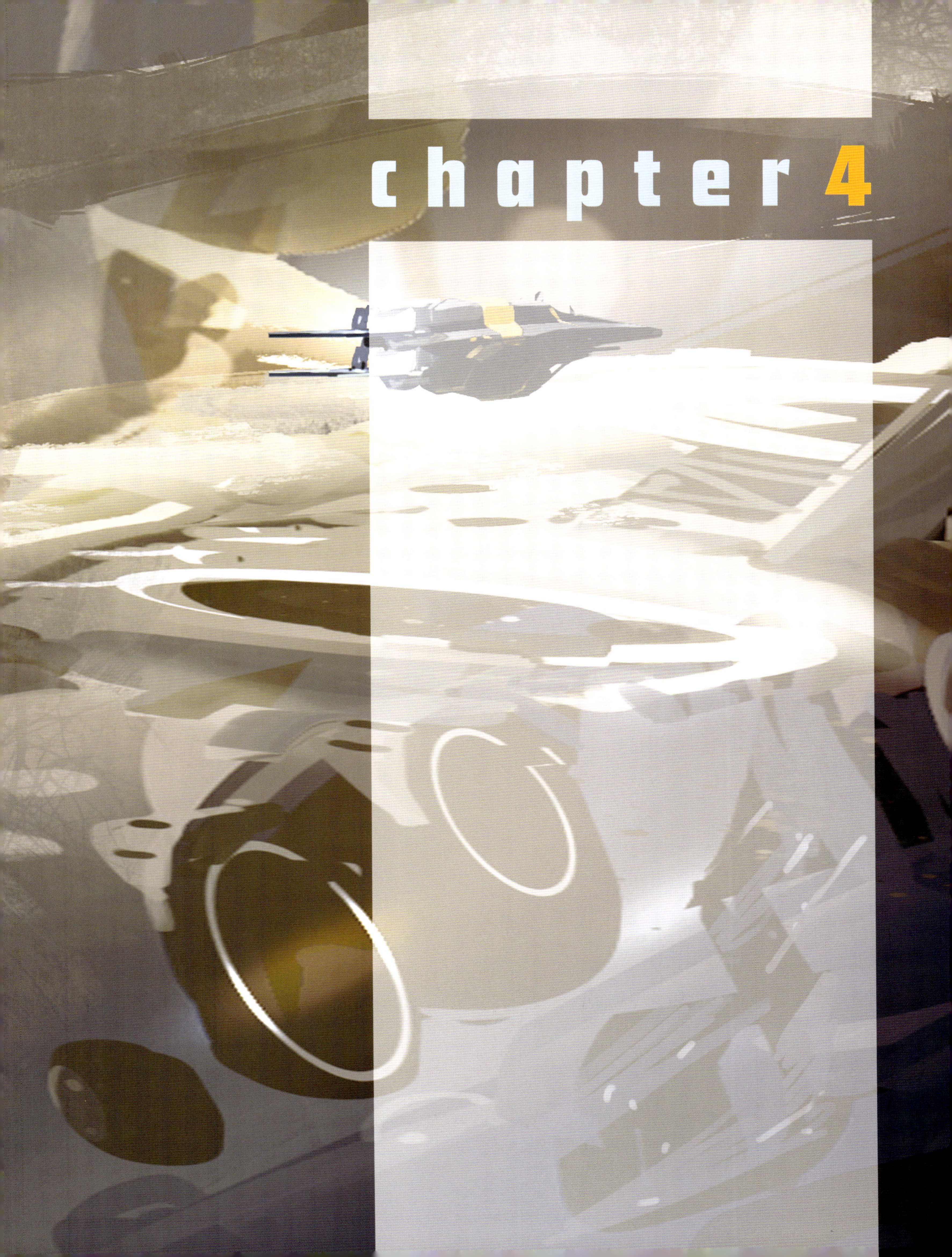
chapter 4

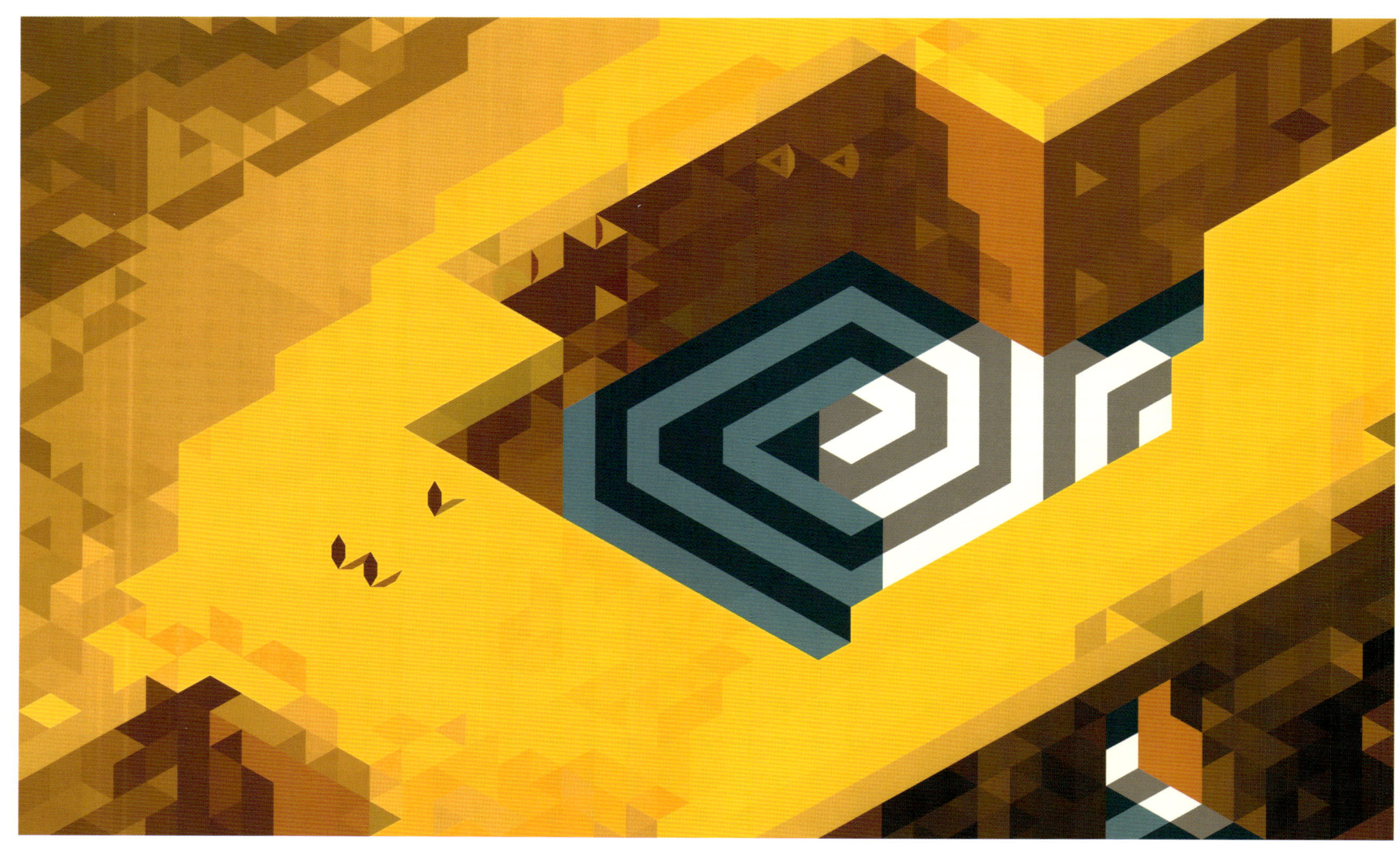

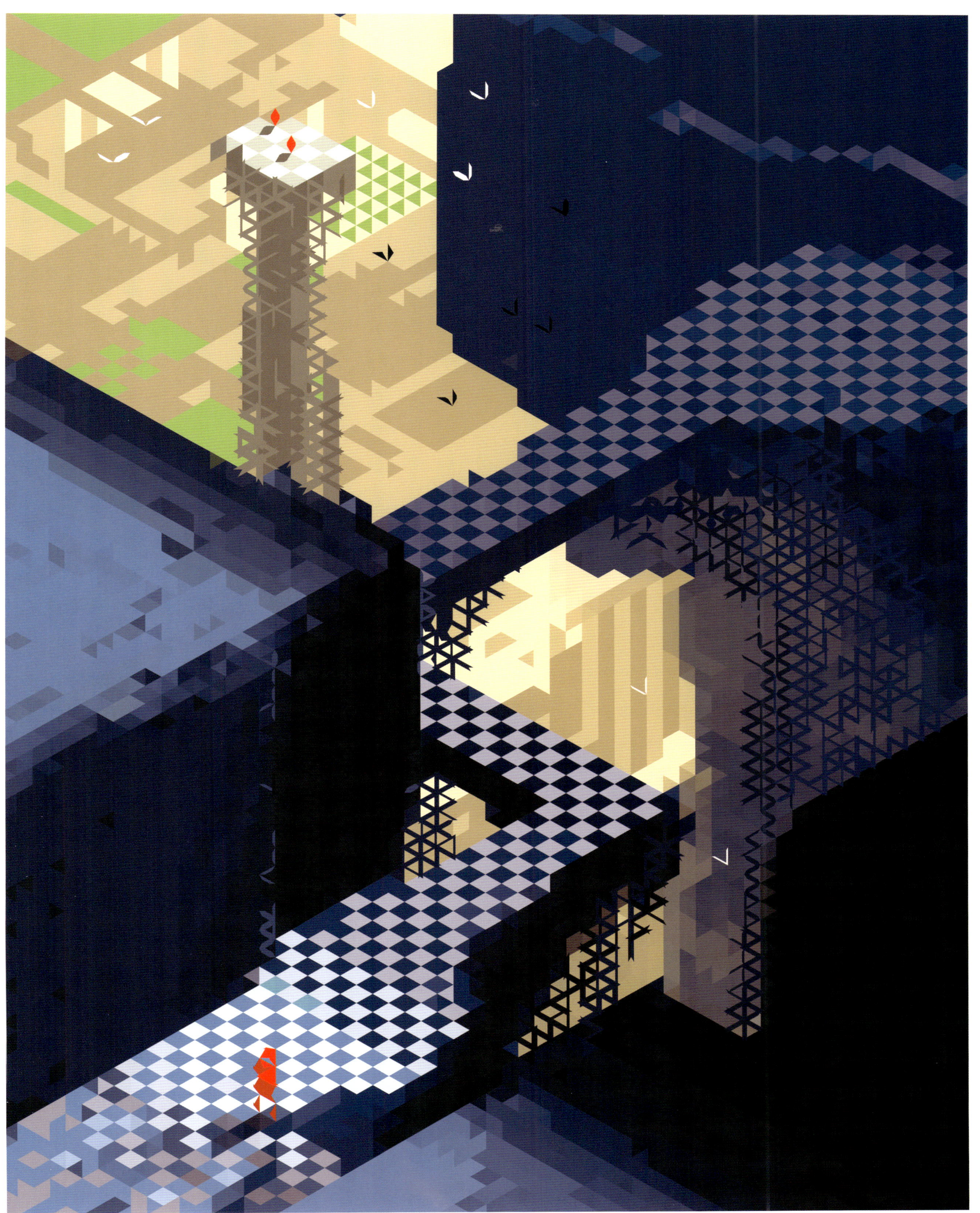

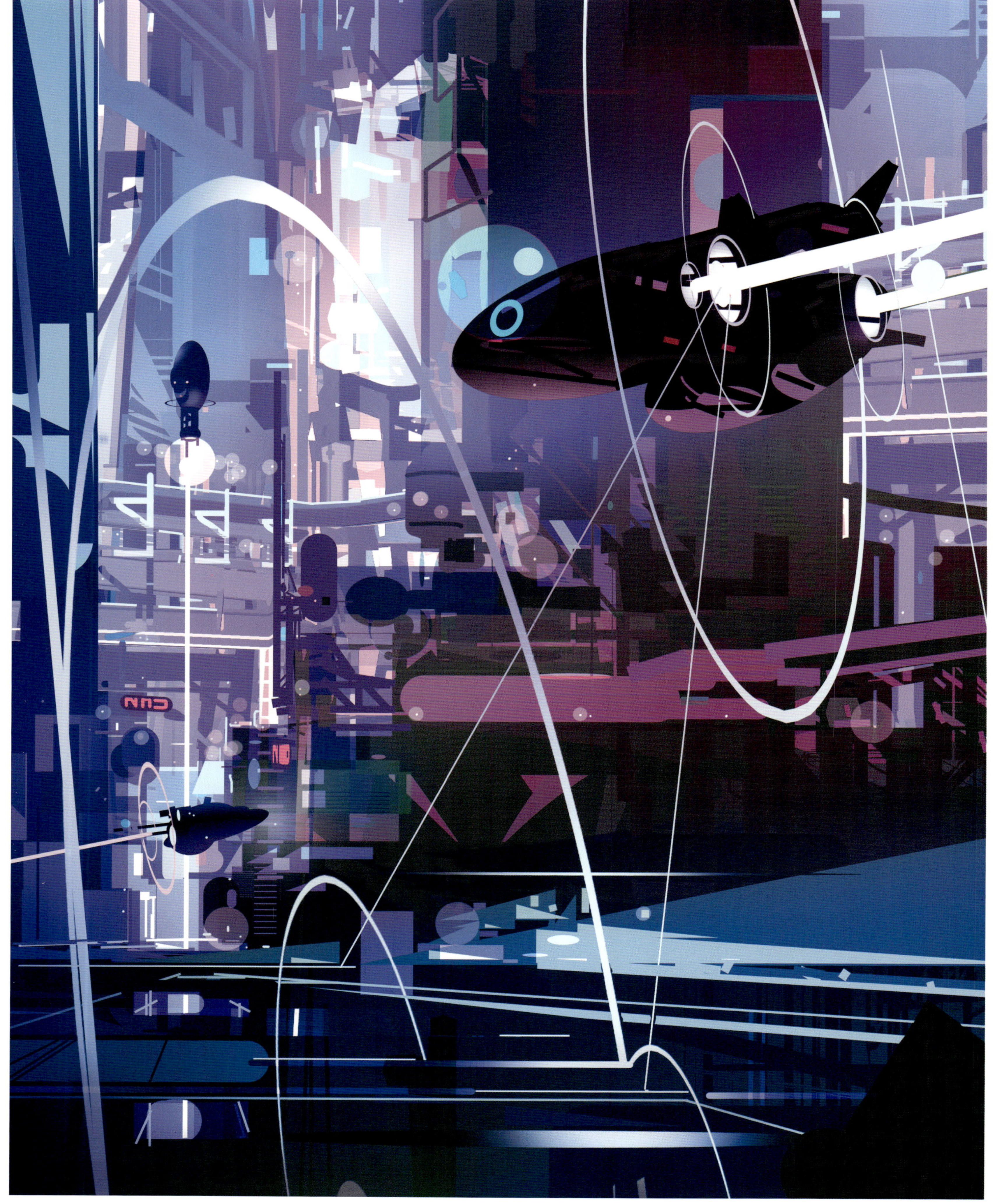

Primitive city 1, 2013

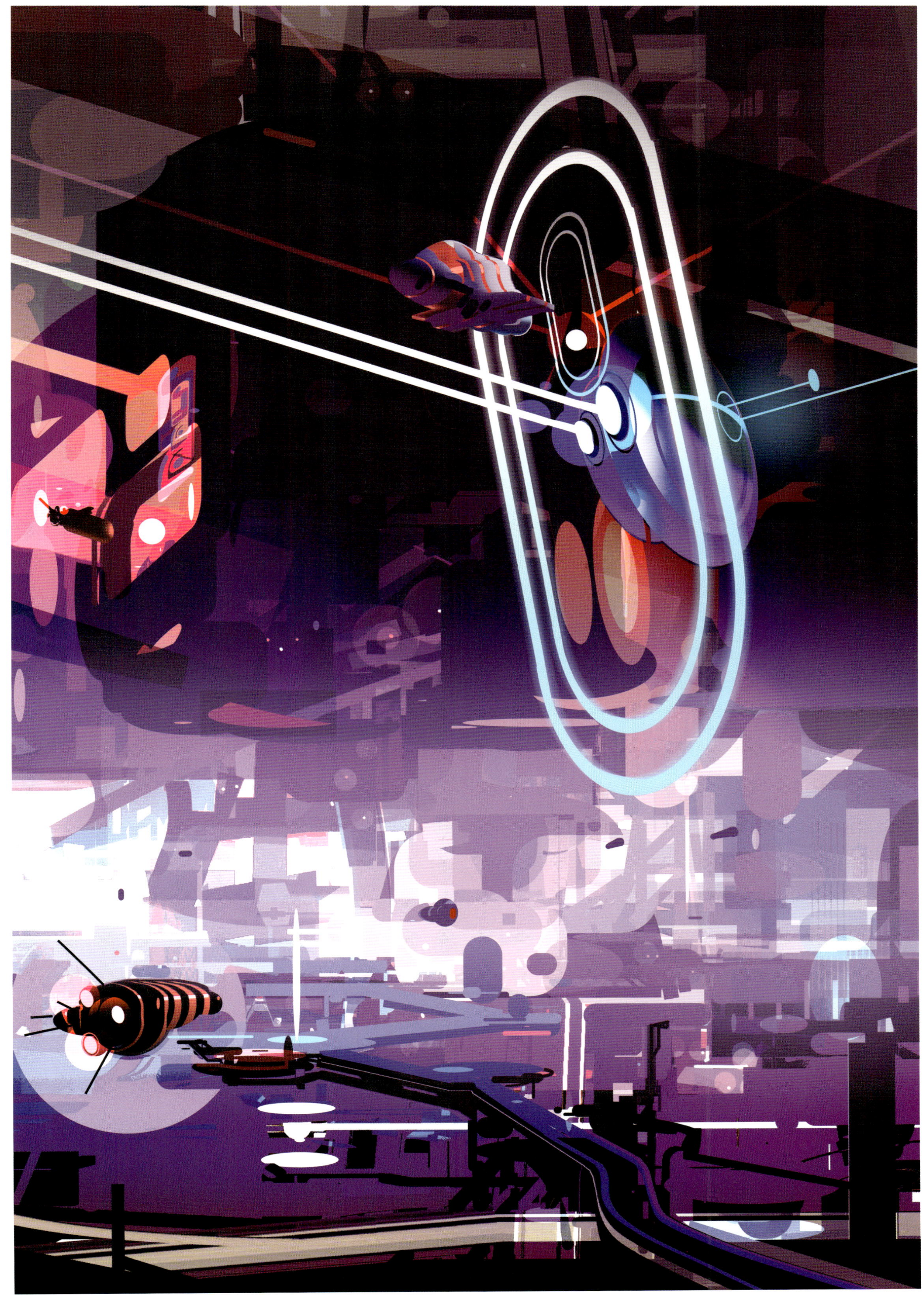

Primitive city 2, 2013

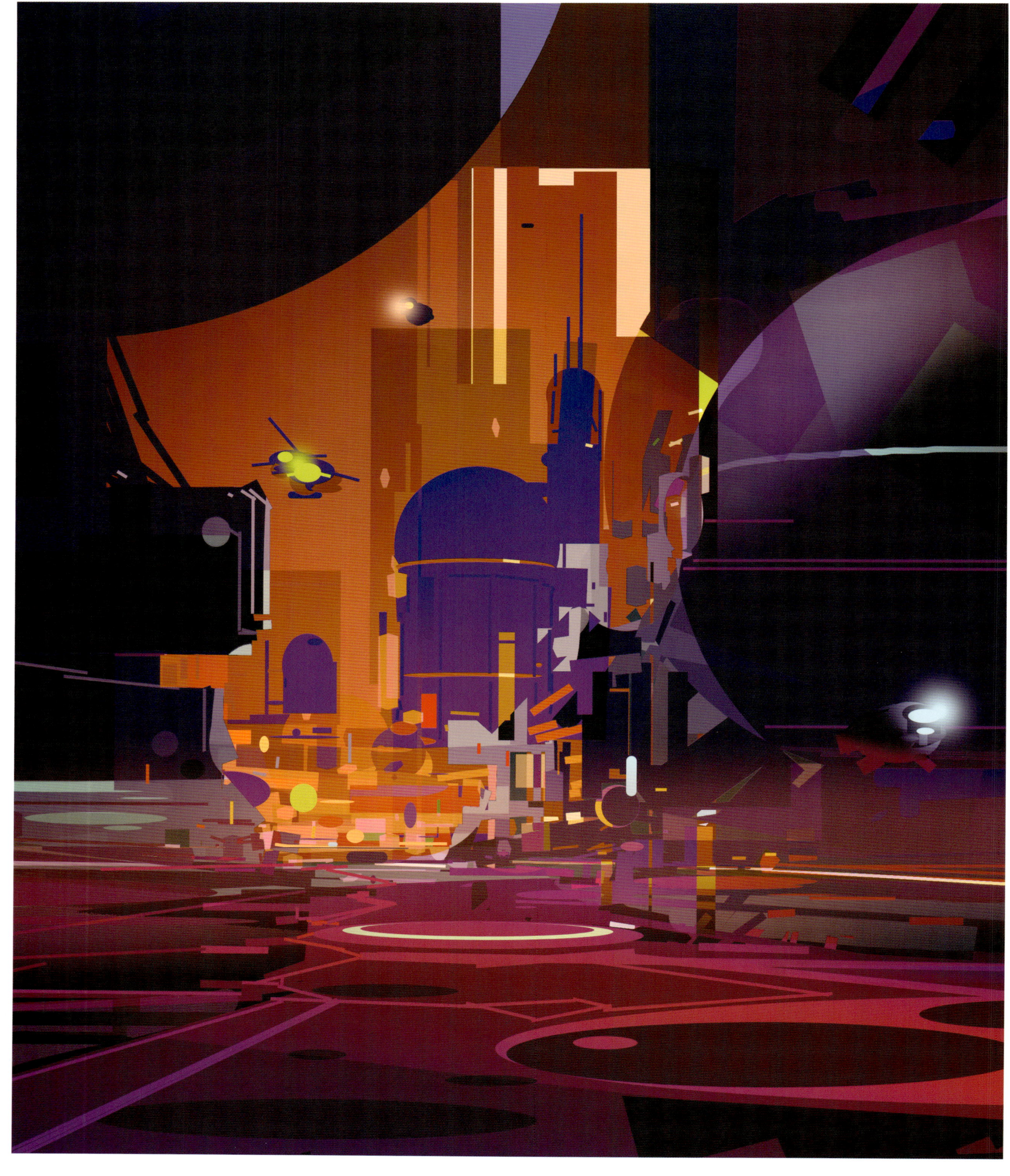

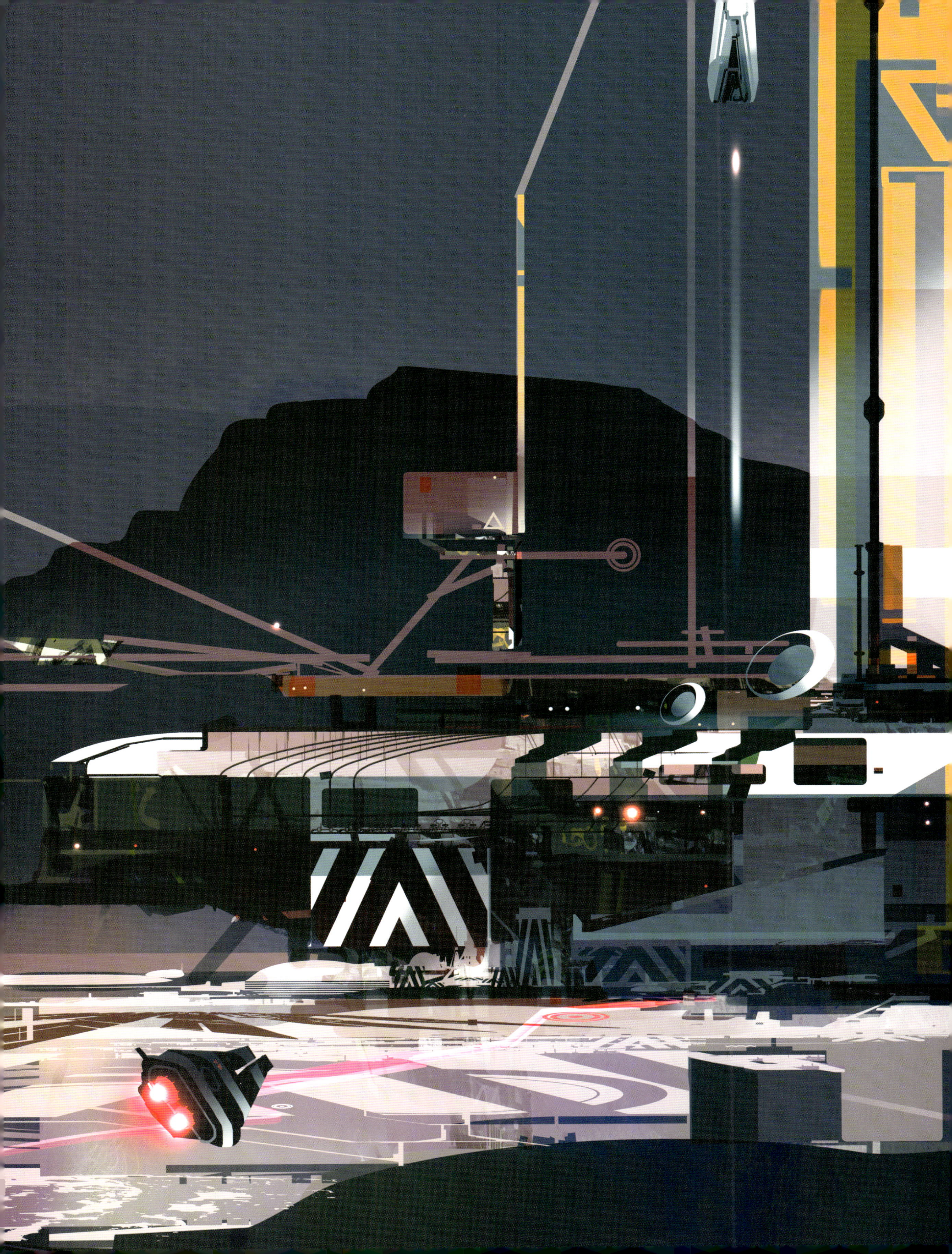

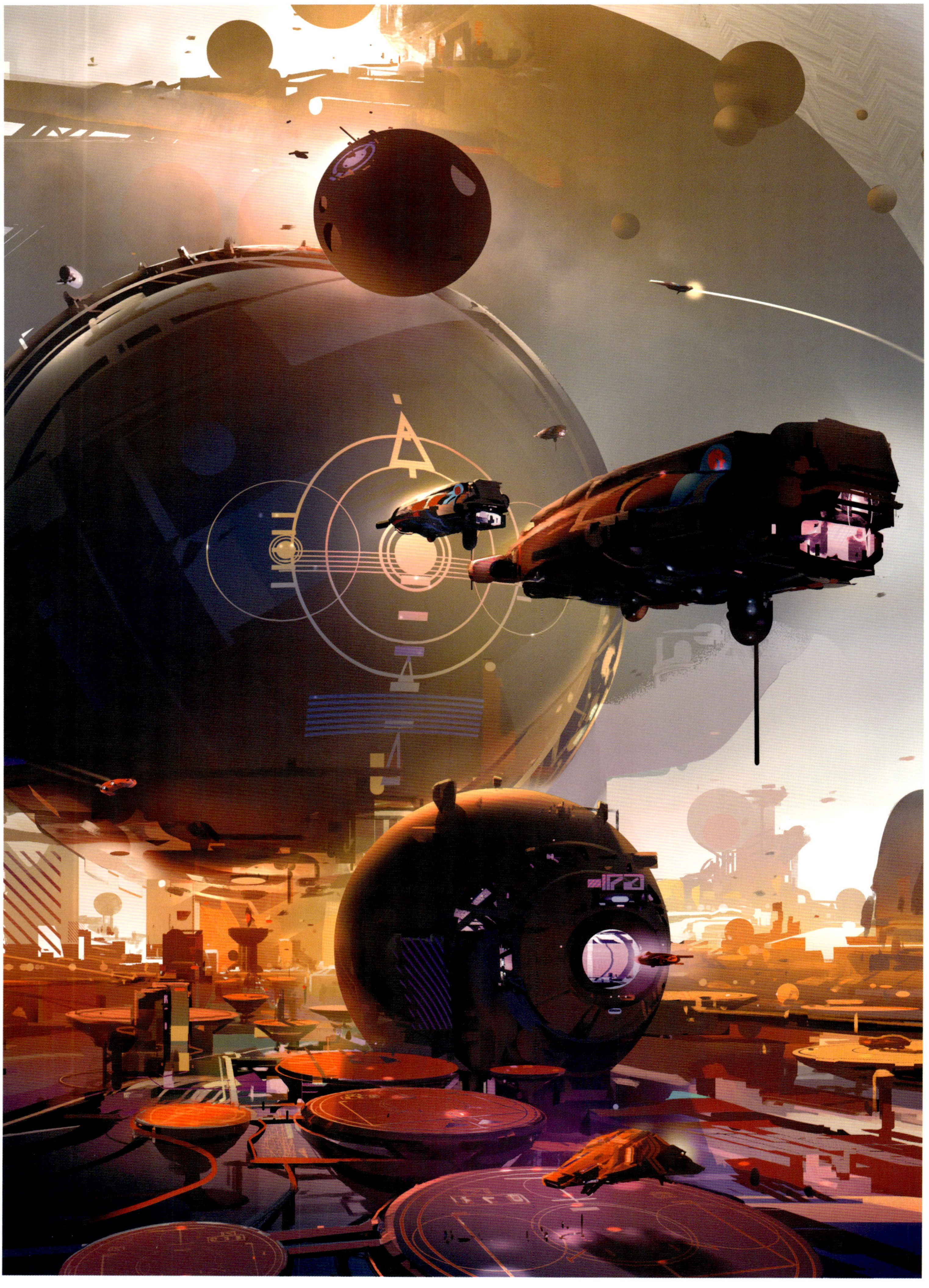

Sphere Monde, 2014

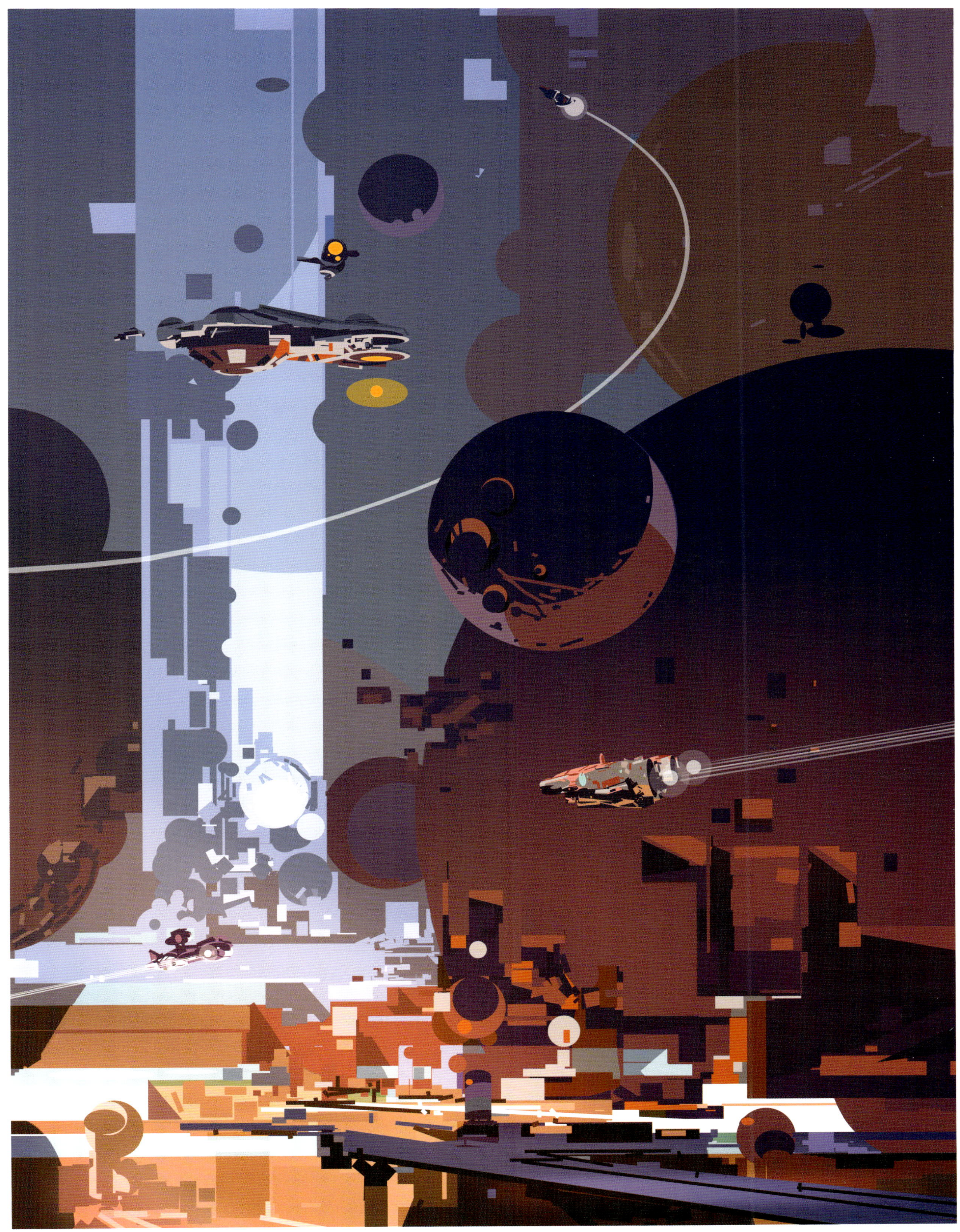

Sinking spheres, 2013

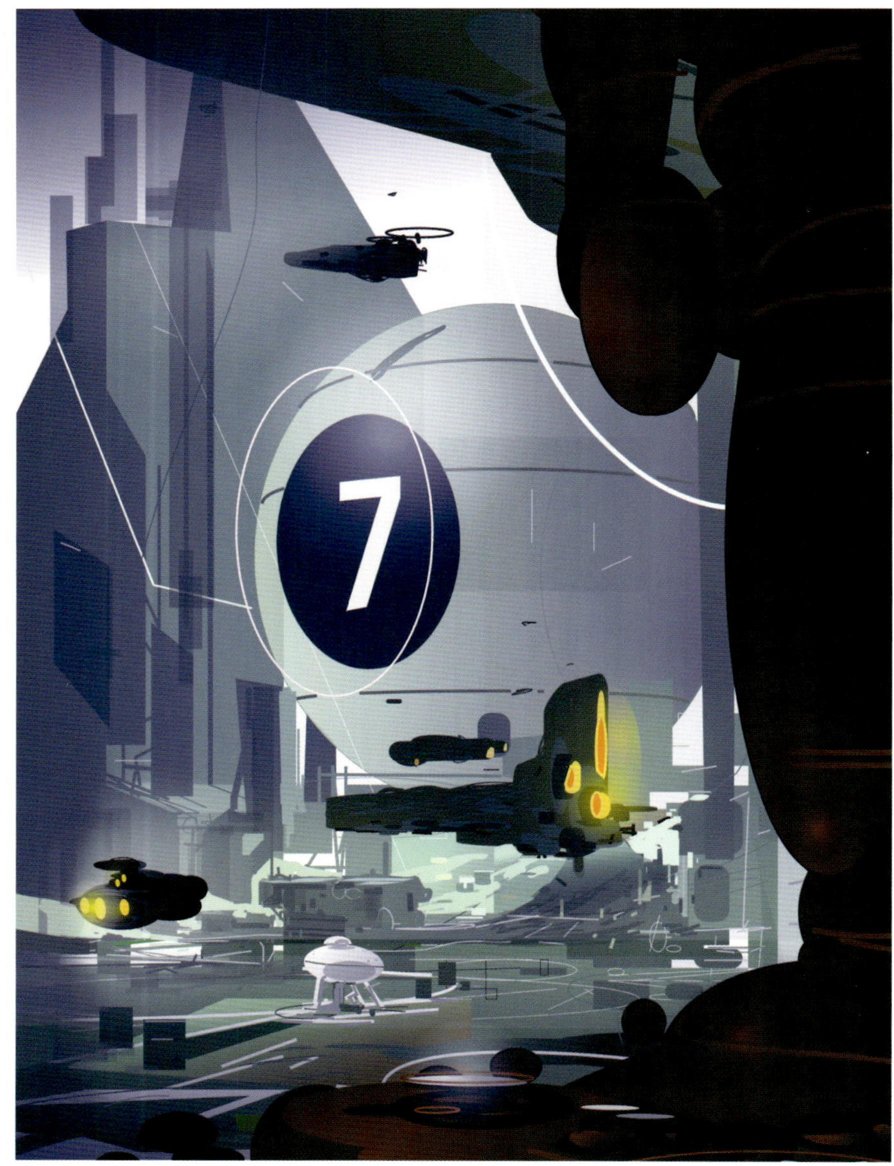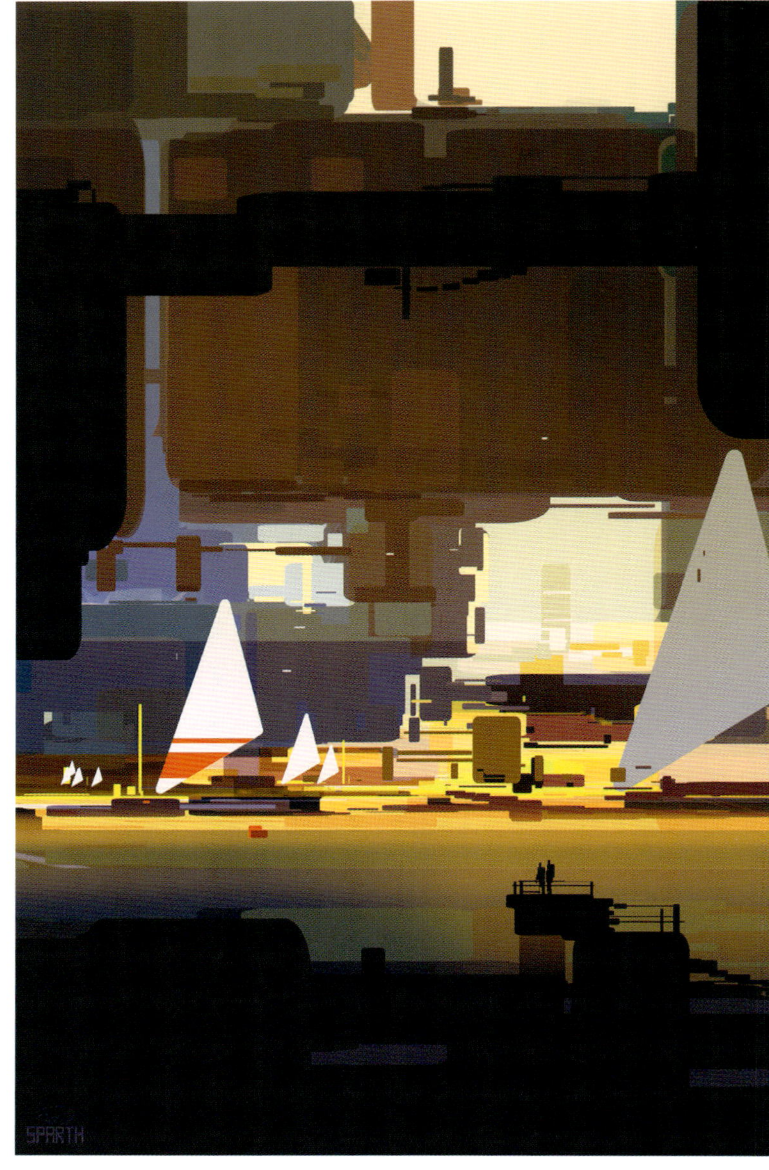

left iPad vector composition, 2013
above Composition with triangles, 2012
opposite Space salt, 2012

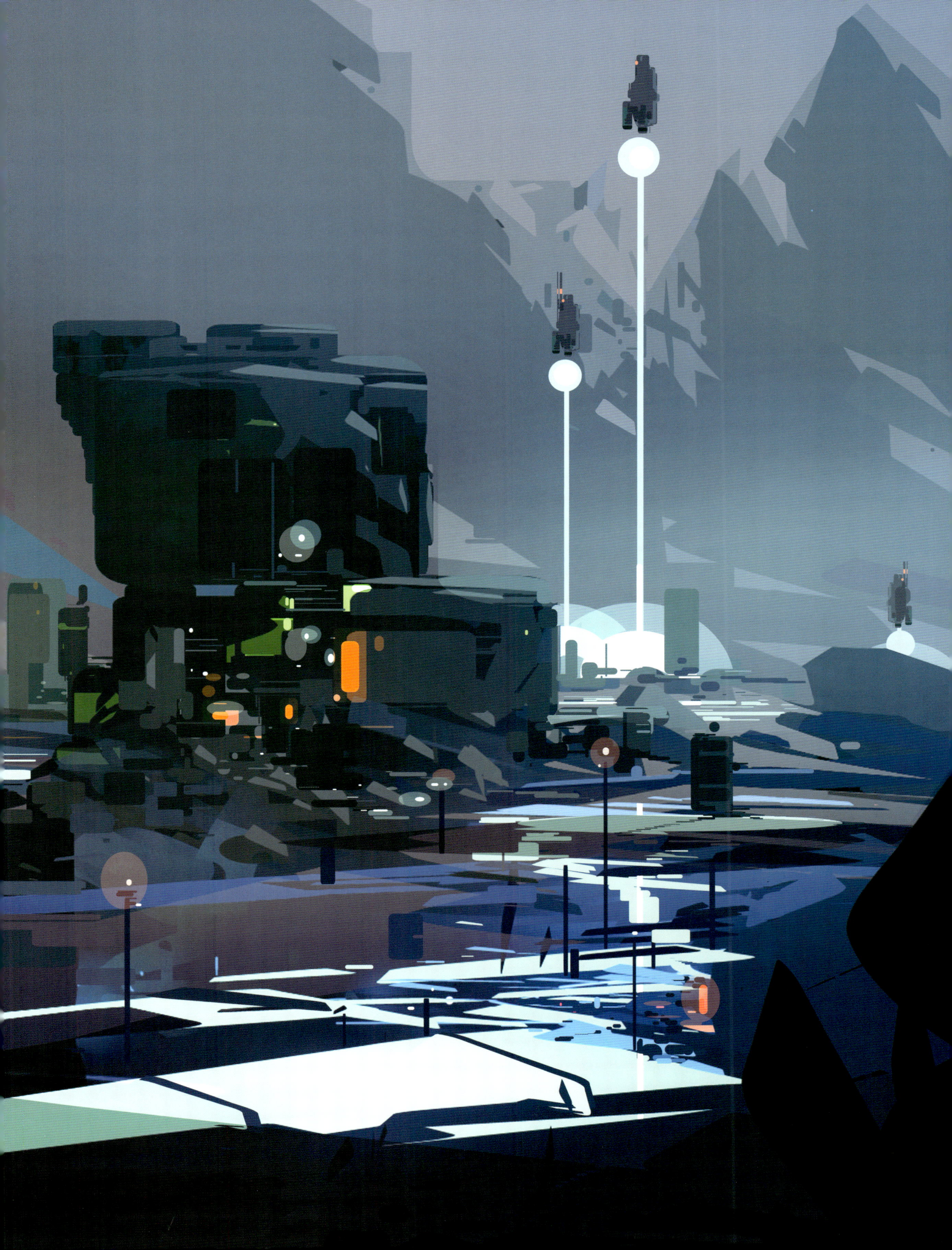

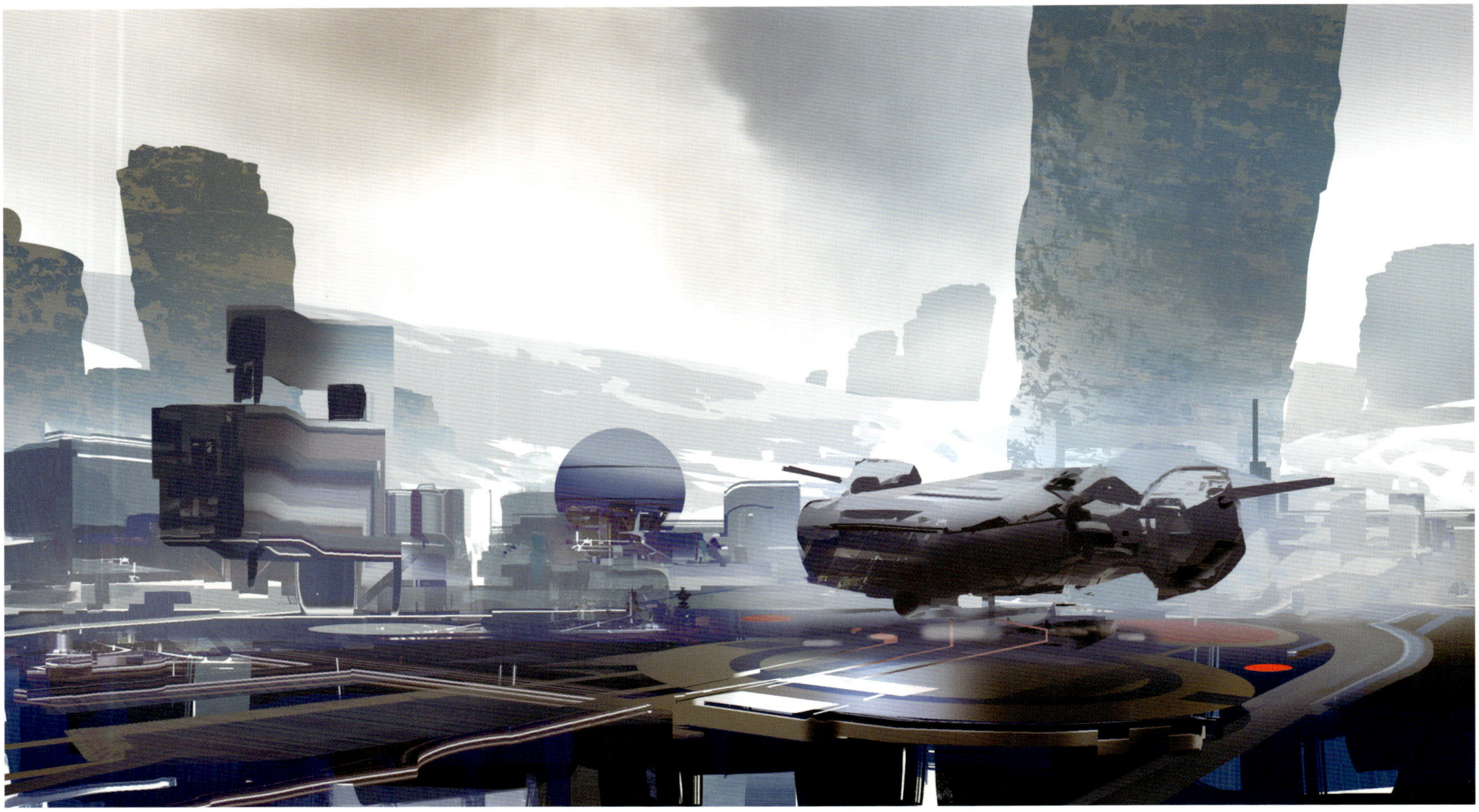

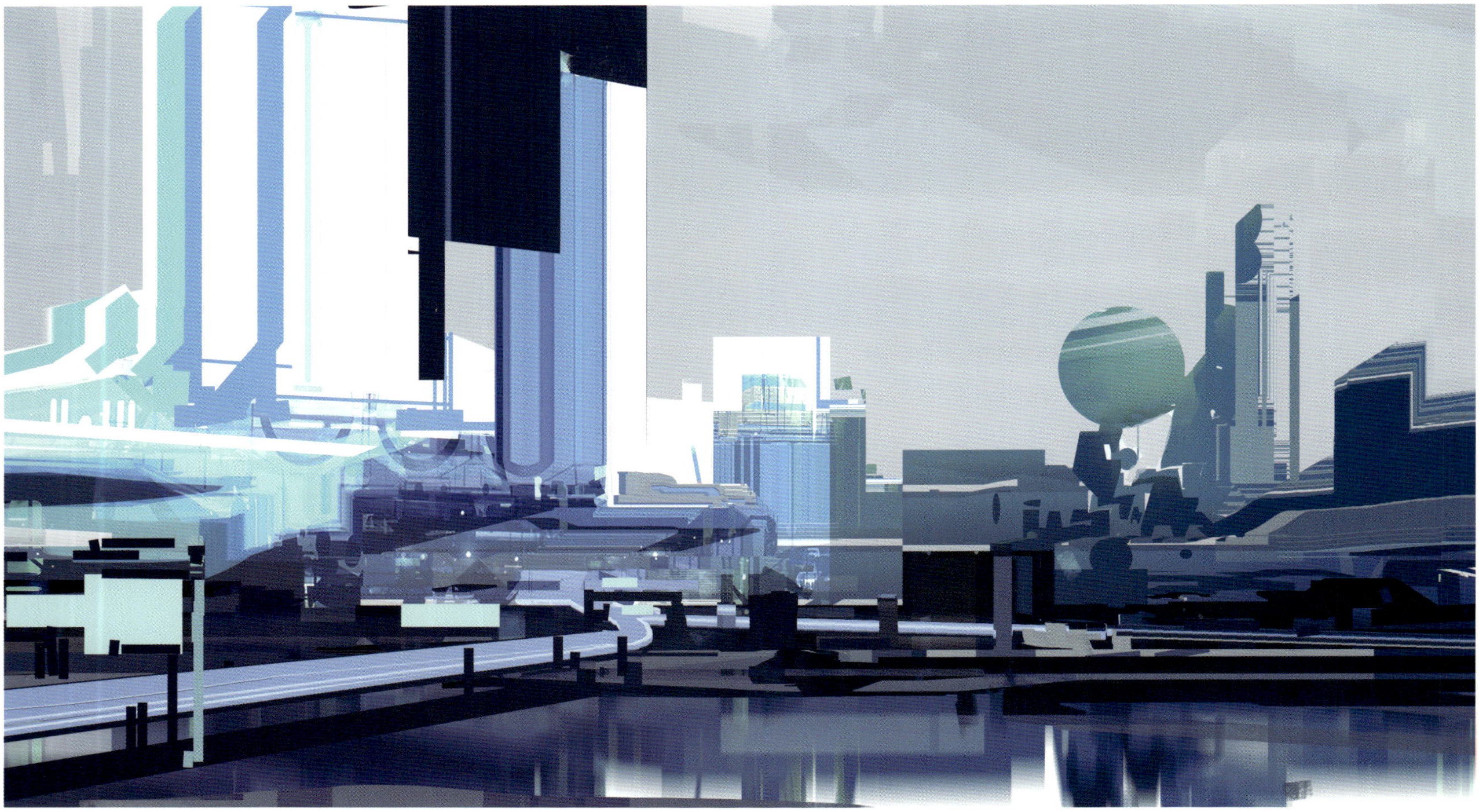

Demo sketches, 2013–2014

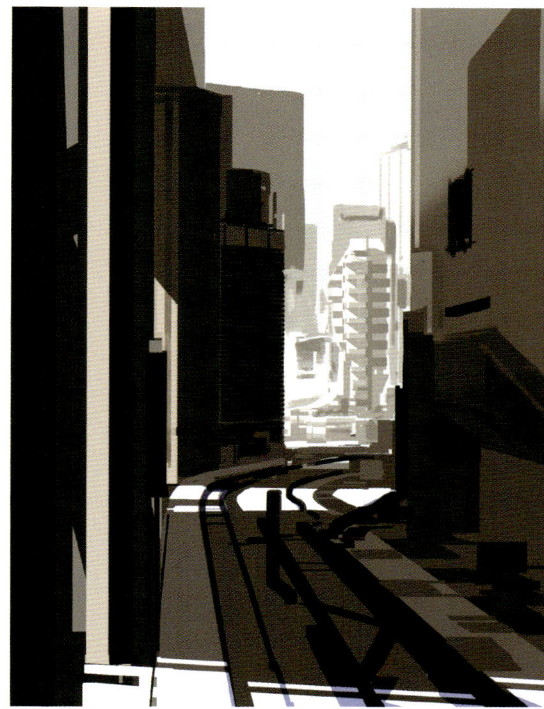

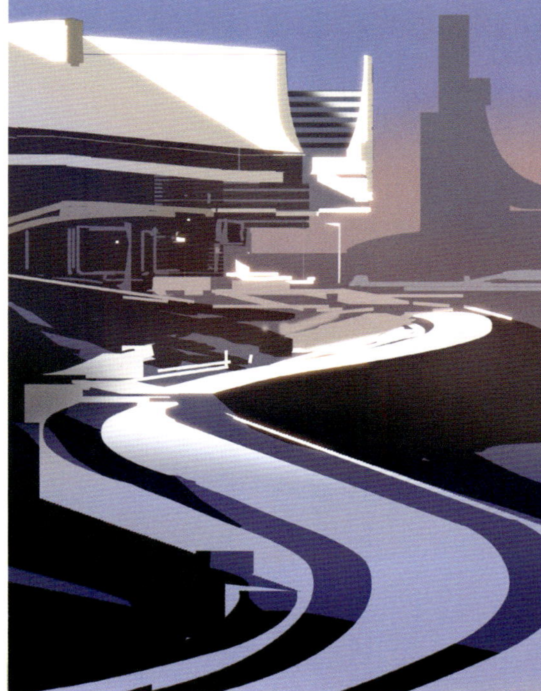

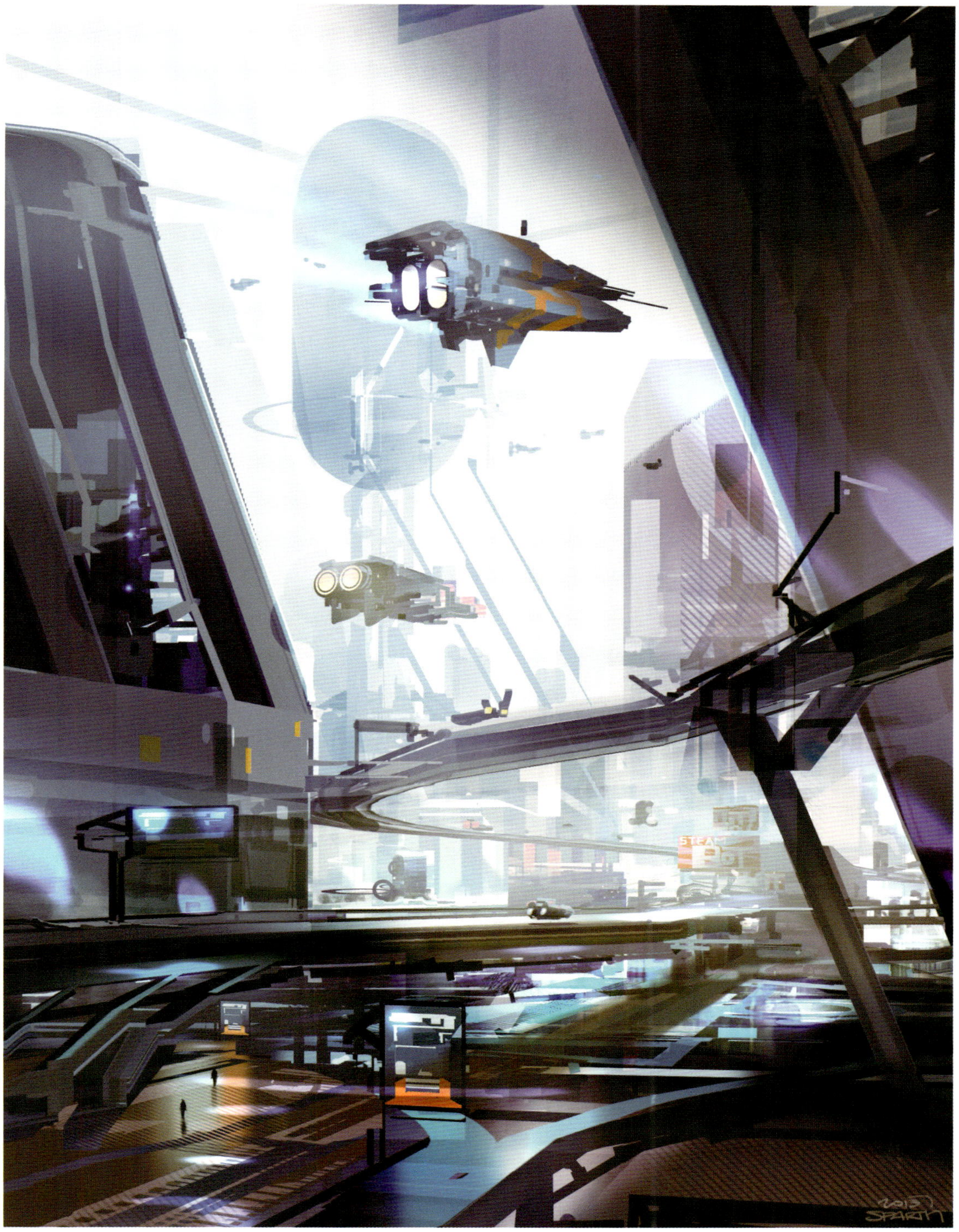

Demo sketches, 2013

Digital art is all about experimenting, testing, breaking things apart, and reconstructing them afterward. It's all about giving fresh material to the eyes.

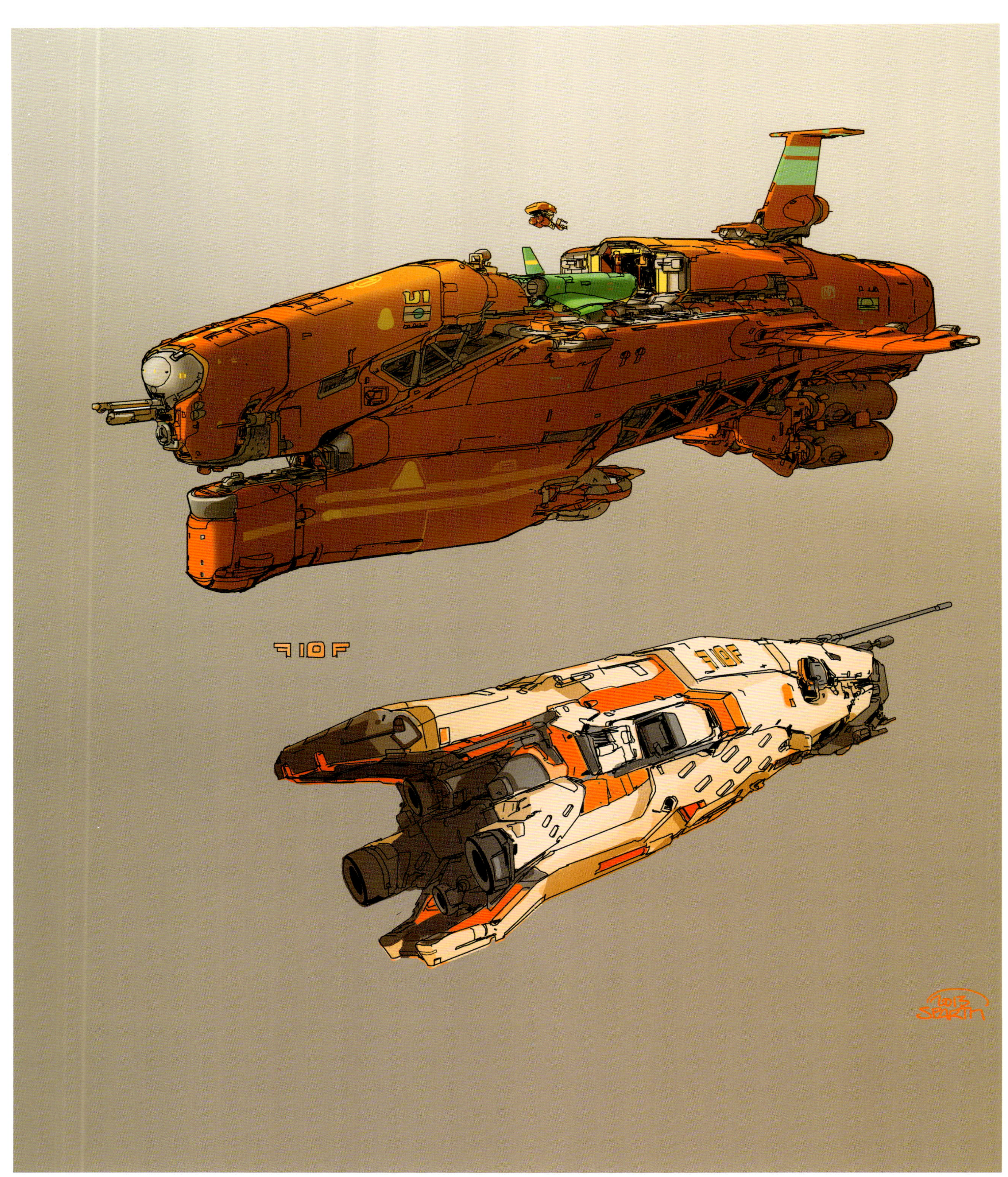

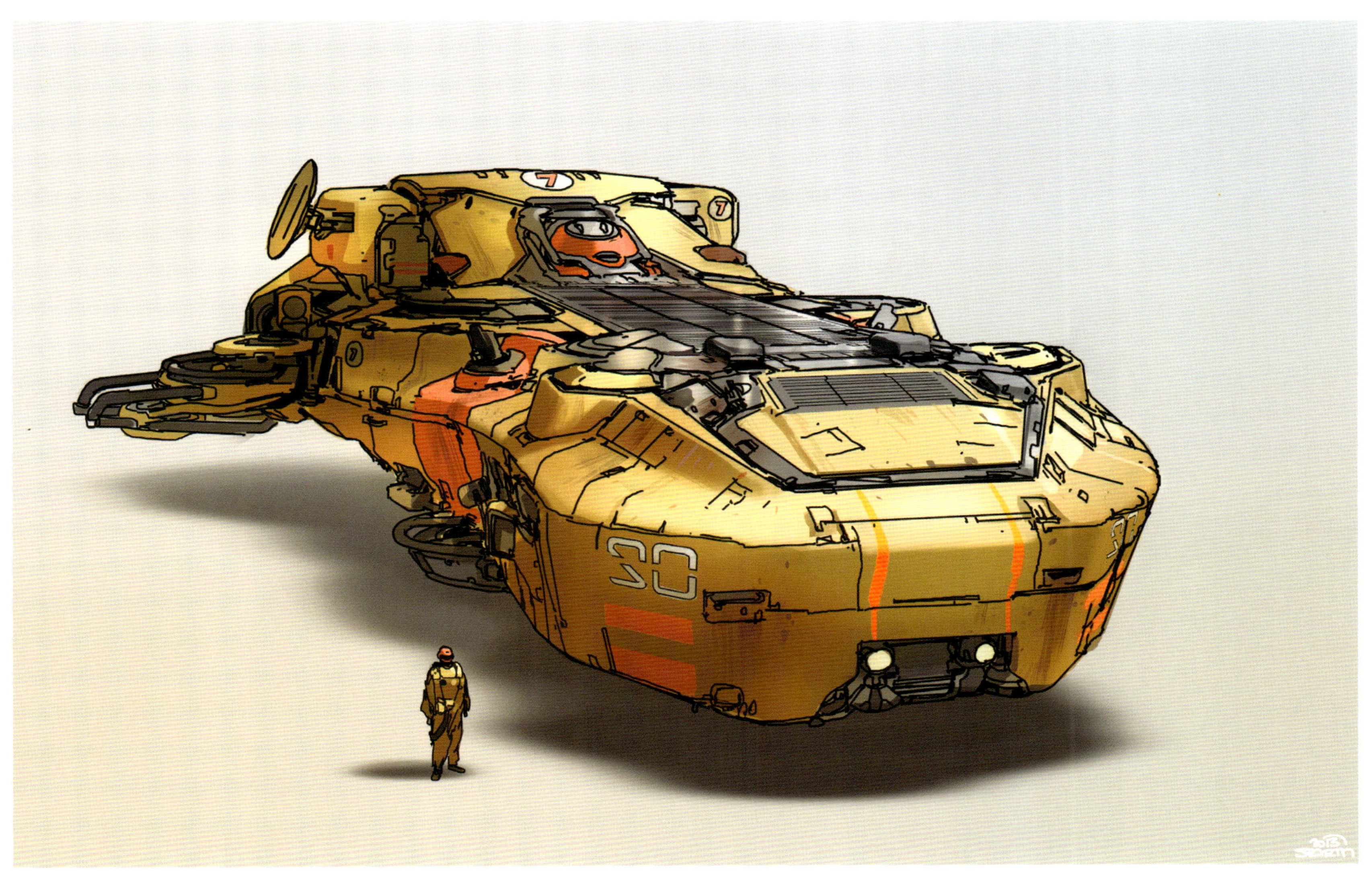

above Small Corvette, 2013
opposite Orange ships, 2013

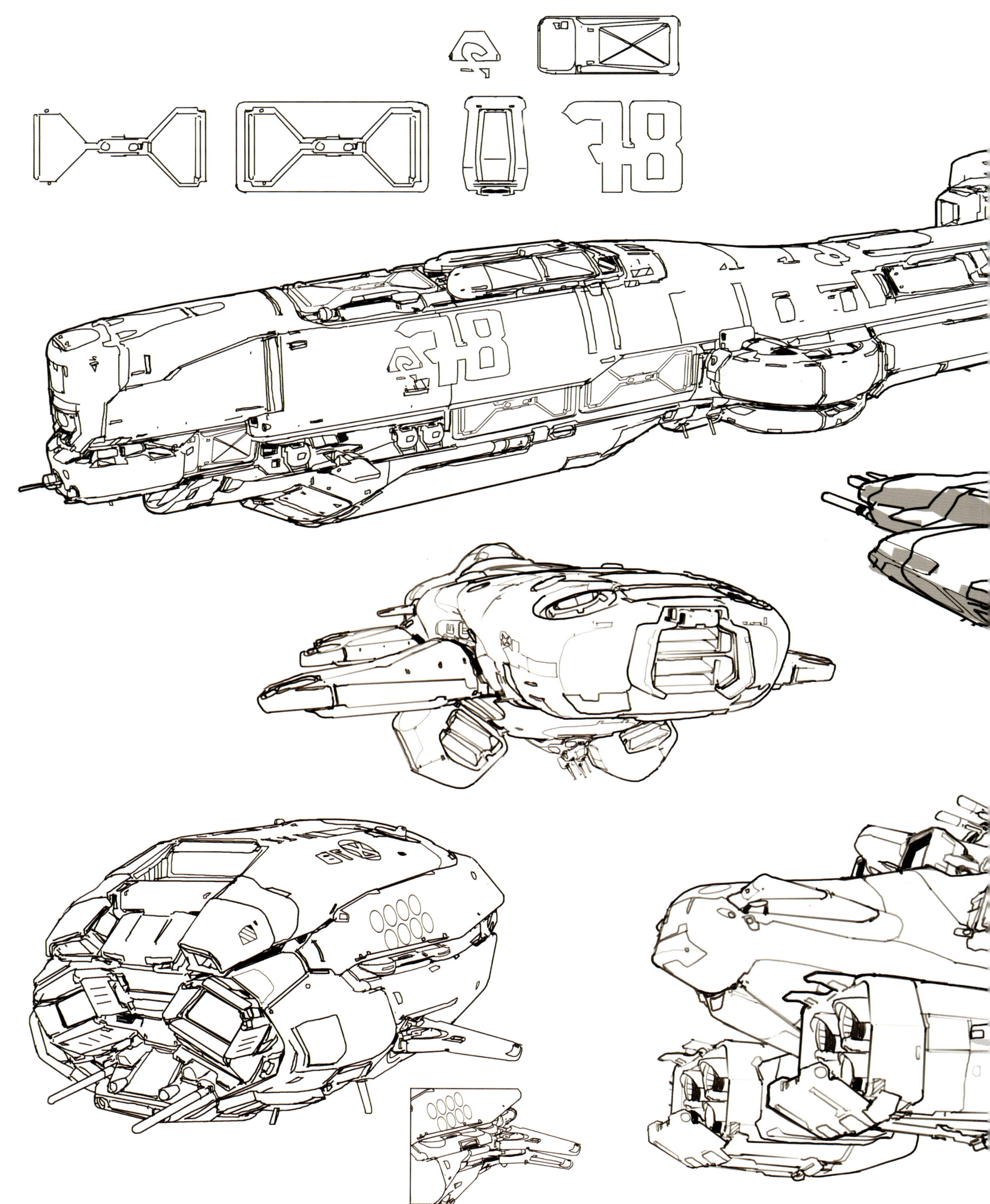

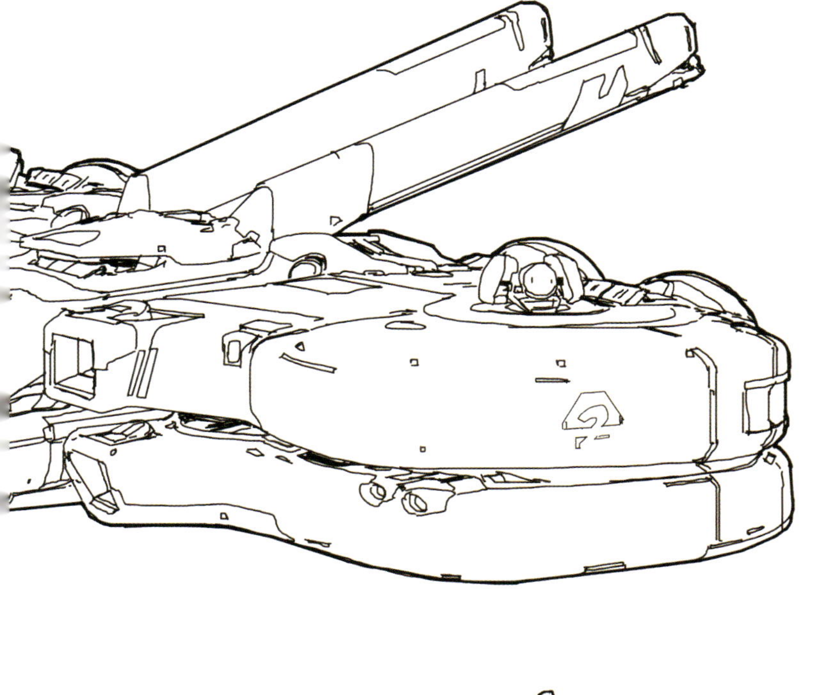

LINE SKETCHES

It is still rare for me to do line work. I have always felt less confident conveying design through simple lines. But it does make a lot of sense when it comes to readability and time constraints.

I usually work in two steps and two layers. On the first layer, I will throw the first sketch in a very loose way. When I feel I have the general shape right, I tone the layer down, and then add a new layer, on which I will redraw the lines in a cleaner way. At the very end, I deactivate the initial "sketch" layer, to obtain a final tighter line work.

When it comes spaceships, I often use bits and pieces of previous sketches, or even patterns and numbers, that I deform according to my needs.

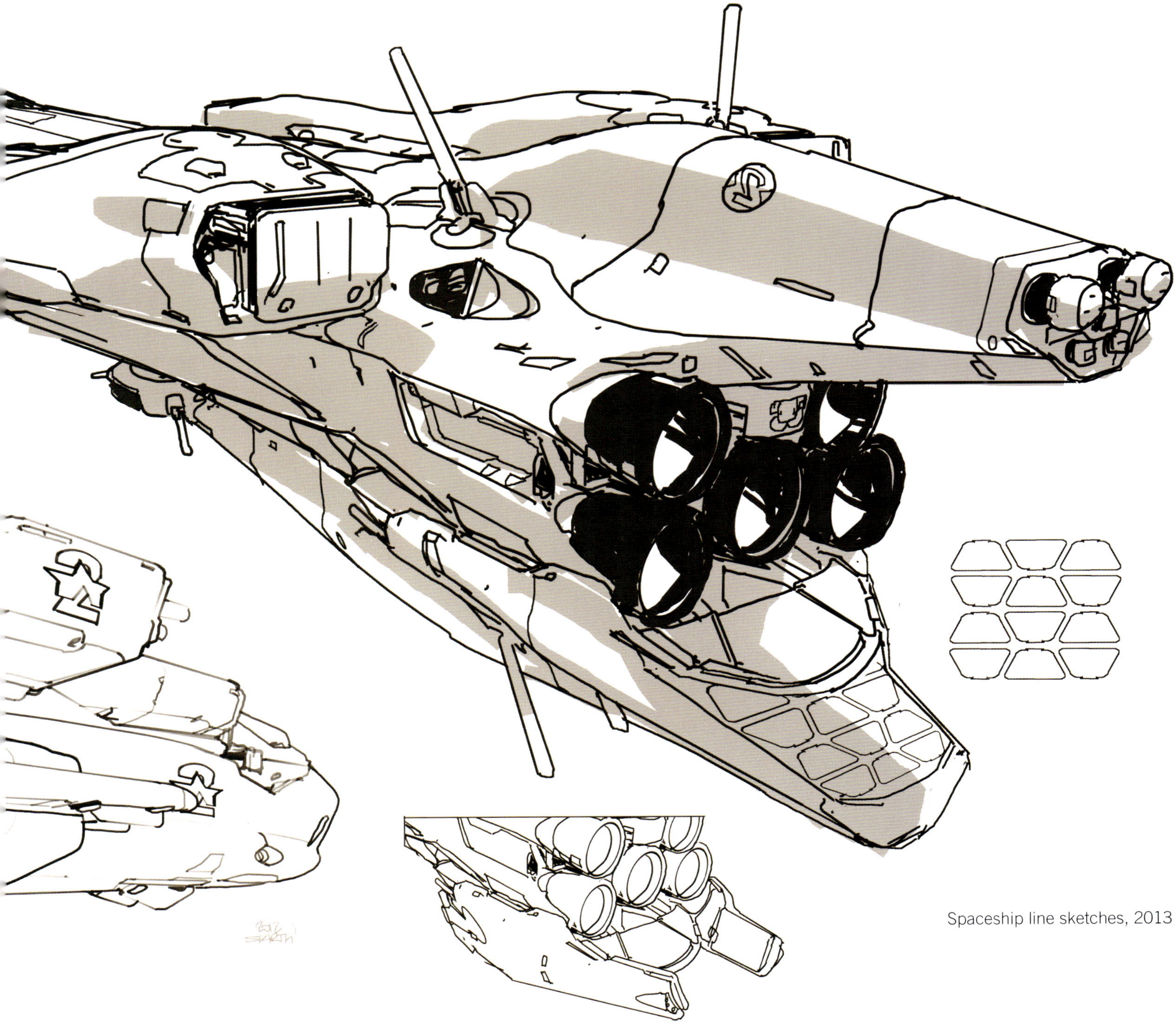

Spaceship line sketches, 2013

I have so much to explain about the digital art explorations I have been experimenting with these last 15 years. Basically, I have always tried to keep the excitement alive through the implementation of changes: Digital art is all about experimenting, testing, breaking things apart, and reconstructing them afterward. It's all about giving fresh materials to the eyes.

There will never be any end to it, since it's tightly connected to the evolution of new art applications and tools hitting the market, not to mention the use of 3-D tools inevitably emerging into the concept art world. But what prevails is the art process based on academic knowledge: shape balance, composition, color theory, narrative themes, and the way we make stylistic decisions to successfully join all these principles together. Beyond the tools and digital techniques, this is truly where the fun begins.

It is nonetheless always insightful to see how artists create their own workflow using a given software. In my case, it's all about Photoshop. This chapter is a mix of technical and artistic tools that I use within Photoshop CS5 and CS6, as well as working habits that are all part of my daily workflow.

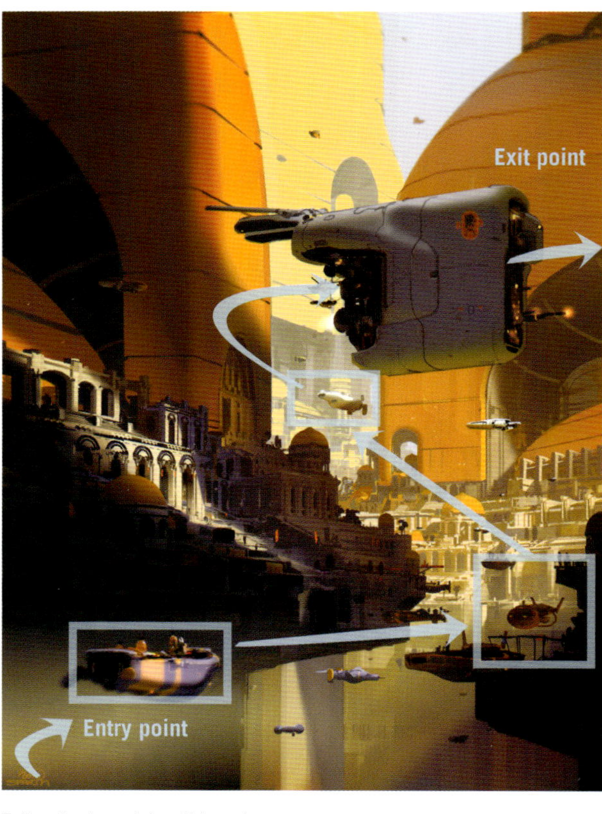

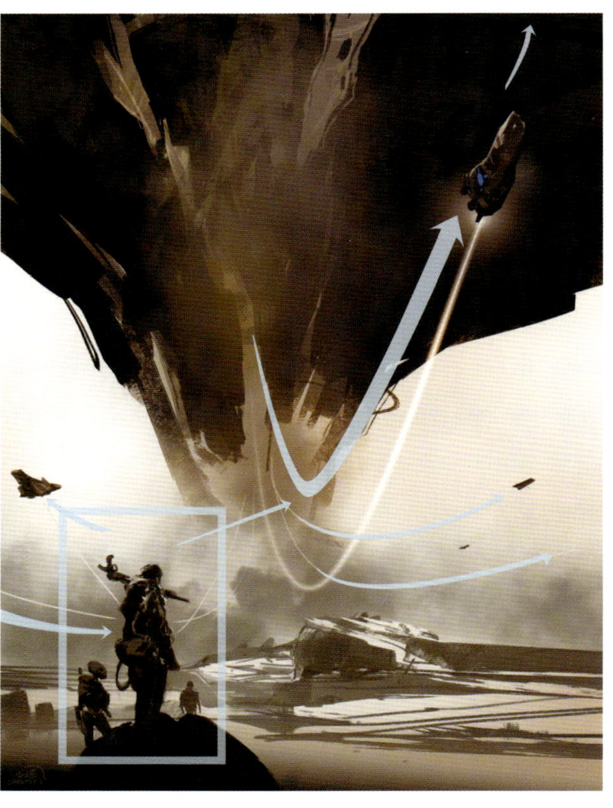

Exit and entry points within an image

COMPOSITION

This is where it all begins, at least for me. I am fascinated by composition. The smart placement of elements within a framed scene is what makes an image successful—rendering comes second. Composition relates to how these elements interact with one another, respecting the rule of thirds, the golden ratio, and implementing what I would call the ubiquitous "visual flow." An image must contain a strong "instant readability" factor, meaning it must be analyzed and understood extremely fast by the viewer. If the eyes want to observe more details in a second read, it's even better, but the first read is the decisive one.

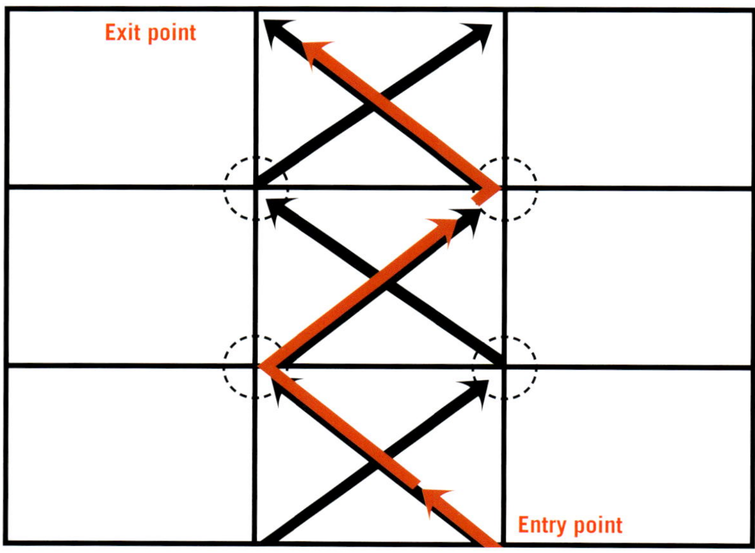

Composition example using the rule of thirds and diagonals

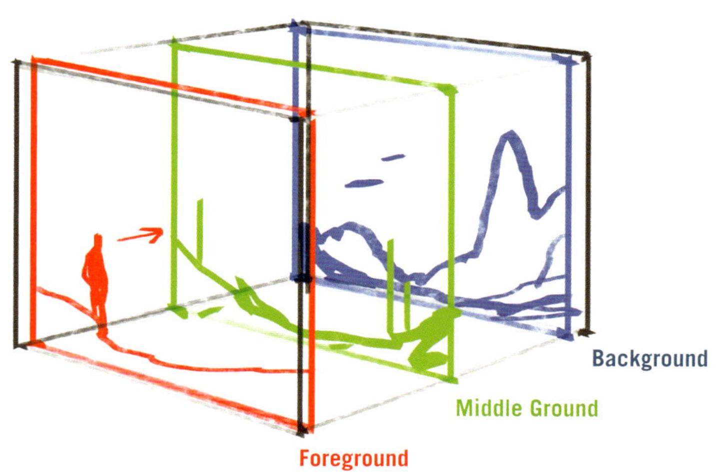

A simple sketch explaining my mental separation of planes

Often I am doing my best to respect this visual flow by always placing an entry point and an exit point in my compositions, with the use of "leading lines" or "guiding lines" within the architecture or the environments to guide the viewer through the image. In the exact same way you would read a sentence in a novel, visual narrative has its own rules based on rhythmical progression and plane differentiation.

This distinct separation of planes is the other element I am always focusing on. With a mental representation, I separate my images into three planes: the foreground, middle ground, and background, where I install my subjects and make them interact. You can have more planes in a composition, as there are no rules ever set in stone. And this applies to all the lessons mentioned in this chapter. Of course, separating planes is a key principle of composition, but you will also need strong perspective knowledge to bind all elements together in order to obtain a cohesive image.

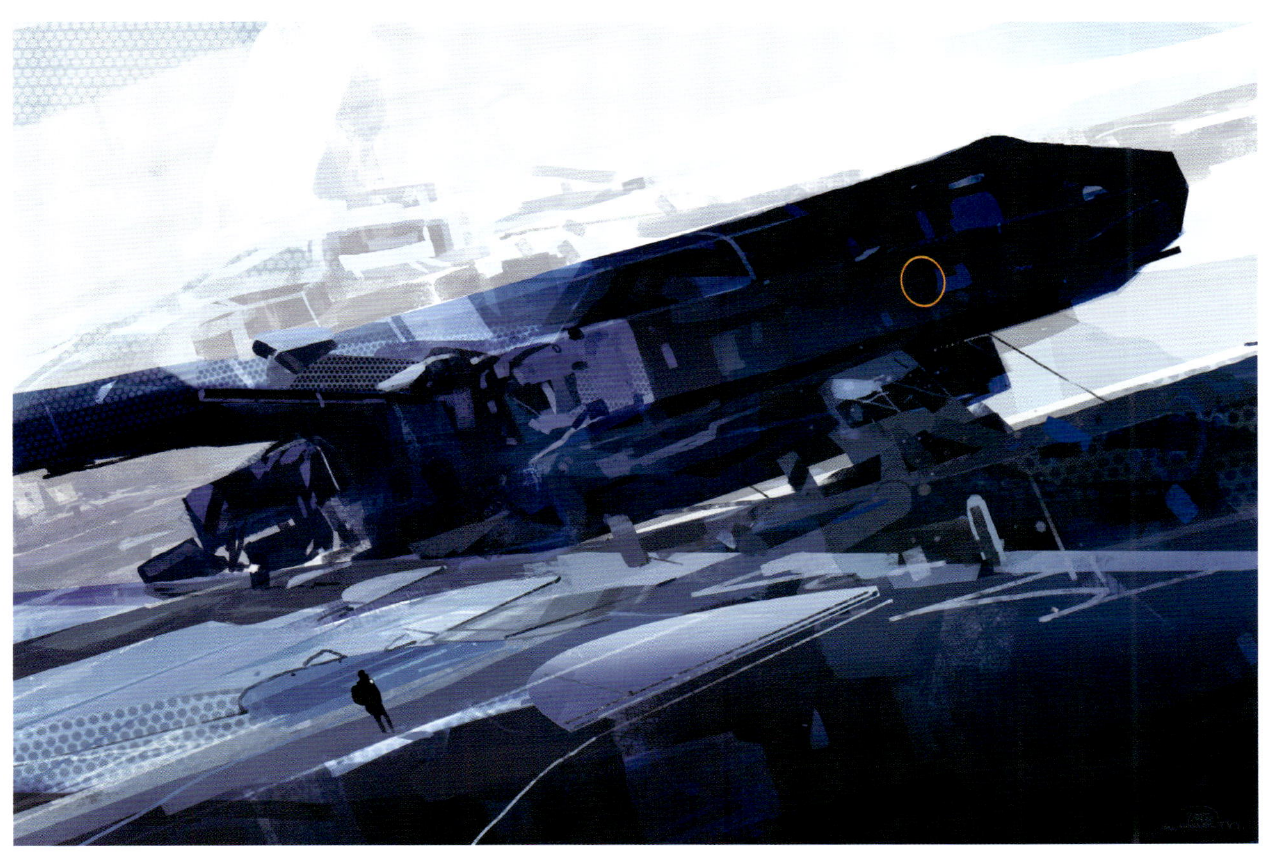

Fast sketch, 2012

COLOR

Complementary tones will help you create compositions with elements that pop. This is the most important principle to respect, but apart from this, it's all about trying to combine theory and practice with talent. The chromatic circle is the key to understanding why specific tones respond with more dynamism compared to others. It is also important to learn the difference between warm tones and cold tones, and how to make them vibrate and interact altogether.

When I switched from traditional to digital painting around 1996, it took me several years to figure out a new workflow for my environment scenes. I was simply unable to transfer my color knowledge from one medium to the other. In theory it's all the same, but in practice, the digital world is so organic by nature that you feel compelled to experiment with multiple layer modes in order to push for a more successful usage of colors. In other words, you can apply all the academic knowledge to the digital side, but messing around with layer modes and adjustments is the best way to push your colors even further, and even reinvent your own creative mechanisms.

During those years, my friend Benjamin Carre helped me to truly understand what was so different about a digital workflow. Stacking layers to randomly find elements that will fit your needs seemed, at first, like an impossible compromise. But with time, you learn to control the accidents, to read within the noise. It's what makes the digital era so fascinating.

INSPIRATION

John Berkey, Ridley Scott, Jeffrey Jones, Vangelis, Stanley Kubrick, Syd Mead, Moebius, Hayao Miyazaki, Katsuhiro Otomo, Ralph McQuarrie, John Harris, Juan Gimenez, Bruce Pennington, Henri Cartier-Bresson, and Craig Mullins—these are the names that automatically come to my mind when I think of inspiration. They are not all artists, but also musicians, directors, and photographers. However, what is most important is to get into the habit of considering the whole world as part of the inspiration process.

Cultures, countries, fashion, or even politics can all be great influencing factors when it comes to design. I personally have always been fascinated by all the space programs that have been organized and ongoing since the '50s, from NASA to the European space programs and the Ariane launches from Kourou, French Guiana. This is what drives my designs, stimulates my visual senses, and encourages me to push my own graphic boundaries further into the unknown.

BRUSHES

You can use brushes in a varied amount of ways: as simple shapes mimicking or emulating real-life paint strokes, or as graphic shapes keeping a digital nature and feel. Most paint software offers a wide selection of both graphic and more painterly options. Unfortunately, graphic brush shapes are often limited to circular or angular forms that artists use with different spacing and rotating parameters. There was an option that was rarely in use back in 2005: complex brushes composed of larger digital or photographic extracts.

The idea was to use brushes as a stamp or pattern tool. I first started experimenting with this technique with a group of concept friends—David Levy, Thierry Doizon, and Sebastien Larroude—while at Ubisoft in Montreal. We were transitioning from *Prince of Persia: Warrior Within* to *Assassin's Creed*, and we had a bit of time to experiment. The goal was to play with the structural accidents within the brushes to obtain random compositions that would then be used as a stable foundation for more rendered concepts. Results were impressive, but the abstract nature of this technique was not always compatible with production work, where you are requested to concept images based on predetermined narratives. Dealing with abstract elements can expand creativity, but pulling the images back into concrete grounds can be tricky. It was nonetheless a technique we used for years, and that the concept art community wholeheartedly adopted.

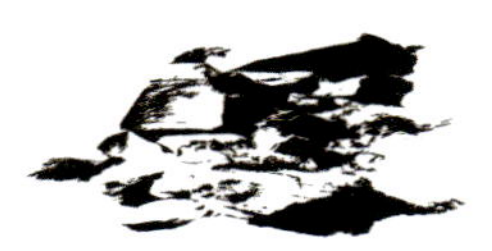
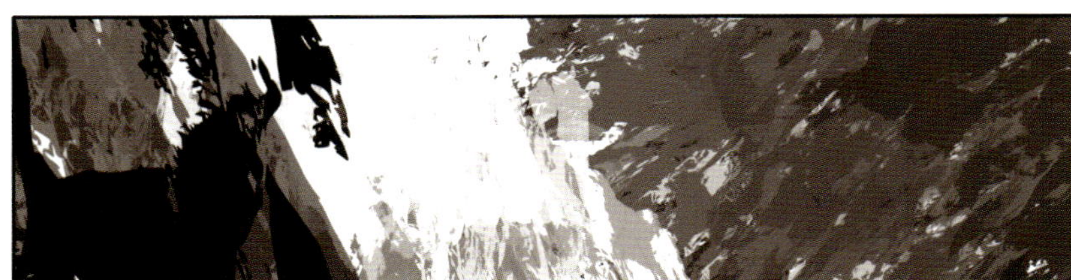
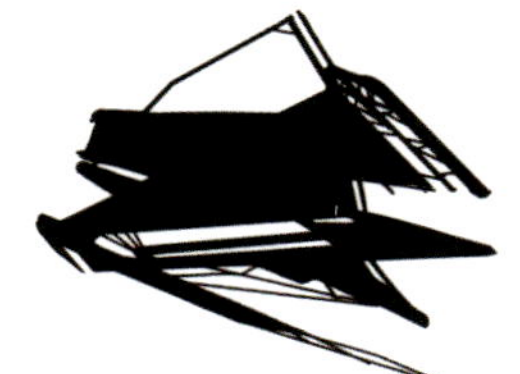
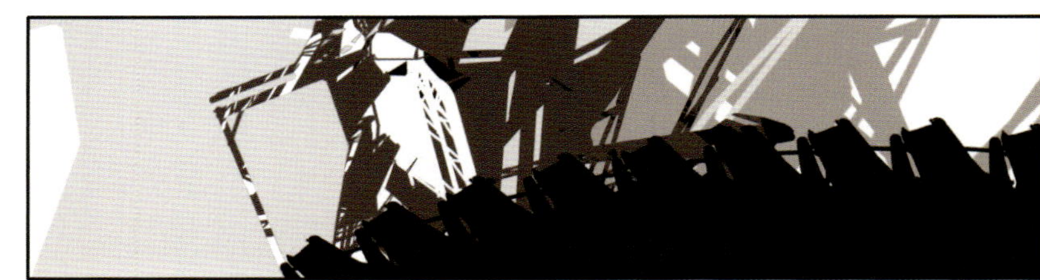

right Complex brushes
far right Examples of their application

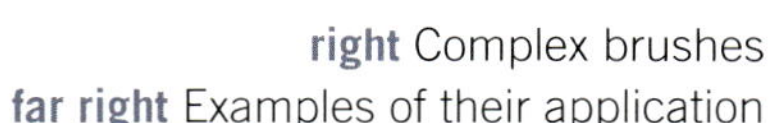
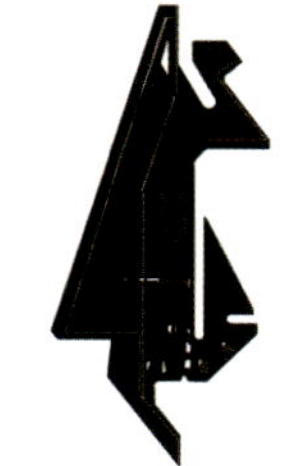
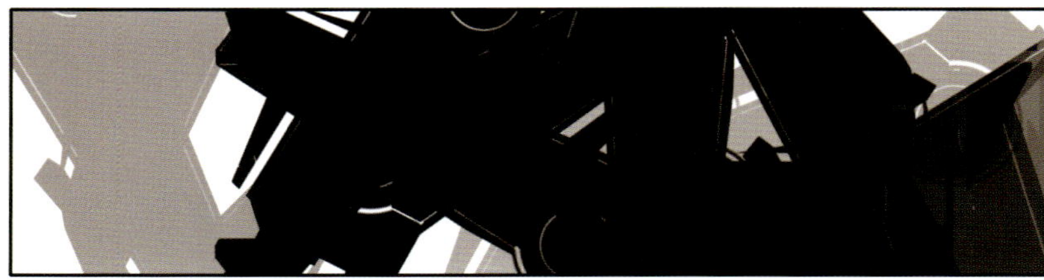
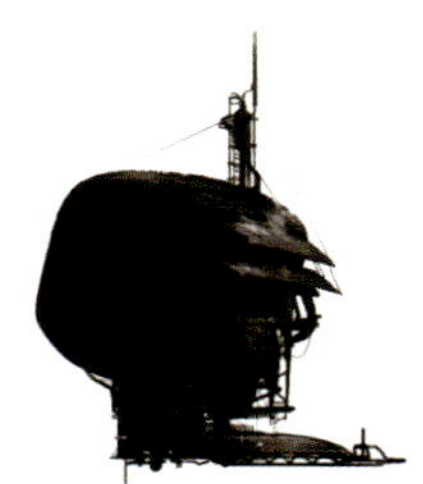
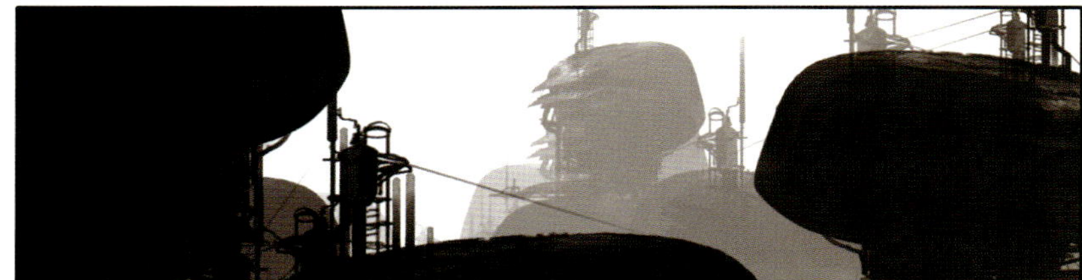
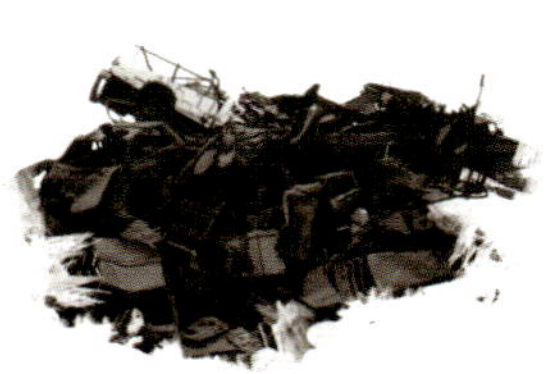
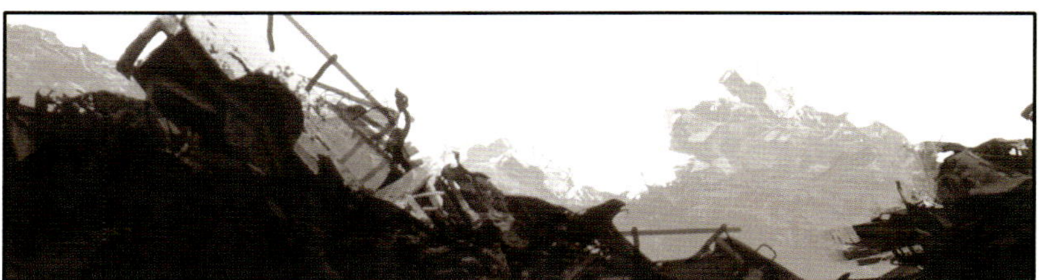

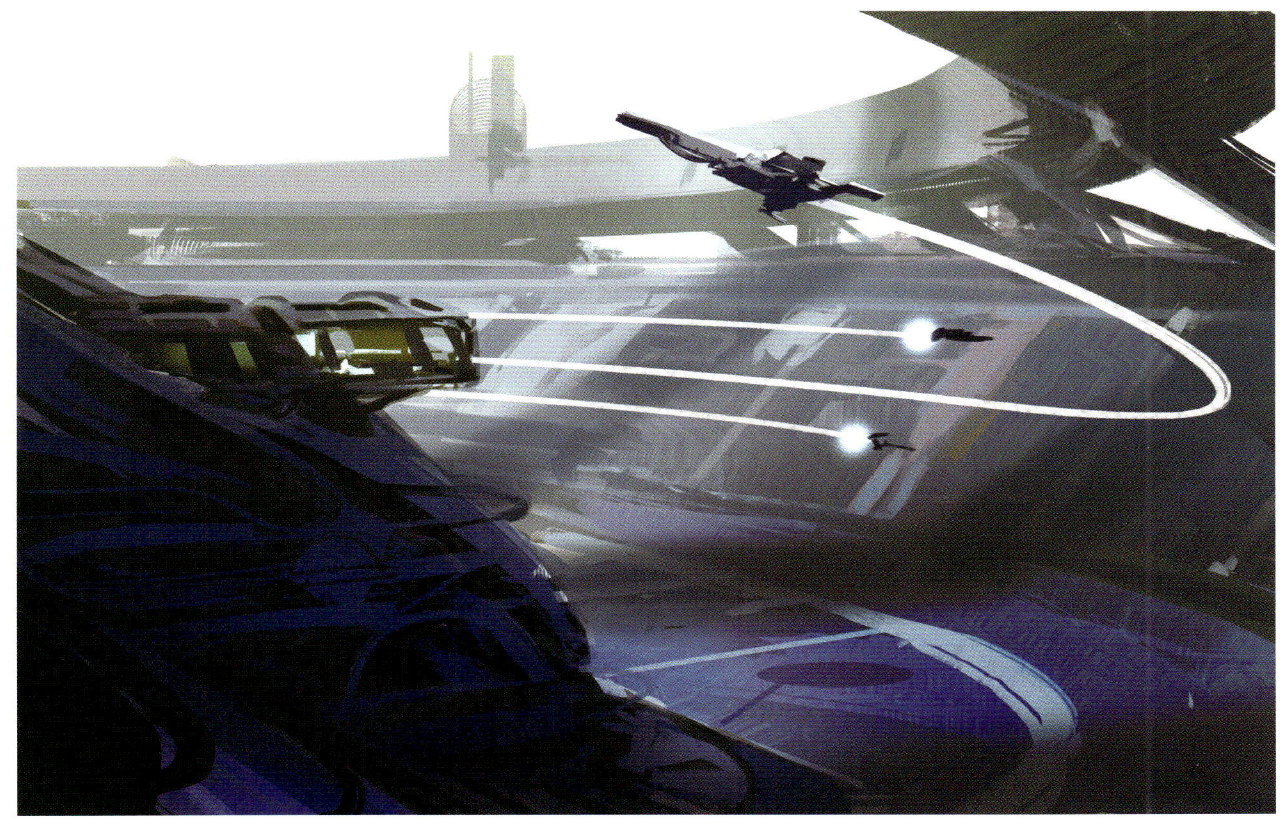

Race sketch, 2013

BRUSH BALANCE

In my opinion, a selection of three to six brushes are more valuable than a set of 30. The reason for this is that you want the viewer's eyes to find patterns and echoing elements throughout the image. If the eyes cannot rely on these echoes, the visual hopping will be nonexistent. Think of it as installing smaller compositions within the larger composition. And it works even better when you add custom shapes or other painting tricks into the mix. It gives more variations to the final image, and this is exactly what the eyes need. I am, of course, aware that a lot of artists will obtain great results out of 50 brushes or more, so this has to do with a personal choice, nothing else.

DESIGN

Design is at the very root of any concept creation. There are infinite ways to define what design is, but when applied to concept art, I would personally describe it as the research of a perfect equilibrium between aesthetic and function within the elaboration of an object, scene, or environment. Whenever I have the task to concept an object, I focus on what the object is used for as well as how it functions. This function will then have an impact on its shape. Let's take the example of a flying vehicle: What is its propulsion method, wingspan, and number of passengers going to be? Will it have wings at all or other particularities? All these parameters will have a definite incidence on its aesthetics. With all these constraints in mind, I apply each new line or stroke of paint, constantly asking myself new questions related to shape and forms in order to stay focused until I am satisfied with the result.

When it comes to design balance, there is also a lot to explain. To be brief, I always explore a new design by keeping in mind a personal golden ratio that I call the "70/30 rule." It simply stipulates that a set of shapes must always contain some type of hierarchy in order to maintain a strong dynamic. The final goal is to always surprise the eyes with pleasing variations and avoid monotony.

If I take the example of a spaceship made of metal platings, for example, this means I would apply the same protective carapace on about 70 percent of its surface, and dedicate the remaining 30 percent to showing more of the internal elements, like

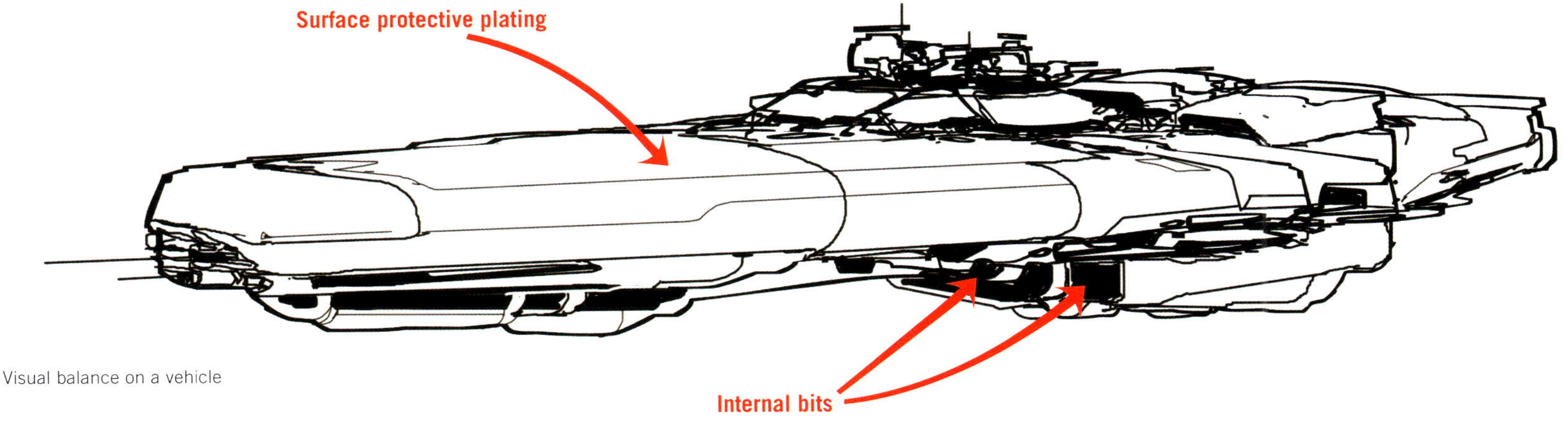

Visual balance on a vehicle

pieces of machinery, valves, or thrusters. This emphasizes the variety among the exterior and interior elements of the vehicle and creates a more pleasing contrast to the overall shape, especially if you apply a darker tone for the interior features.

This 70/30 rule is nothing else than a personal interpretation of the golden ratio combined with the "rule of odds," which stipulates that an odd number of elements within a scene (for example, three, five, or seven) will emphasize dynamic. You still have cases where symmetrical proportions will have a huge impact depending on the composition and narrative intent, so we should never rule out symmetry as a design intent. Rules exist to propose an ideal solution to graphic problem solving. Treating them as a set of constraints would be an error.

Finally, I wanted to discuss "multilayering," or "multilayered objects," a design concept I probably apply to everything I create within the boundaries of science fiction. The idea is simple: I always try to imply that my objects, vehicles, or weapons are made of multiple layers, and I deliberately focus on showing these features whenever I can. An object made of a single layer of material will be, by definition, dull. But if you reveal more of the interior of a vehicle, through cracks, seams, and other visible lines properly integrated to the design, you add to the mystery. You also give the viewer "more to see" in terms of storytelling elements.

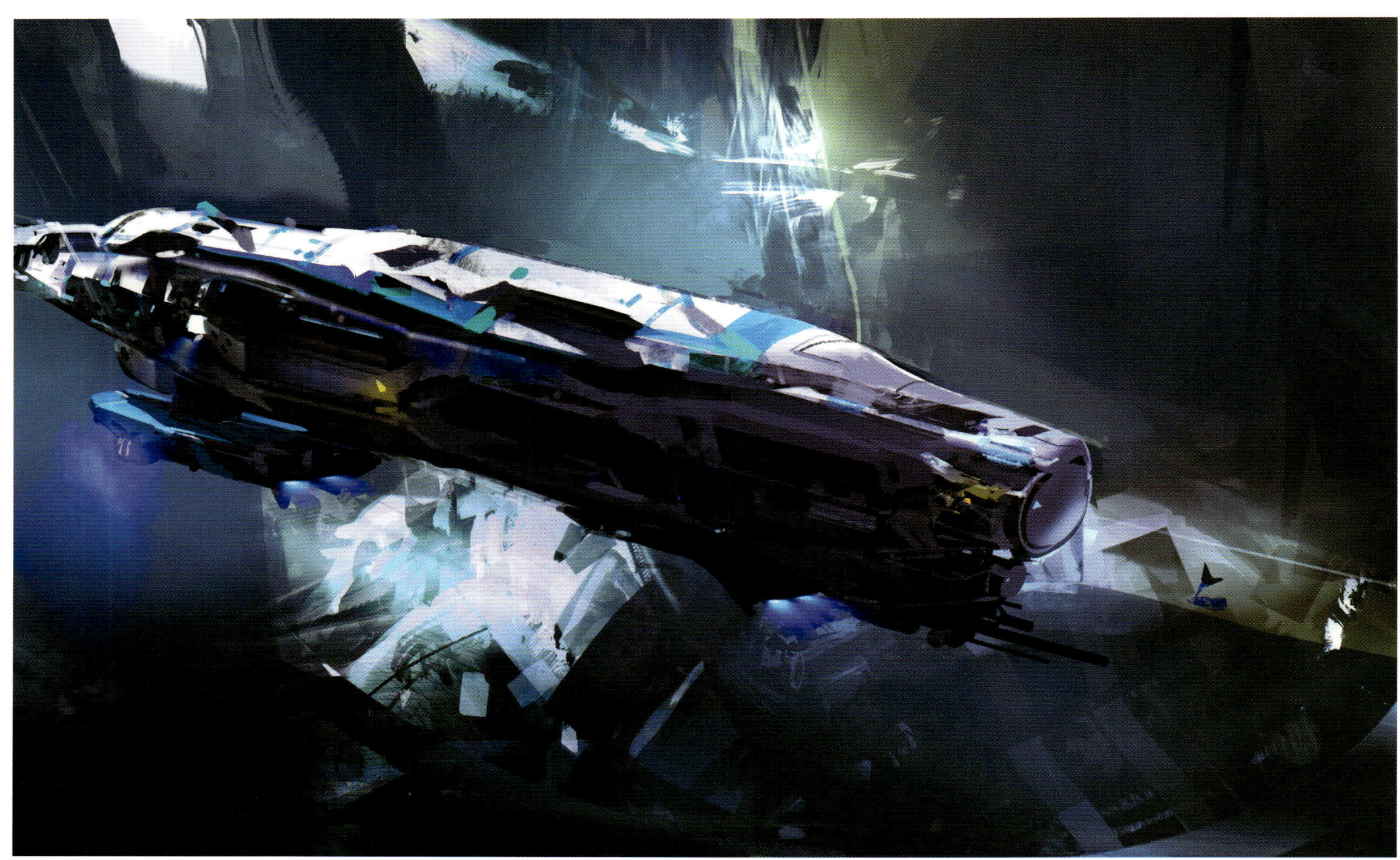

Spaceship sketch, 2012

HORIZONTAL AND VERTICAL FLIP

I have been using these two shortcuts for years. The first shortcut is to flip my canvas horizontally; the second, to flip it vertically, so the image will be upside down. Both can easily be done in Photoshop. The reasoning behind taking these actions is that our eyes often get into a dangerous routine whenever we are painting, and this routine needs to be interrupted at times. It's the exact same method as when we were putting our sketches in front of a mirror to spot potential errors, but more convenient.

Flipping your canvas has the same effect as rebooting your brain, and teaches you to spot the anatomical or perspective issues you would otherwise not pay attention to. It's a vital habit that I have been using a lot. I probably flip my canvas every three or four minutes, to the point that I often forget which side was the initial side I started with!

The vertical flipping is a bit less critical, but still very informative for composition purposes. When you look at your image upside down, you instantly forget about all the storytelling elements within your scene, to only focus on the balance of shapes and contrasts. This is valuable, as you may guess, since these same narrative elements can sometimes negatively influence your composition.

CUSTOM SHAPES

I started experimenting with custom shapes in Photoshop with my friend Thom Scholes in 2010. We wanted to benefit from a very graphic technique that would allow us to obtain extremely sharp edges to counterbalance the more painterly brushes in our sets. Thom had started investigating different layer styles and effects with fascinating results. Later on, our explorations ended up in the Custom Shape Tool window, where we rapidly added our first shapes representing rocks and other natural elements. Prebuilt custom shapes were often used by the graphic design world, but at first glance, its usefulness for concept art was far from obvious.

As it turned out, it worked admirably well for environments and landscapes, so we pushed our research to the point of obtaining several libraries of shapes for architecture and natural organic elements. I now regularly use custom shapes as a complementary technique to my regular brushes. You can actually select and then move custom shapes around by simultaneously pressing the space bar, which is a big advantage since you can position them anywhere in the canvas. You unfortunately cannot flip a custom shape, but I bypass this omission by flipping the whole canvas instead, thanks to my horizontal flip shortcut.

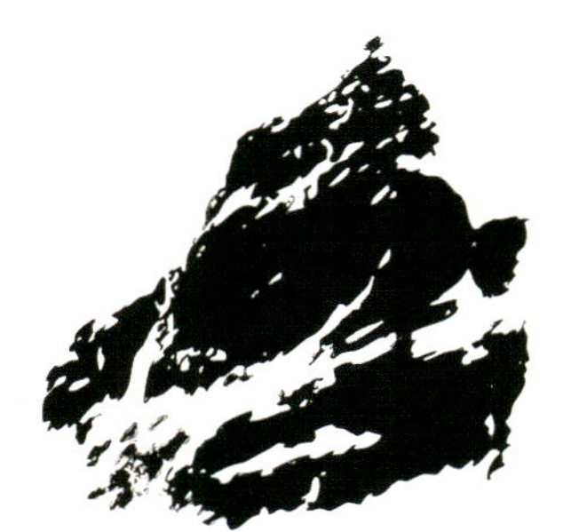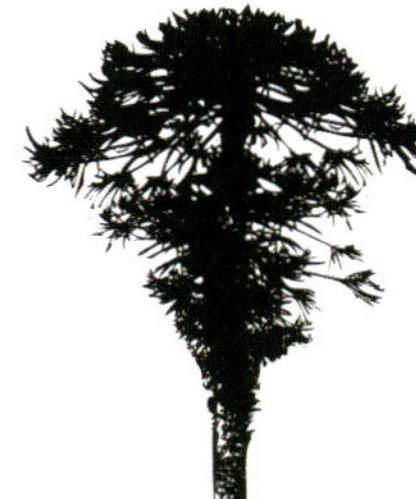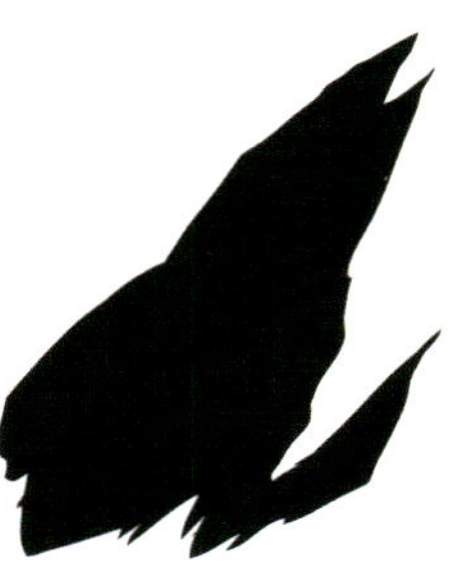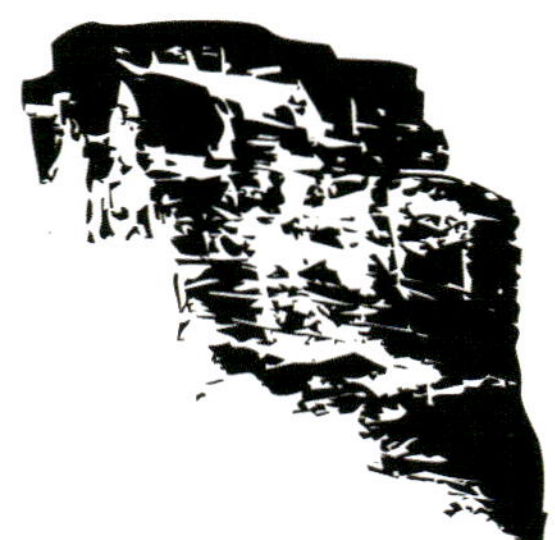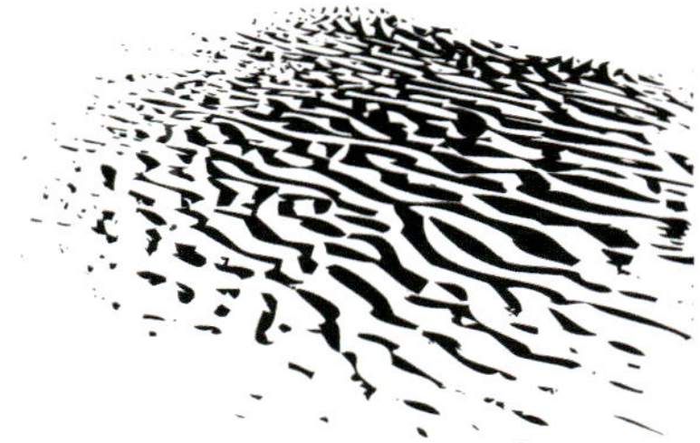

Custom shape examples

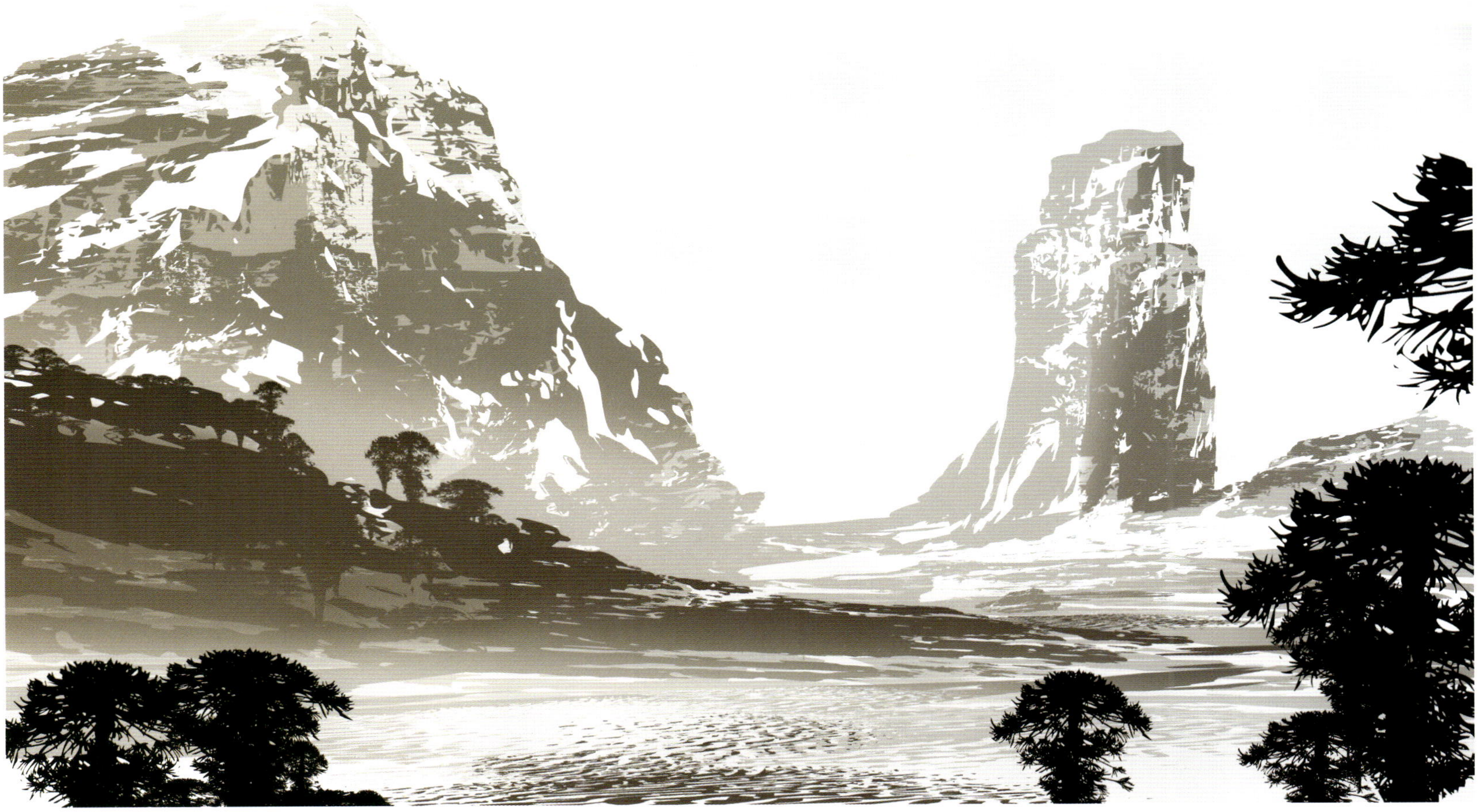

Five-minute sketch with five custom shapes

I mostly use the Smudge Tool as a displacement technique to move around small or large chunks of the image I am working on. It's a vital method when it comes to tight production conditions, as it's extremely fast and practical. The only constraint is to put the smudge strength at 100 percent. Using a square brush is usually very effective, but any brush shape will do the trick. It's all about stretching and moving pixels around.

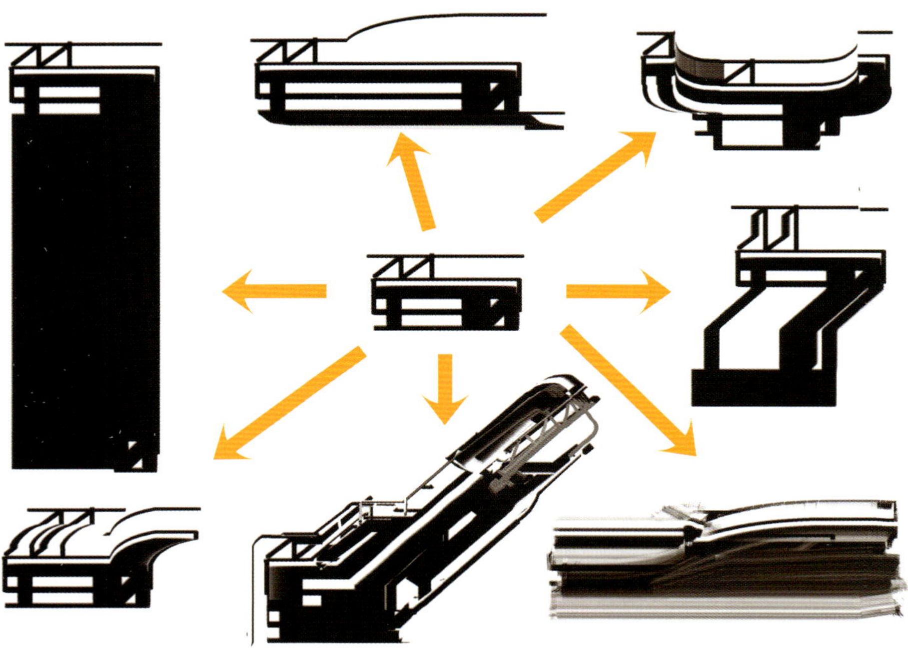

The smudge displacement technique

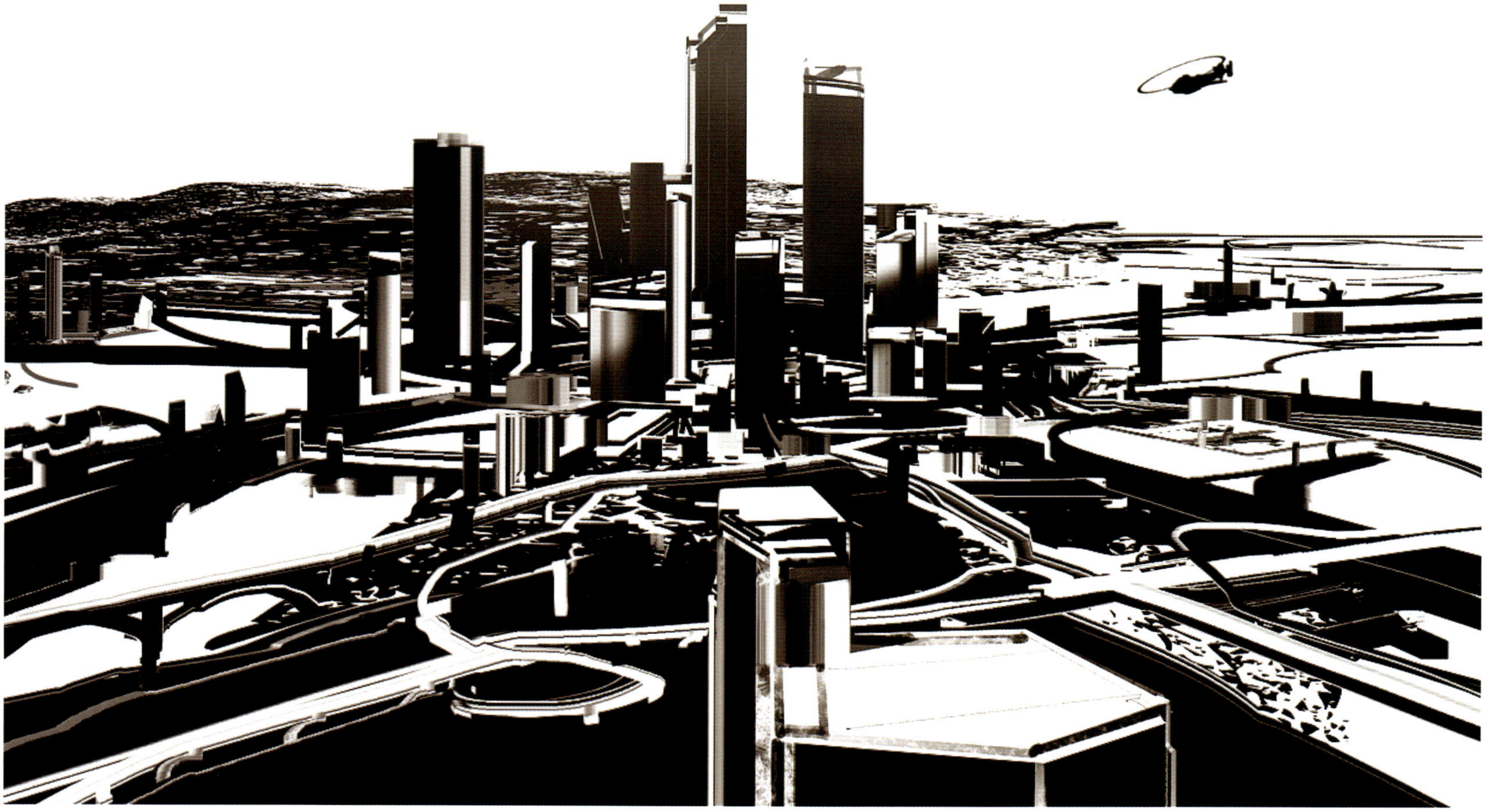

Fast city concept using the Smudge Tool

TEMPLATE TECHNIQUES

In order to speed up my painting process, I also had the idea in 2012 to build myself several template sheets containing elements from previous personal illustrations. This technique was compatible with the construction/deconstruction philosophy I had already experimented in the past, and I tested it on a larger scale by completing several illustrations using only these sheets.

The advantage of using extracts from previous design bits instead of photographs was that these source materials already contained my design language, and the integration process and rendering was extremely simplified as a result. You can also easily stretch and sculpt these bits to your convenience, applying them to the canvas with the appropriate perspective.

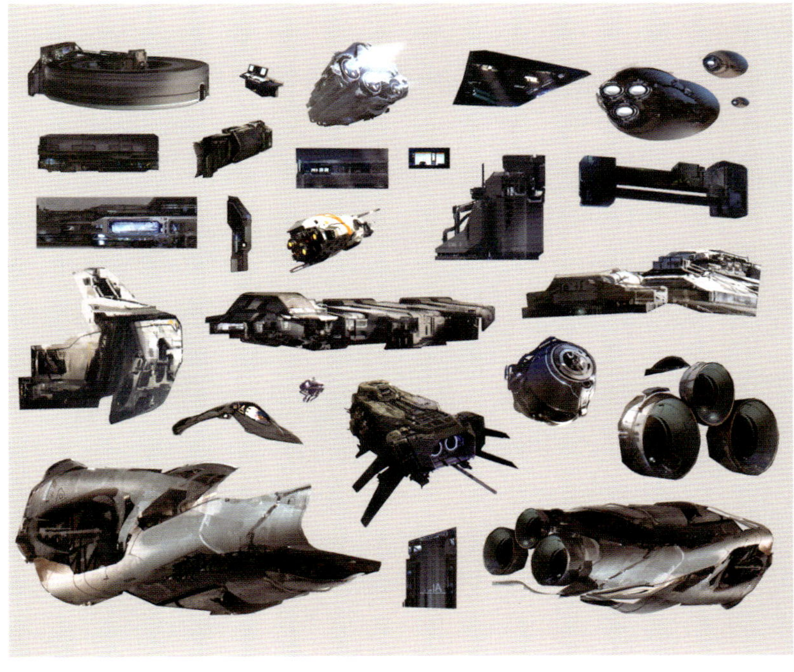

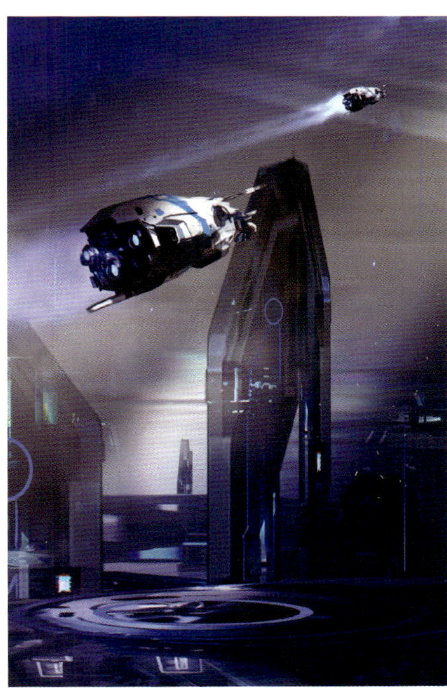

left to right
Personal template sheet
Template sketch, 2012
bottom
Vaisseau, 2012

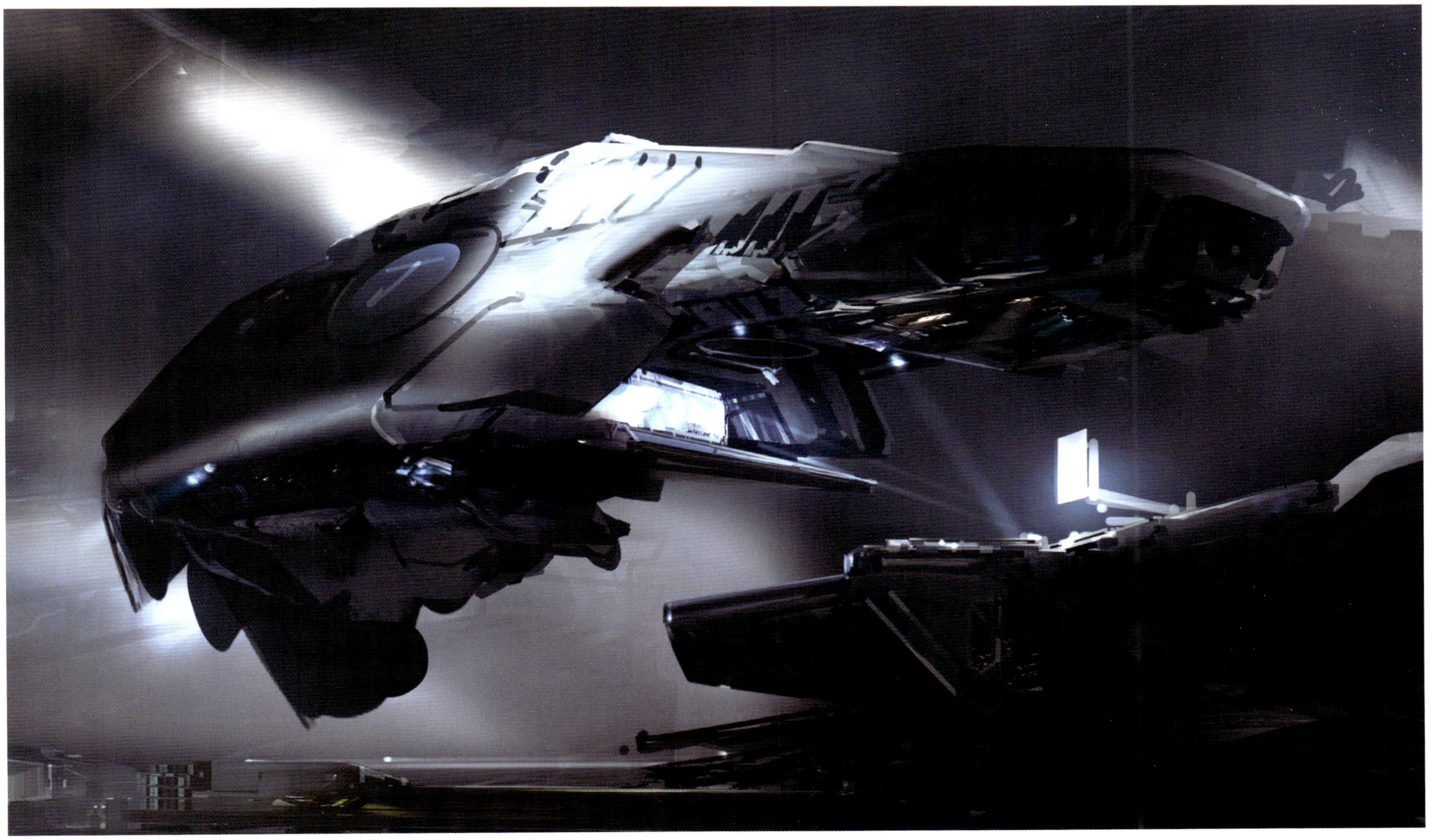

PERSPECTIVE TECHNIQUE

Painting in perspective can be a difficult challenge, and it also requires a lot of time. The simplest option is to use a prebuilt perspective grid that you put underneath your canvas, but another option is to paint everything flat at first, in order to deform it later on with the adequate perspective. In the case of a spaceship, for example, I generally start elaborating a basic structure without too many details. Once I get a general successful silhouette, I then apply the perspective deformation. The last step consists of moving the shapes around to adapt to the new chosen angle. It's tricky at first, but it gets easier when you add the Smudge Tool into the workflow.

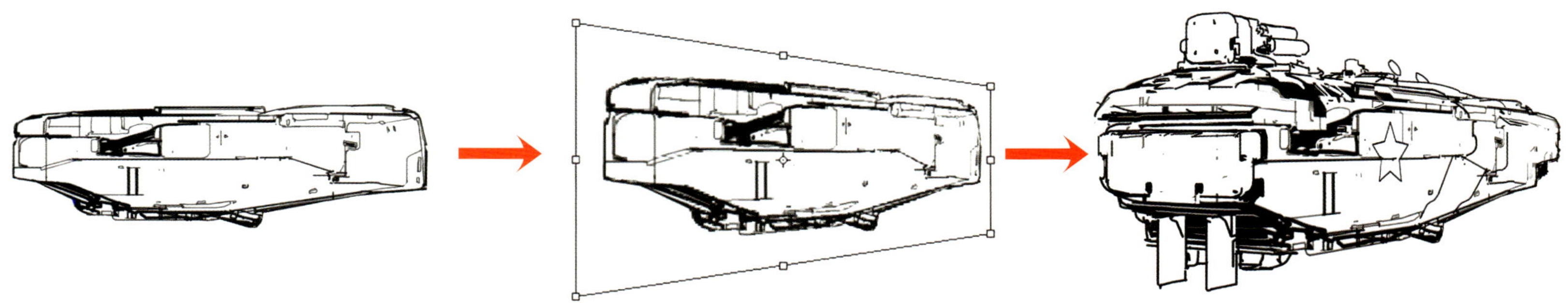

Using perspective with a flat design

LIGHTEN MODE TECHNIQUE

For weapon and vehicle design, I have been using a very simple technique based on the superimposition of two layers, with the one on top in Lighten mode. By moving the top layer around, you can create an infinite amount of design possibilities. True, you must rely on abstraction to spot visual features that make sense. But, again, once you get into the habit of it, you can quickly improve how fast you select the elements that count. Abstraction can provide a fabulous source of valuable materials.

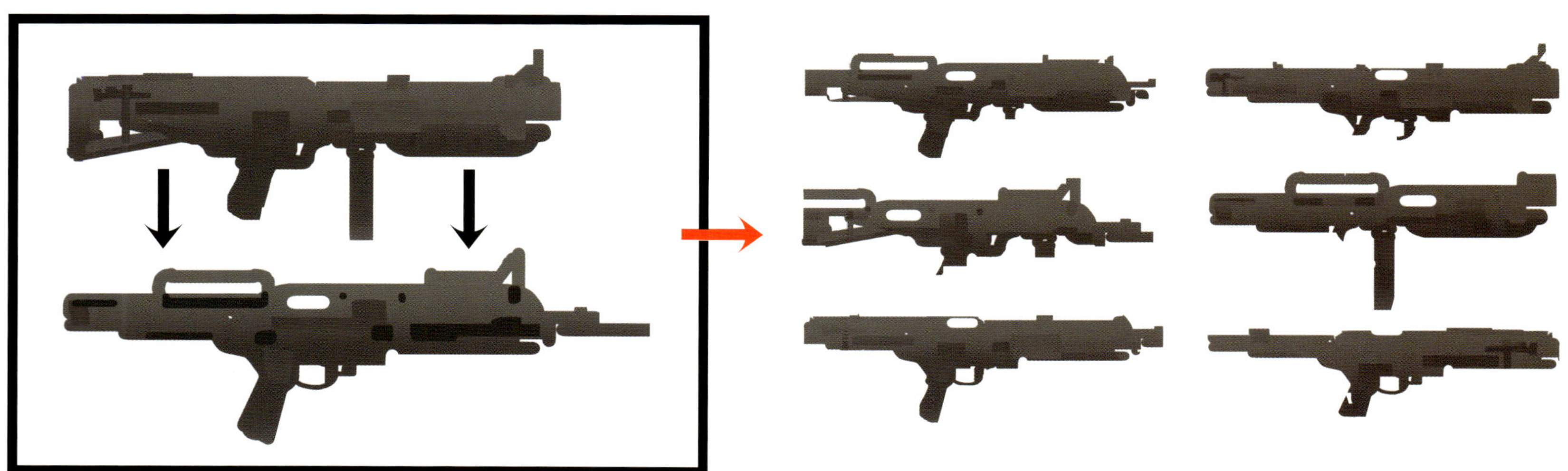

Weapon design example using the Lighten layer mode

DESIGN NOTES

When I'm about 70 or 80 percent into the creation of an image, I often force myself to pause in order to analyze what is left to do to bring a particular concept to completion. The first step is to completely remove my eyes from the image, in order to, once again, break the routine. After 15 minutes or so, I sit back in front of my computer, and start to mentally enumerate all the elements that need to be either perfected or completed. I then proceed to write them down on a Post-it Note, one after the other. My computer screen is often surrounded by these yellow notes: "careful with front subject not being detached enough," "add some atmosphere in the upper sky," or "fix perspective on upper building." I have a very wandering mind, so this is always helpful!

It's a very satisfying process, as it allows you to acknowledge the fact you are nearly done with the heavy bulk of your image, and that it's time to switch to the final rendering phase. It is actually during this phase that I often allow myself to flatten the whole image in order to be sure I will not be tempted to go back to sublayers for further modifications.

TABLET VS WACOM CINTIQ

I often have friends or coworkers asking me why I prefer using a conventional tablet compared to a more advanced Cintiq. The answer is quite simple but definitely interesting. The first time I actually tested a tablet was in Paris in 1993, and I wasn't really convinced. I still ended up buying one in 1996, but it took me another three years to adapt and obtain satisfying results.

The appeal of the tablet is that your hand is located outside the canvas area. It's no longer in your visual pathway leading to your monitor. It allows me to focus on the canvas alone, with no outside distractions. The hand and the way you apply strokes are still important, of course, but what remains is a strict connection between your eyes and the canvas. With years of use, I simply got used to it. It became so natural to paint without seeing my hand, that it sometimes feels awkward sketching with a real pen.

As a concept artist, I have always been fascinated by the idea that I was painting with my eyes, that my brain was tightly connected to a more mental virtual process, and that my hand had become secondary. If I had to switch to a Cintiq, that means I would have to reverse all these habits. I can nonetheless acknowledge the advantages of the Cintiq especially when it comes to making more precise digital sketches.

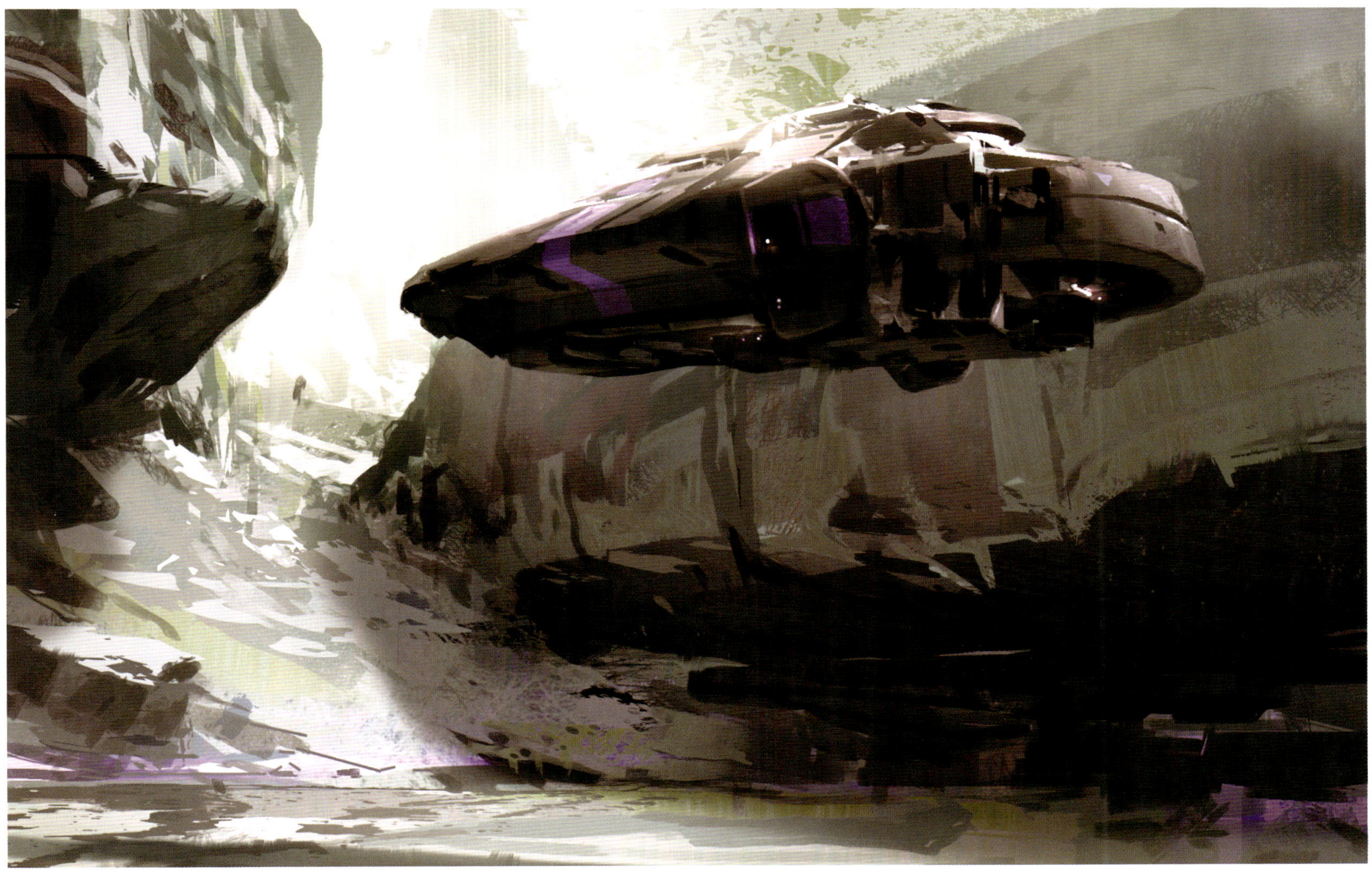

Fast design research, 2013

BRUSH TEST

I wanted to finish this section with a final brush test. When it comes to brushes, it's all about testing. I often grab a few, and see how they interact. I have this bad habit of never finishing these experiments, and end up with folders and folders of "work in progress" images that I rarely share. I try to convince myself that all these experiments are part of a larger picture.

COLONIE

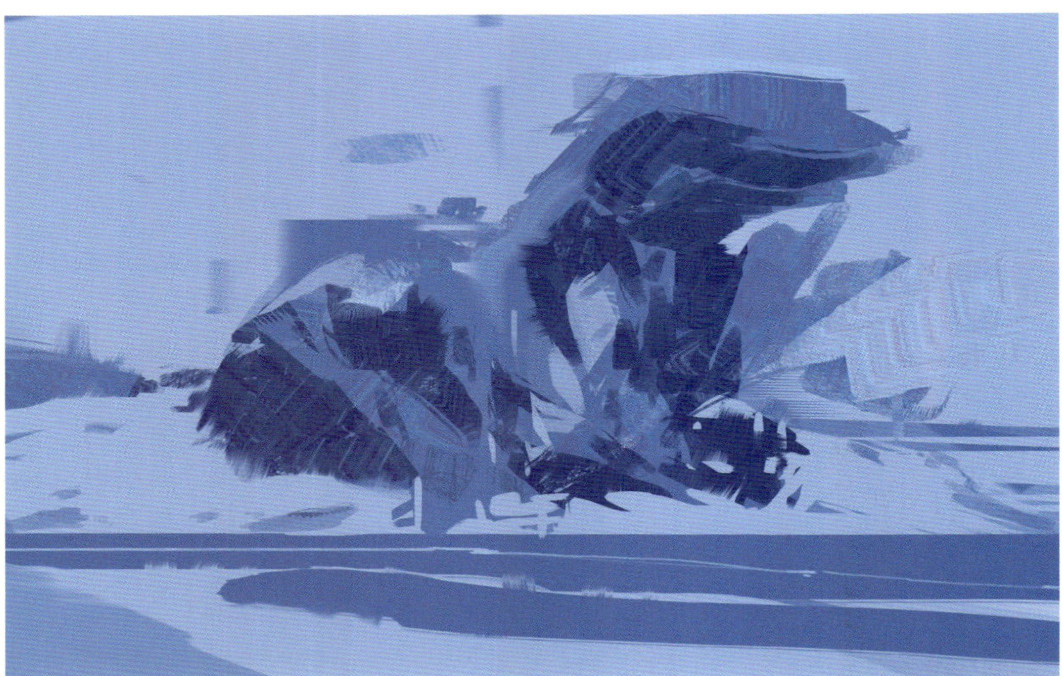

BASIC BLOCKING

I start this Space Opera piece with a mix of environment brushes and custom shapes. The main brush I am using is with the Color Dynamics option on, adding abstract texturing and tones to the canvas. You can also notice the very hard edge coming from the custom shapes in some areas. My goal here is to obtain the best balance and interaction between abstract textures, tones, and shapes.

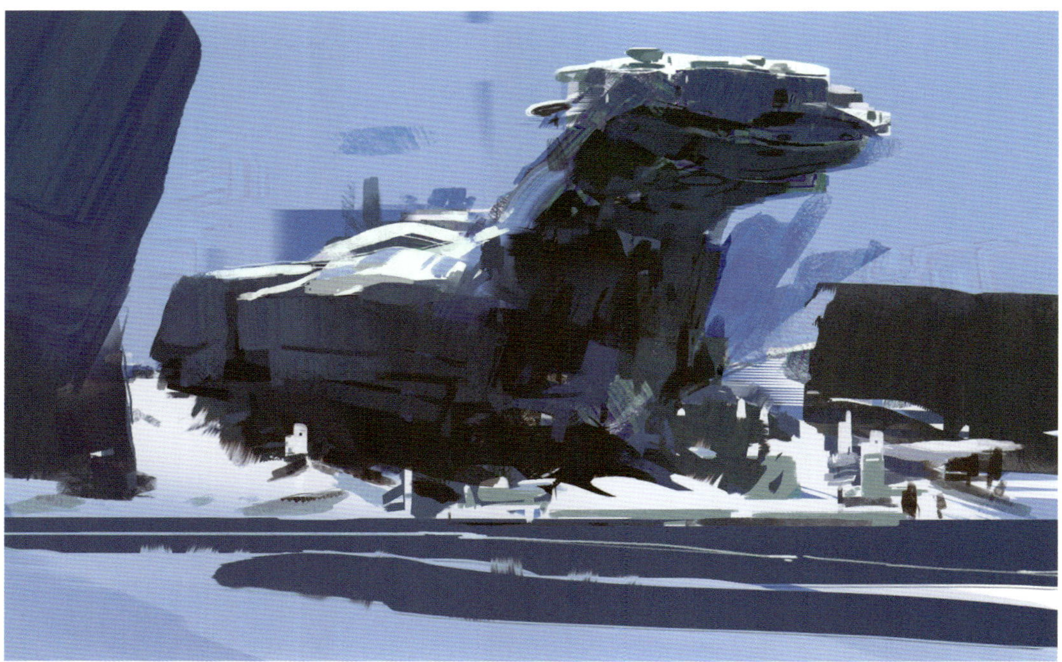

AUTO TONE

The Auto Tone option in Photoshop is a great way to play with new surprising contrasts and values. In this case, I applied it to all layers at once, and erased it in the less effective areas. I am also starting to determine the ground area that now looks like snow, until the next passes.

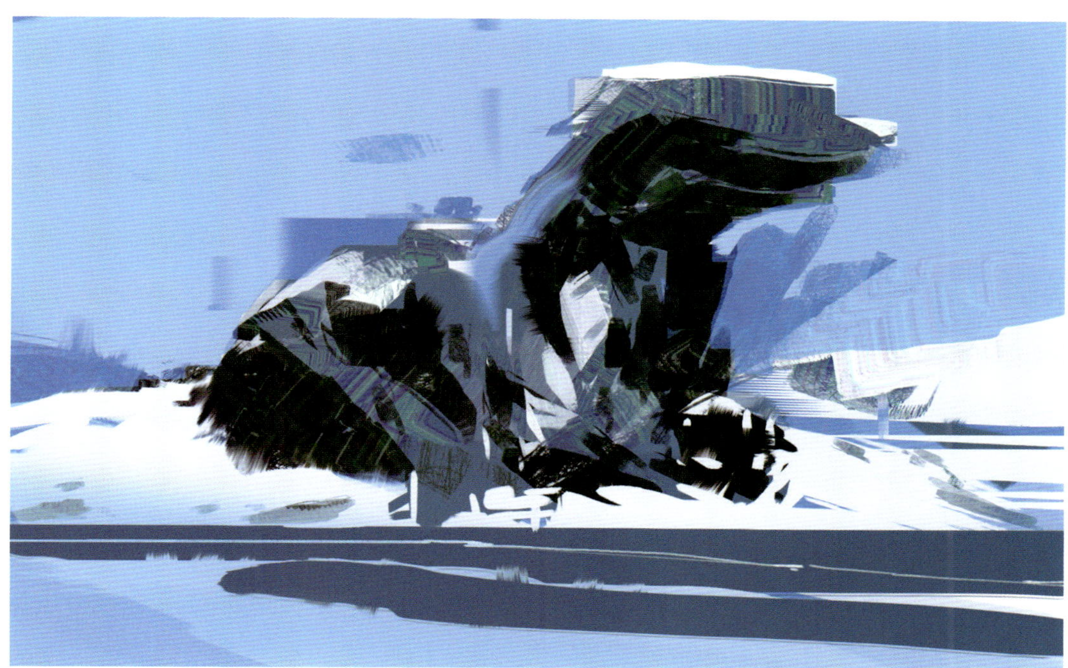

ABSTRACT VOLUMES

I am continuing to add volumes to perfect the composition. Though you can already understand the scene as a large environment, everything is still very undetermined. I straddle the fine line between the figurative and the abstract a lot.

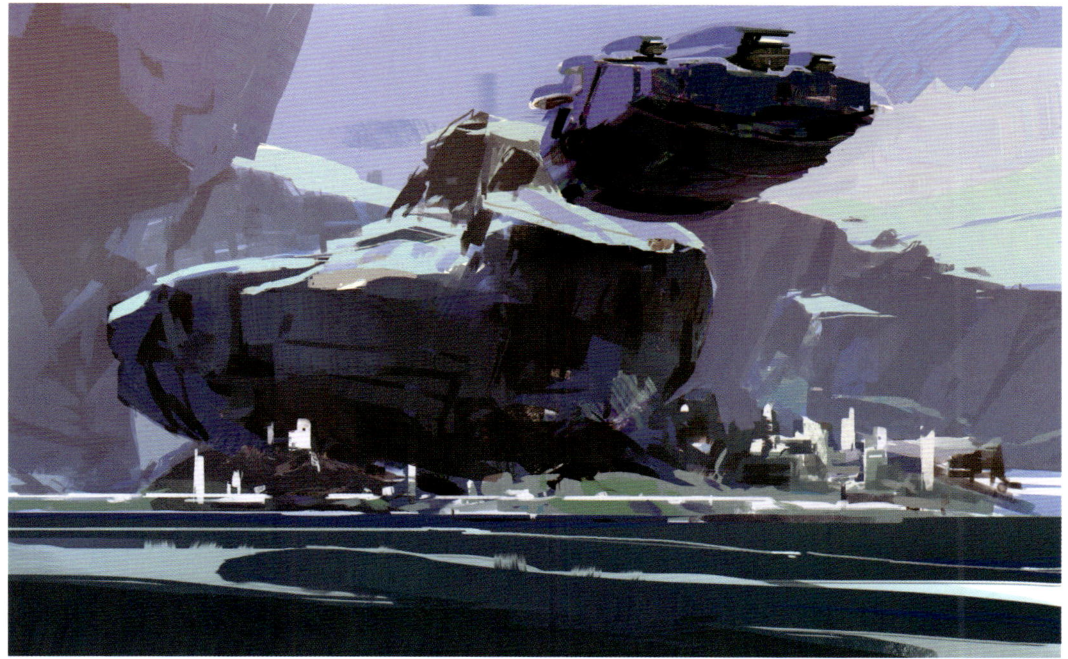

BOLD CHOICES

I always keep my process very organic. For example, below I dissociated the top mountain element in order to create a spaceship, also adding more blue/magenta tones to it in order to clearly determine its narrative importance. The foreground brushstrokes expressing grass or plants were done using a Smudge brush. Finally, notice the white buildings detaching from the central rock structure. They will become important features for the final image.

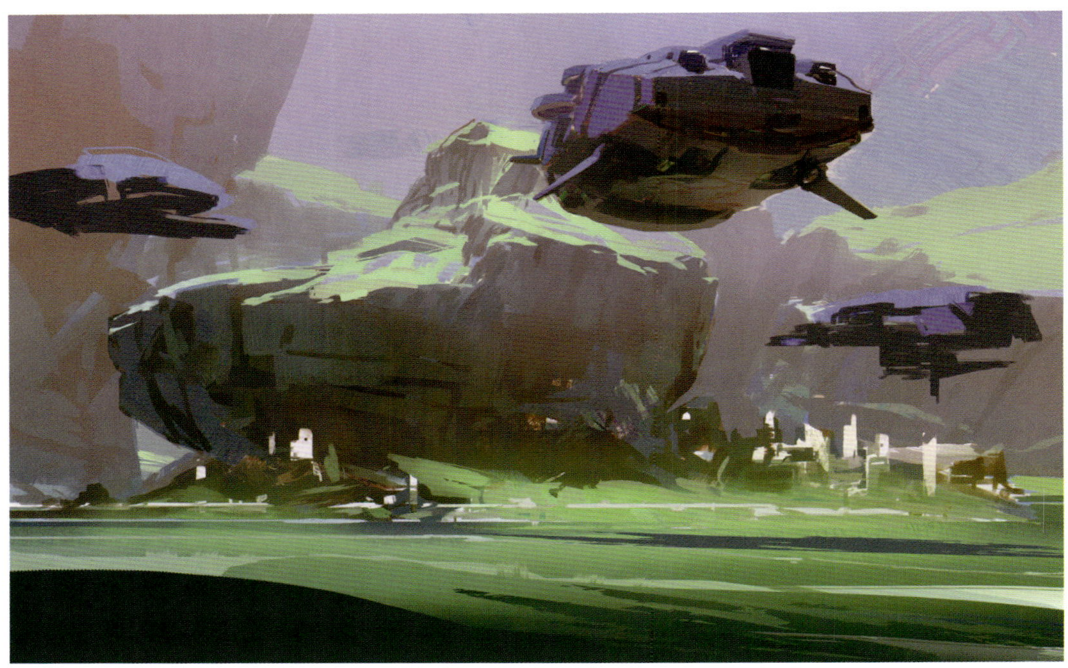

LOCKING FINAL COLORS

The general tones will probably still change slightly until the final steps, but I am now comfortable with the overall green and blue additions. For composition and narrative purposes, I am also adding two new spaceships on both sides of the image. Also, notice how I have painted an additional darker hill in the foreground, in order to prepare an ideal setting for potential characters or vehicles.

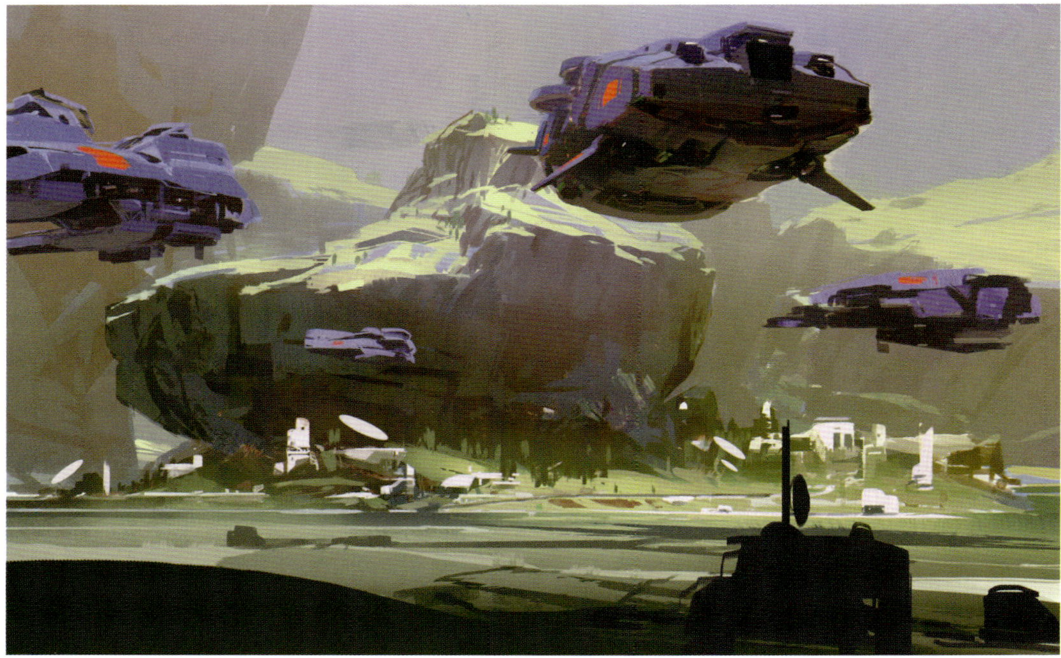

LOCKING FINAL PLANES

The addition of the lower-right foreground building is allowing me to lock down the composition for good. It's only kept as a silhouette for now, until further rendering. I now have a strong distinction of planes, based on shapes and value. I added a fourth spaceship in the background, but I am not convinced yet, as you will soon see.

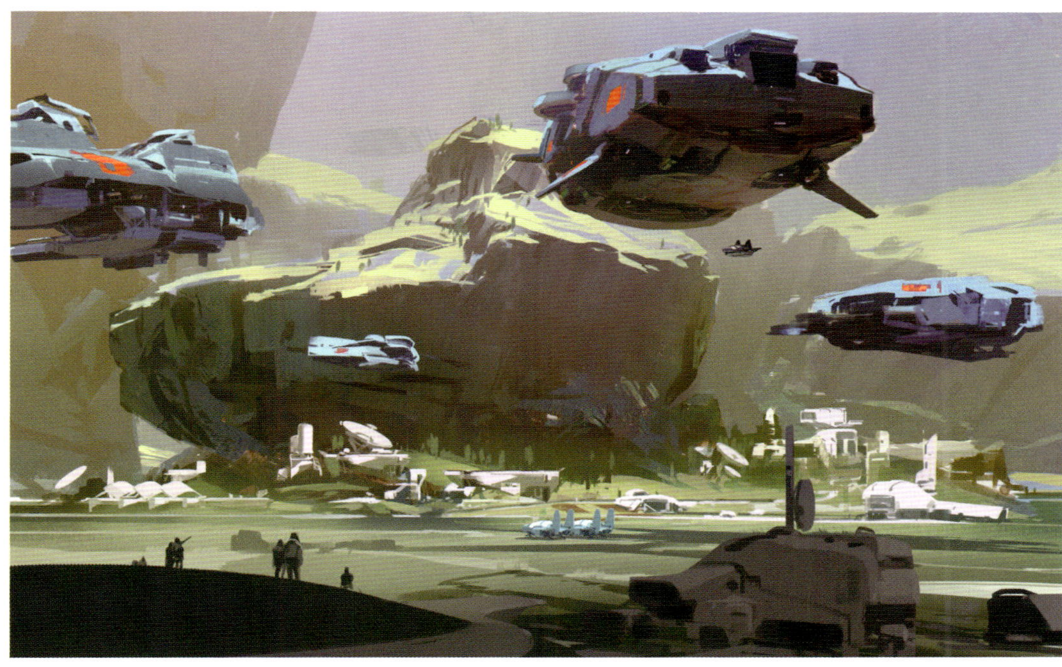

FOREGROUND DESCRIPTION

The lower-right building is now defined. Even more important, I have now added several small silhouettes on the front hill. They are the key elements giving the epic scale to the scene. One of them is raising his arm, pointing at the arriving spaceships. The white architectural structures in the background are now fully described. I kept them very geometric to emphasize modernity and some type of "out of this world" exoticism.

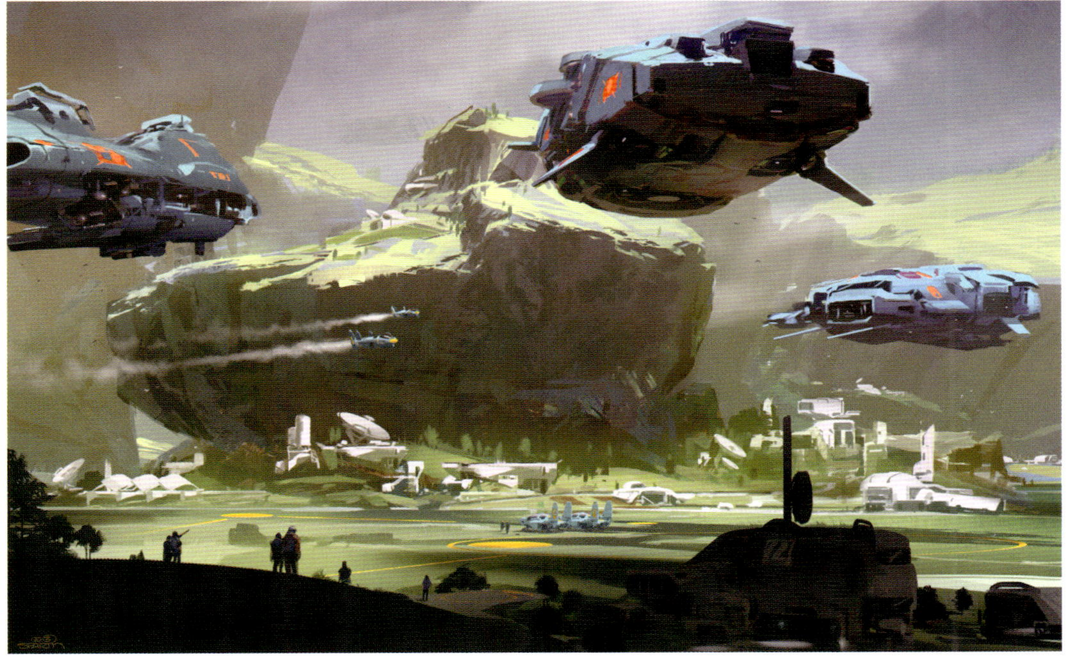

FINAL REFINING

This is always a very pleasant, less stressful step. You know you cannot fail anymore, which makes the whole rendering process even more exciting. I nonetheless decided to remove the left spaceship in the distance to replace it with two futuristic planes that will play a more dynamic role for the composition. As a final touch, I also brightened the area behind the small figures, in order to make them even more visible and to emphasize the narrative impact of the general scene.

DISCOVERY

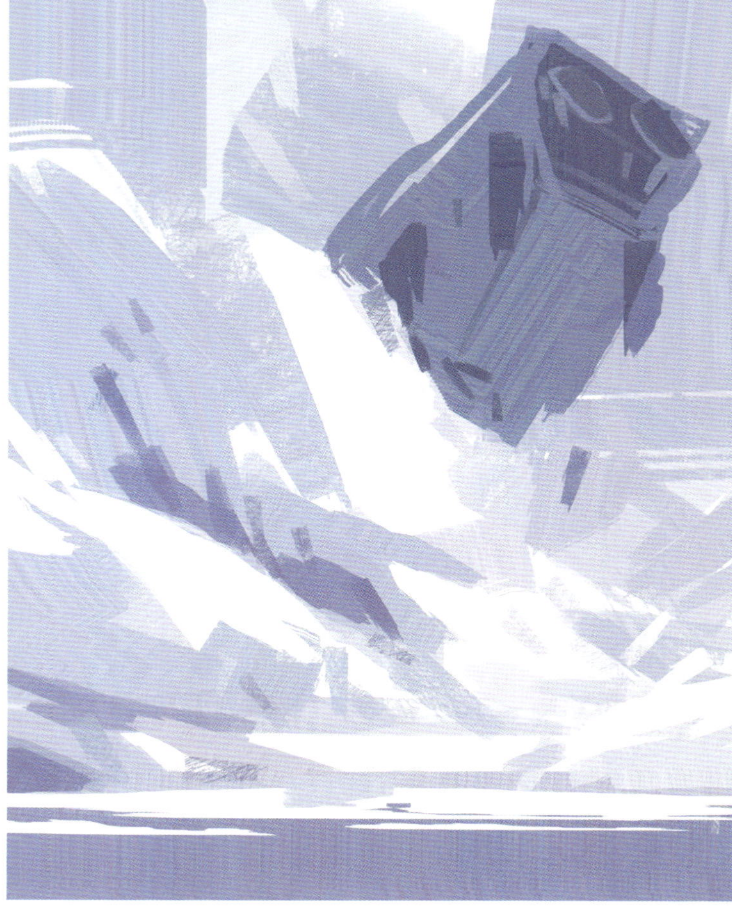

BASIC BLOCKING

This image is a 30-minute exercise based on a preexisting theme: discovery. I must therefore act fast and make some bold decisions when it comes to composition and tones. This time, I already had in mind an arctic scene with a large spaceship structure trapped in the ice cliffs. I will naturally use the white canvas background to my own advantage in order to define bright areas as well as snow.

COMPOSITION

Apart from the foreground elements that I still haven't described, the composition is already locked. You can see the darker blue spaceship in the upper right. I positioned it diagonally to the canvas in order to emphasize dynamism. In the foreground, you can already see ice bits and chunks floating on a blue ocean. These have been done with a few strokes, in a matter of seconds.

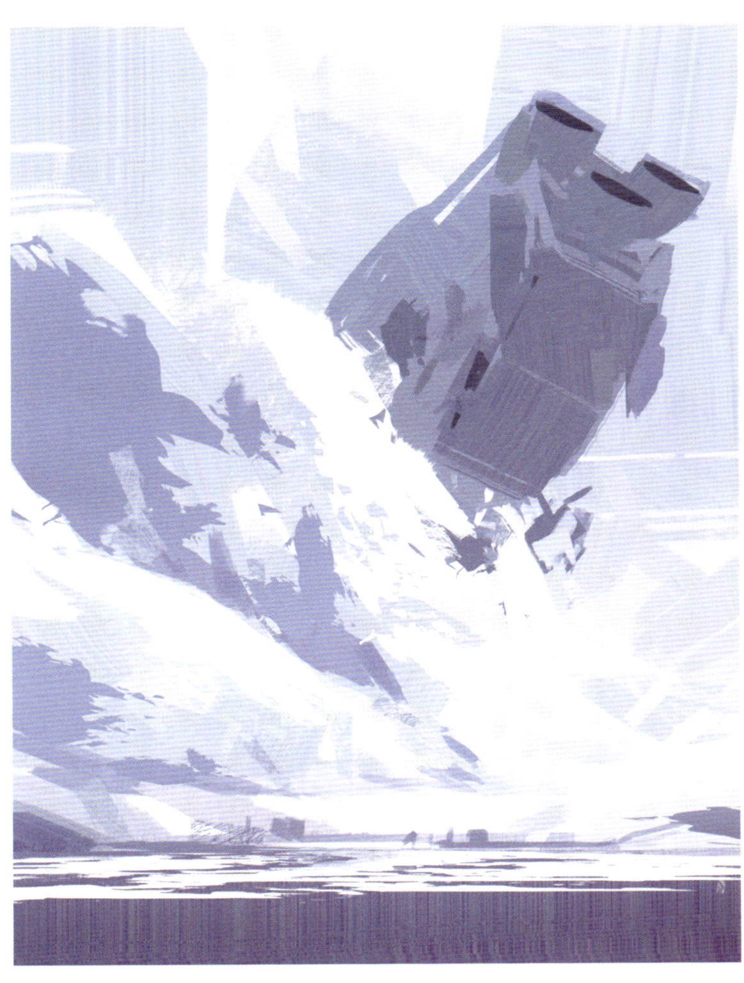

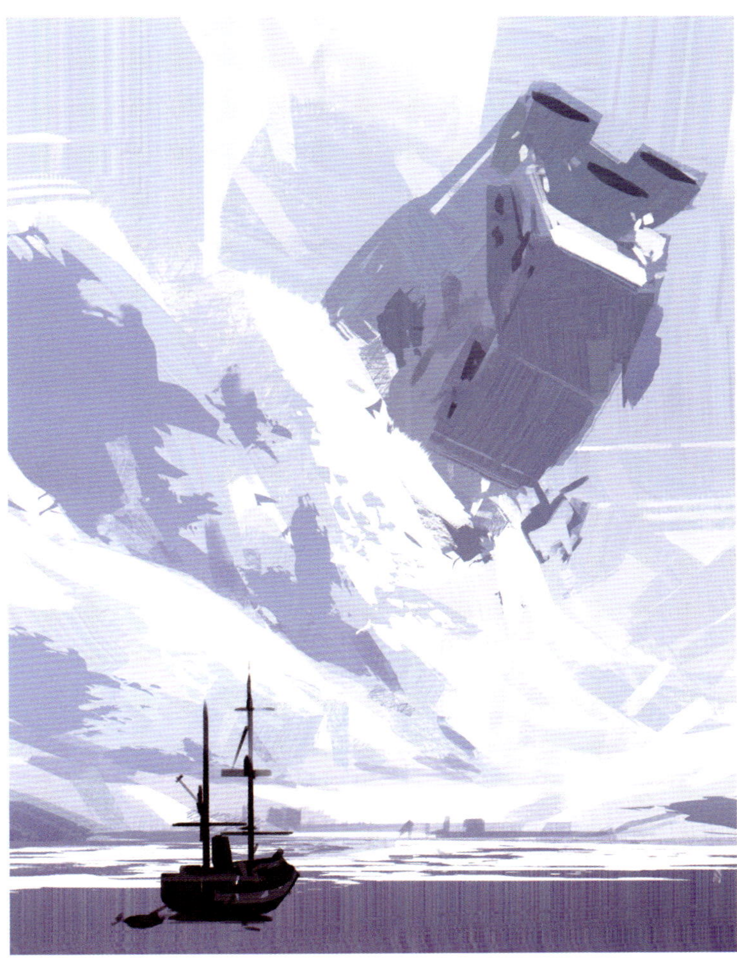

THE CLIFF

With the help of custom shapes, I now focus on the cliff area. My goal is to determine where to put details without breaking the visual flow. Surprisingly, I rarely paint these fast, slowly putting one shape or stroke after the other. My approach is a bit like visual carving, carefully observing where light is going to reach the water, ground, or snow. It's a meticulous process that goes against the idea you have to paint fast to stay within the 30-minute time frame.

THE BOAT

The foreground boat is now in place. I was imagining a 19th century or early 20th century boat like the ones used for the famous Antarctic expeditions. Once again, I positioned it diagonally, compared to the spaceship structure, in order to respect the rule of thirds. Also, the technological difference between both narrative elements will emphasize the surprise and cinematic nature of the scene.

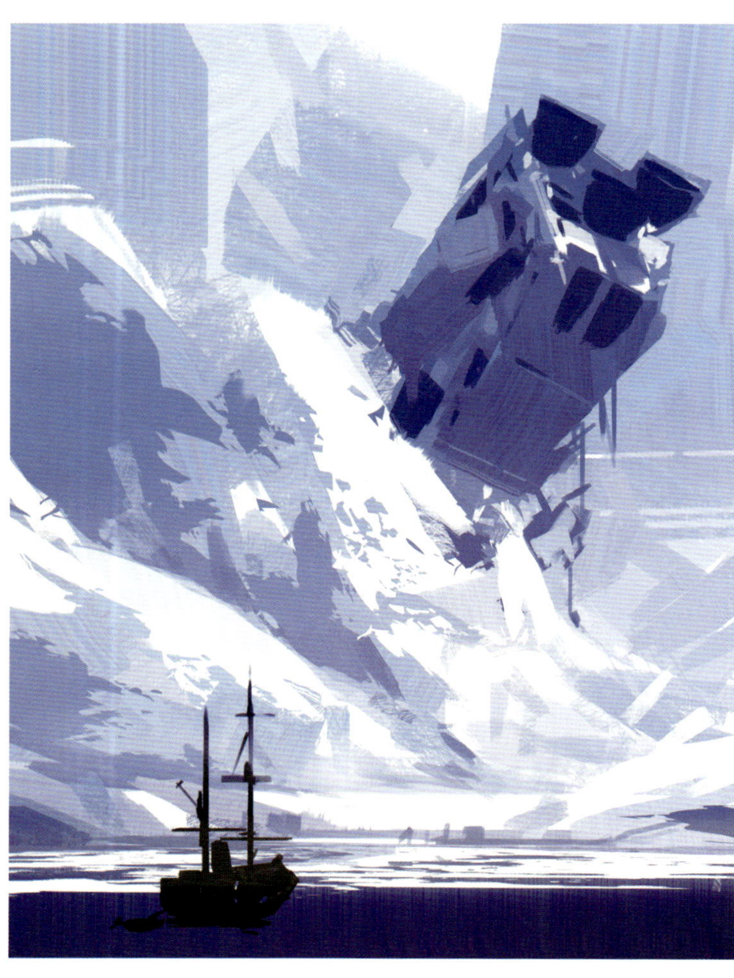

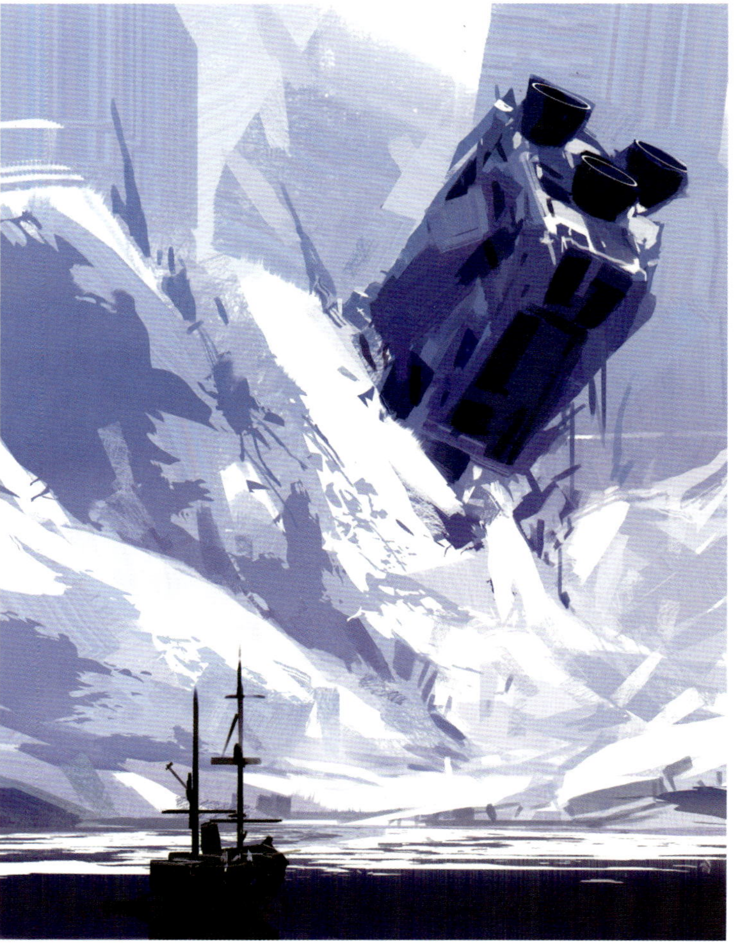

CONTRAST

Keeping everything within 30 minutes can be a challenge, and using tricks and graphic shortcuts is often the way to go when it is done smartly. The Auto Contrast feature can be of great help, as you can first paint without worrying too much about initial contrast. At this point, I have also saved selections for the two main objects: the spaceship and the boat. This way, it will give you fast access to objects you would want to paint selectively.

Pressing the control key while clicking on the layer containing the boat will select it. I will then often create a new channel in order to easily find the selection back. If I do not have enough time left, I will skip this step and keep each object on its own layer, reselecting with the control key whenever necessary.

RENDERING

I am now rendering elements throughout the image, mostly in order to give more "to see," as often said. The eyes really like stopping on specific areas, especially if you render it with more details. In this case, both the boat and spaceship will drive the attention, and receive more details than anywhere else in the image.

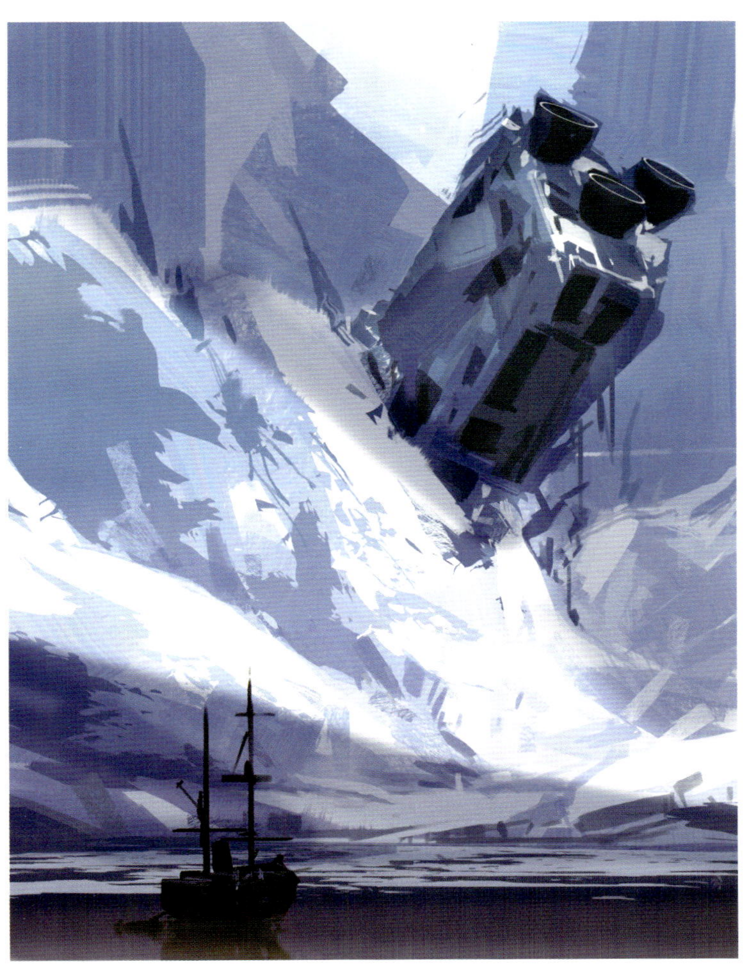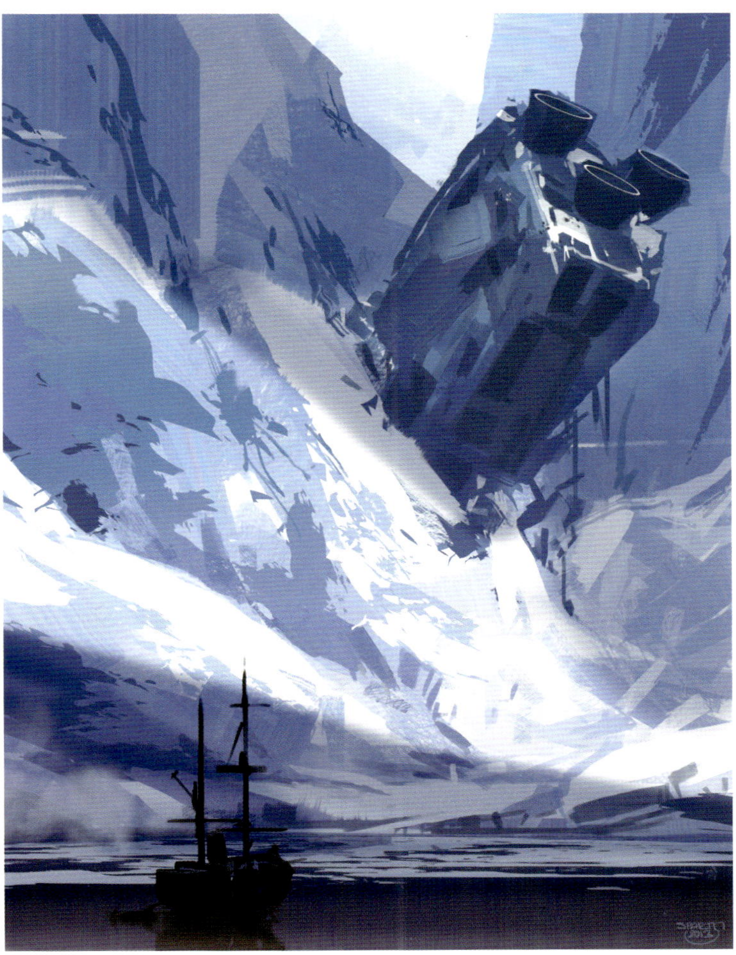

SHADOW PASS

I often add what I would call a "shadow pass" in my images, mostly in order to nail the composition with strong diagonals that will emphasize the visual flow of the image. It consists of determining a good angle for the sun to enter into the scene, and then paint strong dynamic shadows accordingly. In this case, I consciously position the foreground into the shadows, with enough bouncing light coming from the snow to make specific details still recognizable.

You can also notice a slight hue change going toward cyan, added mostly because of a personal preference, as it felt more immersive and believable to me.

ATMOSPHERE

The final pass here consists of adding atmosphere to emphasize the sense of scale. In order to do so, I add a Lighten layer to tone down the dark areas everywhere in the background, for example, on the spaceship thrusters. The goal is to only have darker tones appear in the foreground, in order to establish a strong plane progression between foreground, middle ground, and background.

DEFENSE TURRETS

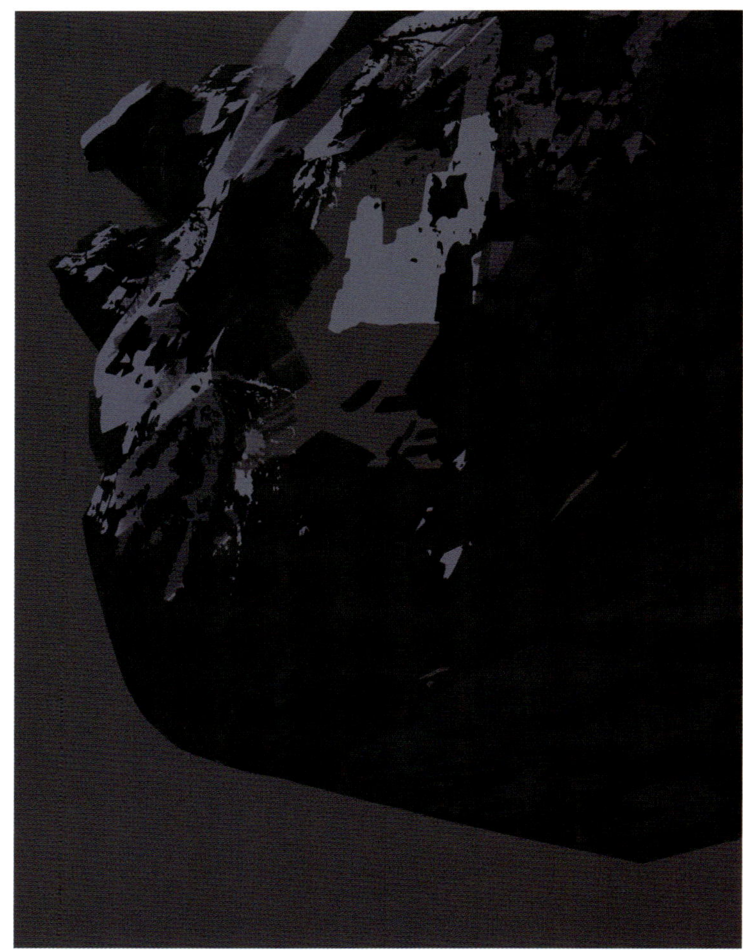

GRAY BACKGROUND

This another 30-minute painting, this time featuring defense turrets. Fast paintings are always informative from a technical and tutorial standpoint because the structure of the image is built with maximum efficiency and coherence. I started this particular image with a dark gray background as I knew I was going to put the scene in deep space. There would be less to paint as a result.

There is also a simple rectangle in perspective drawn in the middle of the canvas. It's barely noticeable, but vital to the future composition.

ASTEROID

You can now see an asteroid occupying most of the image. Painted mostly with custom shapes and regular texture brushes. I keep the asteroid on a single layer in order to better select it in the future.

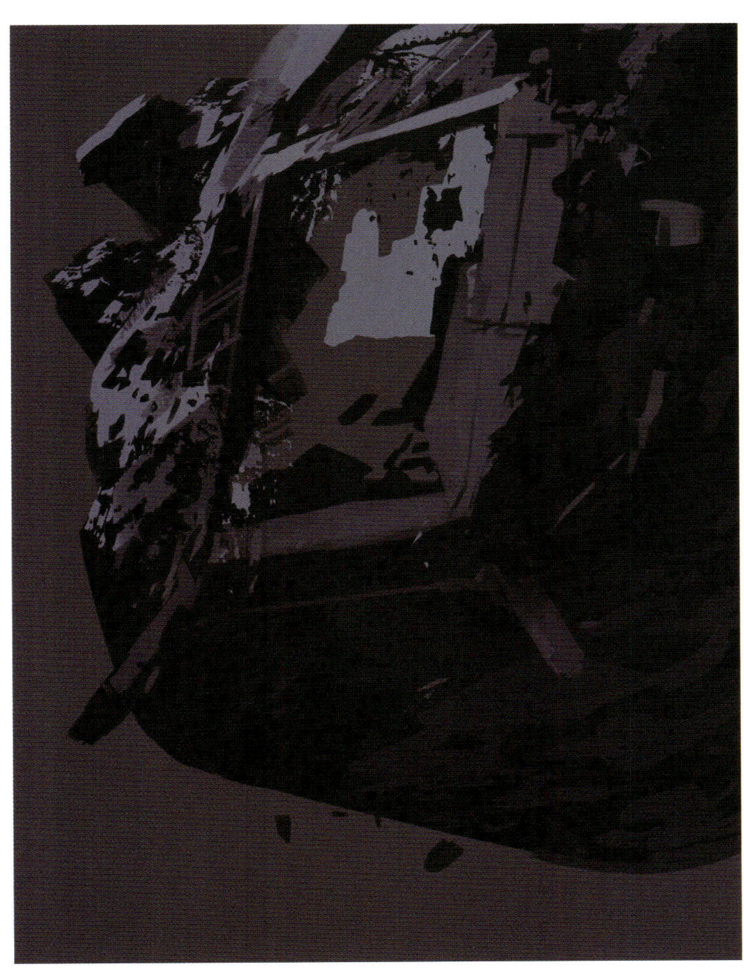

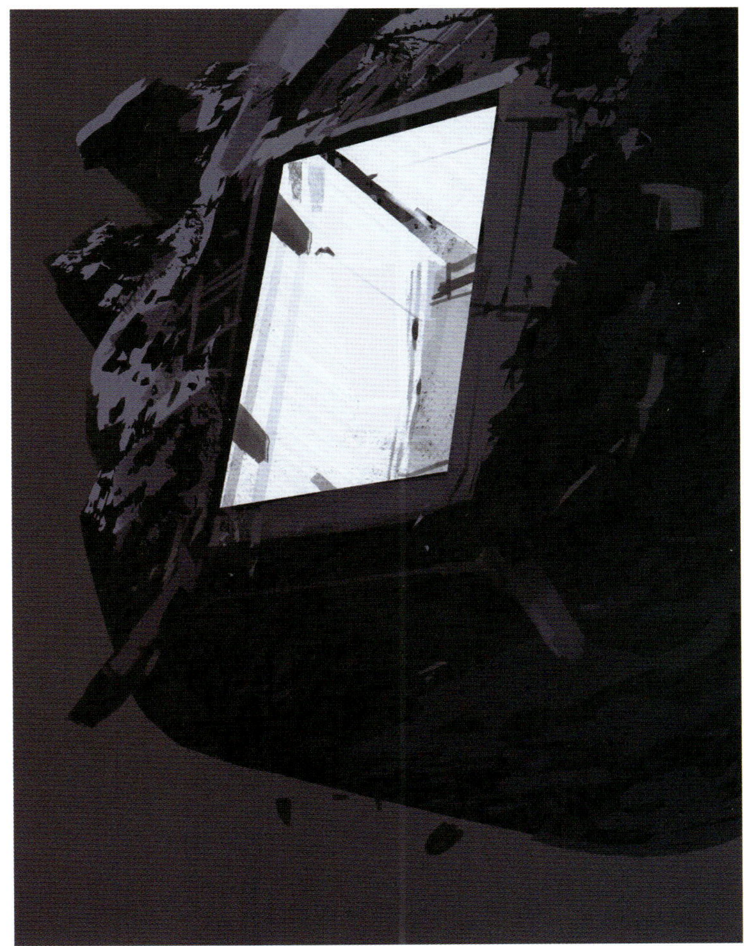

HANGAR BAY

From a storytelling standpoint, I was imagining this asteroid as an inhabited structure with living quarters, bay areas, and spaceships. The initial line rectangle from the first step has now been rendered as some type of a framed window structure.

INTERIOR

It is now time to define the interior of the large opening. Remember that I need to finish everything within 30 minutes, so the fastest option is to select the hangar bay and add a very bright atmosphere and light. As a consequence, it will instantly draw the viewer's attention.

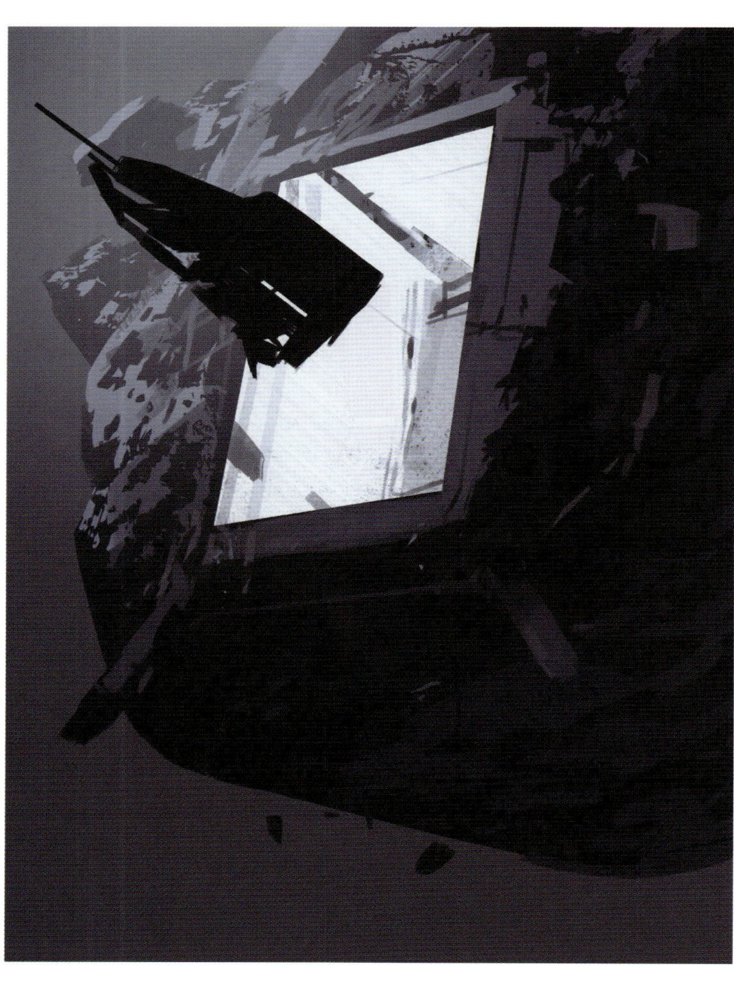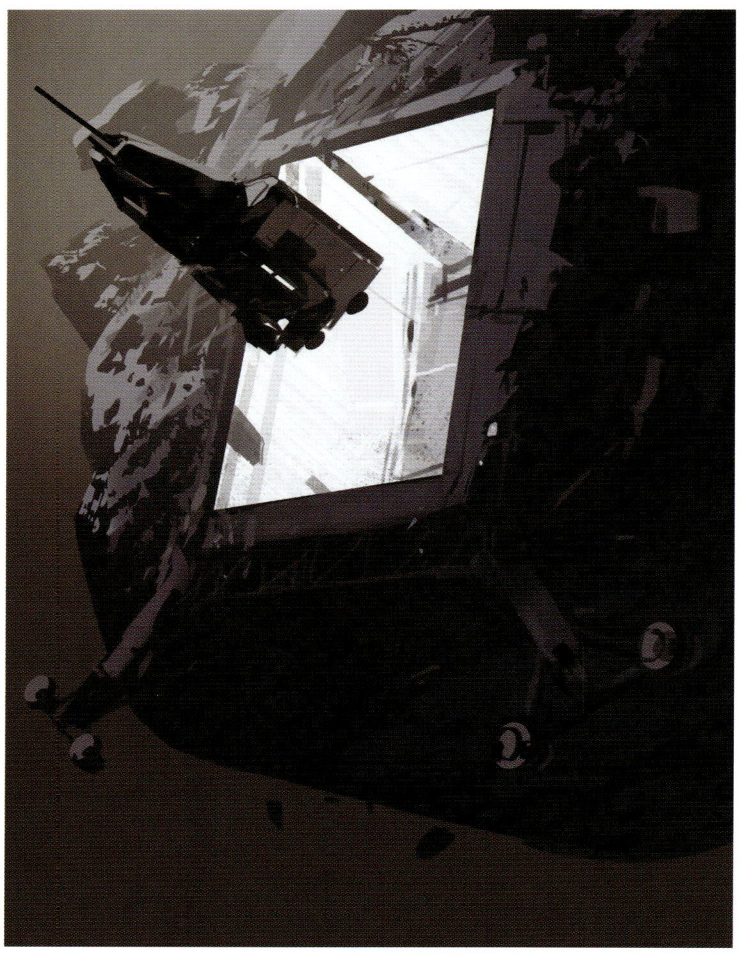

VEHICLE

I add the vehicle in front of the hangar bay. It is here to play a strong narrative role. I chose this specific angle and position for the silhouetted spaceship because it establishes a strong contrast with the highlighted background hangar. Notice how once again it is occupying the upper-left area of the image, according to the rule of thirds.

RENDERING

This is where the real rendering happens. The process here is also very similar to my other images: The fast 30-minute process forces me to keep very clean layers in order to be able to preselect specific elements of the canvas. In other words, I keep one layer for the spaceship, one or two layers for the asteroid, and one layer for the background. It's that simple. On a side note, I shifted the overall color balance towards warmer tones.

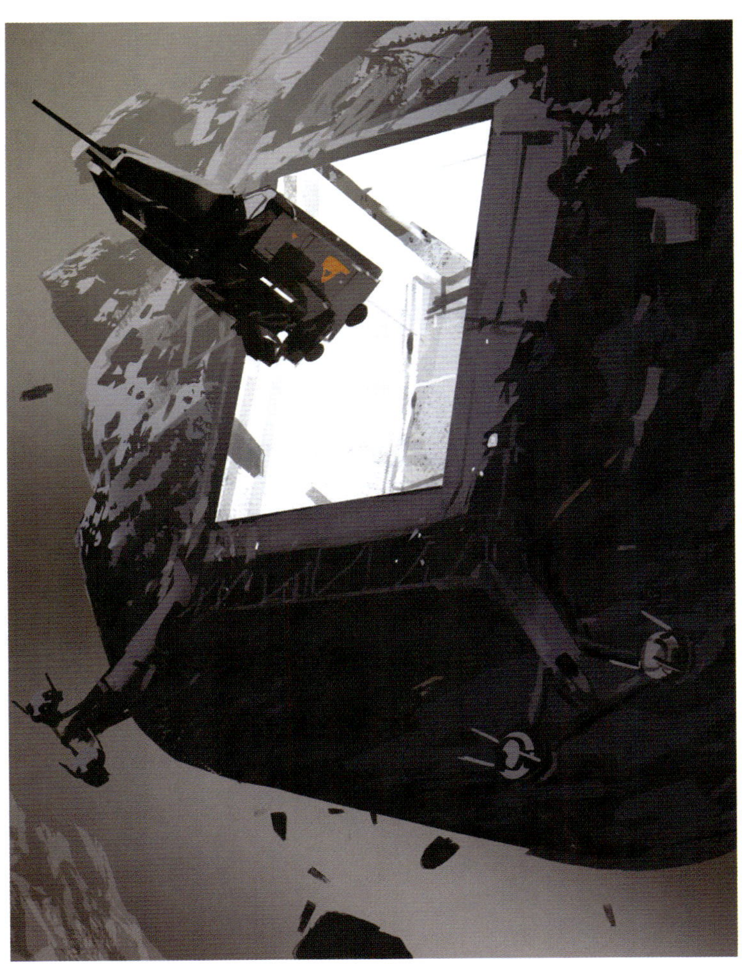 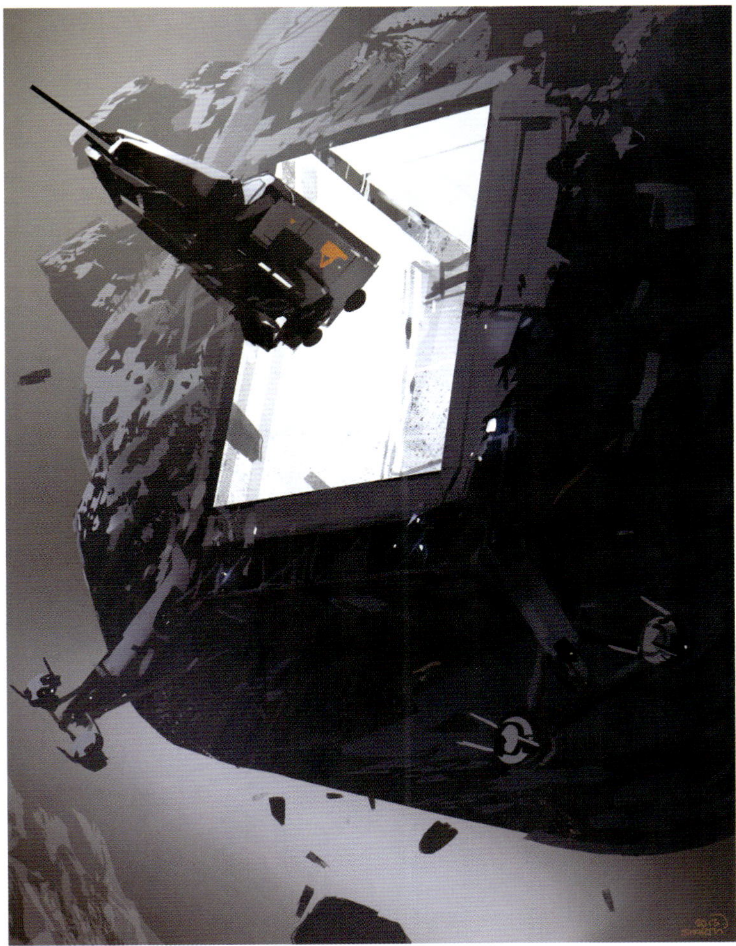

TURRETS

You can now notice tighter details on the front turrets as well as the overall base. I try to convey as much as I can with each new brush stroke, a technique based on economy and visual optimization. I am also improving the overall contrast, with a stronger light coming from behind the asteroid. The orange sign on the spaceship is mostly there to catch the attention. It will become the important focus point of the image.

BACKGROUND LIGHT

I improve the background light once again in order to create multiple planes. A Dodge layer can have great results for details such as lights and over-lit elements, but it must be used smartly to avoid too much unnecessary burning. You can now observe rhythm that is better contrasted, starting from the spaceship and expanding further into the image. The final composition can be read this way: "dark spaceship, bright hangar bay, dark asteroid, bright background."

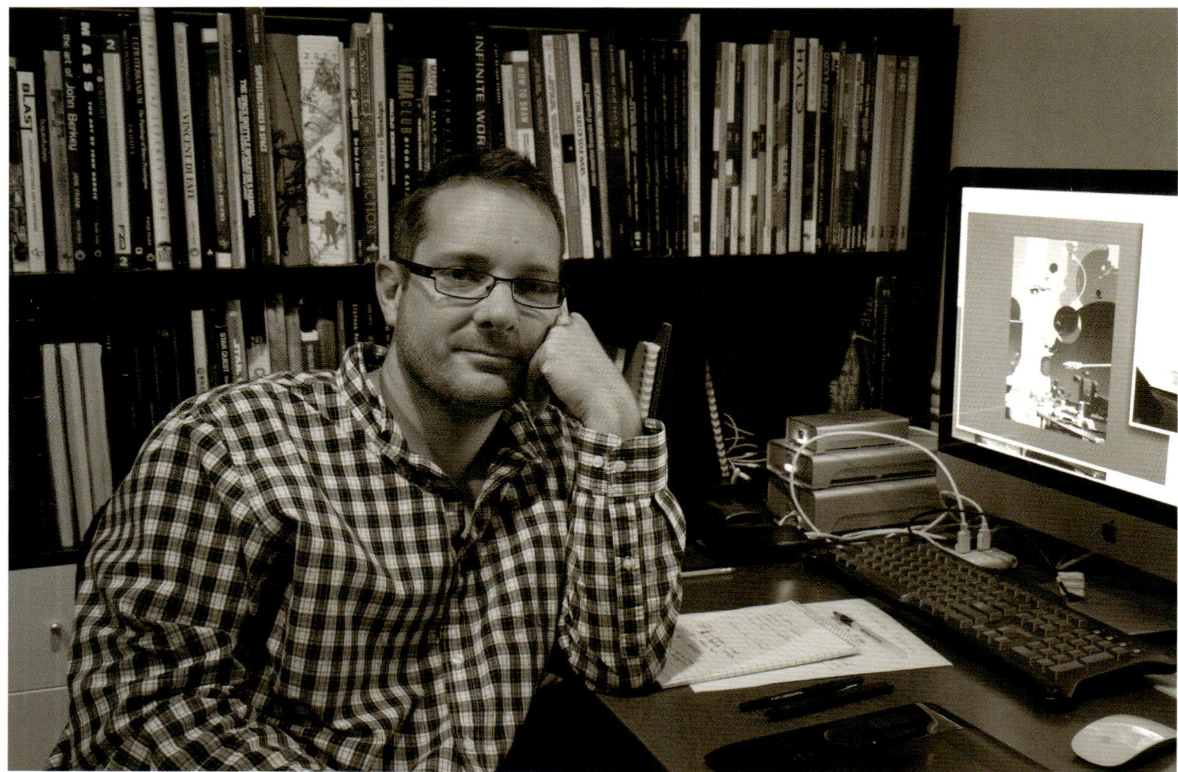

Photo Credit: Lorene Bouvier

BIO

Sparth (Nicolas Bouvier) has been an artistic director and concept designer in the gaming industry for almost two decades. Born in France, he had the privilege to travel extensively at an early age to such places as Singapore, China, and the United States, where he enjoyed observing people and making note of all the tiny details of life that he witnessed. His varied influences are largely responsible for his many creative passions, which range from space and buildings to robotics and beyond.

Professionally, Sparth worked for six years at Darkworks Studio, the Paris-based game studio responsible for *Alone in the Dark 4: The New Nightmare* (2001), before leaving for Montreal in 2003 to join Ubisoft on their ongoing projects, *Prince of Persia* and *Assassin's Creed*. He then left Montreal for Dallas in 2005, where he spent more than three years working for id Software. Finally, in early 2009, he moved to Seattle to work on *Halo* adventures with Microsoft's 343 Industries, where he currently serves as art director of *Halo 5: Guardians*, the next installment in the popular series. Sparth has contributed to the development of several other games since 1997, including *Cold Fear* (2005) and *Rage* (2011), and he has also published more than 80 book covers in France, Canada, and the United States.

There are no limits to Sparth's creativity when it comes to translating forms and concepts. One of his greatest passions continues to be contemporary architecture, the principles of which he applies to his own art, with an experimental and original approach. He also harbors a fascination for modern skyscrapers, although he admits that he himself wouldn't be able to live too high above the ground.

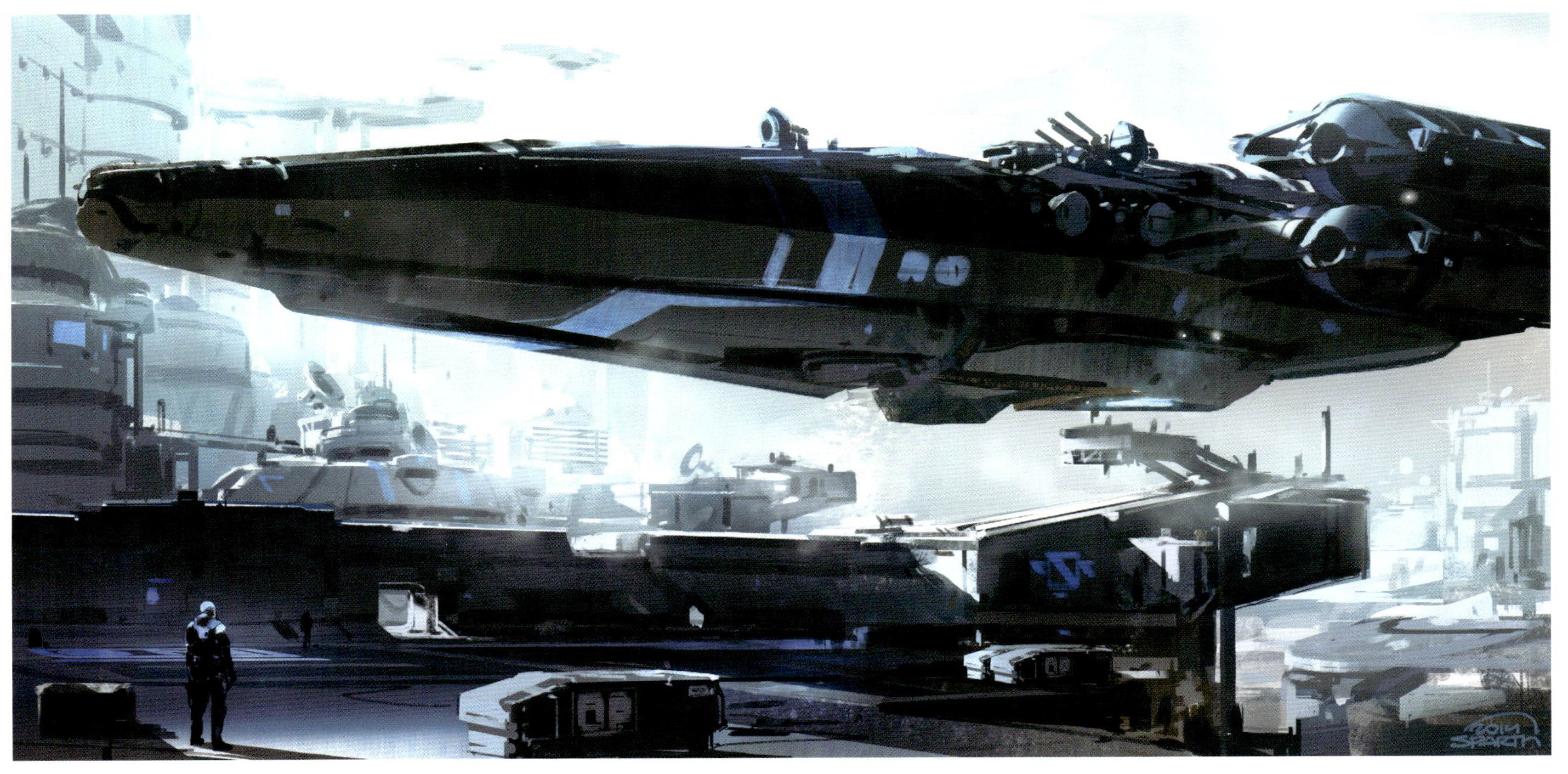

above Blue Strike, 2014
below la Cité Oeil, 2014

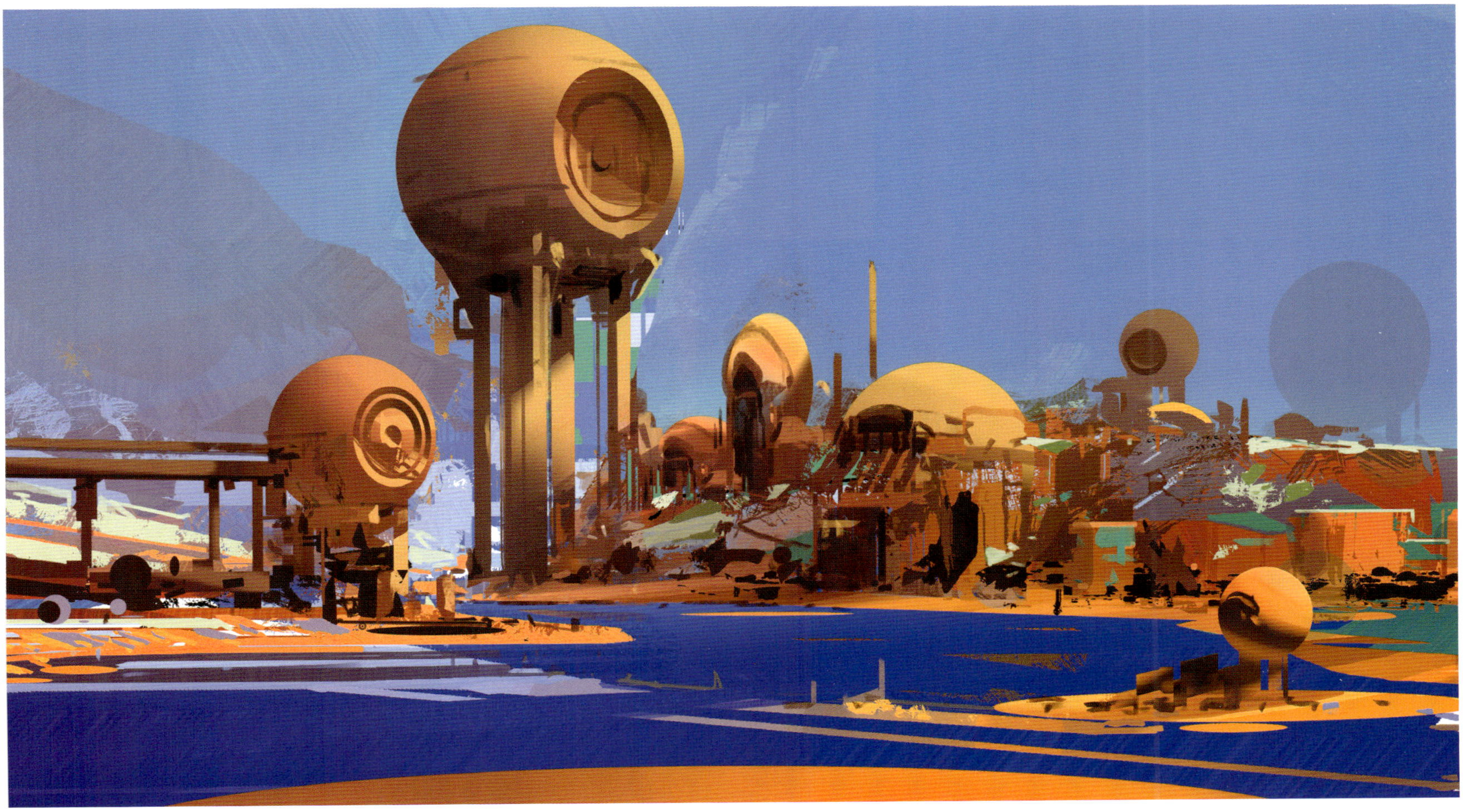

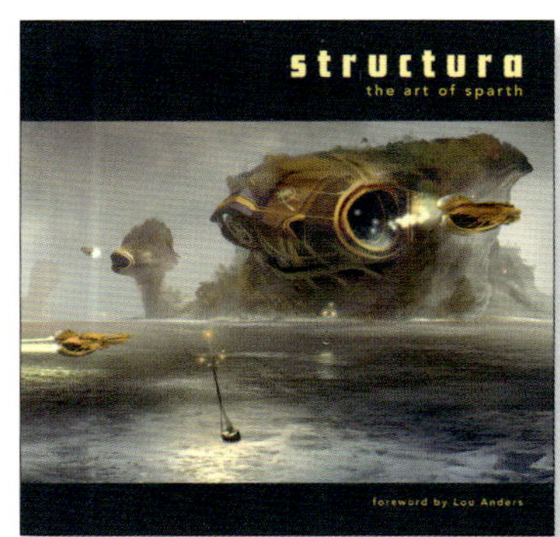

128 pages
paperback
9 x 9 inches
isbn: 978-1-933492-25-4

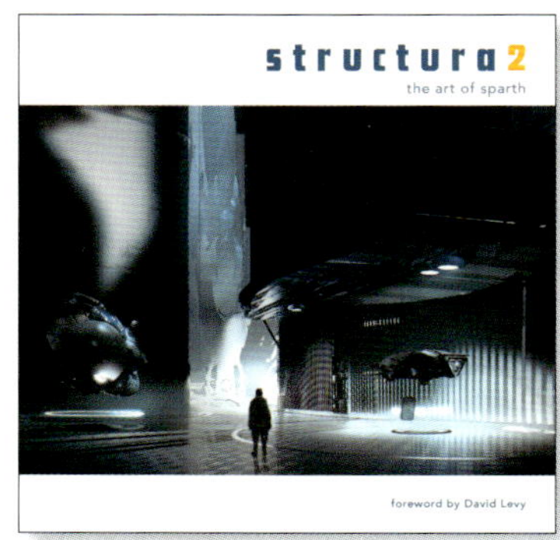

160 pages
9 x 13 inches
paperback isbn: 978-1-933492-65-0
hardcover isbn: 978-1-933492-66-7

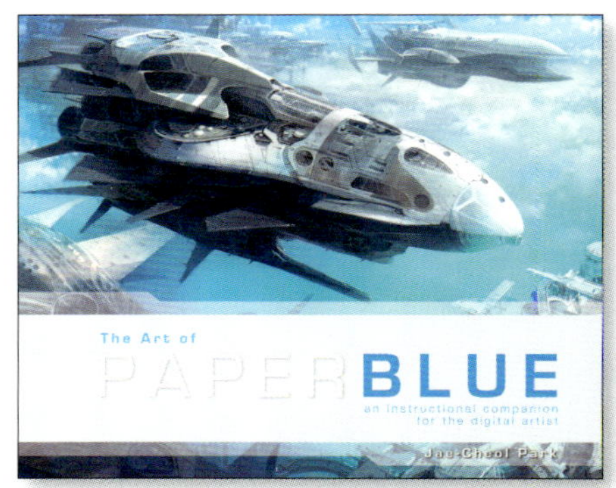

160 pages
paperback
12 x 10 inches
isbn-13: 978-1-933492-70-4

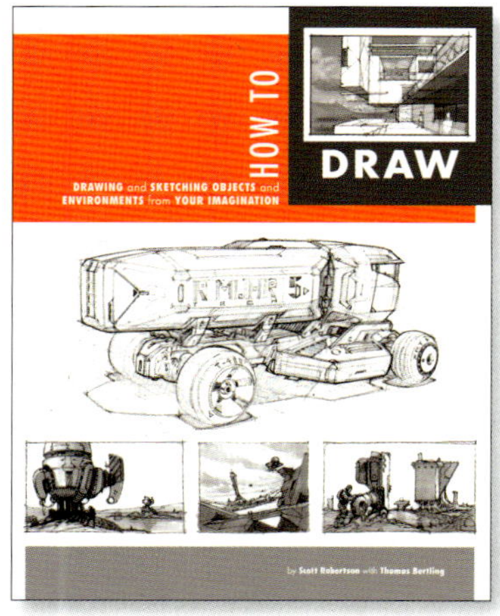

208 pages
9 x 11 inches
paperback isbn: 978-1-933492-73-5
hardcover isbn: 978-1-933492-75-9

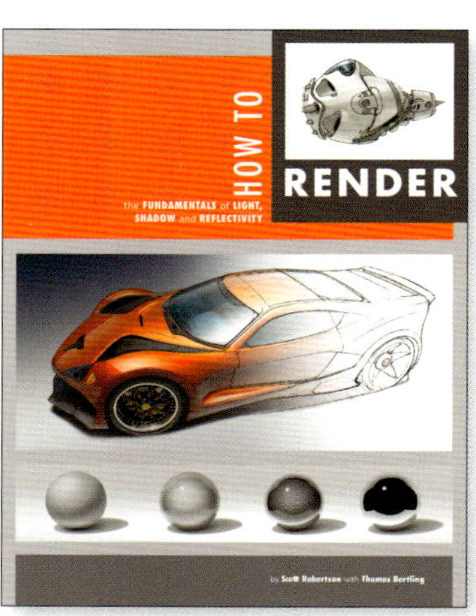

272 pages
9 x 11 inches
paperback isbn: 978-1-933492-96-4
hardcover isbn: 978-1-933492-83-4

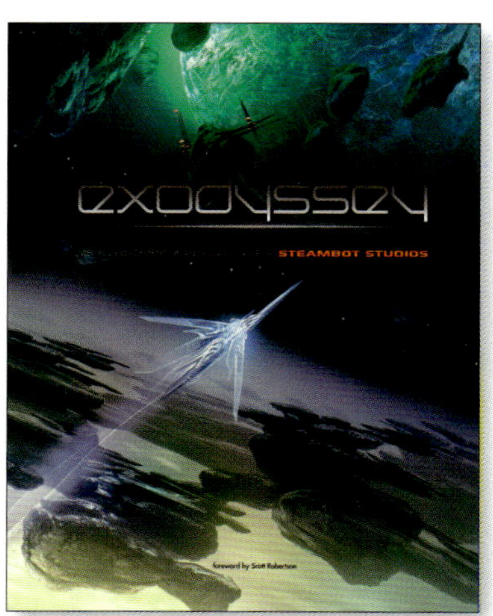

176 pages
paperback
9 x 12 inches
isbn: 978-1-933492-39-1

To order additional copies of this book and to view other books we offer, please visit:
www.designstudiopress.com

For volume purchases and resale inquiries, please email:
info@designstudiopress.com

To be notified of new releases, special discounts and events, please sign up for the mailing list on our website, follow our Facebook page, or follow us on Twitter:

 facebook.com/designstudiopress

twitter.com/DStudioPress

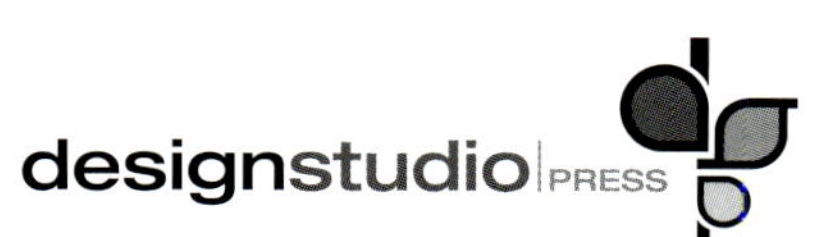